The American Beauty Industry Encyclopedia

The American Beauty Industry Encyclopedia

Julie Willett, Editor

GREENWOOD

AN IMPRINT OF ABC-CLIO, LLC
Santa Barbara, California • Denver, Colorado • Oxford, England

Library of Congress Cataloging-in-Publication Data

The American beauty industry encyclopedia / Julie Willett, editor.
    p. cm.
  Includes bibliographical references and index.
  ISBN 978-0-313-35949-1 (hbk. : alk. paper) — ISBN 978-0-313-35950-7 (ebook)
1. Beauty culture—United States—Encyclopedias. 2. Beauty shops—
United States—Encyclopedias. 3. Cosmetics industry—United States—
Encyclopedias. I. Willett, Julie A.
  TT958.A44 2010
  338.4'76467203—dc22   2010002234

ISBN: 978-0-313-35949-1
EISBN: 978-0-313-35950-7

14 13 12 11 10   1 2 3 4 5

This book is also available on the World Wide Web as an eBook.
Visit www.abc-clio.com for details.

Greenwood Press
An Imprint of ABC-CLIO, LLC

ABC-CLIO, LLC
130 Cremona Drive, P.O. Box 1911
Santa Barbara, California 93116-1911

This book is printed on acid-free paper ∞

Manufactured in the United States of America

Contents

List of Entries

A

Acne
Advertising
African American Beauty Industry
Afro
Androgyny
Animal Rights
Anti-Aging Products and Techniques
Arden, Elizabeth
Asian American Beauty Industry
Aveda
Avon

B

Baldness
Barbers and Barbershops
Bath and Body Works
Beauty Pageants
Beauty Schools
Beauty Shops and Salons
Bed Head
Blondes
The Bob
The Body Shop
Botox
Bouffant
Branding
Brown, Bobbi

C

Calvin Klein
Cellulite
Chanel, Coco
Charm Schools
Cosmetics
Cosmetic Surgery

Cosmopolitan
CoverGirl

D

Dandruff
Dermatology
Designers
Dieting
Display
Dove's Campaign for Real Beauty
Dr. 90210

E

Ebony
Endorsements of Products, Celebrity
Estée Lauder
Extreme Makeover

F

Fashion Magazines
Fat Farms
Feminism
Film
Focus Groups

G

Gentlemen's Quarterly (GQ)
Global Markets, U.S. Trends in
Grooming, Male

H

Hair Care Products
Hairdressers
Hair Shows
Hair Straightening
Hairstyles

List of Entries by Topic

CLOTHING

Androgyny
Branding
Designers
Klein, Calvin
Natural Look
Teen Market
Tween Market
Undergarments
Vogue
What Not to Wear

COMPANIES

Arden, Elizabeth
Aveda
Avon
Bath and Body Works
The Body Shop
Chanel, Coco
CoverGirl
Dove's Campaign for Real Beauty
Estée Lauder
Johnson Products
Klein, Calvin
Mary Kay Cosmetics
Max Factor
Organic Trends and Products
Procter and Gamble
QVC
Revlon
Rubinstein, Helena
Sally's Beauty Supply
Sassoon, Vidal
Skin Care Lines, Men's

Trade Journals and Publications
Walker, Madam C. J.

HAIR

Afro
Androgyny
Bed Head
Blondes
The Bob
Bouffant
Grooming, Male
Hair Care Products
Hair Shows
Hair Straightening
Hairstyles
Hairstylists, Celebrity
Natural Look
Permanents
Religion and Beauty
Sassoon, Vidal
Wigs and Hairpieces

HEALTH

Acne
Cosmetic Surgery
Dandruff
Dieting
Health and Safety
Organic Trends and Products
Spas
Tanning
Vitamins and Beauty Supplements
U.S. Food and Drug Administration

INDUSTRY

Advertising
African American Beauty Industry
Asian American Beauty Industry
Branding
Display
Focus Groups
Global Markets, U.S. Trends in
Infomercials
Internet
Labor
Latina Beauty Industry
Manufacturing
Nail Salons
Organic Trends and Products
Packaging
QVC
Retail
Teen Market
Trade Journals and Publications
Trade Shows
Tween Market

INSTITUTIONS

Barbers and Barbershops
Beauty Pageants
Beauty Schools
Beauty Shops and Salons
Charm Schools
Fat Farms
Hair Shows
Nail Salons
Spas
Trade Shows
U.S. Food and Drug Administration

MAGAZINES

Cosmopolitan
Ebony
Fashion Magazines
Gentlemen's Quarterly (GQ)
Magazines, Men's

Maxim
Men's Health
Seventeen
Teen Market
Trade Journals and Publications

MALE BEAUTY

Androgyny
Gentlemen's Quarterly (GQ)
Grooming, Male
Klein, Calvin
Magazines, Men's
Maxim
Men's Health
Metrosexuals
Models, Male
Piercing
Queer Eye for the Straight Guy
Skin Care Lines, Men's
Tanning
Tattoos
Vitamins and Beauty Supplements
Wigs and Hairpieces

MEDIA

Advertising
Branding
Fashion Magazines
Film
Infomercials
Internet
Magazines, Men's
Makeovers
QVC
Teen Market
Trade Journals and Publications
Tween Market

MOVEMENTS

Animal Rights
Feminism
Hip Hop

Preface

Whether one is flipping through the pages of a magazine or watching the latest tween music video, it is no surprise that beauty is a multibillion-dollar industry and the business of beauty is ubiquitous in American society. Consciously or not, men and women, regardless of age, invoke a sense of aesthetics that brings into bold relief the intersection of beauty and commerce. Indeed, a quick glance at any high school yearbook will lead to conversations about the hair, makeup, and clothes of the day and how those fashions have changed. In the past several decades, the study of the beauty industry has also come into fruition and an abundance of new research is now available that transcends a number of different disciplines. This encyclopedia benefits from this new research, as well as from a diverse range of scholars and professionals whose research backgrounds reveal the profound influence the industry has had on the social, cultural, and economic terrain of daily life. These contributors represent fields as diverse as medicine, labor, film and media studies, philosophy, sociology, anthropology, and history, as well as fashion studies. Entry topics range from the institutions, entrepreneurs, styles, trendsetters and technology to the contemporary mores inextricably bound to religion, feminism, and other global concerns such as the health and safety of those creating and consuming the industry's products, and the animal rights and environmental issues that have been affected by these processes. Each entry reveals precedents as well as contemporary trends, exploring the meaning of beauty practices and products, and often making analytical use of categories such as gender, race, religion, and sexuality, as well as stages of the lifecycle.

More than 100 entries were chosen specifically to illuminate the most iconic aspects of the beauty industry's past and present. The introduction offers a summary of the major themes that have shaped the beauty industry and reflects on the themes that run through the encyclopedia. Front matter also provides an alphabetical and topical list of all entries. A chronology highlights important dates in the history of the American beauty industry. Cross-references are bolded or called out in order to direct readers to related entries. A Further Reading section follows each topic and includes sources such as academic and governmental studies, company and consumer group websites, and newspaper and magazine articles, as well as documentaries, blogs, and YouTube postings. Throughout the encyclopedia, photographs and sidebars are also designed to illuminate the complexity of various trends, products, processes, and the individuals who have defined the industry. Two appendices provide industry data. Finally, the encyclopedia concludes with a selected bibliography and an index to provide additional means to access information within this publication as well as to find additional research on related topics.

Introduction

It is both humiliating and humbling to discover that a single generation after the events that constructed me as a public personality, I am remembered as hairdo. It is humiliating because it reduces a politics of liberation to a politics of fashion.

—Angela Davis[1]

When former Black Panther and political activist Angela Davis complained that she did not want to be known simply for a hairdo, she was specifically thinking of her infamous Afro—a style that seemed to be more readily emulated and understood than the nuances of the Black Power movement. To be sure, the Afro remains a symbol of radical politics, but it has long been a beauty commodity, bought, sold, and processed like any other mainstream accessory. Davis's concern that her public self had been reduced to a fashion statement reflects much of the contradictions and complexities that have defined the beauty industry. Beauty is often associated with narcissism and vanity, but as style it transcends cultural space and engages in a dialogue that mixes politics and social movements, as well as cultural and technological transformations. And it is the intersection of culture and society, beauty and business, that fosters the industry's multimillion-dollar reach into pocket books and headlines (see Appendix 1 and Appendix 2).

Beauty, fashion, and style have been a means to assert and challenge the status quo. To be sure, much of the industry's history has made the blue-eyed blonde with her Barbie figure a pinnacle of beauty. Thus, altering one's complexion, hair texture, or body images has led to debates that draw upon feminism, and critical race theory, for example, leaving producers and consumers of beauty to dance around fears of overt sexuality, objectification, health and safety, and racism. At the same time, beauty and style challenge social norms that are viewed as stagnant. In the 1920s, the bob was a popular hairdo and a rejection of the social constraints still lingering from 19th-century Victorian propriety. For some women, entering a barbershop and adopting a boyish bob was as much about being a new woman as smoking, dancing, or voting. Similarly, during World War II, Latino and African American zoot-suiters asserted their disdain for wage work, racial apartheid, and patriotism through clothing, hair, and a stance so provocative they were beaten and their long hair shorn in a series of race riots. Most recently, the influence of hip hop speaks to global connections that link the subaltern with black Americans' rich history of resistance.

Nevertheless, the beauty industry has often been relegated to a world of female pursuits and dismissed as inconsequential. Yet, the invisibility of women's work in beauty culture created opportunity and community not typically found in businesses deemed more male, more professional, and thus more important. Within a beauty economy, a litany of female entrepreneurs, many immigrant or African American, became movers and shakers in the business world. Madam C. J. Walker and Elizabeth Arden, along with the late 20th century's proliferation of female-dominated, Korean- and Vietnamese-owned nail salons, exemplify how women with often meager resources have initiated a range of business and marketing trends. Even the neighborhood hairdresser has been central to the social well-being of her clients and, in some places, so strikingly independent that she could assert change in local and national politics. Thus, beauty sales and production have been a stepping stone for women challenging many economic, gender, and racial constraints that place them in positions that seem to reinforce as well as alter prevailing stereotypes.

Of course, some of the most famous designers and entrepreneurs have been men, but as consumers of beauty trends, men have also been ignored or mocked, depending on how they negotiate prevailing gender conventions. Entrenched in femininity, male beauty trends that hint at alternative masculinities have too often been subject to ridicule or defined as something other than beauty. The male beauty industry, however, is not a contradiction in terms, nor is it simply the response to metrosexuality. Instead, it is rooted in one of the oldest occupations, barbering, and includes everything from Gillette razors to men's magazines, all of which have a rich and dynamic history. Although male beauty consumption has not been fully recognized, male designers, stylists, and entrepreneurs have been hailed as the gods of the industry and the epitome of professionalism. Max Factor, Vidal Sassoon, and Calvin Klein, just to name a few, are known well beyond the beauty industry for their artistry and business savvy. Ultimately, men who enter the world of beauty and fashion have often found tremendous success, while their gendered identities are both lampooned and liberated.

Regardless of gender or innovation, industry leaders have been met with the harshest of criticism. In the realm of advertising, style and beauty move swiftly across cultural terrain, but marketing practices often seem more invasive as of late. The use of Hollywood and music icons who transform the off-beat to Main Street is not new. However, thanks to beauty blogs, reality shows, home shopping channels, and the less-regulated children's programming, celebrity endorsement and branding seem even more pervasive. From scantily dressed blonde divas to hypersexual teenage rebels, every generation seems to have new concerns over youth culture and that generation's embrace of style and attitude. Like the shift from push-up bras to breast implants, surgical makeovers, tattoos, and piercings make the once extreme seem as mundane as the suburban home's multi-car garage. It is far too easy to blame the beauty industry for asserting changing mores, especially since cultural transmission ebbs and flows in multiple directions; since it is an industry that thrives on name recognition and profit, many worry that too high a price is paid for hope in a jar.

Global concerns thus address the consequences both for consumers and producers in the industry. Each generation scoffs at early beauty practices deemed archaic, unsafe, or simply uncomfortable; yet many still question current laws and regulations that do not seem to take a serious enough look at the effects of cosmetics or vitamins. The conditions of labor within and beyond U.S. borders bring to bear another side of the beauty industry. Brands like Nike are associated with some of the most successful advertising campaigns, but also stand out as symbols of exploitation and global sweatshops that manufacture cheap goods at high human cost. From factory to service jobs, beauty is a business often completely devoid of glamour. The continued growth of the beauty industry and its consumption also bring up debates over sustainability. Increasing numbers of companies have found a new market niche with a commitment to organic ingredients, recycled packaging, and products that are designed to bring health benefits to consumers. From massage oils to solar-powered salons, green industry production is a particularly poignant part of the beauty business. Hand in hand with concerns over the safety of labor and consumption are protests and boycotts that have condemned the use of animal testing and animal by-products in the production process. Concerns over the exploitation of animals have been one of the most powerful social movements in the beauty business, and have for some time caused many in and outside the beauty business to pay close attention to the suffering and sacrifice that go into the production of beauty products.

It is thus understandable that Angela Davis did not want to simplify the politics of liberation that continues to fight for equality and social justice, but it may indeed be problematic to dismiss the politics of fashion. On the one hand, the industry provides a means for men and women to tease out their sense of self and create identities that may or may not be more than skin deep. On the other hand, it markets artificiality and self-expression, and encourages consumers to mask as well as reveal their true self. Still, it does not operate in isolation. A multitude of daily interactions and popular assumptions create the context of consumer choices, making them infinitely complex and contradictory. Indeed, beauty goods and services can make the process as important as the final product. Events like the Triangle Shirt Waist Fire, ads that ask, "Does she or doesn't she?" and reality shows like *Queer Eye for the Straight Guy* are all part of an industry whose past and present often blur distinctions between beauty and politics.

NOTE

1. Angela Davis, "Afro Images; Politics, Fashion and Nostalgia," *Critical Inquiry,* 21 no. 2 (1994): 37–45.

Chronology

30,000 B.C.E.	Haircutting tools have been located from this era.
c. 3500 B.C.E.	Egyptians use eye makeup and cosmetics and have a rich array of beauty and health regimens.
600 B.C.E.	The nose (rhinoplasty) becomes the first part of the body to be surgically altered for aesthetic purposes, by the Indian surgeon Sushruta, and the procedure remains popular today.
296 B.C.E.	The Greek colony of Sicily introduces barbering to Rome; frequenting a tonsorial becomes a daily social ritual.
100 C.E.	Makeup on the eyes and cheeks, as well as the use of hair dyes, are common in the male grooming regimen in Rome.
1597	The first Western manual of plastic surgery (*De curtorum chirurgia*) by Italian physician Gaspare Tagliacozzi describes the procedure of using a flap graft to replace a missing nose.
1616	Puritan Thomas Tuke warns of women who embrace falsehood with a "painted face."
1770	The English parliament annuls marriages in which women have used "scents, paints, cosmetic washes, artificial teeth, false hair, Spanish wool, iron stays, hoops, high-heeled shoes and bolstered hips" to lure men into marriage.
1700s	Tattooing has become an established aspect of the commercial economies that have appeared in port cities across Europe.
1700s	Wig making remains a thriving artisanal craft in the American colonies until the wig, which has long been a symbol of status, begins to diminish in popularity during the early national period.
1820s	Mass-produced, ready-made gentlemen's clothing is first produced, primarily in New York and along the eastern seaboard.
1830	*Godey's Lady's Book* is published and affords fashionable American women the latest styles from Paris. It includes poetry, current events articles, and sheet music, as well as patterns for needlework designs and clothing.
1851	American women's suffrage pioneer Amelia Bloomer popularizes Turkish trouser–like pantaloons for women that gain popularity in the early 1900s.

1867	*Harper's Bazaar* is the first American magazine devoted specifically to fashion. It debuts as a weekly gazette with a mix of fashion illustrations, colored plates, and reports on what society's elite is wearing.
1875	Parisian Marcel Grateau perfects the use of a curling iron and popularizes the Marcel wave.
1879	Procter & Gamble introduces Ivory Soap, intended for both personal hygiene and laundry. It is not meant to be a beauty product and is sold on its purity and ability to float.
1879	French hairdresser Alexandre Godefroy invents the hot-blast hair dryer.
1886	The Journeymen Barbers International Union of America (JBIUA) is established and affiliates with the American Federation of Labor.
1886	Avon begins as the California Perfume Company. The company would change its name to Avon in 1939.
1886	The fashion magazine *Cosmopolitan* is first published.
1891	The first beauty school, known as the Harper Method Shop, opens in Rochester, New York.
1891	New Yorker Samuel O'Reilly patents the first electronic tattoo machine—a modification of Thomas Edison's electronic engraving machine.
1892	*Vogue,* the single best-known fashion magazine title in the world, is first produced as a weekly gazette.
1899	Bernarr Adolphus Macfadden (1868–1955) publishes the magazine *Physical Culture* to promote healthy diets, regular exercise, and the acquisition of muscle.
1901	Founding of the American Safety Razor Company, which will revolutionize men's shaving.
1904	Madam C. J. Walker, African American beauty industry leader, begins to produce her own products and sell them in person and by mail order. Her company's earnings will reach six figures by the 1910s.
1906	The Pure Food and Drug Act of 1906 allows the federal government to regulate the cosmetics industry and crack down on faulty marketing practices.
1906	German inventor Charles Nessler patents the original electric permanent wave machine.
1907	French chemist Eugene Schuller is credited with developing the first commercial hair color product that is safe for human use. The company he founds becomes known as L'Oréal.

1908	The first appearance of the bob can be traced to Paris and Polish-born Monsieur Antoine (Antek Cierplikowski) who cut the hair of actress Eve Lavallière into a short cut, which Antoine dubbed Jeanne d'Arc.
1908	Beauty entrepreneur Elizabeth Arden opens her first salon on New York's Fifth Avenue.
1911	The Triangle Shirt Waist Fire in New York City is a catalyst for anti-sweatshop campaigns of the era.
1914	Max Factor develops a foundation for actors that will not crack, cake, or crepe under the harsh studio lights, and soon afterward becomes a highly sought-after makeup artist in the film industry. He is credited with coining the term *makeup*, based on the phrase "to make up one's face."
1914	When war erupts in Europe, Helena Rubinstein and her husband immigrate to New York City, where she opens a Fifth Avenue beauty salon.
1916	Elizabeth Arden (1878–1966), known for founding and operating a chain of high-end beauty spas and salons, marked by her trademark red door, ranks first in the nation in prestige skin care sales.
1918	Lulu Hunt publishes the first popular weight-control book titled *Diet and Health with a Key to the Calories*.
1918	Annie Minnerva Turnbo Malone, one of the most successful black female entrepreneurs of the early 20th century, opens Poro College—an institution that will include a factory and store for hair and cosmetic products, hairdressing school, dormitory, and auditorium, as well as dining and committee rooms used for meetings, banquets, lectures, and entertainment.
1921	The first Miss America pageant promotes the tourist commerce of Atlantic City, New Jersey.
1924	Anna May Wong, the first Asian American movie star, becomes internationally known and revered as a fashion icon.
1924	*Modern Beauty Shop*—now known as *Modern Salon*—a trade journal, is first published and reflects the dramatic growth of popularly priced beauty shops across the country.
1926	French designer Coco Chanel's little black dress is introduced to the world of fashion.
1926	Proctor & Gamble introduces its first personal beauty soap, Camay, a perfumed bar.
1929	Lastex, a rubber elastic thread manufactured by Dunlop Rubber Company, replaces whale bone in corsets.

1931	The American Society of Plastic and Reconstructive Surgeons (ASPRS) is organized.
1932	The Revlon Cosmetics Company is founded.
1933	Estée Lauder, one of the most prominent 20th century entrepreneurs in the beauty industry, begins a home-based cosmetics business during the Great Depression.
1933	Animal testing for cosmetic safety begins in the United States after an eyelash-darkening treatment called Lash Lure blinds a woman.
1938	The Food and Drug Administration (FDA) passes the Federal Food, Drug, and Cosmetic Act to provide safeguards against the harmful effects of cosmetic use.
1939	The first Mr. America contest, held in Amsterdam, New York, celebrates the muscular male body.
1944	The Draize test by John Draize is the most commonly used test on rabbits to evaluate eye damage in shampoos, deodorants, laundry detergents, and other soaps.
1944	*Seventeen* magazine, a beauty and lifestyle magazine designed for American teenagers, makes its debut.
1945	*Ebony* is first published. This is a monthly magazine that chronicles the social, political, economic, and cultural activities of people of African descent in the United States and abroad, self-described as one the "earliest and most passionate defenders of Black beauty."
1946	Estée Lauder and her husband expand the sales business to beauty salons and hotels, founding the Estée Lauder Company.
1947	French fashion designer Christian Dior (1905–57), who began his career over a decade earlier, launches his first collection.
1951	Clearasil, a popular brand of acne medication, is first mass marketed to teens.
1952	Proctor & Gamble begins to manufacture Gleem toothpaste, followed by the even more popular Crest toothpaste, marketed in 1955.
1952	The merry widow, a foundation garment, is invented for and worn by actress Lana Turner in *The Merry Widow*. The film brings a renewed attention to the breast, depicting the ideal mid-century hourglass feminine figure with a cinched waistline.
1953	Hugh Hefner first publishes *Playboy* magazine, a lifestyles magazine for urban men, featuring the nude centerfold of Hollywood actress Marilyn Monroe.

1954	The Johnson Products Company is founded in Chicago and focuses initially on the African American male hair care market.
1955	Revlon reveals the power of television advertising when it successfully begins a lipstick war against competition to secure its domination of the market.
1955	Clairol dominates the hair color market with Shirley Polykoff's ad campaign that rhetorically asks "Does she or doesn't she . . . ?"
1957	*Gentlemen's Quarterly (GQ)* is launched as a new publication intended to whet the consumer appetites of fashion-conscious men of style and provide a broad range of lifestyle advice to its decidedly prosperous readers.
1957	Ultra Sheen, a chemical relaxer designed for women, helps to revolutionize the African American female hair care industry.
1958	CoverGirl, a cosmetics company, is founded by the Noxzema Chemical Company.
1959	An international organization, Beauty Without Cruelty (BWC), is formed to educate people about the suffering of animals.
1959	Du Pont's invention of Lycra increases comfort of the girdle.
1962	*Newsweek* reports that the popularity of the bouffant among teenagers is troubling to parents who think their daughters are wasting too much time rolling and combing their hair.
1963	Weight Watchers, one of the best-known dieting programs, is launched.
1963	Mary Kay Cosmetics, a direct sales company known for its conservative corporate culture and the pink Cadillac, is launched, specializing in beauty products, especially skin care and makeup.
1963	British Hairdresser Vidal Sassoon rises to celebrity fame with his geometric bob cut.
1965	Mary Quant introduces the miniskirt at her London clothes shop, *Bazaar*.
1968	Feminists protest the Miss America Beauty Pageant by filling a trash can with bras, makeup, curlers, and other popular beauty products of the era.
1974	Fashion designer Calvin Klein prints his logo on t-shirts for the use and amusement of staffers at his company. The logo is soon in hot demand and ushers in the era of designer labels.
1976	Anita Roddick founds an earth-, animal-, and community-friendly cosmetic and skin care business, The Body Shop, in Great Britain.

1976	Farah Fawcett first appears in *Charlie's Angels*, a popular television detective series. Her feather-blown hairstyle and her iconic swimsuit poster make her an international fashion sensation.
1978	Environmentalist Horst Rechelbacher, who wanted to create personal care products using ingredients found in nature, establishes Aveda.
1981	Fifteen-year-old model/actress Brooke Shields appears in a provocative Calvin Klein jeans commercial that defines the designer's edgy approach to advertising.
1983	The Jenny Craig program, a popular system that focuses on weight loss, weight management, and nutrition, is marketed.
1983	Jockey International revolutionizes men's underwear sales by relying on revealing photographs of Baltimore Orioles pitcher Jim Palmer.
1984	In the spirit of laissez faire, the Reagan administration deregulates advertising on children's television.
1987	*Men's Health* magazine is launched, providing male readers with how-to advice for achieving the perfectly sculpted body.
1988	Rogaine, a product designed to encourage hair growth, especially for men, is mass marketed.
1990	The FDA bans 27 unsafe or ineffective ingredients commonly found in dandruff shampoos.
1990s	Korean and Vietnamese artisans and entrepreneurs make popularly priced pedicures and manicures the latest rage. By the end of the decade, the number of nail techs has tripled and nail salons are deemed one of the fastest-growing industries in the United States.
1991	The International SPA Association (ISPA) is the first professional organization to represent the industry and an indication of the newest trends in the beauty business.
1991	Naomi Wolf publishes *The Beauty Myth,* in which she argues that the notion that beauty equals liberation is false and constructed by the beauty industry as a marketing tool.
1994	British cultural critic Mark Simpson coins the term *metrosexual* in an article for the *Independent*.
1994	The J. Sisters Salon in New York City, a salon owned by seven Brazilian sisters, first offers the Brazilian wax in the United States.
1995	*Maxim,* a monthly men's magazine, is launched. It features articles about men's health, fashion, sports, and consumer goods, along with other male activities and men's culture.

1996   A scandal involving talk show host Kathy Lee Gifford and her brand of sportswear exclusively sold by Walmart reflects renewed media interest in sweatshop labor conditions at home and abroad.

1996   The Coalition for Consumer Information on Cosmetics (CCIC), an agglomeration of citizen groups, including the Humane Society of the United States, develops the Corporate Standard of Compassion for Animals in an effort to create an international non–animal testing standard.

2002   *Extreme Makeover,* a reality TV makeover program, debuts on ABC and features individuals who consider themselves ugly submitting videotapes that detail their facial and bodily flaws in hopes of being flown to Hollywood for an extensive makeover. A wave of similarly themed reality shows soon follows.

2002   The U.S. FDA approves the use of Botox, a derivative of the botulinum bacterium, an increasingly popular cosmetic treatment that reduces wrinkles by paralyzing the underlying facial muscles responsible for wrinkles around the forehead and eyes.

2002   Abercrombie & Fitch face ridicule for marketing thong underwear to tweens.

2004   The U.S. Department of Agriculture begins regulating organic personal care products; the first organic standard specifically targeting the beauty and personal care industry emerges in 2008.

2006   Uruguayan model Luisel Ramos dies of a heart attack brought on by anorexia nervosa during a fashion show; just a few months later, anorexia also claims the life of Brazilian model Ana Carolina Reston.

2006   The National Latino Cosmetology Association, a nonprofit organization founded by CEO Julie Zepeda, is established.

2008   The FDA Globalization Act is established to provide the FDA with the authority to regulate food, cosmetics, drugs, and medical devices in a global marketplace.

2009   The European Union bans all animal testing for cosmetics and the sale of animal-tested cosmetics.

2009   First Lady and fashion icon, Michelle Obama, is featured on the cover of *Vogue.*

A

ACNE

Pimples or zits, as they are so commonly known, have been considered the bane of teenage complexions since the early 20th century. Whether teens and young adults pop them, cover them with makeup, or use a steady stream of commercial products, much time and money has been spent trying to reduce the appearance of blemishes. An obsession with breakouts reflects the degree to which acne is associated with unclean or impure thoughts: in the early 20th century, popular belief held that acne was a sign of some internal spiritual struggle or sexual immorality. This only fueled the need to combat acne medically, because young women were particularly concerned with their reputations and did not want to be seen as immoral. Acne, physical beauty, and marriage were inextricably bound, and girls sought treatments for acne because they feared that without clear skin they would wind up as spinsters or old maids. Boys and men were also the target of innuendos. Male acne sufferers, for example, were called pansies, and it was assumed that they engaged in questionable activities like masturbation. Acne, when not seen as a spiritual concern, was an indicator of dirtiness, linked with the lower classes, especially at the turn of the century when scientists and Progressives began to talk about germs and the unsanitary conditions of the working class. Today it is known that acne is not caused by dirt, but rather by bacteria. However, some of the most effective treatments are available by prescription only and can be quite expensive. Thus, acne can still be seen as an affliction of the lower classes, those who cannot afford the pricey treatments to attain clear skin and are more likely to be subjected to critiques of lifestyle.

Causes and Types

Acne vulgaris is a skin disease caused by overproduction of the sebaceous glands surrounding hair follicles. There are different types of acne that vary in severity, but all acne lesions can pose problems for the afflicted. Acne is most common during adolescence, but frequently continues into adulthood. For most people acne begins to disappear once they are in their early 20s. Acne usually forms on the face and upper neck, but the chest, back, and shoulders can also be affected. The sebaceous glands are found on the face, neck, back, and chest and produce sebum, which is necessary for keeping skin healthy. If one of these follicles, or pores, gets clogged with impurities or dead skin cells it can lead to a buildup of sebum, which causes a pimple to form.

Acne pimples come in many forms and vary according to the severity of each case. Non-inflammatory acne is defined as acne lesions that are not accompanied by redness of the skin. The most common forms of non-inflammatory acne are blackheads and whiteheads. Blackheads are blocked pores, which have a dark appearance. Whiteheads appear as small white bumps on the skin. Papules are the mildest form of inflammatory acne and appear as small pink bumps on the skin, which can be painful to the touch. Pustules and nodules are the most severe forms of acne. Pustules are small, round lesions that are inflamed. Nodules are large, painful lesions deep within the skin. These will sometimes last for months and often harden into cysts. Some forms of acne are caused by hormone imbalances and can be treated with hormone therapy or the birth control pill. Periodic flare-ups of acne in women can be traced to hormonal imbalances as part of the onset of puberty, the menstrual cycle, or pregnancy.

Treatments

In the early 20th century, an emerging **advertising** industry began to target young people with acne, who were part of a new **teenage consumer market**. And although youth have relied on many do-it-yourself remedies, over-the-counter medications became the preferred and most widely available treatment. These treatments include the use of sulfur, salicylic acid, and benzoyl peroxide. Sulfur has been used in the treatment of acne since the 19th century and works simply by absorbing excess oil on the skin's surface. It is a common ingredient in facial masks and many other over-the-counter treatments. Sulfur is one of the mildest acne treatments, but is not as commonly used as others due to its smell. Salicylic acid is a mild acid that encourages the shedding of dead skin cells. It works well for milder acne by keeping pores from becoming clogged and is the most commonly available over-the-counter treatment. For the more severe cases of acne, harsher and more effective medications have been sought out. In the 1920s, benzoyl peroxide began to be used by **dermatologists** and became available over the counter in the 1950s. Clearasil, a popular brand of acne medication, first appeared on the scene just as complexion-conscious baby boomers were coming of age in the 1950s. Benzoyl peroxide works by killing the bacteria *P. acnes* that causes outbreaks. It also reduces the number of blocked pores by working as an antiseptic. One of the more effective but controversial treatments is isotretinoin, sold under the brand name Accutane. It is considered to be a last-resort treatment for patients who have tried everything else with limited or no results. Accutane was introduced in 1982 and continues to be a popular treatment for patients suffering from moderate acne to severe nodular acne. While it has been considered a breakthrough miracle drug for the treatment of acne, Accutane has been known to cause serious side effects and has therefore remained controversial. In some cases, the drug causes a worsening of the symptoms before an improvement is seen and, in women, has been linked to severe birth defects. In some cases, use of the drug has been linked to an increased risk of depression.

Natural treatments such as the use of tea tree oil in place of the harsher chemical, benzoyl peroxide, may be effective in some cases. Caring for one's overall health is also recommended. This includes drinking the recommended daily amount of water in order to flush the system and to keep skin moisturized. It is widely accepted that the most effective means of combating mild to moderate acne is to simply keep the skin clean and to refrain from touching one's face. A lot of the greener treatments have become popular as a result of a renewed focus on natural health and the rejection of harsh chemicals in beauty rituals. These natural remedies are often more expensive than the traditional treatments, and therefore have yet to tap in to the teenage consumer market.

"The early Clearasil campaigns in *Seventeen* demonstrate how marketers spoke to girls. At first, Clearasil did not do much more than tout itself as a 'revolutionary, new skin colored miracle medication.' At that time, the advertisements showed a small line drawing of a worried face, a doctor at a microscope, and a dancing couple. Clearasil's promoters explained how their product was both a medication and a cosmetic: 'Clearasil works while it hides pimples amazingly!' A bubble above the head of the happy female dancer proclaimed (ungrammatically): 'No more embarrassment of blemishes.' In order to entice *Seventeen* readers to try it, the manufacturer promised a money-back guarantee if Clearasil did not 'amaze you.' When this advertisement first appeared, in 1951, a tube of Clearasil cost fifty-nine cents, which was affordable for girls who had even a small allowance or some weekly baby-sitting money."

Joan Jacobs Brumberg, historian

Source: Jacobs Brumberg, Joan. *The Body Project: An Intimate History of American Girls.* New York: Vintage, 1997, 86.

There are many popular theories as to what actually causes acne, but youthful indiscretions have often been blamed because it tends to peak during the teenage years. To be sure, these theories have changed over time as part of a constantly evolving medical, political, and cultural discourse. For example, sexual immorality is no longer readily linked to poor complexions. Instead, parents are more likely to urge their children to avoid eating greasy food or chocolate, thus holding teenage self-indulgence accountable. Although this has been disproven, poor eating habits remains the most popular explanation, blaming blemishes not on bacteria but on the lifestyle choices of children and families. In reality, effective treatments are expensive and time consuming and, much like unnaturally white teeth, they reveal less about the daily habits and much more about a segmented market that reflects the growing division between those who can afford costly beauty treatments and those who cannot.

Further Reading: Acne.com, sponsored by Proactive Solution. http://www.acne.com/prevention/medications.php; Banner, Lois. *American Beauty.* New York: Knopf, 1983; Brumberg, Joan Jacobs. *The Body Project: An Intimate History of American Girls.* New York: Vintage, 1997; Kern, Daniel. *What is Acne?* http://www.acne.org

http://health.yahoo.com/skinconditions-medications/isotretinoin-oral/healthwise—d01245a1.html;

Krystal A. Humphreys

ADVERTISING

Advertising is a communication method designed and intended to promote a product or service for consumer purchase and use. Although advertising takes many forms, in the beauty industry its aim involves targeting men and women with stereotypical idealized images of physical appearance and attractiveness, along with an ideology that consumers are expected to exhibit when and after using that product. However, the images presented and methods promoted typically convey a singular, stereotypical message. As a result, advertising in the beauty industry has faced harsh criticism for being racist, sexist, detrimental to society, and unrepresentative of the targeted audience or the status quo.

History

Beauty advertising in the 20th century follows the development of modern advertising throughout the late 18th and 19th centuries. Modern advertising developed with the rise of education, print capitalism, and Western economies. New groups

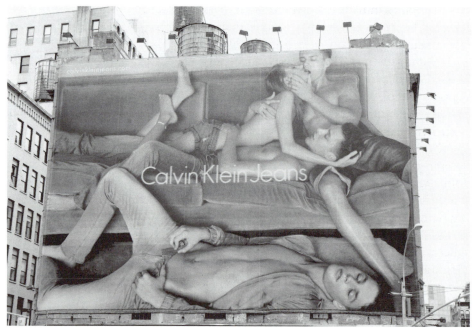

Calvin Klein billboard at Houston and Lafayette in Manhattan, 2009. (AP Photo/ Seth Wenig)

and business agencies emerged to facilitate, organize, and develop advertisements as the practice expanded during the 19th century. Industrialization in the latter half of the 19th century further changed the purpose and outlook of large-scale advertising and created a business environment for the advertising of specific industries like beauty to emerge. In the 20th century, imagery and ideology were the primary factors that contributed to advertising campaigns. The availability of new products in the first decades of the 20th century contributed to the growth of advertising, and beauty products were present to change the cultural and social dynamics of Americans lives. In the early decades of the 20th century, new manufacturers and companies were set up to produce, specialize in, and advertise new and specific products. Unique to the beauty industry is the litany of female entrepreneurs shaping early advertising practices. In 1890, **hairdresser** Martha Matilda Harper licensed her Harper Method, which became the foundation for 300 **beauty salons** in the Northeast. And the most successful of her time, **Madam C. J. Walker** relied on her own rags-to-riches story, along with Walker agents, to promote her products, processes, and the occupation of beauty culture. While her husband Charles initially helped her start the business, it was she who made it national in scope. Many female entrepreneurs transformed beauty methods and **beauty schools** into franchises.

Embracing a new ethos and style, beauty products attempted to cash in on the panache of the modern girl. Her bright smile, bobbed hair, and embrace of boyish adventure made the flapper the It girl for advertising a string of products from deodorant to toothpaste and face cream. However, when it came to **cosmetics**, the main tool used for advertising in the roaring '20s was radio, because many women's magazines initially refused cosmetic advertising. The taint of wearing rouge, however, began to fade, and the end of the decade witnessed a dramatic increase in the amount spent on advertising, from $300,000 in 1927 to $3.2 million in 1930. Additionally, **African American beauty products** expanded dramatically in the 1920s beyond those designed for **hair care** and hairdressing. Madam C. J. Walker's company introduced face powder and skin-care products in the 1920s to capitalize on modern sensibilities and the demands of drugstore **retailers**. Most controversial, however, was the company's decision to sell skin bleachers such as Tan-Off, something Walker refused to market before her death, but which later became popular.

By the 1920s and 1930s, companies were introducing and reconfiguring new products and methods of cosmetic application and use, and new technologies like motion pictures contributed to a multitude of cultural and social shifts in attitudes that forever changed the industry. **Films** and images of celebrities reflected and created new standards of female beauty, especially with manufacturers like **Max Factor** who sold celebrities products that did not cake or crack. Factor used this reputation and the appearance of his products on stars like Alice White to sell his methods and products to the average consumer. The flawless complexions of celebrities and their sexual allure caused an interest in cosmetic products as a way to improve one's appearance, both as a measure of personal taste and a method of attracting the opposite sex. Although this had been projected as a female world of commerce, Factor was marketed as the lab-coat-wearing expert who exemplified the male image of authority, even in a decidedly feminine pursuit.

After World War II, advertisements promoted new goods and products to a population that had been wary of material and consumer culture during the crises of the previous two decades. The introduction of the television furthered the power of advertising, as the TV radically changed how Americans experienced entertainment and the proliferation of numerous new goods and products. Programs produced for television, as for radio, were backed by money offered from companies that would promote specific products and **brands** during the program's broadcast. Beauty products were no exception, and television helped advertisers to choose what products were advertised and which audiences were exposed to those products. **Revlon** revealed the power of television advertising when it successfully conducted a lipstick war against Hazel Bishop between 1955 and 1958, eventually growing to become the top cosmetics manufacturer by the end of the 1960s, with six separate product lines designed to appeal to different classes of consumers.

In the 1960s and 1970s, advertising was still male dominated, but not immune to **feminist** critiques that drew attention to women's objectification in all advertising, as well as opposing the use of cosmetics altogether. In response, **Estée Lauder** introduced Clinique in 1967, which was a product line designed to promote skin care and cosmetic use as a regular, everyday, healthy cleansing product. Many of the new more **natural looks** in beauty were accompanied by new advertising messages, sometimes selling the same old merchandise but recast to reflect a more feminist stance. L'Oréal's "I'm Worth It" campaign for hair color, for example, was followed by other ads attempting to capture the mixed consciousness of female consumers. One of the more memorable 1980s advertisement was Enjoli's "8-Hour Perfume" that featured a career-minded gal touting that she "can bring home bacon, fry it up in pan . . . and never, never, never let you forget you're a man."

Criticisms and the Future

Images of sex and sexuality have long been used as powerful tools in advertising products and services and raised critiques about the beauty industry as a whole. These images range from highly explicit displays of sexual activity to products designed with the intention of improving physical appearance and attractiveness. Sexual images may have little to do or little in common with the product in question, and are used only because the image sparks interest in the product. Overt images have accompanied fragrance products, for example, where men and women are depicted semi-clothed or nude and in sexually explicit or suggestive positions. In 1981, when **Calvin Klein** featured 15-year-old Brooke Shields evocatively announcing to the world that "nothing comes between me and my Calvins," the consuming public was infuriated yet titillated. Over the next several decades, CK jeans, fragrances, and even children's underwear would present a litany of all-too-young-looking, at times **androgynous**, always sensual Calvin Klein **models**. In the 1990s, for example, British model Kate Moss came to epitomize a heroin chic that invoked accusations of anorexia and a reprimand from President

Bill Clinton. Most recently, in 2009, the latest CK controversy erupted over images of oiled-down topless models in sensual play that feature a teenage-looking girl presumably being passed around from one man to the next, all of whom, once again, were wearing nothing but their Calvins. Calvin Klein may be one of the better-known advertisers when it comes to pushing the envelope, but such ads are indicative of the larger beauty industry and its precarious balance between the erotic, exotic, and constantly changing mores.

Critics have been especially fearful of any and all advertising to children, an industry that represents nearly $600 billion a year. Fears include worries over body image and obesity, poor nutrition, and alcohol and tobacco use. Advertising tools have come under fire as a result, especially cartoon characters that brand specific products for the youngest of audiences. Some psychologists have even reported that advertising to children under a certain age should not be conducted at all, since it could result in feelings of inferiority if they do not possess specific or numerous products. The fashion industry's quest for the new **tween market** fuels debates over selling sexuality to preadolescents.

New Technologies

The growth of advertising throughout the 20th and into the 21st century brought numerous criticisms and attempts to avoid or detach the influence of advertising fueled by the latest technology on American life-concerns. Some groups looked at how advertisements targeted specific groups, with the major concern being what kind of influence advertising could hold. During the last decades of the 20th century and in the early 21st, the cropped and airbrushed images of persons used to promote the use of brands and products created unobtainable body images that could distort expectations of self-worth and well-being. Critiques of advertising have also increased with the introduction of new technological methods to dispense advertisements and products, in particular the **Internet**. The Internet also allows advertising for a range of beauty products to enter into consumers' lives on a very regular basis, as trial use can be tracked in manufacturer Web sites and different methods can be assessed in demonstration animations.

The growth of advertising into the 21st century and the development of new technologies and media indicate that advertising is not in any position to decrease or lose momentum. Global developments in communications also suggest that advertising will take on new meanings for consumers as manufacturers are forced to compete in new markets and for new customers. However, the criticisms have not been ignored. In 2007, Dove created the Self Esteem Fund, intending to promote healthy body images and build conversations with consumers about what they need and how they feel about the products offered and used on a daily basis. Regardless of the controversy, advertising is an essential element of material culture and the development of new technologies that create new methods and mediums to advertise products. Advertising promotes and helps construct the culture around Americans, creating systems for that culture to grow through the continuous consumption and production of beauty goods and fashions, the meanings of which remain part of complex and controversial dialogues.

Further Reading: APA Task Force on Advertising and Children. "Television Advertising Leads to Unhealthy Habits in Children." *American Psychologist Association Online.* http://www.apa.org/releases/childrenads.html. (Accessed October 21, 2008); Barlow, Tani E., Madeleine Yue Dong, Uta G. Poiger, Priti Ramamurthy, Lynn M. Thomas, and Alys Eve Weinbaum. "The Modern Girl around the World: A Research Agenda and Preliminary Findings." *Gender & History,* 17 no. 2 (August 2005): 245–94; "Brooke Shields in the Calvin Klein Jeans Commercial 1981." www.youtube.com/watch?v=YK2VZgJ4AoM. (Accessed June 17, 2007); "Calvin Klein: A Case Study." http://www.media-awareness.ca/english/resources/educational/handouts/ethics/calvin_klein_case_study.cfm. (Accessed July 6, 2009); "Calvin Klein CK One/CK BePromo-'Altered States.'" www.youtube.com/watch?v=BKvjAUAPve4. (Accessed July 12, 2006); Clay, Rebecca A. "Advertising to Children: Is it Ethical?" *Monitory on Psychology,* 31 no. 8. http://www.apa.org/monitor/sep00/advertising.html. (Accessed October 21, 2008); Committee on Communications. "Children, Adolescents, and Advertising." *Pediatrics,* 118 no. 6. http://pediatrics.aappublications.org/cgi/content/full/118/6/2563. (Accessed October 21, 2008); Donaldson James, Susan. "Calvin Klein Taps Foursome Sex." Abcnews.go.com/business/story?id=7854000&page=1. (Accessed June 17, 2009); *Gallup and Robinson: Sex in Advertising.* http://www.gallup-robinson.com/essay1.html. (Accessed October 21, 2008); Hill, Daniel Delis. *Advertising to the American Woman, 1900–1999.* Columbus: Ohio State University Press, 2002; Johnson, Fern L. *Imaging in Advertising: Verbal and Visual Codes in Advertising.* New York: Routledge, 2008; Kilbourne, Jean. "Beauty . . . and the Beast of Advertising." *Media & Values,* 49. http://www.medialit.org/reading_room/article40.html. (Accessed October 21, 2008); Nakayama, Tom. "Images of Men in Advertising." *Media & Values,* 48. http://www.medialit.org/reading_room/article438.html. (Accessed October 21, 2008); Peiss, Kathy Lee. *Hope in a Jar: The Making of America's Beauty Culture.* New York: Metropolitan Books, 1998; Pope, Daniel. "Making Sense of Advertisements." *History Matters: The U.S. Survey Course on the Web.* http://historymatters.gmu.edu/mse/ads/. (Accessed October 21, 2008); Purifoy, Jennifer. "Understanding the History of Cosmetics." *History of 20th Century Fashion.* http://www.digitalhistory.uh.edu/do_history/fashion/Cosmetics/cosmetics.html. (Accessed October 23, 2008); Quart, Alissa. *Branded: The Buying and Selling of Teenagers.* New York: Basic Books, 2004; "Retro Enjoli Commercial." www.youtube.com/watch?v=4X4wbVfOA. (Accessed March 7, 2006); Schor, Juliet. *Born to Buy: The Commercialized Child and the New Consumer Society.* New York: Scribner, 2004; "The Beauty Business: Pots of Promise." *The Economist,* May 22, 2003, 71–74; Walker, Susannah. *Style and Status: Selling Beauty to African American Women, 1920–1975.* Lexington: University Press of Kentucky, 2007; Weitz, Rose. *Rapunzel's Daughters: What Women's Hair Tell Us about Women's Lives.* New York: Farrar, Straus and Giroux, 2004; Wren, Christopher. "Clinton Call Fashion Ads' 'Heroin Chic' Deplorable." *New York Times,* May 22, 1997.

Richard D. Driver

AFRICAN AMERICAN BEAUTY INDUSTRY

The African American beauty industry comprises cosmetic and hair product companies, beauty salons, and professional organizations engaged in the business of selling commercial beauty products and services to black women. A specialized African American beauty industry emerged in the late 19th and early 20th centuries due to segregation and because entrepreneurs, black and white, sought to build markets for products and services geared specifically toward African American women's hair textures and skin tones. Initially, African American women dominated the product-**manufacturing** industry and used agent sales and other direct marketing techniques to distribute them. In conjunction with this, agents often trained through company programs to style black women's hair, while other women received beauty training independently, leading to a proliferation of small **beauty shops** and home-based businesses in African American neighborhoods. Migration to urban areas and rising black consumerism in the early 20th century encouraged this trend, and generally led to greater demand for beauty products. This, along with the increasing use of print **advertising** and **retail** venues to market and distribute products, attracted significant numbers of white-owned companies to the industry by the 1920s and 1930s. By the beginning of World War II, white-owned companies controlled a large market share and continued to have a strong presence after the war, even as new black-owned companies emerged and African American beauty salons, **beauty schools**, and professional organizations enjoyed unprecedented growth and success in the same era. The industry adjusted to shifting beauty standards in the late 1960s and into the 1970s, offering products and services for **Afros** and other natural **hairstyles** while significantly curtailing the promotion of skin-lightening products. Into the 1980s and 1990s, black-owned product companies struggled to maintain independence as large national and multinational personal care corporations bought out many of the most prominent African American firms.

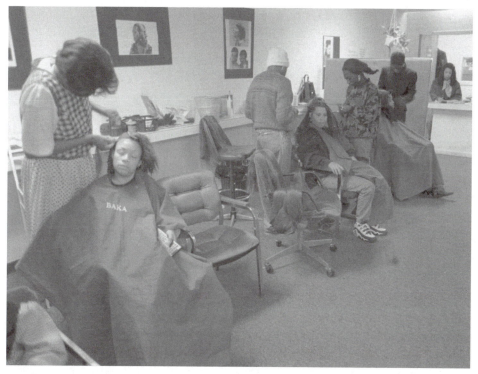

Women have their hair braided at the Baka Beautiful Braiding Salon and Boutique in Philadelphia, 1995. (AP Photo/H. Rumph, Jr.)

Before 1920

Until the late 19th century, most African American women, like white women in the United States, did their own hair at home; when they used hair or cosmetic products at all, they used homemade preparations more often than commercially produced products. During slavery, black women in the South used braiding, twisting, and wrapping techniques, many drawn from African traditions, as both decorative and practical means to care for and manage their hair. Several developments, including the growth of black populations in towns and cities, increasing numbers of African American women working for wages, and the broader proliferation of commercially produced and marketed beauty products in general by the late 19th century, contributed to the emergence of the African American beauty industry.

In the era of Jim Crow, African American entrepreneurs were able to carve out a space for themselves in spite of (and to a significant degree because of) racial segregation and economic discrimination. This was particularly the case in personal care businesses including funeral homes, **barber** and beauty shops, and grooming/cosmetic product manufacturers. The early growth of the African American beauty industry is in part documented in African American newspapers, which often carried advertisements for products in these years. The advertising represented dozens of small, mostly mail order businesses whose stories do not survive in the historical record; a few, however, notably Overton Hygenic, Poro Company, and **Madam C. J. Walker** Manufacturing Company, gained national success and widespread notoriety. Later, by the 1920s, Sara Washington's Apex Company would also be founded. **Annie Malone** (founder of Poro) and Madam C. J. Walker were probably the most famous and successful marketers of hair and cosmetic products to black women at this time. This was due to their marketing strategy, which involved training black women to use a heated iron comb, oils, and pomades to straighten African American women's hair, and employing these women as beauticians and sales agents across the country. Agents worked independently, paying the company for training and products, a business strategy that predated agent sales–based companies like **Avon** and **Mary Kay Cosmetics**.

In this period, **hair straightening** was a growing but quite controversial practice for African Americans, even in urban areas where it was most popular. Given this, black-owned companies like Poro and Walker downplayed straightening products and methods in newspaper advertising, stressing instead that their products improved hair health and promoted good grooming, and emphasizing their role in helping black women to gain financial independence as agents and **hairdressers**. These black-owned companies did not produce many cosmetic products, although they all sold face powders in darker shades. By the early part of the 20th century many of these black-owned companies did produce skin-bleaching creams, but they almost never advertised them, which many white-owned companies did at the same time, often using crude images such as a woman's face split in half, one side black and one white.

1920 to World War II

During the 1920s and 1930s, new more sophisticated advertising techniques and the proliferation of chain stores transformed the African American beauty industry. Overall, using commercial hair and cosmetic products became more common for women across racial lines in this period, a trend that reflected a variety of changes in women's lives, including urbanization, increasing participation in the waged workforce, and shorter hairstyles that required more professional care. The industry used sophisticated advertising that linked beauty and beauty products to female popularity, glamour, and romantic success. African American–owned beauty product companies expanded product lines and adopted the new advertising strategies as well, in part as a response to white-owned companies like Golden Brown and Plough's, which placed extensive advertising in black publications, and in part due to a new emphasis on the retail sale of beauty products in drugstores and five-and-tens, which increased the need for **brand** recognition and introduced the pressure of side-by-side brand competition. Many white-owned companies portrayed themselves as black-owned in advertisements, a trend that would not have been as successful in a market dominated exclusively by agent sales. In spite of this, the service side of the African American beauty industry continued to grow and employ black women, a trend reflected in the proliferation of beauty colleges (both independent and company sponsored), as well as beauty salons in black neighborhoods.

Post-World War II to the Present

World War II brought a new wave of African American urban migration and economic growth that supported a booming African American beauty industry in the late 1940s and 1950s. Many new companies emerged, often white-owned, but significant exceptions to this included the **Johnson Products** Company and Supreme Beauty Product Company. All of the new companies advertised in newly started black magazines like ***Ebony*** and *Hue,* and most began to market, with increasing success into the 1960s, new products for chemically straightening hair (rather than using pressing combs and oil). African American beauty salons enjoyed widespread growth as neighborhood shops and as large, well-publicized beauty shops that employed dozens of beauticians in cities like New York, Chicago, and Detroit. Beauticians and product manufacturers worried, initially, about the popularity of Afros in the wake of the civil rights and Black Power movements, but were able to market products and services for caring for unstraightened hair.

By the late 1970s, and certainly by the 1980s, while other natural styles such as braids emerged, products and services for chemical straightening dominated the industry. Especially by the 1970s, several new companies emerged that claimed to be the first to produce **cosmetics** for African American skin tones, even though companies such as Madam C. J. Walker had advertised such products for decades. Articles on the subject in black magazines, from the 1940s into the 2000s, perennially complained about the lack of good foundations for darker skin tones, although recent authors acknowledge that the chemical technology (especially in the creation of sheer foundation bases) has improved significantly in recent years.

Non-African American ownership of African American beauty products continued to be a controversial issue into the 1990s and 2000s on a variety of fronts. In the 1990s, the entry of Asian and **Asian American** entrepreneurs into the business of manufacturing and marketing hair extensions and **wigs** for black women became increasingly commonplace. On a larger scale, national cosmetics and hair product companies such as L'Oréal and **Revlon** were buying out black-owned companies, sometimes keeping brand names and product lines, and at other times launching new product lines, using prominent African American celebrities as spokespeople.

Further Reading: Blackwelder, Julia Kirk. *Styling Jim Crow: African American Beauty Training during Segregation.* College Station: Texas A&M University Press, 2003; Craig, Maxine B. *Ain't I a Beauty Queen? Black Women, Beauty, and the Politics of Race.* New York: Oxford University Press, 2002; Peiss, Kathy. *Hope in a Jar: The Making of America's Beauty Culture.* New York: Metropolitan Books, 1998; Rooks, Noliwe. *Hair Raising: Beauty, Culture, and African American Women.* New Brunswick, NJ: Rutgers University Press, 1996; Walker, Susannah. *Style and Status: Selling Beauty to African American Women, 1920–1975.* Lexington: University Press of Kentucky, 2007; Willett, Julie A. *Permanent Waves: The Making of the American Beauty Shop.* New York: New York University Press, 2000.

Susannah Walker

AFRO

The Afro is a **hairstyle** that was popularized by African Americans in the late 1960s and 1970s, and signaled racial pride and the embrace of a new aesthetic. Characterized by stretching tightly coiled or kinky hair into a large round crown, the Afro is one of the most recognizable hairstyles in American culture. Alternately heralded for liberating African Americans from decades of self-hatred and torturous beauty regiments and vilified as a symbol of militancy and racial separatism, the Afro has been a part of some of the most important debates concerning black beauty and politics.

While the Afro was a style worn by African American men and women at the height of its popularity, it was seen as a greater departure from aesthetic norms for African American women. For decades leading up to the late 1960s, the only acceptable way for an African American woman to wear her hair was to have it straightened with a hot metal comb and then curled into style. Men, on the other hand, often wore their hair in its unstraightened state, but cut close to their heads, unlike the Afro which usually involved longer hair that was stretched, though not straightened, to reveal maximum height. Breaking with conventions that deemed that the only acceptable way for African American women to wear their hair was straightened, a small group of artistic women in urban areas began wearing what they called the *natural,* a shorter version of what would become the Afro, as early as 1952. However, the style did not become widely worn until disappointment with the failed promises of the modern black freedom struggle of the 1950s and early 1960s gave rise to a more nationalistic black politics that encouraged not only political engagement, but cultural markings in the form of clothing and hairstyles. While the style was popular among those who came of age during the civil rights movement, it was never fully embraced by older African Americans, who rejected it as radical and a reflection of poor grooming.

While the Afro gained in popularity throughout the late 1960s and 1970s as a hairstyle associated with those who were shifting away from integration and toward black self determination, the style was also popular among those who did not share such politics. Some beauticians who originally eschewed the style because they thought it would cut into their profits soon began adopting the Afro as a fashion trend, promoting an extensive bevy of products designed to maintain the style, and even selling a line of **wigs** designed to mimic the fullness and roundness of the Afro.

By 1977, however, the *Washington Post* declared that the Afro was "doing a graceful fadeout," making way for the increased popularity of hairstyles that relied on

Black militant Angela Davis, with her iconic Afro, New York City, 1973. (AP Photo)

chemical **hair straightening**. However, even as the rise of a more conservative national politics rendered the nationalistic racial politics represented by the Afro virtually obsolete, **African American beauty culture** was forever changed by the style. While most African American women currently wear their hair straightened, the Afro introduced a new black aesthetic that celebrated the beauty of black hair in its natural state.

Further Reading: Byrd, Ayanna, and Lori Tharps. *Hair Story: Untangling the Roots of Black Hair in America.* New York: St. Martin Press, 2001; Craig, Maxine Leeds. *Ain't I a Beauty Queen: Black Women, Beauty, and the Politics of Race.* New York: Oxford University Press, 2002; Rooks, Noliwe. *Hair Raising: Beauty Culture and African American Women.* New Brunswick, NJ: Rutgers University Press, 1996; Walker, Susannah. *Style and Substance: Selling Beauty to African American Women, 1920–1975.* Lexington: University of Kentucky Press, 2007.

Tiffany M. Gill

ANDROGYNY

Throughout different periods in Western history, men and women have both embraced what today is considered to be androgynous fashion. Prior to the Industrial Revolution and before the decline of the aristocracy in the late 18th century, aristocratic men indulged in **cosmetics**, preferred perfectly coifed hair and powdered **wigs**, and adorned themselves in lace, velvets, and silk. Increasingly, the elaborate outfits of aristocratic males embodied the slothfulness and leisurely abominations of the upper classes. Proletarian men dressed in austere and distinct clothing to distance themselves from the aristocracy; they dressed in a manner that represented their class and Protestant work values. Women's fashion remained largely unaffected by the restructuring of men's fashion; nevertheless, women often embraced cross-dressing (although distinct in many ways from androgyny) to slip into male worlds of leisure, romance, work, and politics. However, it would not be until the counterrevolutions of the 1960s and '70s that directly challenged long-standing assumptions about sex and gender that the fashion industry would fully embrace androgyny as a marketing strategy.

Attempts at androgyny have often reflected social and cultural movements in the 1960s and 70s. Second-wave **feminism**, for example, opened traditionally male professions to the working girl who, in the name of equality, sought pantsuits, slacks, ties, and pressed dress shirts to signify her transition from domesticity to a position of authority. Working women's use of androgynous style, however, proved to be a double bind. Women with long hair and a conventionally feminine appearance often represented less of a threat to the male-dominated workforce, which increased her employment and advancement opportunities. To ensure the continuation of women's femininity, today's **designers** soften women's work clothes to prevent women from losing their feminine identity. Thus, a blazer may be thrown over a blouse to support a professional appearance.

In the 1960s, males once again began to play with androgynous styles, but this time it was all about hair. Men's visits to **barber shops** declined and, more often than not, they simply grew their hair long or frequented unisex salons. In order to adapt to this new trend, beauty salons often dropped traditional symbols of effeminacy, such as a pink and frilly décor, and transformed the **beauty shop** into a more gender-neutral space. While long hair stood in contrast to the crew cut, something that was highly significant against the backdrop of the Vietnam War, rock and rollers contributed to androgynous fashion trends on both sides of the Atlantic. The Beatles' girlish mop tops gave rise to an older generation's concerns that "you can't tell the boys from the girls." Indeed, a hippy aesthetic seemed to create as much debate as any political stance. By the 1972 Nixon-McGovern campaign, politics and style had completely intertwined and returning POWs (prisoners of war) were sometimes shocked by pictures of their long-haired adolescent sons and their support of antiwar politics. The Vietnamese, cast through the gaze of war, were caricatured as inverting gender norms, making men effete and women masculine, all of which, it has been noted, added to the sense of shock for returning POWs while fueling conservative reactions that associated a decline in traditional American values with women wearing unisex pants, shaggy-haired men, and left-wing movements. And in popular culture, the most visible symbol of androgyny in 1972 was rock star David Bowie, whose hot-orange Ziggy Stardust look gave rise to the 1980s mullet—a style popular regardless of gender.

A gay aesthetic would also have profound effects on the **advertising** industry. In the 1970s, the nude male photography exhibited by Wilhelm Von Golden, Robert Mapplethorpe, Arthur Tress, and other gay photographers also influenced designers to use the male body to advertise their men's lines in ways that challenged prevailing notions of gender distinction. **Calvin Klein**, the famous fashion designer and founder of Calvin Klein, Inc., integrated masculine depictions of the male body into fashion advertising and merchandising after visiting the Flamingo bar in New York City. Not only did CK ads recast the male body in erotic poses of vulnerability and sensuality commonly associated with the female **model**, but ads selling CK One, a fragrance for either sex, relied on the youthful embrace of androgyny to sell its product.

In the late 1980s, some fashion observers doubted androgyny would fully reemerge, but recent trends have proven them wrong. Blue jeans, for example, once the epitome of working-class masculinity, were transformed decades ago into mainstream attire for either sex. However, a younger generation of men are providing a bit of a twist on the once exclusively male fashion by not simply rejecting the baggy style that has recently dominated men's lower half, but also purchasing women's skinny jeans such as those introduced by Hedi Slimane of Yves Saint Laurent. As well, both Emo culture (coming from style, music, and an ethos that embraces rather than masks emotion) and the conspicuous consumption of **metrosexuality** encourages an array of fashion trends and processes that blur, if not completely undermining, dichotomous notions of gender and sexuality.

Further Reading: Bordo, Susan. *The Male Body: A New Look at Men in Public and Private.* New York: Farrar, Strauss and Giroux, 1999; Bruck, Kathy. "Men Wearing Jeans, for Her." *The Massachusetts Daily Collegian.* October 10, 2006. http://www.dailycollegian. com. (Accessed November 11, 2008); "Calvin Klein CK One/CK BePromo-'Altered

States.'" www.youtube.com/watch?v=BKvjAUAPve4. (Accessed July 12, 2006); Cox, Caroline, and Lee Widdows. *Hair and Fashion.* London: V & A Publications, 2005; Davis, Fred. *Fashion, Culture, and Identity.* Chicago: University of Chicago Press, 1992; Emo Style. http://emo-style.info/; Entwistle, Joanne. *The Fashioned Body: Fashion, Dress and Modern Social Theory.* Malden, MA: Blackwell Publishers, 2000; Kefgen, Mary, and Phyllis Touchie-Specht. *Individuality in Clothing Selection and Personal Appearance.* New York: Macmillan, 1986; Kidwell, Claudia Brush, and Valerie Steele. *Men and Women: Dressing the Part.* Washington, D.C.: Smithsonian Institution Press, 1989; Steele, Valerie, ed. *Encyclopedia of Clothing and Fashion,* 3 vols. New York: Charles Scribner's Sons, 2005; Schelat, Leslie. "Man, I Dress Like a Women." *Kent News Net.* October 25, 2005. http://www.kentnewsnet.com. (Accessed November 11, 2008); Willet, Julie A. *Permanent Waves: The Making of the American Beauty Shop.* New York: New York University Press, 2000; Zaretsky, Natasha. *No Direction Home: The American Family and the Fear of National Decline, 1968–1980.* Chapel Hill: University of North Carolina, 2007.

Brian Robertson

People for the Ethical Treatment of Animals (PETA) activists wearing masks sit next to a stuffed animal, representing a dead rabbit, in a coffin to protest cruel cosmetic testing on animals, 2009. (AP Photo/Bidas Dais)

ANIMAL RIGHTS

Animal rights proponents have been concerned about the treatment of animals in the production of beauty and personal care products. This includes the testing of beauty products and the wearing of fur and leather. Lotions, shampoo, mascara, and other **cosmetics** are routinely tested on animals to assess their effectiveness and any side effects such as itching or burning. Animal rights and consumer groups oppose animal testing on the grounds that it is ethically wrong because of the harm imposed on animal subjects.

Animal Testing

Animal testing is a common practice in the cosmetic industry to test the safety of products applied to the human body for cleansing or beautifying. Testing of cosmetics involves evaluating either a finished product or its individual ingredients by applying the substance to animals, usually rabbits, but also mice, rats, and other animals. Ingredients are typically applied to the animals' mucous membranes, such as the eyes, nose, and mouth to evaluate any adverse reactions. The Draize test, developed in 1944 by John Draize, is the most commonly used test to evaluate eye damage in shampoos, deodorants, laundry detergents, and other soaps. This test requires the application of the substance to the eye of a rabbit. Evidence of irritation is observed over hours or days, and any damage to the eye area is scored numerically. Based on the outcome of the Draize test and others, companies determine whether a beauty product is safe for human use.

"Government statistics, where available, indicate that product testing accounts for approximately 10 percent of all animal use for scientific purposes, which amounts to many millions of animals per year worldwide. Such testing calls into question the ethics and humaneness of deliberately poisoning animals (sometimes to death), the appropriateness of harming animals for the sake of marketing a new brand of mascara or moisturizer, the applicability of animal data to humans, and the possibility of sparing millions of animals by developing alternatives to a handful of widely used procedures."

The Humane Society of the United States

Source: The Humane Society of the United States. "Animal Testing." 2010. www.hsus.org/animals_in_research/animal_testing/.

Regulation of Animal Testing

Animal testing for cosmetic safety began in the United States in 1933 after an eyelash darkening treatment called Lash Lure blinded a woman. The resulting outcry over this news prompted Eleanor Roosevelt to campaign for the stricter regulation of beauty treatments. In 1938, the **U.S. Food and Drug Administration** (FDA) passed the Federal Food, Drug, and Cosmetic Act to provide safeguards against such harmful effects of cosmetic use. The United States and many other countries now require testing to ensure the safety of cosmetic products for human use. While the United States does not require such tests to be conducted on animals, cosmetic companies commonly test their products on animals to evaluate toxicity and to test the hypoallergenic properties of cosmetics.

In 1966, Congress passed the Laboratory Animal Welfare Act, which governed the humane treatment of animals, including in relation to animal research. Subsequent amendments to the act (renamed the Animal Welfare Act) expanded it to include the treatment of animals in venues besides experimentation and created exclusions for mice and other animals. One of the issues in regulating testing is that beauty companies contract production of ingredients to third parties who, if not located in the United States, may operate in entirely unregulated markets. Companies that do so may label their products as "finished product not tested on animals." The lack of regulation means that consumers may have difficulty in determining the amount and/or type of testing conducted in the creation of beauty products.

There is an international call to ban animal testing entirely. In 1963, an international organization, Beauty Without Cruelty (BWC), was formed to educate people about the suffering of animals. The company works to eliminate animal testing, including in the cosmetic industry, and seeks a ban on the fur and ivory trades. In 1996 the Coalition for Consumer Information on Cosmetics (CCIC), an agglomeration of citizen groups, including the Humane Society of the United States, developed the Corporate Standard of Compassion for Animals in an effort to create an international non–animal testing standard. The group designed the Leaping Bunny Logo, featured on the products of all companies who pledge to uphold this standard.

Animal testing for cosmetics is banned in the United Kingdom, the Netherlands, and Belgium, and in 2002, the European Union banned all animal testing for cosmetics and the sale of animal-tested cosmetics by 2009. While L'Oréal, the world's largest cosmetic company, has lodged a legal protest against the EU's ban, numerous other beauty companies promote cruelty-free products.

Reasons for Animal Testing

The FDA does not require animal testing, but data from animal toxicity tests are considered the benchmark for cosmetic safety. The U.S. National Academy of Sciences declares that toxicity tests on animals provide crucial information for evaluating the hazardous potential of products used by humans. Data from animal toxicity tests represent the most complete set of information regarding consumer products. Advocates of animal testing further argue that doing such tests on humans could risk the safety of the human subjects, endangering their health and well-being. The primary reason given for animal testing is the protection of the **health and safety** of human consumers. Companies argue that, given the enormous pressure to ensure consumer safety, animal testing is ubiquitous, and necessary for maintaining a competitive edge in the **global market**. According to some proponents of animal testing, in cases where significant pain or discomfort could be caused to the animal, painkillers should be used.

Arguments against Animal Testing

The main arguments against animal testing concern the ethical treatment of animals and the reliability of tests performed on animals when evaluating the safety of a product for human use. Researchers have found that animal tests do not reliably predict the risk of cosmetics to humans given the differences in human and animal tissue, particularly the distribution of fine blood vessels and skin reactions. Variability in the dosage given to laboratory animals compared with those used by humans does not accurately reflect the toxicity for humans. Consumer groups and animal rights activists argue that testing cosmetics on animals is inhumane because the cosmetics have severe effects on animals, including allergic reactions, bleeding, and discomfort. Some beauty companies and activist groups promote cruelty-free products and business practices in an effort to protect animal welfare. Cosmetic companies that have taken a strong stance against animal testing include **Aveda**, **Avon** Cosmetics, Clinique Makeup, **Estée Lauder**, Urban Decay, and **The Body Shop**.

Alternatives to Animal Testing

Alternatives to animal testing exist and are held up by critics of the practice as evidence that it is unnecessary. Cell cultures, donated eye tissues, and computer modeling are examples of alternative animal testing. Advocates of alternatives also note that companies could use existing ingredients that have already been tested for safety. Human volunteers for clinical trials would create an additional alternative to animal testing. Some activists call for the United States to institute a total ban on all animal testing. Other, less total regulations of the practice include using non-animal alternatives whenever possible, reducing the number of animals used in procedures, and altering procedures to reduce animal suffering.

Fur

While the main debate over animal rights in the beauty industry concerns animal testing, there is controversy over the wearing of fur as well. Fur has long been a staple of the fashion industry. Fox, chinchilla, and mink are just a few of the types of fur that are popular with **designers** and consumers. Animal rights groups, such as People for the Ethical Treatment of Animals (PETA) have staged protests and campaigns in an effort to reduce the use of fur in fashion. Most animals used for fur are raised and slaughtered in factory farms, which keep animals confined and use electrocution and suffocation to kill them while keeping fur intact.

Philosophy of Animal Rights

The debate over animal rights is rooted in a debate about the ethical implications of experimentation on animals. In 1975, Peter Singer published *Animal Liberation,* which offered a new ethics for the humane treatment of animals. Singer posited the moral status of animals as sentient beings, and his book provided a foundation for a growing animal rights movement. In *The Case for Animal Rights* (2004), Tom Regan argued that beings with inherent value, that is, value independent of their usefulness or benefit for others, have rights. For this reason, animals, like humans, have rights as sentient beings. Animals have the capacity to experience pain, and there is no ethical justification for ignoring their potential for suffering when evaluating human actions such as animal testing.

Those making the case for the ethical permission of animal experimentation argue that animals are not part of the moral community, and therefore humans are not morally obligated to them. Singer and Regan both argue against animal testing; Singer on the basis that it is wrong because of its consequences (the suffering of animals), and Regan on the grounds that animal testing is wrong in and of itself because humans have an obligation to respect the moral rights of animals.

Further Reading: Food and Drug Administration. *History of the FDA: The 1938 Food, Drug, and Cosmetic Act.* http://www.fda.gov/oc/history/historyoffda/section2.html. (Accessed September 24, 2008); Food and Drug Administration (Center for Safety and Nutrition/Office of Cosmetics and Colors). *Authority over Cosmetics.* http://www.cfsan.fda.gov/~dms/cos-206.html. (Accessed September 24, 2008); Haugen, David M., ed. *Animal Experimentation.* San Diego, CA: Greenhaven Press, 2000; Johnson, Steve. "Finding Options to Animal Testing." *San Jose Mercury News.* August 10, 2008. http://www.mercurynews.com/lifestyle/ci_10156583. (Accessed September 24, 2008); Regan, Thomas. *The Case for Animal Rights.* Berkeley: University of California Press, 2004; Sunstein, Cass R., and Martha C. Nussbaum. *Animal Rights: Current Debates and New Directions.* New York: Oxford University Press, 2005.

Anne Marie Todd

ANTI-AGING PRODUCTS AND TECHNIQUES

Anti-aging products are one of the most fundamental aspects of the modern beauty industry. While **cosmetics** often enhance or conceal physical features, anti-aging products and beauty techniques tend to take a more proactive—and oftentimes clinical—approach to beauty and health. While cosmetics have existed for at least seven thousand millennia, anti-aging techniques were traditionally tied to longevity practices in Eastern medicine that originated in present-day China and India. Anti-aging techniques associated with longevity tended to focus on nutrition and exercise techniques as ways to increase the lifespan.

In the 20th century, by contrast, *anti-aging* generally refers to techniques developed by cosmetics **manufacturers** and some beauticians to focus more on the outward signs of aging. Most anti-aging products tend to be related to skin care and the prevention or reduction of visible wrinkles and blemishes associated with aging and sun exposure, although some anti-aging products are targeted for **hair care**.

Development and Marketing

The cultural associations between youth and beauty, particularly for women, and the growth of visual media like **film** and television have greatly influenced the beauty industry and the development and marketing of anti-aging products.

"Coco Chanel had great eyebrows. 'When one reaches 50, everything becomes difficult,' she said. She was a realist. Me, too. I expected sag, jowls, hair dye, five unshiftable pounds, and the likelihood of having to pass on a six-inch Louboutin heel. What I didn't expect was my damn eyebrows to go walkabout. Who would? I thought eyebrows were a permanent fixture, like earlobes or eye color. I am uncontent with most of my facial features, but my brows never worried me. They were dark, thick, and smooth enough not to need daily makeup. Now they're traveling—up, down, sideways. Some individual hairs have gone crazy—bulking up, like they're on steroids, and spiraling around."

Vicki Woods

Source: "She's Come Undone: The Subtle Signs of Aging go well Beyond Wrinkles. Four Women Face Their (Not-So Fatal) Flaws." *Vogue,* August 2009, 176.

The growing population of older people and the increase in life expectancy has also indirectly affected the marketing of anti-aging products.

Perhaps the earliest attempt to develop and market an anti-aging cream, as opposed to a lotion or moisturizer, was with the collaboration of a South African chemist Graham Wulff and his wife, Dinah. Using his wife as both inspiration and test subject, Graham Wulff developed Oil of Olay in 1949 as an alternative to heavier face creams and lotions. Unlike other face creams, Oil of Olay marketers emphasized its healing abilities and even suggested that the product had medical benefits. Oil of Olay developed a unique **advertising** campaign in the 1950s that appeared to show doctors' endorsements of the product, thus blurring the lines between the cosmetic and the clinical. Since the introduction of Oil of Olay, numerous other cosmetics manufacturers began to market anti-aging and anti-wrinkle creams, including RoC, Lancôme, and **Estée Lauder**.

The primary component of Oil of Olay, lanolin, or wool fat, was already used as a moisturizer. In the past three decades, scientists also began to understand the relationship between **vitamins** and the process of oxidation, a biological process that can damage cells. Since the late 1980s, most anti-aging products use retinol, or Vitamin A, and Vitamin E, because of their clinical ability to repair damaged skin. In the 1990s, RoC introduced alpha and beta hydroxy acids for their ability to exfoliate dead skin cells, although whether they can definitively reduce wrinkles has been questioned by some scientists. In the last decade, many anti-wrinkle products have begun to use Coenzyme Q_{10}, or Q10, as the active ingredient because of its potency as an anti-oxidant. Some products even use caffeine for its ability to make the skin appear taut, in part from dehydration. However, the most significant development in anti-aging products has been the addition of ultraviolet protection from solar radiation, one of the primary causes of wrinkles and blemishes associated with aging. Although cosmetics producers continue to market anti-aging and anti-wrinkle products most aggressively to women, in the last several years, anti-aging products have also been introduced for men. Although not markedly different in ingredients, the special attempt to market anti-aging products to men suggests both the difficulty manufacturers have had in opening a male market to anti-aging products and the increasing pressure on men to maintain a youthful appearance.

In addition to the mass marketing of anti-aging products by major cosmetics producers, many smaller cosmetics boutiques and even **spas** have begun to offer alternative treatments to reduce the appearance of aging. Often times, such boutiques and spas incorporate non-Western techniques and products into their businesses in order to individualize beauty treatments and compete with mainstream cosmetics manufacturers.

Cosmeceuticals and the Debate over Anti-Aging Products

More than any other beauty products, the cosmetics industry markets anti-aging products as clinically developed and tested. In part because aging represents a biological process with a correlate in professional medical practice, many manufacturers have begun to market anti-aging products as *cosmeceuticals,* a neologism combining the words cosmetic and pharmaceutical. The cosmetics industry has come under fire for the use of the word in advertising campaigns, as scientists cast doubt on the clinical veracity of manufacturer reports demonstrating a link between anti-aging products and the reduction of visible signs of aging.

Because of the scientific and clinical aspects of anti-aging, the governments of many industrialized nations have begun to regulate the marketing and distribution of anti-aging products. In the United States, the legislature has responded by broadening regulations for the industry with oversight boards like the **U.S. Food and Drug Administration** (FDA). Furthermore, the United States Senate Special Committee on Aging, founded initially in 1977 to study Medicare and Social Security programs for older Americans, has begun to take an increasing interest in the effects of anti-aging products as they become more widespread and the population of older Americans increases.

While cosmetics manufacturers often fund and publicize their own scientific studies, the industry continues to follow the looser regulations developed for cosmetics as opposed to pharmaceuticals. While cosmeceuticals might potentially mislead consumers, anti-aging products marketed as such do not require the lengthy FDA test process or waiting period for drugs.

Since 2002, the FDA has approved the use of **Botox**, a derivative of the botulinum bacterium. Botox, which has become an increasingly popular cosmetic treatment, reduces wrinkles by paralyzing the underlying facial muscles responsible for wrinkles around the forehead and eyes. Prior to use as a cosmetic, Botox was also a common treatment for muscle spasms and related disorders. Although a number of studies have questioned the safety of Botox, the product remains the most common alternative to cosmetics products or **cosmetic surgery**.

Further Reading: Dayan, Nava, ed. *Skin Aging Handbook: An Integrated Approach to Biochemistry and Product Development.* Norwich, NY: William Andrew, 2008; Elsner, Peter, and Howard I. Maibach, eds. *Cosmeceuticals and Active Cosmetics: Drugs versus Cosmetics.* 2nd ed. Boca Raton, FL: Taylor & Francis, 2005; Weingarten, Rachel C. *Hello Gorgeous!: Beauty Products in America '40s–'50s.* Portland, OR: Collectors Press, 2006.

Christopher A. Mitchell

ARDEN, ELIZABETH

Elizabeth Arden (1878–1966) was known for founding and operating a chain of high-end beauty **spas**, Maine Chance, and **beauty salons**, marked by her trademark red door. She is credited with establishing makeup as proper for a ladylike image during a period when such use associated the wearer with the lower classes and unrespectable professions; this new image included the subtle application of **cosmetics** with a lighter touch, a more refined look for the high-class woman. During her lifetime, Arden's company was known for its fine line of high-end cosmetics and **perfumes**. Along with her chief rival, **Helena Rubinstein**, Arden helped establish early cosmetics marketing practices and a female presence in the male corporate world during the first half of the 20th century. Arden also had a second career—she owned a stable of thoroughbred race horses, Maine Chance Farms, which gained prominence in the 1940s and 1950s.

Early Years

Born Florence Nightingale Graham to tenant farmers in Canada, Arden never finished high school but held a series of low-paying jobs while living in Toronto. An early attempt at nursing exposed her to various skin salves and creams used to treat skin injuries or maladies. While living at home, she often experimented with various ingredients in her private laboratory, attempting to turn the salves into beauty skincare products. In 1908, at the age of 30, Arden

Elizabeth Arden, 1939. (Courtesy of Library of Congress)

moved to New York City with her brother, where she was employed for a time as a bookkeeper by the Squibb Pharmaceutical Company. By 1910, she had found work in Eleanor Adair's beauty salons, and there she became a specialist in facial treatments.

Early Career and Beauty Philosophy

Arden opened up a shop on Fifth Avenue with new partner Elizabeth Hubbard, where she developed a line of Venetian beauty preparations, an identity choice lending the pricey lotions and powders prestige—this strategy would become her trademark. When the partnership broke up, Florence Graham became Elizabeth Arden, taking her former partner's first name, and legend has it, the last name of the title character in Alfred, Lord Tennyson's poem "Enoch Arden." This is also when the door to her beauty salon became red, to distinguish her entrance from the more common doorways around her shop. Among the products from this early period around 1912 were Arden's first rouges and tinted powders.

Arden formulated her marketing and product philosophy very quickly through research and experimentation. In these early years Arden added fragrances to her lotions and powders, and hired a chemist to lighten the texture of the greasy and heavy creams commonly found at the time. Her development of the *total beauty* concept led her to expand her salon by including the services of a **hairdresser** and a milliner within one location, thus providing easy access to supplementary beauty routines. This idea would later lead to her founding of beauty spas. She also trained her workers to apply makeup, and to teach their customers to apply it, with a lighter touch and subtlety. Understated makeup became classier and thereby more respectable for ladies to wear. Arden was an early proponent of the beauty routine and the shared meanings and rituals that that entailed within female culture.

In 1914, Arden traveled to Paris, studying Parisians' more sophisticated cosmetics techniques, ingredients, and, especially, their use of eye makeup. This last was harder for Arden's American clientele to accept than rouges and face powders. It is believed that Arden's eye products were the first to be introduced in the United States and that they were a difficult sell. In 1914, she opened a second salon in Washington, D.C., which proved a success, and her creams and line of cosmetics were sold in department stores all along the East Coast. By 1916, the Arden Company ranked first in the nation in prestige skincare sales.

Middle Career and Company Expansion

At age 37, in 1918, Arden married Thomas Lewis and became a U.S. citizen. Also in 1918, she expanded her salon services into product sales; her husband supervised production and distribution while Arden dealt with the more public image of the company by attending to the exclusive salons. Arden pink became her signature color, though any allusions to pink femininity would be wide off the mark, as Arden gained a reputation as a tough manager and was the sole stockholder in her company throughout her life.

In 1925, the Arden Company topped $2 million in sales, and by 1929 that figure had doubled. In a bold move, Arden expanded during the Great Depression; she believed that women would still be seeking ways to lift their spirits, and brought out such innovations as a lipstick kit, which contained several different shades. This, along with different perfumes for different times of the day, enabled women to change their cosmetics along with their dress; this may have led to today's predilection for day makeup and night makeup. In 1934, Arden opened Maine Chance Beauty Resort, accessing the beauty ritual culture she had helped to establish. The Maine spa was a varied treatment facility where women lost weight, immersed in Arden's new bath salts, and slathered themselves with her bath lotions, all for $500 a week. During the Depression she also marketed her first fragrance, Blue Grass (1935). By the mid 1930s, Arden owned, **manufactured**, and marketed around 108 different products. She also owned approximately 29 salons around the world. Arden extended her reach by making the first cosmetics commercial shown in movie houses in 1939.

World War II and Late Career

During World War II, Arden expanded her domestic market coast to coast, and her lines went into all of the major department stores at that time. Arden also directly addressed the needs of a growing female workforce; new cosmetics and beauty routines emerged that helped women to present a more professional appearance. As women entered the armed services, Arden created Montezuma Red lipstick to match the red trim on women's uniforms. The company remained a pacesetter, even during the height of the war. In 1945, Arden entered into a new enterprise, couture clothing, and thereafter continued to challenge her competitors by adding men's fragrances and opening a men's boutique in the 1950s. Her men's lines included designs by Charles James, Antonio Castillo, Fernando Sarmi, and Oscar de la Renta.

Thoroughbred Racing

While Arden had no children, she owned a thoroughbred racing stable, Maine Chance Farms. During the 1940s and 1950s it was a big contender in the racing world and in 1945, Maine Chance Farms was the top money-winning stable in the United States. In 1954, her filly Fascinator won the Kentucky Oaks. Her biggest win, however, was with Jet Pilot, a colt, who won the Kentucky Derby in 1947, ridden by Eric Guerin and trained by Tom Smith. Legend relates that one of Arden's best creams (Eight Hour Cream) resulted from formulas concocted for her thoroughbreds; she noticed their effect on the stable handlers' hands, and modified the formula for human marketing.

Arden's Company after her Death

Before her death in 1966, the Elizabeth Arden Company grossed an average of $60 million per year. Her empire consisted of 17 corporations and over 40 salons worldwide, with an additional 100-plus smaller establishments. It is thought that she created and manufactured upward of 300 cosmetics and fragrances. Since her death, the Elizabeth Arden Company has passed through several hands. Eli Lilly & Company acquired it in 1970, cut costs and streamlined procedures. and then sold it in 1987. After changing hands twice more, Unilever PLC purchased Elizabeth Arden in 1990. In 1992, **Calvin Klein** joined Elizabeth Arden as part of Unilever's Prestige Personal Products Group. Between 1987 and 1993, Joseph Ronchetti, president and CEO of Arden, greatly expanded **advertising**. Those years also brought about research and development of new products, including skin protection care products, which were recognized and given awards by the Skin Cancer Foundation. In 1991, Arden's product Elizabeth Taylor's White Diamonds was the nation's number one fragrance. Today, the company has addressed issues of social concern and does not conduct **animal testing**. The company also contributes large donations to child welfare causes and AIDS research.

Further Reading: Elizabeth Arden Corporate Web site. http://www.corporate.eliza betharden.com. (Accessed September 4, 2008); Gavenas, Mary Lisa. *Color Stories: Behind the Scenes of America's Billion-Dollar Beauty Industry.* New York: Simon & Schuster, 2002; Kepos, Paula, ed. *International Directory of Company Histories.* Vol. 8. http://www. fundinguniverse.com/company-histories/Elizabeth-Arden-Co-Company-History. html. (Accessed October 15, 2008); Peiss, Kathy. *Hope in a Jar: The Making of America's Beauty Culture.* New York: Metropolitan Books, 1998.

Christina Ashby-Martin

ASIAN AMERICAN BEAUTY INDUSTRY

Until very recently, Asian American women have been virtually ignored by the U.S. beauty industry. Although a few Asian American beauty icons were recognized in the cinema of the 1920s and '30s, even those who managed to find some success in the United States tended to be pigeon-holed into certain stereotypes. Anna May Wong, the first Asian American movie star, managed to break into **films** in her late teens. In 1922, at the age of 17, she won the lead role in the first color

feature to be made in Hollywood, *The Toll of the Sea.* In it, Wong played Lotus Flower, a young woman who rescues a white man from the sea. In a Madame Butterfly, Puccini-esque turn, the two fall in love and he promises to take her home with him. But his xenophobic friends prevent him from doing so, and the Asian woman is left behind. When they meet years later, too much has changed for them to ever reunite. By 1924, Wong had appeared in enough films to be recognized internationally and be revered as a style icon. She continued to star in major films, including Josef von Sternberg's *Shanghai Express* with Marlene Dietrich, but Wong was frustrated with the stereotypical roles—either Dragon Lady or Butterfly— she was offered in Hollywood. She received her most devastating blow when studio heads

Anna May Wong, 1939, photographed by Carl Van Vechten. (Courtesy of Library of Congress)

refused her the role of O-Lan in Pearl Buck's *The Good Earth;* it was offered instead to Luise Rainer, a white woman who played the lead in yellowface.

Other Asian American women found some success, including Nancy Kwan, a biracial actress, whose first role was as a Hong Kong prostitute who mesmerized a white artist in Richard Quine's 1961 film adaptation of *The World of Suzie Wong.* In 1962, Kwan played Linda Low, a manipulative and seductive Chinese American showgirl involved in a complicated arrangement of affiances and affairs in Henry Koster's *Flower Drum Song.* Her roles in these two movies solidified her status as a sex symbol, and her **Vidal Sassoon** asymmetrical **bob** helped make her a style icon for the 20th century. Asian American women became increasingly visible in the 1990s and 2000s, with Margaret Cho, Tamlyn Tomita, Connie Chung, Ming-Na Wen, Lucy Liu, Parminder Nagra, Sandra Oh, Lisa Ling, Padma Lakshmi, Vanessa Hudgens, and others earning more lead roles, more prime-time specials, and more minutes in front of the camera than before.

Growing Visibility and Markets

The relative lack of Asian Americans on television and in film and the selection of those who are fortunate enough to appear are linked to the conceptions of beauty and aesthetics in the United States. The overwhelming cultural imperative to define beauty as something that is inherently Caucasian and therefore out of reach for most people of color has informed the **advertising** campaigns of the beauty industry, the development of goods and products, and the availability and popularity of treatments and surgeries that physically alter the human body. Most recently, the beauty industry has begun to recognize the incredible consumer voice and buying power of the Asian American public, and a concerted effort has been made on the part of certain **cosmetics** giants to tap into a large and profitable market.

Skin-lightening creams are among the most popular cosmetic and skin-care product purchases in East Asia. The contrast between pale skin, dark hair, and red lips is an aesthetic that has historically permeated Asian art and aesthetics. From the white makeup of the Geisha to the use of nightingale droppings to clarify skin, Asian women have valued a lighter skin tone as a sign of social status and beauty. Since the 1970s, Asian beauty companies have been producing products that promise to fulfill this desire for paler, fairer complexions. While the products were geared for the Asian market, as recognition of the growing Asian American demographic grew, the number of products offering brightening increased in the United States.

Susan Yee, the founder and president of Zhen cosmetics, was one of the first entrepreneurs to create a line of cosmetics designed to fit the needs of the women with skin with yellow undertones. In 1994, Yee and her sisters developed beauty products that they thought would best complement Asian American women—and they soon became popular via word of mouth among young Asian Americans who were frustrated with unflattering **makeovers** at department stores, where the sales staff did not know how to enhance East Asian features such as the single-lid eye.

Cosmetic Surgery

The perception that Asian features are unattractive and unappealing has led to an increase in **cosmetic surgery** procedures that specifically target Asian Americans and, in particular, Asian American women. The American Society of Plastic Surgeons noted that in 2004–5, Asian American plastic surgery patients increased by 58 percent. As an Asiancemagazine.com article cited, in 2006, Asian Americans accounted for 6 percent of all cosmetic surgery patients in the United States. Among the most popular surgical procedures requested by Asian Americans were rhinoplasty, breast augmentation, and eyelid surgery. An entire website, Asiancosmeticsurgery.com, is dedicated to the various procedures that might fix specific Asian American features. It has been noted that the idea that Asian Americans traditionally asked for procedures that would make them look more Caucasian made the discussion of plastic surgery taboo. The eyelid surgery, blepharoplasty, by which a single lid eye is made more Caucasian by stitching a double lid crease permanently into the eyelid, is the number one plastic surgery procedure in Asia and is fast growing in the United States. In 2000, the American Academy of Facial Plastic and Reconstructive Surgery reported that 125,000 blepharoplasty procedures were performed in the United States. As plastic surgeons have become more aware of the changing demography of their patient groups, some have become more sensitive to Asian American concerns and more open to tailoring procedures specifically to Asian Americans. For example, plastic surgeons use **Botox** injections to reduce wrinkles in many Caucasian women—in East Asian women, the same injections can be used to relax the masseter muscle of the jaw, thus creating a more streamlined jawline and reducing the lower half of the face. As well, plastic surgeons have become more aware of sensitive skin, scarring, and hyperpigmentation, especially among South Asians.

While in the United States, Asian Americans are discussing the meaning behind these physical transformations, the masking of ethnicity, the whitening of race; in Asia, the stigma of being labeled a sell-out is not as pronounced. With the increased awareness of the concerns and desires of Asians, plastic surgery procedures have also become more radical and more controversial. Most at issue is a newly developed Korean procedure to reduce the size and thickness of Asian women's legs. The term *Daikon legs*, a reference to a long, thick radish popular in Asian kitchens, describes a perceived aesthetic problem for Asian women by which they look shorter and more obese because of their thick legs. In an attempt to create longer, more Western legs, Asian women are having muscle fiber removed from their calves according to the patient's desired calf shape, reducing the bulk of the gastrocnemius muscles. Another extreme procedure, leg lengthening surgery, was just recently banned in China, despite its growing popularity. In China, being taller is seen as a sign of beauty, conforming to more Western ideas of height and body type. The procedure entailed the breaking of the patient's legs and the insertion of steel pins into the bones just below the knees. The pins were attached to a metal frame that the patient could tighten little by little, constantly forcing the ends of the broken bones apart so that new bone would fill in the gaps, creating more length at the price of excruciating pain.

Resisting Stereotypes

Calvin Sun recently directed a documentary on Asian American standards of beauty titled *Asian American Beauty: A Discourse on Female Body Image* (2007). In the short film, Sun examines the inconsistencies of defining Asian American beauty. In the director's notes to the film, he writes: "We also must reveal the contradiction of how Asian American girls are pressured in this society to look both 'western' and 'Asian.'" He highlights the tension between "play[ing] up this well-known image of looking innocent, weak, and petite as 'attractive'" and the construction of the mainstream media "depict[ing] Asian American females as alluring, 'exotic,' and 'sexy.'" In the film, Sun examines not only the beauty constructs that are more specific to Asian Americans, he seeks to expand the more general discussion of female body issues, psychological concerns, and eating disorders to include Asian American women, a group that has usually been ignored or rendered peripheral in these discussions.

Although Asian American **models** still play a relatively small role within beauty campaigns, Asian Americans have become increasingly present as workers within the beauty industry itself. Korean and Japanese hair salons have popped up in most major cities—New York, Houston, San Francisco, Los Angeles, Cleveland, Chicago—specializing in treatments that have been made popular in Asian countries and are now available to Asian Americans. Chemical hair processes such as Japanese **hair straightening**, Japanese thermal conditioning, Korean **permanents**, and Japanese digital perms have recently become popular among a younger Asian American clientele. Even more pervasive have been the **nail salons** that have opened across the country, owned and operated by Asian Americans, especially Vietnamese Americans. The ubiquitous Asian American–owned and operated nail salon is so popular an image that it appeared in a *Seinfeld* episode titled "The Understudy," first broadcast May 18, 1995. The character of Elaine, convinced that the Korean nail technician is talking about her behind her back in Korean, asks Mr. Costanza, fluent in Korean after his experiences in the Korean War, to accompany her and eavesdrop on the women. Even more recently, *Sex and the City* featured the August 8, 1999 episode "The Caste System," in which the four women argue about the existence of a class system in the United States as they are having their feet serviced by Asian American workers.

Asian American women especially, but also Asian American men, have had to confront deep-seated misconceptions about immigration, integration, and unassimilability. The supposed interchangeability of people of East Asian descent, the assumption of close ties to the mother country, and cultural stereotypes about the Orient and Orientals have contributed to a larger call by Asian Americans for recognition and political and cultural voice. To that end, a number of glossy print magazines have attempted to provide a medium for Asian American voices. Some of the initial attempts met with financial difficulty—magazines such as the now defunct *A Magazine*, *Yolk*, and *Noodle* attempted to meet the needs of young, hip Asian Americans and found that the market had not yet developed and advertisers were not convinced of profitability. Today, magazines such as *Hyphen*, *Audrey*, and *AsianWeek* bring Asian American issues and concerns to the forefront and allow Asian Americans to better control and contribute to their cultural space.

Further Reading: Chung, Philip. "Where Are the APA Movie Stars?" http://www. asianweek.com/2007/12/14/where-are-the-apa-movie-stars/; Shah, Sonia, ed. *Dragon Ladies: Asian American Feminists Breathe Fire.* Cambridge, MA: South End Press, 1999; Devayya, Dhaya. "'She's Got the Look': Cultural Beauty Ideals from the Asian American Woman's Perspective." https://www.ideals.uiuc.edu/handle/2142/3631; Farmer, Melanie. "What's Missing in Mainstream Media: Where are all the Asian-American Magazines?" DiversityInc.com. www.magazine.org/content/files/AsianMags.pdf; Hodges, Graham. *Anna May Wong: From Laundryman's Daughter to Hollywood Legend.* New York: Palgrave, 2004; Kimura, Margaret. *Asian Beauty.* New York: Collins, 2001; Kobrin, Sandy. "Asian Americans Criticize Eyelid Surgery Craze." www.womensenews.org/article.cfm/dyn/aid/1950/context/archive; Lee, Robert G. *Orientals: Asian Americans in Popular Culture.* Philadelphia: Temple University, 1999; Sun, Calvin, dir. *Asian American Beauty: A Discourse on Female Body Image*; Asian American Beauty— Female Body Image (Part 1 of 2). www.youtube.com/watch?v=mv-WI6Vlrpk; Asian American Beauty—Female Body Image Part 2 of 2). www.youtube.com/watch?v= L8XWQ62HdCs; Takeuchi Cullen, Lisa. "Changing Faces." *Time Magazine.* www. time.com/time/asia/covers/1101020805/story.html.

Aliza S. Wong

AVEDA

Aveda is a beauty company that **manufactures** flower- and plant-based beauty products. Aveda, which is translated from the Sanskrit as "all knowledge" or "knowledge of nature," is based on the fundamental connection of health and beauty and the healing properties of nature. Through its commitment to environmental responsibility in its products and business practices, Aveda is an example of environmental leadership for the beauty industry.

History

Aveda was founded in 1978 by environmentalist Horst Rechelbacher, who wanted to create personal care products using ingredients found in nature. Rechelbacher worked in a **beauty salon** in Minnesota and founded the company with the goal of providing beauty industry professionals with high performance, botanically based products. The company launched its first **hair care product**, clove shampoo, in 1978, and later expanded to institutes and salons. In 1989, Aveda opened its first Environmental Lifestyle Store on Madison Avenue in New York City and endorsed the Coalition for Environmentally Responsible Economies (CERES) Principles. In 1997, **Estée Lauder** bought Aveda for $300 million. Today, Aveda is one of the fastest-growing brands in Estee Lauder's portfolio.

Products

Aveda products are designed according to the company's slogan: The Art and Science of Pure Flower and Plant Essences. Aveda products are only sold in licensed salons or Aveda stores. Aveda's product lines include hair products, such as shampoos, conditioning agents, and styling gels; skin care, including moisturizers, toners, and exfoliants; a full line of makeup; and scents based on pure natural ingredients. In addition to the extensive line of products, Aveda has also developed **spas**, which provide services based on Aveda's mission, and created institutes to teach salon professionals the Aveda principles. Aveda emphasizes using natural ingredients in its products and using responsible **packaging** as a way to promote sustainability.

Environmental Sustainability

Aveda advocates sustainable business practices. Their mission and values are designed to foster awareness and create change in individuals and society to protect biodiversity and promote sustainable living practices. Aveda was the first company of its kind to endorse the CERES Principles, which promote higher environmental standards for corporations. The CERES Principles include sustainable use of natural resources, reduction of waste, energy conservation, environmental restoration, informing the public, and assessment and reporting. Aveda publishes CERES annual reports to inform the public of its progress in meeting these goals.

Community Partnerships

Aveda's commitment to sustainability extends beyond its products into community partnerships. In 1993, Aveda formed a partnership with the Yawanawa tribe, indigenous to the Amazon rainforest in Brazil, to source *uruku,* a red dye used in the company's **cosmetics**. In 2007, Aveda became the first beauty company to use 100 percent wind power in its manufacturing and is the largest corporate purchaser of wind energy in Minnesota. At the 2008 New York fashion week, Aveda handed out refillable bottles filled with New York tap water. Aveda's newest environmental campaign is CAPS, which asks consumers to bring their plastic caps from water bottles to Aveda stores to recycle.

Further Reading: Belli, Brita. "Aveda Gets Active during NYC's Fashion Week." *E Magazine.* http://www.emagazine.com/view/?4369. (Accessed September 24, 2008); Candey, Dana. "Estée Lauder Is Acquiring Maker of Natural Cosmetics." *New York Times.* November 20, 1997. http://query.nytimes.com/gst/fullpage.html?res=9D01E3D8173BF9 33A15752C1A961958260. (Accessed September 24, 2008); DePass, Dee. "For Aveda, the Problem with Common Scents." *Minneapolis Star Tribune.* August 17, 2008. http://www.startribune.com/business/27027359.html. (Accessed September 24, 2008); Rechelbacher, Horst. *Aveda Rituals: A Daily Guide to Natural Health and Beauty.* New York: Owl Books, 1999.

Anne Marie Todd

AVON

Known to many as the ding-dong company for its door-to-door sales approach, Avon began as the California Perfume Company in 1886. Its founder, David Hall McConnell, originally a bookseller, started giving out **perfume** samples to his book costumers and found that they thought the samples were more attractive than the literature. Avon's products center on fragrances, **cosmetics**, and toiletries; they also sell some specialty items such as jewelry, clothing, and toys. Today, the Avon company markets its products in over 100 countries, with 5.5 million sales representatives and 42,000 corporate employees. No longer tied to marketing door-to-door, Avon has updated its company workforce, its management workforce, its corporate vision, and its selling models to effectively deal with the early 21st century.

History

For most of its 123-year history, the company known as Avon was staffed by women and run nearly entirely by men. Founder McConnell marketed his first five fragrances in 1886: lily of the valley, violet, heliotrope, white rose, and hyacinth. They were so successful that McConnell abandoned books in 1892 to concentrate on fragrances. Credited with much of the early successful history of selling the California Perfume Company products was Mrs. P.F.E. Albee, who was not only Avon's first official salesperson, but also began the practice of recruiting other women to sell the product. The company honors her memory today with the Albee statuette for its top sales representatives. Shortly after perfumes took off, shampoo cream, witch hazel cream, almond cream balm, and small household items including toiletries were added to the product lineup. By 1906, the first cosmetics were added with a rouge in liquid and powder form.

By 1920, the company had reached the $1 million sales mark; during the Great Depression, the company received the Good Housekeeping Seal of Approval, switched to a three-week sales cycle (rather than four weeks), and created sales territories for its representatives to maximize sales. In October 1939, the California Perfume Company ceased to exist and was renamed Avon, in honor of the founder's liking for Stratford-Upon-Avon, which was already one of the **brand** names of the company. As a public corporation in 1946, Avon then expanded into international markets beyond Canada (which it entered in 1914). By 1972, the door-to-door sales juggernaut began to expand into non-related endeavors, such as buying Tiffany's in 1979. This also initiated the company's financial decline through the 1980s until 1990. The company went through hostile takeover attempts by its chief rivals, Amway and **Mary Kay**.

At the same time that the company was experiencing its most traumatic economic decline, it was also trying to deal with a non-modern workforce, as well as seemingly antiquated product lines and customer marketing. Well past the 1954-to-1967 Ding Dong **advertising** campaign, the public identified Avon as solely a door-to-door selling company, and during the social changes of the 1970s and 1980s, it fell behind the times. During the late 1980s and through the 1990s, Avon modernized its product lines, market distribution, and diversity of workforce, and finally broke the gender barrier in its management team. The company of women working for men came to an end and Avon consciously redirected its mission toward the "World's Premier Company for Women." The company's first female CEO and president was Andrea Jung, appointed in 1999.

Current Status

Today, Avon is one of the international companies most heavily dependent on technology for sales, distribution, and **manufacturing**. Because its U.S. catalog (new products) turns over every two weeks and the international catalogs change every three to four weeks, the company's research, production, and distribution sectors are some of the most complex and active in the sales world. Approximately 70–75 percent of sales business is currently international, while the U.S. market is handled by 650,000 sales representatives. The company's sales model has been redefined, paralleling the old direct-sales with a new sales leadership structure that will, the company hopes, be able to improve Avon's dismal retention rate in representatives by offering women a career choice rather than a strictly part-time supplemental income. Because of the negative reputation of pyramid structures, Avon's Sales Leadership program started small in 1990, and is slowly being expanded into full integration into the U.S. market and, more slowly, into appropriate international markets. This is a three-tiered system where representatives recruit others to work under them, while they work under an upward management layer. In contrast to some of Avon's competitors, Avon representatives in the Sales Leadership program must continue direct selling themselves, not just living off their downline commissions. Another difference between Avon's selling methods and those of its competitors is that sales representatives do not have to purchase the products in advance of customers. Avon extends what amounts to credit to its representatives and waits for reimbursement from the customer once the product has been delivered.

The foundation of Avon's business today remains the top three: cosmetics, fragrances, and toiletries. Avon's initial reputation was made and is maintained through its fragrance lines, and the company strength is still scents, although recent expansions have changed the look of the company. Today its key brands are Anew skin care, Avon Color, Skin-So-Soft, Advance Techniques hair care, and Avon Wellness. Most long-term successes have been found among the skin-care products. Skin-So-Soft was launched in 1962 as a bath oil, but has found its most loyal following over the last 40 years as a bug repellant. In 2004, Avon recognized that the company was not fully accessing a fast-growing market, and launched *M: The Men's Catalog*. Avon is also attempting to more fully recruit and market to black and Hispanic women, as well as younger women, and especially to recruit college-age sales representatives to ensure the future of the sales force.

Avon was an early (1980s) innovator in adding UVA/UVB protection to its moisturizers (often without labeling it), came out with the retinol product BioAdvance in 1985 after learning how to stabilize a pure form of **vitamin** A, patented its process for stabilizing vitamin C, and launched **anti-aging products** in 1987. In 1992, Avon became the first mass producer of Alpha Hydroxy products. While the company's main research facility remains in Suffern, New York, it also has one in Europe, two in Asia, two in Latin America, and one in Japan.

Philanthropic Endeavors

Like many other beauty companies, Avon contributes significant monies toward breast cancer research and treatment foundations. The Avon Foundation (1955) is its main avenue through which to fund not only breast cancer issues (since 1995), but also more recently, an anti–domestic violence campaign. Because of the breadth of Avon's sales force and market areas, these campaigns are global in nature. In addition to health philanthropy, the Edna McConnell Clark Foundation funds educational and developmental programs for young people from low-income backgrounds. At the same time, controversy has surrounded the company. For example, during the Campaign for Safe Cosmetics in California in 2005, the company lobbied against efforts to implement a regulatory framework for the use of chemicals in beauty products that would require companies to report all toxic ingredients used in their products.

Further Reading: Avon. www.ca.avon.com; www.avoncompany.com; Klepacki, Laura. *Avon: Building the World's Premier Company for Women.* Hoboken, NJ: John Wiley & Sons, 2005; Walker, Susannah. *Style and Status: Selling Beauty to African American Women, 1920–1975.* Lexington: University of Kentucky Press, 2007.

Christina Ashby-Martin

B

BALDNESS

Baldness refers to excessive hair loss from the scalp. Although it is normal to lose 50 to 100 hairs per day, hair loss becomes noticeable after approximately 50,000 hairs are lost. One of the major cases of baldness is alopecia, a genetic condition affecting more than five million people in the United States that may result in hair loss on the scalp or body. Baldness may be caused by other factors such as heredity, side effects from medication, certain medical conditions, hormone imbalances, stress, hair pulling, aging, poor nutrition, chemotherapy, tight **hairstyles**, chemical relaxers, pregnancy, or menopause.

Common

People may react to baldness by feeling isolated, withdrawn, anxious, depressed, sad, fearful, angry, ashamed, embarrassed, or helpless. They may lose self-esteem or self-confidence, feel unattractive to others, or become self-conscious. Men's baldness tends to be viewed more positively as a sign of masculinity or virility, while women's baldness tends to be viewed more negatively as a loss of femininity or sexuality. For people experiencing cancer-related baldness, hair loss represents a loss of vitality, health, and physical strength.

Remedies

Baldness remedies vary by the amount of time or expertise required by users and cost. People with patchy or partial hair loss can experiment with a variety of styling options. Men may comb over their hair to cover the balding area or wear long hairstyles, while women may use hair extensions or weaves, wear short hairstyles, or dye their hair a light shade to conceal bald areas. Unisex options include head shaving or the use of hats/scarves, laser combs, hair thickeners, volumizing hair products, ointments, and vitamins. There are several prescription drugs that people can use to combat balding. Rogaine, a line of **hair care products** that can be used by men or women, has been clinically proven to grow hair. These products are available by prescription or over the counter. Propecia is a daily pill for men that treats male pattern hair loss. Hairpieces such as wigs or toupees are also a popular method of hair replacement. Hairpieces come in a variety of colors, textures, densities, and styles, and may be used to cover temporary or permanent hair loss. The cost, durability, comfort, and appearance of hairpieces vary based on the materials used and the level of craftsmanship in their creation. Hairpieces are usually made from horse or human hair, wool, feathers, or synthetic material. Another remedy for baldness is a hair transplant, a medical procedure where a surgeon removes hair from a part of the scalp that has abundant hair growth and places it in areas that have thinning or no hair. Hair transplants may need to be repeated as other areas of the scalp lose hair over time. A related procedure is scalp reduction surgery, which involves decreasing the areas of bald skin by removing hairless portions of the scalp and covering them with hair-covered scalp. A variation of scalp reduction involves folding hair-covered scalp over bald skin.

Further Reading: American Hair Loss Association. http://www.americanhairloss.org; Mayo Clinic. http://www.mayoclinic.com/health/hair-loss/DS00278/DSECTION=treatments-and-drugs; National Alopecia Areata Foundation. http://www.naaf.org.

Priya Dua

BARBERS AND BARBERSHOPS

Barbers have had an influence on the evolution of the American beauty industry that is disproportionate to their numbers. As members of the oldest trade in the beauty industry, they have, until the 1970s, maintained a system of occupational segmentation that let them serve the most lucrative customers. They controlled the hair care market through apprenticeships, licensing laws, trade associations, and unions. These institutions relied, in turn, on a male work culture, which helps to explain why so few women worked as barbers. Moreover, as custodians of masculinity, barbers have played a role in defining male identity that gives them an outsized influence in American society.

Although, until recently, barbers have fended off competitors from other trades, the competition between different groups of men has long been fierce. Immigrants and African Americans flocked to the trade, attracted by the small initial outlay of capital needed to set up a barbershop. Because of the competition between these groups, the ethnic and racial identity of the American barber has changed repeatedly since colonial times. Each large wave of European and later Asian and Caribbean immigration to the United States intensified the struggle to control the trade. Other factors also influenced which group had the upper hand, such as changes in the services offered by barbers, who went from coiffing wigs and bloodletting to cutting and styling hair. The one exception to the rule of change within the tonsorial trade has been black barbers, whose enduring appeal makes them central figures in the African American community.

Colonial Origins

In Africa and Europe, **hairstyles** indicated status within hierarchical societies, making barbers arbiters of class distinctions. European barbers, in particular, earned a reputation as witty bon vivants, even though they were servants. When colonial merchants and planters sought recognition as gentlemen in Anglo-American culture, they donned wigs and relied primarily on enslaved waiting men to attend to their appearance. The link between African Americans and barbering

Senate office building barbershop, 1937. (Courtesy of Library of Congress)

had two important consequences. First, the trade became stigmatized. What had been a class relationship in Africa and Europe became a race relationship in the United States. As a consequence, white men generally rejected working as barbers, which created an occupational niche for black men. Second, black barbers had the chance to become fluent in European genteel culture, making them some of the most acculturated slaves in North America. Slave barbers learned genteel ways and negotiated the permission to hire out their own time, which gave them more independence and sometimes let them save the money to purchase their freedom. During the antebellum period, slave barbers tended to be the sons of white fathers, who arranged for them to be apprenticed as barbers and freed them at manhood. Free black barbers accepted the sons of family members and friends as apprentices, raising the young men in their own households and fostering close ties among black barbers.

Race and Barbering in Antebellum America

Race largely determined how barbers interacted with their customers during the antebellum period. Since black men lacked the money to pay for haircuts, they cut each other's hair informally. Almost all barbershops consequently served white men. Part of the appeal of black barbers to white customers was their willingness to provide deferential service that validated white superiority. By contrast, white barbers treated their white customers with an air of easy familiarity. Most American barbers were black until 1850, when German immigrant barbers supplanted them, at least numerically. Black barbers, however, continued to serve affluent white men until the early 20th century in increasingly palatial barbershops that featured bath houses and luxurious furnishings. These first-class barbershops represented the most consistently successful black-owned businesses in the 19th century.

The trade also bolstered the self-esteem of black barbers. As *knights of the razor,* a nickname that emphasized their link to the cosmopolitanism of European barbers as well as their tonsorial skills, black barbers enjoyed a positive occupational identity. Their success also let them serve as the breadwinners in their household, a role denied to black men at that time due to low wages and underemployment. Within the African American community, where their wealth and connections to powerful whites made them influential leaders, black barbers promoted an alternative version of respectability based on the shopkeeper's virtues of discipline, honesty, and thrift. Barbering, in sum, gave African Americans the opportunity to contest negative racial stereotypes and reformulate their identity.

Trade Transformed in the Gilded Age

Following the Civil War, several developments changed the marketplace for barbers. The proliferation of barber schools created a surplus of poorly trained barbers who eked out a meager living by charging low prices and working long hours. After several false starts at forming a union, white, mainly German American, barbers formed the Journeymen Barbers International Union of America (JBIUA) in 1886 and affiliated their union with the American Federation of **Labor**. In 1896, the JBIUA began lobbying for laws requiring that barbers have a state license. Black barbers such as Cleveland's George Meyers objected that licensing laws were designed to exclude African Americans from the trade serving white men. In Ohio, Meyers defeated the union effort, but licensing laws became the norm over the next 30 years. In the Atlanta Race Riot of 1904, tensions between white union barbers and black barbers led to violence. A white mob ransacked the barbershop of Alonzo Herndon and murdered one of his bootblacks; the black community maintained that the mob was led by white union barbers. During the 1920s, Herndon was the target of another campaign to regulate barbering. White women had gone to the black man to have their hair bobbed, scandalizing public opinion. In response, the Atlanta City Council enacted a law prohibiting African Americans from serving whites in a barbershop, and the local newspapers attributed the proposal to the barbers' union. The courts subsequently overturned the law. Public health had provided the rationalization for the licensing campaign, and the union benefited from a white tendency to associate African Americans with disease. Ironically, Gillette Razors used the same argument against union barbers in the company's successful campaign to get middle-class men to shave themselves during the 1920s.

Small Businesses in a Corporate Era

During the 20th century, barbershops exemplified trends in small business and in the service sector. Every main street had at least one barbershop where men gathered to talk. Unlike in the past, these shops, with a few exceptions, were segregated. Black barbers, pushed by Jim Crow and pulled by the growing urban black market, switched to a black clientele. Because of the personal service involved in barbering, the locally owned barbershop was not easily replaced with corporate chains. During the Great Depression, the federal government exerted influence over the trade for the first time, regulating hours, prices, and wages under the National Recovery Administration. In addition, the armed forces imposed new standards for grooming and haircuts on millions of American soldiers. The military created a significant niche for barbers who worked on bases as independent contractors. Following the return of prosperity in the 1950s, the JBIUA encouraged its members to upgrade their skills and learn how to style hair. Techniques developed by female beauty culture, such as coloring and **permanents**, were increasingly adopted by barbers.

Gradually, the differences that had separated barbershops from beauty salons broke down. Not all barbers embraced change, which left them ill prepared for the 1960s when young American men let their hair grow long. The **Afro** hairstyle best illustrates the change brought by long hair. Young black barbers such as Nathaniel Mathis, aka the Bush Doctor, of Washington, D.C., and Willie Morrow of San Diego understood that the Afro was an important symbol of black pride. Their Afro shops celebrated African heritage and the counterculture of the 1960s. Both men started corporations that sold Afro-care products, and existing companies such as Johnson Hair Products also capitalized on the style with Afro Sheen. Although the Afro and longer hair on white men would be depoliticized by the mid 1970s and become just another style, the baby boom generation had been exposed to a new type of business—the unisex salon—and they liked it.

During the 1970s, barbering finally experienced the same corporate transformation as other traditional service businesses. Entrepreneurs capitalized on the trend by franchising salons in chains such as Fantastic Sam's. Hiring primarily female graduates straight from **beauty schools**, the chains offer low prices and untested talent. These chain salons have increasingly attracted white men away from the traditional barbershop, which is a dying institution. In sharp contrast, a significant portion of women have remained faithful to their neighborhood beauty shop. Black men also rejected corporate standardization and overwhelmingly support their neighborhood barbershop. Functioning as a men's club, black men gather at the local barbershop to air opinions, share gossip, and tell off-color jokes. As one of the few spaces controlled by and reserved for black men, the black barbershop is at once a refuge and a community institution.

Further Reading: Bristol, Doug. *Knights of the Razor: Black Barbers in Slavery and Freedom.* Baltimore: Johns Hopkins Press, 2009; Hall, W. Scott. *The Journeyman Barbers' International Union of America.* Baltimore: Johns Hopkins Press, 1936; Harris-Lacewell, Melissa Victoria. *Barbershops, Bibles, and BET: Everyday Talk and Black Political Thought.* Princeton,

NJ: Princeton University Press, 2004; Walker, Juliet E. K. *The History of Black Business in America: Capitalism, Race, Entrepreneurship.* New York: Twayne Publishers, 1998.

Doug Bristol

BATH AND BODY WORKS

Bath and Body Works is a part of the Limited Brands company, which also owns Victoria's Secret, C. O. Bigelow, Henri Bendel, La Senza, and The White Barn Candle Company. Limited Brands distributes in Canada and in 40 other countries worldwide. Bath and Body comprises slightly over 1,500 of the company's 2,900 specialty stores nationwide. Bath and Body specializes in "fragrant flavorful indulgences," with an emphasis on innovation from nature. It focuses on incorporating simple rituals into daily life to improve emotional and physical well-being; it builds on earlier spa entrepreneurs' innovations and updates them by incorporating natural ingredients into personal care products.

Bath and Body Works subcategorizes its products into Body & Bath, Spa & Aromatherapy, Beauty, Accessories, Home & Candles, Kids, Gifts, and Sales. The product lines and brands listed under its categories demonstrate the interconnectedness with other Limited Brands' companies; C. O. Bigelow, Victoria's Secret, Henri Bendel, and Candles are all available through the Bath and Body Works online shopping links. The company's products reflect current concerns and trends in its clientele. There are lines of antibacterial products, B & B Works for Men, as well as bath and beauty products for tweens and young children. Its Aromatherapy category can be searched via Stress Relief, Sleep, Energy, Optimism, or Sensuality. While the company continually introduces new scent lines, to keep loyal customers happy, old favorites may be ordered through the Signature Collection and CLASSICS. The Web site includes many coupons and sales options to encourage repeat customers.

The Limited Brands company, and Bath and Body in particular, has gained a reputation for environmental responsibility and especially, non-testing of their products on animals. PETA, the **animal rights** group, awarded Bath and Body the Best Animal-Friendly Retailer Proggy Award in 2007, and the parent company, Limited Brands, has received numerous environmental recognition awards for the reduction of its footprint and its successful recycling procedures in **manufacturing**, **advertising**, **packaging**, and distribution. Of the six categories of "Social Responsibility" on its Web site, "Environment" is the longest, and the section on "Inclusion" is revealing in terms of the company's stated values, with special mention of its INROADS partnership to recruit minority college students, and pledge to continue supporting supplier diversity through relationships with minority- and women-owned businesses.

Further Reading: Bath & Body Works. http://www.bathandbodyworks.com; Home Business Expo. http://www.home-business-expo.com/wiki/BathBodyWorks.asp; Limited Brands. http://www.limitedbrands.com; People for the Ethical Treatment of Animals. http://www.peta.org/feat/proggy/2007/winners/asp.

Christina Ashby-Martin

BEAUTY PAGEANTS

Beauty pageants or beauty contests are competitions that more often than not judge the beauty of women. Although beauty pageants rank women according to physical appearance, organized pageants also give awards for congeniality or personality in order to emphasize inner beauty. Although beauty contests have existed in multiple historical and cultural contexts, modern, commercialized beauty pageants emerged in the late 19th and early 20th centuries in the United States. Today, beauty pageants for women are held in most regions and countries of the world, and international competitions like Miss World have also become increasingly popular. While there has been limited interest in male beauty pageants since the early 1990s, most contests that feature men tend to focus on bodybuilding.

History

Beauty contests in the United States began to appear as part of a broader culture of commercial leisure in the late 19th and early 20th centuries. Throughout the 19th century, cities and towns—particularly on the northeastern coast—began to expand as a result of industrialization and immigration to the United States. As Americans spent more of their time and money on leisure activities, entrepreneurs like P. T. Barnum began to establish an entertainment industry on boardwalks and main streets. Beauty pageants emerged within this economy of commercialized entertainment in the 1880s, when beach communities on the Mid-Atlantic coast began to sponsor them in order to encourage tourism. Competition among bathing beauties also provided the public the opportunity to see women's bodies exposed to a greater degree than Victorian norms allowed. Although public decency campaigns often curtailed efforts to hold such events, beauty pageants nonetheless became a ritual of the leisure culture in many beach communities throughout the early 20th century. In addition to beauty pageants, numerous community gatherings such as county fairs, holiday celebrations, and even football games, began to feature competitions that combined elements of civic virtue with beauty.

Arguably the most famous beauty pageant, the Miss America pageant, originated in the tourist commerce of Atlantic City, New Jersey, in an attempt to lure beach-going tourists after Labor Day weekend. The first competition was held over two days in September 1921. Known at first as the Inter-City Beauty Contest, the name of the winner was crowned Miss America at the next year's pageant. The early pageant emphasized different styles of dress, in particular a bathing suit,

Bathing beauty pageant, 1925, Huntington Beach, California. (Courtesy of Library of Congress)

as the most important criterion for the competition. However, in 1935 the pageant added a talent contest, and in 1939, a Miss Congeniality award was added. Throughout most of the history of the Miss America Pageant, until 1970, non-whites were either excluded or chose not to participate in the competition. Nonetheless, competitions like the Miss Chinatown USA and Miss Black America pageants emerged in the 1950s and 1960s.

As the pageant spread in popularity in the 1920s, Miss America began to sponsor preliminary competitions in states and territories that became elaborate public rituals in their own right. As the pageant gained in notoriety, many Miss America winners went on to significant earnings in endorsements and guest appearances. Due to a lack of funds during the Great Depression, the pageant was suspended for several years. However, throughout the 1940s and 1950s, Miss America enjoyed increased popularity as a national symbol during a period of wartime and postwar patriotism. Although the pageant officially encouraged the most prevalent and socially acceptable image of woman as housewife and mother, the organizers of the pageant introduced scholarships for women in the 1940s. In 1951, Catalina Swimwear withdrew commercial support from the competition when that year's winner refused to compete in a swimsuit. The following year, the Miss USA and the internationally expanded Miss Universe pageants, sponsored by Catalina manufacturer Pacific Mills, emerged as the biggest competitors to the Miss America brand. Nationwide beauty pageants that emerged in other countries after the 1950s tended to espouse the patriotism and national values of their American counterparts.

In 1955, the Miss America Pageant was first televised for a national audience. The telecast attracted significant numbers throughout the late 1950s and 1960s. Several Miss America winners have gone onto become actresses and some have enjoyed celebrity status. In the 1960s, changing attitudes toward women's status led to a resurgence in women's activism known as second-wave **feminism**. This era of women's liberation movements saw a number of organizations openly protest employment practices, the legal status of women, the social treatment of women, and the representation of women. In 1968, a group of feminist activists held a prominent protest in Atlantic City, where they crowned a sheep Miss America. Protestors also disseminated a widely read pamphlet that criticized the pageant's organizers for demeaning women, racial discrimination, and uncritical support for the military. The protest attracted a large amount of undue media scrutiny, and ratings and interest in the program declined throughout the 1970s. In many other countries, women also protested the pageants as an affront to the dignity of women and public piety.

Although ratings for the telecast dipped in the 1970s and 1980s, changing attitudes saw some unconventional candidates crowned. Some Miss America winners made headlines by supporting feminist causes. In 1984, Vanessa Williams became the first African American to win the competition, although she gave up the crown when nude photographs emerged. Arguably the most famous winner, Williams went on to become a top-selling musician and a widely recognized actress. Since the 1990s, the Miss America foundation has devoted much of its attention to women's scholarships, although the beauty competition remains the centerpiece of the organization.

Commercialization

The expansion of beauty pageants to other countries also saw the emergence of a global beauty pageant circuit. The spread of competition and the media scrutiny of the pageants led many competitors to spend more time in training. In addition, a large network of commercial support from **cosmetics** and clothing manufacturers became a major part of beauty pageants.

Beauty pageant circuits have become common for many competitors, who spend tremendous amounts of time and effort on preparing for the competition. Although the most prominent beauty pageants feature adult women in their early 20s, nationwide beauty pageants for children and teenaged girls have been common since the 1960s. Criticism has focused on inappropriate attention to children's bodies and undue pressure based on physical appearance. Since the sensationalized murder of child beauty contestant JonBenét Ramsey in 1996, children's beauty contests have also come under tremendous scrutiny because of their potential for abuse by sexual predators. In recent years, dwindling television ratings and the rise of professional modeling has seen a major decline in popularity for beauty pageants.

Gay and Male Culture

With the decriminalization of cross-dressing and homosexuality in the 1960s, female impersonators and transgender women began to organize drag pageants at bars in cities like San Francisco, Los Angeles, Chicago, and New York. Early gay rights activist and notable performer José Sarria organized the Imperial Court System in 1965 as a nonprofit foundation for gay liberation organizations in the San Francisco area. The structure of the Imperial Court System spread to numerous other cities and remains a major fundraiser in the LGBT (Lesbian, Gay, Bisexual, and Transgender) community. Since the late 1960s, male and drag beauty pageants have become a prominent feature of many gay male cultures in the United States. One of the earliest of these, Miss Gay America, was first held in 1971 in Nashville, Tennessee. In the early 1980s, Miss Continental became a major beauty pageant for transgender women. In addition to drag pageants, the last 20 years has seen a number of tongue-in-cheek male beauty pageants. Often, such pageants emphasize a subcultural aspect of the gay community, such as International Mr. Leather or Mr. Bear USA. The competitions often support local LGBT charities. Most gay beauty contests are campy, tongue-in-cheek parodies of female beauty pageants.

Since the 1950s, there have been a number of contests that have been viewed as the male equivalent of female beauty pageants. However, most of these, like the Mr. Universe competition, tend to focus on bodybuilding rather than male beauty. Since the 1990s, there have been various attempts to promote mainstream male beauty pageants. The Manhunt International competition originated in Singapore in 1993 and represented one of the earliest attempts to establish a contest based on male beauty and charm, modeled heavily after female beauty pageants. The Miss World organization also began to host a Mister World pageant in 1996. Despite serious efforts to gain wider recognition for male beauty pageants, they attract little recognition from any mainstream media sources.

Further Reading: Banet-Weiser, Sarah. *The Most Beautiful Girl in the World: Beauty Pageants and National Identity.* Berkeley: University of California Press, 1999; Craig, Maxine Leeds. *Ain't I a Beauty Queen? Black Women, Beauty and the Politics of Race.* Oxford: Oxford University Press, 2002; D'Emilio, John, and Estelle B. Freedman. *Intimate Matters: A History of Sexuality in America,* 2nd Ed. Chicago: University of Chicago Press, 1998; Riordan, Teresa. *Inventing Beauty: A History of the Innovations that Have Made Us Beautiful.* New York: Broadway Books, 2004; Watson, Elwood, and Darcy Martin, eds. *"There She Is, Miss America": The Politics of Sex, Beauty, and Race in America's Most Famous Pageant.* New York: Palgrave MacMillan, 2004.

Christopher A. Mitchell

BEAUTY SCHOOLS

In the United States, the first beauty schools emerged near the end of the 19th century in tandem with the development of commercially produced and marketed beauty products. Initially, women trained for beauty culture with other women who were established in hairdressing and skin care enterprises. The apprenticeship system continued well into the 20th century, but some beauty culturists established beauty colleges as well. At the same time, many successful female beauty product entrepreneurs were expanding their businesses from locally distributed homemade preparations to factory-made beauty systems sold regionally, and eventually nationally, by mail order and door-to-door sales agents. Offering beauty services was an important marketing tool for sales agents. At first, beauty company founders trained sales agents themselves, but as their businesses grew, they increasingly depended on experienced agents to train new recruits. Eventually, the biggest companies founded beauty, or what were more professionally known as cosmetology schools in major urban centers, allowing graduates to open salons using the company name and advertise that they were certified in that particular product line's "system." Martha Matilda Harper's Harper Method and the Marinello Company, founded by Ruth Maurer, represent two prominent and early examples of this sort of training, licensing, and franchising system.

Educators and Entrepreneurs

African American female beauty entrepreneurs offer particularly good examples of how beauty schools developed from particular brand name beauty product lines in the early 20th century. **Madam C. J. Walker** and **Annie Turnbo Malone** (founder of the Poro Company) started out by traveling across the country, training women to act as both sales agents and **hairdressers**. Walker was so successful that she was able to hire some of her best agents to travel and educate potential agents on her behalf. For African American beauticians, this system was something of a necessity. This was due in part to segregation, which barred them from pursuing training at established beauty parlors, but it was also a function of the particular systems both women offered. Malone and Walker pioneered products and methods for straightening African American women's hair using oils and heated metal pressing combs. Such hairdressing practices were relatively new for black women in the early 20th century, and were certainly not taught in white-owned beauty schools at this time. Marjorie Joyner became the first African American to graduate from Chicago's A. B. Molar Beauty School in 1916. While she was an accomplished and innovative beautician (Joyner patented one of the first permanent wave machines), Joyner left Molar and ran a beauty shop for several years without knowing how to work with tightly curled hair. After training with Madam Walker, and introducing Walker to methods of Marcel waving and hair weaving that she had learned at Molar, Joyner became the Walker Company's leading traveling educator. By the 1920s, Malone and Walker (and Apex founder Sara Washington) had established beauty colleges in cities with significant African American populations.

From Beauty Schools to Beauty Colleges

In the context of limited educational opportunities for working-class women, and limited opportunities for women generally to train for professions, beauty schools in the first half of the 20th century often portrayed themselves as institutions of higher learning akin to women's colleges rather than as vocational schools. Schools called themselves beauty colleges, offered dormitories, hosted formal dances, fielded sports teams, published yearbooks, and put on elaborate graduation ceremonies. Claims of professional legitimacy gained ground during the 1930s and 1940s, when states began to establish training requirements and certification exams for beauty culturists. In many states, certification required 1,000 hours or more of training in cosmetology, and beauty college programs that once took a few weeks to complete expanded to fill one or even two years. This led to a proliferation of beauty schools and cosmetology courses by the 1940s and 1950s, as well as broadened opportunities to take courses in beauty culture in high schools and at some two-year colleges. Beauty school students took courses in anatomy, **dermatology**, business, and accounting, and they were required to learn an array of hairstyling and skin care methods. African American leaders in the beauty culture industry fought for places on state cosmetology boards and to make sure that hair care methods for black women were included in state standards and taught at all beauty schools that offered preparation for certification exams. In spite of this, and even after legal segregation in beauty schools ended throughout the United States in the 1960s, beauty training remained a racially divided activity.

In the wake of the civil rights and women's liberation movements, women strove to realize broader educational and occupational possibilities. Although such opportunities were not equally available to all women across racial and class lines, it is clear that women who might have trained to be beauty culturists in the 1950s had many other options by the 1970s and 1980s. Those women who wanted and had access to a university education (and to professions that required college and graduate school) were less likely to look to beauty school by this time.

Beauty schools did not necessarily lose rigor or status as educational institutions as a result, but they were less likely to highlight beauty culture as a prestigious profession, and more likely to stress their practical and vocational missions. In the later decades of the 20th century, beauty schools remained an important educational route for many women (and an ever-increasing number of men) to train for a skilled and creative occupation that continued to be in demand. Amid an encumbering recession, beauty schools also offer bargain prices for customers who don't mind their hair in the hands of hairdressers in training.

See also: African American Beauty Industry

Further Reading: Blackwelder, Julia Kirk. *Styling Jim Crow: African American Beauty Training during Segregation.* College Station: Texas A&M University Press, 2003; Peiss, Kathy. *Hope in a Jar: The Making of America's Beauty Culture.* New York: Metropolitan Books, 1998; Walker, Susannah. *Style and Status: Selling Beauty to African American Women, 1920–1975.* Lexington: University Press of Kentucky, 2007; Willett, Julie A. *Permanent Waves: The Making of the American Beauty Shop.* New York: New York University Press, 2000.

Susannah Walker

BEAUTY SHOPS AND SALONS

Beauty shops have long been seen as a place for women to temporarily escape the problems of labor and love, literally washing away the blues in search of a new look and attitude. Thus, beauty shops quickly gained the reputation as bastions of gossip that mixed seemingly mundane conversation with the smells of hairspray and perms. Often located in front parlors and tenement flats, many shops have mistakenly been relegated to the periphery of a larger political economy, but few institutions more profoundly fueled the growth of the beauty industry while providing women an institution that offered them such a unique degree of independence as both consumers and producers of beauty. Because beauty shops were often located in or adjacent to homes, they allowed mothers and wives with households to maintain an entrepreneurial niche that fit the changing demands of the lifecycle.

Beauty shops have also tended to reflect the distinct cultures and communities to which they are inextricably bound and, just as race profoundly shaped the American landscape, beauty shops came of age with segregation, creating a racially segmented industry. At the same time, women's desire to create a social space that stood in bold relief to the barbershop's masculine milieu defined beauty salons regardless of race and class distinctions.

"When I go to my mom's shop, I find out who's going to college, who's graduated from college, who got a job, who's in prison. You find out a lot of information is traded there: job searching, networking, happens, social events . . . Like if Mr. Farrakhan is coming to town . . . or if something's going on where we're selling tickets."

Derrick Williams (pseudonym), hairstylist

Source: Willett, Julie. *Permanent Waves: The Making of the American Beauty Shop.* New York: New York University Press, 2000, 189.

Early Roots

The history of the beauty shop owes much to technological and stylistic changes, as well as the ebb and flow of women's roles as consumers and workers in American society. In the 19th century, posh salons were few and far between, and ladies' **hairdressers** frequented the private homes of the well-to-do where they washed, fan-dried, and arranged hair. Free and enslaved household laborers were also routinely asked to care for their employer/owner's personal and hygienic needs, something that often included dressing hair. Men with more access to money and public space frequented barbershops, while washing and styling hair was often part of mother and daughter's routine relegated to the private realm of the family. When women began frequenting barbershops for the short and carefree **bob**, first popular in the 1920s, they posed a threat to distinct gender roles and the once exclusively male bastion of the barbershop. Bobbing hair and fears over respectability were coupled with the development of electric permanent wave machines that further delineated ladies' hairdressing and beauty shop services as distinct from barbershops.

Work Cultures in the 1920s and 30s

By the 1920s and 30s, beauty shops were easily found even in out-of-the-way places. While many were owner-operated businesses that relied on kitchen sinks and homemade ingenuity, other salons were stylish art deco retreats that hired dozens of beauty workers who specialized in everything from color to perms. Renting just a booth was also a common practice and offered a measure of independence with little economic risk. Coloring hair and painting nails, as well as facial and skin treatments, were common features of beauty shop services, although many shops thrived on just doing hair. Pampering the well-to-do or catering to working-class neighbors meant work cultures varied greatly, yet pleasing a picky customer easily transgressed class boundaries. Permanent machines, one of the most iconic features of these early shops, were often unreliable. Curls did not come out the same, and dyes and other products could be unpredictable. Hair type and hairdressers' skills varied, as did the creams, colors, and rinses used in these different beauty rituals. Heat and humidity could ruin styles as quickly as they were finished, and beauty shop profits could decline with the weather or fashion trends that made previous investments in supplies and skills obsolete. Some shops strategically operated in cooler basements, but even then chemical and thermal combinations could make the smells unbearable at times and strikingly unhealthy for hairdressers who worked in salons day in and day out.

Social and Political Space

African American entrepreneur **Madam C. J. Walker** understood that offering beauty services to working-class women was about providing more than style. It was about giving Black women the chance to brush aside or straighten out the racial politics of the day. Like churches, beauty shops helped transform, in the words of so many black leaders, "segregation into a form of congregation," making hairdressers more than a sympathetic ear but movers and shakers in their communities. In African American communities especially, beauty shops have been the locus of politics and community organization throughout the 20th century. During the long civil rights movement, for example, beauty operators manned voter registration drives, housed a plethora of African American literature, and cleaned up protesters after violent attacks at sit-ins. Thanks to their rich history of independence from white control, African American hairdressers' legacy continues today. Whether with information on breast cancer or AIDS, beauty shops often provide more successful kinds of outreach than institutions that seem too distant, impersonal, or untrustworthy.

Golden Age of Owner-Operator Shops

Beauty shops have also thrived despite the ebb and flow of politics and economy in part because they have never been a static institution. During World War II, Beauty shops visibly contributed to charities, sold war bonds, saved scrap metal, and dressed store front windows in red, white, and blue. Doubting the iconic Rosie the Riveter's war worker's femininity ensured that trips to beauty shops were cast as patriotic acts. In fact, some war industries made sure their factories provided beauty shop services to their female employees even though they failed to offer working mothers day care for their young children. Women who were able to avoid being absent too many days or made it to work without being tardy might even receive a bonus in the form of a trip to the factory-owned beauty shop. Similarly, the cold war's emphasis on domestic containment resurrected quasi-Victorian styles along with high maintenance hair-dos that meant weekly standing appointments at most salons. Even when drugstores offered more inexpensive do-it-yourself products, **bouffants** and beehives helped to make the 1950s and 1960s the golden age of independently owned beauty shops that boasted names like Bertha's Temple of Beauty.

Unisex Salon and Corporate Chains

The most direct challenge to beauty salons came in the 1970s, with the rise of unisex salons and the corporate reorganization of the beauty industry that attempted to break down gender distinctions in style and process. Longer hair in males was devastating to barbershops, which began to wane in numbers as a younger generation of men rejected their father's crew cuts. An ever increasing number of salons redesigned themselves by changing their names and décor to cater to a male clientele. Unisex salons brought not only male and female customers into the same salon, but fostered direct competition between female and male stylists, the latter often deemed more professional and still occupying a disproportionate number of managerial/ownership positions. Although this is something of a stereotype, gay men found salons a unique work space that embraced homosexual identities and masculinities often chastised in more conservative businesses.

Other corporate trends have been designed to break down the bonds between hairdressers and their clients, making customers' loyalty rest with a chain salon rather than an individual. Some salons advertise that appointments are not necessary and that walk-ins are welcome, adding excitement and aggravation to the stylist's day-to-day routine. Regardless of the length or condition of hair, these businesses guarantee a new look faster than a pizza delivery. Stylists were often prohibited from using their own names, providing any personal information, or making small talk, to ensure that profits would not be disrupted by high rates of employee turnover. Although low-budget chains may be the places where the newest cosmetology graduates first find employment, they often provide benefits like health insurance and other benefits that smaller, independently owned business have not always been able to afford. Despite the corporate reorganization of the salon, many follow their stylist from salon to salon and retain relationships that defy most other kinds of service work.

Contemporary Marketing Trends

Today, hair salons are as diverse as they were in the early 20th century, and just as likely to be marketed to different pocketbooks, but they are not without competition. Businesses that specialize only in hair compete with **nail salons** and **spas** for consumer dollars. Full-service salons once employed a single manicurist who managed both her wealthy regulars and customers celebrating special occasions like proms and weddings. Now the same salon may employ a number of specialists who provide manicures, **waxing**, and facials. The visibility of an ethnic market has also meant that businesses, with varying success, have blurred some of the race and ethnic boundaries that had long divided the hair care industry. Head-to-toe beauty salons have also courted a male clientele seeking everything from sport facials to MANicures. Some businesses that advertise "for men only" alter more than the names of their services to adopt a more manly bearing. They also tout flat-screen TVs and decor that would revival any sports bars. Of course, many beauty salons operate just as they did 30 or 40 years ago and thrive in private homes and residential neighborhoods. Whether businesses market cheap and fast service for family budgets, **hip hop** chic to white suburbia, or **organic** products for a green consciousness, salons continue to be the heart and soul of many communities, caring for customers from cradle to grave, ensuring that beauty workers are always more than just a hairdresser to their clientele.

Further Reading: Banks, Ingrid. *Hair Matters, Beauty, Power, and Black Women's Consciousness.* New York: New York University Press, 2000; Banner, Lois. *American Beauty.* New York: Knopf, 1983; Blackwelder, Julia Kirk. *Styling Jim Crow: African American Beauty Training during Segregation.* College Station: Texas A&M Press, 2003; Furman, Frieda Ke. *Facing the Mirror: Older Women and Beauty Shop Culture.* New York: Routledge, 1997; Peiss, Kathy. *Hope in a Jar: The Making of America's Beauty Culture.* New York: Metropolitan Books 1998; Rooks, Noliwe. *Hair Raising: Beauty, Culture, and African American Women.* New Brunswick, NJ: Rutgers University Press, 1996; Walker, Susannah. *Selling Beauty to African American Women, 1920–1975.* Lexington: The University Press of

Kentucky, 2007; Weems, Robert. *Desegregating the Dollar*. New York: New York University Press, 1998; Willett, Julie. *Permanent Waves: The Making of American Beauty Shop*. New York: New York University Press, 2000.

Julie Willett

BED HEAD

Bed Head is a line of hair, makeup, body, and nail products that transformed a playful insult into high fashion and sought-after name brand. Bed Head is known for catering to a hip, trendy, and modern customer. Its one-of-a-kind **packaging** and unforgettable product names have given Bed Head its reputation as a company pushing the limits of marketing and **branding**. It gets its name from a popular trend of the 1990s in which hair was meant to look like one "just got out of bed." The bed head hairdo is one that looks effortless and not overly styled. The look relies on styling products to achieve its no-fuss appearance.

History

TIGI Bed Head was founded by hairstyling giant **Toni&Guy** in 1995 in Dallas. Kyara Mascolo, wife of Bruno Mascolo, one of the four brothers who started Toni&Guy, was the mastermind behind the Bed Head logo and its savvy **packaging** and product names. The colorful containers and distinctive bottle shapes have appealed to a wide array of consumers. Its originality is seen throughout its total marketing campaign, including self-service cosmetic displays. Linking the products to celebrities and magazines has bolstered its cutting-edge reputation. Bed Head evolved from Toni&Guy's original TIGI hairstyling line that began in 1986. It was a way to support Toni&Guy's emphasis on fashionable and stylish hair design. Unilever purchased TIGI, which includes the Bed Head, Essensuals, and Classic lines for $411.5 million in 2009.

Products

The first Bed Head hair product was the Bed Head stick, used to create texture and hold for hair. The line sells shampoos, conditioners, gels, mousse, volumizers, straighteners, curl enhancers, hair wax, hair sprays, and styling appliances. Bed Head's marketing focus is on fun and entertainment, while providing the customer with a top-of-the-line, quality product. Names like Hook-up, a mousse wax, Power Trip, a hair gel, and Dumb Blonde, a color enhancer for blonde hair, drive its reputation for creativity and innovation. The Bed Head makeup line sells foundations, powders, lipsticks, eye shadows, eyeliners, and nail polishes. The Body by Bed Head line sells body washes, body butters, lotions, scrubs, and fragrance. Pet Head by Bed Head offers stylish dog accessories, apparel, and grooming products.

Further Reading: Cuellar, Catherine. "Bruno Mascolo—Raising Toni&Guy's Status in a Cutting-Edge Industry." *Dallas Morning News,* April 9, 2000. http://infoweb.

newsbank.com.lib-e2.lib.ttu.edu/iw-search/we/InfoWeb?p_product=NewsBank&
p_theme=aggregated5&p_action=doc&p_docid=0ED822308DBC8B23&p_doc
num=1&p_queryname=1. (Accessed May 6, 2009); King, Ian. "Unilever Gels with
Brothers over $411m TIGI Deal." *Times* (London). January 27, 2009. http://www.
mediapost.com/publications/?fa=Articles.showArticle&art_aid=99180. (Accessed
May 4, 2009).

Corye Perez Beene

BLONDES

Whether or not blondes have more fun, blondeness has been a crucial component in the hair care industry, the world of fashion, and popular imagination.
While blondeness has for centuries been associated in art and literature with the
fairer sex, and thus inextricably bound to all the race and cultural implications
that have long privileged light complexions, bleaching hair blonde was not readily
embraced until the middle of the 20th century. Changing hair color, much like the
use of makeup, was associated with deception, artificiality, and sensuality, all of
which violated middle-class ideas about respectability. In the 20th century, Hollywood made blondeness the crowning glory of **film** icons like Jean Harlow and
Marilyn Monroe, who epitomized both feminine vice and virtue. Clever **advertising** campaigns made dying hair acceptable for the girl next door and cashed in
on the inherent contradictions that such a bold look implied to make millions for
the hair color industry.

Hollywood Blondes

Against the backdrop of decades of deteriorating race relations that relegated
blackness and ethnic identities to that of other, 1930s Hollywood turned to the
blondest of blondes to sell films and fantasy amid economic depression. Jean
Harlow titillated moviegoers in films like *Platinum Blonde* (1931) and *Blonde Venus*
(1932), in which she achieved her trademark blondeness with the help of bleach,
soap, and ammonia that was so damaging that she had to resort to a wig. Nevertheless, Harlow and Hollywood paved the way for a series of blonde starlets who
ranged from the sassy Mae West to demure Marlene Dietrich. The most famous
20th-century blonde, however, was Marilyn Monroe. Her famous nude calendar
shot made her the first and most famous *Playboy* centerfold and blondeness a
symbol of unabashed sexuality. Blondes were turning heads but they were not
without their critics who mocked blondeness along with other narcissistic beauty
practices. Assuming brains and beauty were a rare combination, an ever-growing
litany of dumb blonde jokes could be heard in bars and businesses, especially
as increasing numbers of women directly challenged the prevailing sexism. By
the 1970s, liberation movements coupled with the rise of the **natural look** also
threatened the bottled blonde, but California tans and sun-kissed highlights made
weaves and frosted tips all the rage. By the 1980s, artificially had lost much of its
taboo in the realm of beauty consumption. At the one extreme, Princess Diana
coupled purity and humility with her look, and at the other, stars like Madonna and

"The white American GIs who had been dreaming of Alberto Varga's blond pinups and Betty Grable during the war returned and of course, married women with hair of every tint. But as Graham McCann comments in *Marilyn Monroe* [his 1988 book], 'Fifties movie moguls demanded the stereotype of a blonde, a dream (so they said) of returning soldiers and of Men Only, something Michelangelo might have carved out of candy'. . . . Blondes were, QED, the whitest, most desirable of whites. And so the bleach that had been all the rage in the '30s was applied liberally to many heads—not only those in Hollywood—now readily accessible to middle-class women through the new 'Miss Clairol,' products. Bristol-Myers Ltd., parent company of 'Miss Clairol,' assisted in editing ethnicities other than Anglo-Saxon and Nordic—If only until the next application of its products."

Ellen Tremper, Professor of English

Source: Tremper, Ellen. *I'm No Angel: The Blonde in Fiction and Film.* Charlottesville: University of Virginia Press, 2006, 185.

Pamela Anderson unapologetically embraced blondeness as a symbol of personal ambition and sensuality.

Advertising Campaigns

Hollywood sex symbols made iconic, advertising campaigns marketed to fit an ever-changing political milieu: blondeness inspired some of most innovative advertising campaigns in the beauty industry and privileged female innovation in the almost exclusively male world of advertising. Clairol quickly dominated the market thanks to an easy home rinse process and the advertising genius of Shirley Polykoff. In the late 1950s, Polykoff's innovative ads toyed with an ambiguity that balanced sexuality and respectability. The slogan "Does she or doesn't she . . . only her hairdresser knows for sure," reassured the girl next door that she too could be blonde and beautiful. Polykoff followed with other iconic ad campaigns such as the rhetorical catchphrase that asked "Is it true blondes have more fun?" and "If I've only one life, let me live it as a blonde." Competition from other companies was quick to follow. Advertising agencies were male dominated in the 1960s and '70s, and Ilon Specht, a female copywriter, grew irritated with male colleagues who insisted, for example, that she only use "girl" rather than "woman" in all of her copy. Frustrated personally and professionally, she came up with L'Oréal's "I'm worth it" campaign that captured the mood of the women's liberation movement and a major share of the market. Most recently, L'Oréal's "Feel the Power of Color" ad campaign captured the same vein for a generation of women looking to crack more glass ceilings. Today, Western fascination coupled with global marketing strategies have made blondeness popular in countries as diverse as Brazil, Japan, and China, expanding a hair color industry into previously untapped markets around the globe.

Further Reading: Flyin, Natalia. *Blonde Like Me: The Roots of the Blonde Myth in Our Culture.* New York: Simon & Schuster, 2000; Jones, Geoffrey. "Blonde and Blue-Eyed? Globalizing Beauty c. 1945–1980." *Economic History Review,* 61 no. 1 (2008): 125–54; Pitman, Joanne. *On Blondes.* New York: Bloomsbury, 2003; Tremper, Ellen. *I'm No Angel:*

The Blonde in Fiction and Film. Charlottesville: University of Virginia Press, 2006; Weitz, Rose. *Rapunzel's Daughters: What Women's Hair Tells Us about Women's Lives.* New York: Farrar, Straus and Giroux, 2004; Willett, Julie. *Permanent Waves: The Making of the American Beauty Shop.* New York: New York University Press, 2000.

Julie Willett

THE BOB

An ear-length blunt cut, worn with or without bangs, the bob became a widely popular hairstyle for women during the 1920s. Associated with the young women known as flappers, the bob became a visual metaphor for the social changes taking place during this period. Prior to the 1920s, a woman's hair was considered her crowning glory and was generally worn long, uncut, and styled into heavy arrangements that incorporated both real and false hair. Females with short haircuts were either very young, invalids, or those who functioned on the margins of society. The popularity of the bob changed this perception of the short-haired woman and moved her into the mainstream.

The first appearance of the bob can be traced to 1908, when the French hairstylist Antoine cut the hair of actress Eve Lavallière into a short cut that Antoine dubbed Jeanne d'Arc. In 1909, French fashion designer Paul Poiret cropped the

Young women sporting the bob, 1923, Washington, D.C. (Courtesy of Library of Congress)

hair of his models for a fashion show. From this point on, the bob began to appear on the heads of women associated with the arts. Dancer Irene Castle Isadora Duncan, author Colette, actress Louise Brooks, and fashion designer **Coco Chanel** all sported bobs during the teens or '20s.

The bob truly came into its own as the fashionable silhouette began to move toward a slim, streamlined, almost boyish look in the late teens and the early '20s. The sleek, neat lines of the bob perfectly complemented these styles, and helped propel the cut into widespread popularity. Bobs were particularly popular with young women, who considered the easy-care cut more practical and hygienic than the styles favored by older generations. From the original blunt-cut, numerous variations emerged, many of which were named. These included the coconut, the orchid, the garçon, the French swirl, and the Eton crop, which was an extremely short, slicked-back style. For women who were hesitant to have their hair cut, bob wigs were widely available.

The bob became a genuinely international style, with fashion periodicals noting its appearance in countries as diverse as France, China, Mexico, Germany, and the United States. As the bob became more widespread, it also became more controversial. Religious leaders railed against it; doctors warned that the exposed neck would lead to more frequent colds; while hairstylists feared that it would put them out of business. Many young women whose parents refused to allow them to bob their hair invented tales of assaults that ended in their crowning glory being shorn into a short bob. This distaste for the bob pointed to a general discomfort with the ways in which young women were adopting new behaviors and pastimes such as dancing publicly, working outside the home, and engaging in sporting activities.

Despite the hopes of some critics, the bob was not simply a passing fad. Though the extremely severe variations of the bob faded from popularity, many women persisted in keeping their hair relatively short. In fact, the bob ushered in an era of popularity for short hair that lasted until the late 1960s, when long hair moved back into fashion's spotlight; nevertheless, the bob remains a sought-after style and a symbol of a carefree attitude.

Further Reading: Cox, Caroline, and Lee Widdows. *Hair & Fashion.* London: V&A Publications, 2005; Weitz, Rose. *Rapunzel's Daughters: What Women's Hair Tells Us about Women's Lives.* New York: Farrar, Straus and Giroux, 2004; Willett, Julie. *Permanent Waves: The Making of the American Beauty Shop.* New York: New York University Press, 2000. Zdatny, Steven. "The Boyish Look and the Liberated Woman: The Politics and Aesthetics of Women's Hairstyles." *Fashion Theory,* 4 (1997): 367–98.

Rachel Harris

BOBBI BROWN. *SEE* BROWN, BOBBI

THE BODY SHOP

The Body Shop, founded in the mid 1970s, is a beauty company that offers vegetable-based products and a strong ethical mission. It is the second largest cosmetic franchise in the world. The Body Shop emphasizes its stance against animal testing and for fair trade and promotes positive environmental and social change through its products and community investment.

History

In 1976, Anita Roddick founded The Body Shop in Great Britain. Currently, The Body Shop has over 2,400 stores in 61 countries, and offers 1,200 products. In 1986, the company formed an alliance with Greenpeace, joining the group's campaign to save the whales. Greenpeace and The Body Shop ended their alliance a few years later after London Greenpeace published a treatise criticizing The Body Shop for prioritizing corporate values over community. The Body Shop responded with a leaflet extolling the ways in which it promotes environmental responsibility. The company rejoined with Greenpeace in 2001 to promote clean energy. In 1990, the Body Shop Foundation was formed for the purpose of providing financial resources for nonprofit activist groups working for the protection of human rights and the environment. In March 2006, L'Oréal bought The Body Shop for $1.1 billion. **Animal rights** groups protested the takeover, since other products produced by the parent company are alleged to be tested on animals; L'Oréal, however, states that the company has not tested on animals since 1989.

Animal Rights

The Body Shop takes a stance against animal testing. The company's slogan reads: "Our products are not tested on animals, never have been and never will be." Critics note that the actual policy on animal testing is to use ingredients that were tested on animals before 1991 (when their policy was introduced) or ingredients that were tested on animals after 1991 for non-cosmetic reasons. However, the company insists that its products are cruelty free. The Body Shop was the first international company to be recognized under the Humane **Cosmetics** Standard, sponsored by the British Union for the Abolition of Vivisection (BUAV). While The Body Shop carries a range of personal care products, including lotions, cleansers, and fragrances for the home, all of its products have been 100 percent vegetarian as of June 2007. Conducting research on natural preservatives, the company is working toward a goal of having 80 percent of its products free from artificial preservatives.

Community Trade

The Body Shop has a long-established program called Community Trade, which is the company's own fair trading network. The company does business with more than 30 community suppliers in 20 countries for its ingredients. By purchasing community-produced ingredients, the Body Shop supports fair trade, providing a fair price for community-produced ingredients. As of 2008, 65 percent of the company's products contain Community Trade ingredients. In addition to securing product ingredients from such community partners, the Body Shop has offered handcrafted items supplied by small communities. The first such product was a foot massager developed by a community in southern India. Critics note that the company's actual payments to such communities resulted in less than one percent of its costs.

Further Reading: Associated Press. "L'Oréal is Paying $1.1 Billion for Body Shop." *New York Times,* March 18, 2006. http://www.nytimes.com/2006/03/18/business/worldbusiness/18body.html. (Accessed September 24, 2008); Roddick, Anita. *Business as Unusual: My Entrepreneurial Journey, Profits with Principles.* London: Anita Roddick Books, 2005; Vallely, Paul. "Dame Anita Roddick: Idealist Entrepreneur who with The Body Shop took 'Cruelty-Free' Products into the High Street." *Independent,* September 12, 2007. http://www.independent.co.uk/news/obituaries/dame-anita-roddick-402053.html. (Accessed September 24, 2008).

Anne Marie Todd

BOTOX

Botox, a diluted form of the neurotoxin botulinum A, is, according to the statistics of the American Society for Aesthetic Plastic Surgery, the most popular cosmetic procedure (including surgical and non-surgical procedures) ever to exist. While in the year 2000, one million people had had Botox injections in the United States, by 2002, when the FDA approved the drug as successfully reducing the severity of frown lines for up to 120 days, the number of users had already risen to over 1.6 million, and to 2.4 million by 2008. This represents an increase of over 4,000 percent for men and around 3,600 percent for women since 1997. Botox is injected subcutaneously, and as a non-surgical cosmetic procedure it is followed in its popularity by the use of hyaluronic acid and such rejuvenation procedures as chemical peels and laser skin resurfacing.

The drug, which is manufactured in the United States by Allergan, is dedicated to reducing the appearance of fine lines and wrinkles on the face, particularly the forehead, for aesthetic purposes. It is named after the Latin *botulus* (sausage). The substance was identified in 1895 by the Belgian physician Emile van Ermengem, who named it after its identification in some sausages that had been poisoned with *clostridium botulinum,* a group of bacteria commonly found in soil. Consumed in larger doses, botulinum causes a form of botulism, a serious paralytic illness. In the late 1980s, the substance was originally tested for eye problems like muscle spasm, tics, and blinking by the Canadian doctors Alastair and Jean Carruthers, who published the ground-breaking article "Treatment of Glabellar Frown Lines with C. Botulinum-A Exotoxin" (1992), which formed the basis of today's cosmetic application of the toxin.

For doctors, Botox treatments are a cash cow. In 2005, doctors paid $488 for a vial that generated revenues of up to $3000. For the U.S. consumer, costs vary between $450 and $800 per treatment, or between $2,700 and $4,800 per year. Variations of Botox can be found for much less on the black market. Overall, Botox is well over a billion-dollar industry.

The number-one selling point of Botox is the effect of a youthful appearance, due to the disappearance of wrinkles and strong frown lines. But the importance of communicating with precisely these facial features during speech or on the stage—which by the legendary Roman rhetorician Quintilian was held to be absolutely indispensable for a successful presentation—is seriously undermined by the use of this paralyzing substance. Indeed, some Hollywood directors have been known to say that they cannot work with actresses and actors who have lost the ability to express emotion in the face due to Botox (Nicole Kidman has been thought to have had Botox). Botox, according to one scholar, can be understood as a *pharmakon* because of its ability to cure while poisoning. The cure in question is of a psychological nature, and appears to be stronger in the minds of its users than the damage it causes. The person who uses Botox expresses that he feels younger inside and wants to have that feeling reflected in his face. The toxin can hence be understood as a necessary evil for the modern self, who lives in the zeitgeist of makeover.

Further Reading: Cooke, Grayson. "Effacing the Face: Botox and the Anarchivic Archive." *Body & Society,* 14 no. 2 (2008):23–38; Kuczynski, Alex. *Beauty Junkies: Inside our $15 Billion Obsession with Cosmetic Surgery.* New York: Doubleday, 2006.

Bernadette Wegenstein

BOUFFANT

Lacquered puffiness, usually on top of the head but sometimes also on the sides, to increase the hair's height and volume characterizes the bouffant hairstyle. The hairstyle's name comes from the French verb *bouffer,* meaning to puff out or to swell. An urban legend, known to folklorists as "The Fatal Hairdo" or "The Spider in the Beehive," alleges that black widows, cockroaches, or other small creatures are likely to nest inside the darkness and warmth of the lacquered bouffant, feeding off the blood of their hosts, especially when the hair is uncombed or unwashed for extended periods of time. None of these legends have any basis in fact and can be traced to English tales from the 13th century in which spiders inhabit the elaborate hairdos of excessively vain women.

Although the bouffant can be traced to late 18th century France, it achieved its greatest popularity in the United States from the late 1950s to the mid 1960s. Its rise was aided in large part by two consumer innovations of the time: the plastic hair roller, which was used for winding and curling the hair (usually overnight) before teasing or backcombing it to increase volume, and the aerosol can of lacquer hairspray, which was applied liberally to create a rigid shell that held the bouffant in place. During the 1960s, the bouffant could be seen on the heads of first ladies Jacqueline Bouvier Kennedy and Pat Ryan Nixon, **film** and television actresses Audrey Hepburn and Mary Tyler Moore, singing groups such as the Supremes and the Shangri-Las, and many other influential models of fashionable style.

Not all appreciated the new style. *Newsweek* reported in 1962 that the bouffant's popularity among teenagers was troubling to parents, who thought their daughters were wasting too much time rolling and combing their hair; to teachers, who observed a correlation between low grades and high hair; and to **hairdressers**, who cautioned that the scalp underneath a lacquered shell was not able to breathe properly. An exaggerated version of the bouffant, known as the beehive or B-52 (because of its resemblance to the bulbous nose cone of this particular aircraft), was popular around the same time—and has subsequently been spoofed in various forms of popular culture, such as the film and Broadway musical *Hairspray,* Marge Simpson's hair in *The Simpsons,* and the New Wave rock band the B-52s.

By the late 1960s and early 1970s, more natural **hairstyles** that did not require rollers, teasing combs, and hairspray had become increasingly popular, causing the bouffant to fall out of fashion. The women's liberation movement, along with carefree and often more gender-neutral fashions, fit the workaday lives of a younger generation of wage-earning women who seemed less interested in and/ or less likely to be able to afford the time and cost associated with weekly trips to a beauty shop or salon so familiar to an older generation. However, thanks to certain celebrities in the 2000s, such as Jennifer Lopez, Gisele Bündchen, and even Sarah Palin, the bouffant may be making a comeback along with the emulation and condemnation that has long been associated with such exaggerated feminine style.

Further Reading: Brunvand, Jan Harold. *The Vanishing Hitchhiker: American Urban Legends and Their Meanings.* New York: Norton, 1981: "Real Regal." *Newsweek,* March 12, 1962, 92; Sherrow, Victoria. *Encyclopedia of Hair: A Cultural History.* Westport, CT: Greenwood Press, 2006; Turudich, Daniela. *1960s Hair: Hairstyles for Bouffant Babes and Swingin' Chicks.* Long Beach, CA: Streamline, 2003.

James I. Deutsch

BRANDING

From Calvin Klein's designer jeans to Nike's infamous swoosh trademark, branding is an integral component of the **advertising** industry in which a collection of images and ideas connect consumers with specific attitudes, feelings, and perceptions about products and companies, invoking a sense of trust and status. Branding has transformed advertising, culture, and the economy, changing the ideas that consumers have about the products they use, the companies that produce them, and ultimately their relationships with the product and company.

Since the 19th century, manufacturers branded products with logos and slogans intended to attract consumers and develop a system where consumers bought only that brand and ultimately other products from the company. Manufacturers struggled with the challenge of making sure the brands of their products were the first chosen by consumers. Many companies launched extensive marketing campaigns designed to define the brands and the quality of the product. These types of campaigns continued throughout the 20th century, to the point where specific brands became a stand-in for the actual names of products. Levi's, for example, is a particular brand but often used as a stand-in for jeans.

Characters and celebrities further the disconnection between brand and product, creating new stand-ins for products, while they instill more value and brand recognition. Celebrity endorsed and named perfumes, for example, demonstrate the level of cross-industry branding that occurs in the **cosmetics** industry; Halle Berry and Britney Spears did not necessarily start as models or cosmetics spokespersons, but their perfume lines attempt to tap a market ruled by name recognition. Brand recognition of beauty products extends beyond perfumes, with entire product lines of beauty and health products recognized by the manufacturer as the first priority. For example, **film** actress Catherine Zeta-Jones is the current face of **Elizabeth Arden** products. The marketing and selling of these products has also extended to branding the sales associates working at cosmetic counters or driving a pink Mary Kay Cadillac.

"I was in Grade 4 when skintight designer jeans were the be-all and end-all, and my friends and I spent a lot of time checking out each other's butts for logos. 'Nothing comes between me and my Calvins,' Brook Shields assured us, and as we lay back on our beds Ophelia-style and yanked up the zippers on our Jordache jeans with wire hangers, we knew she was telling no word of lie. At around the same time, Romi, our school's own pint-sized Farrah Fawcett, used to make her rounds up and down the rows of desks turning back the collars on our sweaters and polo shirts. It wasn't enough for her to see an alligator or a leaping horseman—it could be a knockoff. She wanted to see the label behind the logo. We were only eight years old but the reign of logo terror had begun."

Naomi Klein, Journalist

Source: Klein, Naomi. *No Logo.* New York: Picador, 2000, 27.

Critics have argued that brand advertising and branding have created new forms of monopoly, especially where price competition and ownership is involved. Since a logo or product name can be associated as a popular name for a generic product, the company that owns the trademark and copyrights to those symbols and images profits from further connection and usage. Branding is also criticized for the degree to which it has entered popular culture and shaped the daily lives of consumers.

In modern advertising, manufacturers and companies continue the extensive marketing campaigns that have roots in 19th-century industrial America. Today's advertisements seek to connect brands and products with much more than consumer expectations or experiences. In addition to addressing consumer hopes and reactions to products, manufacturers have also created characters to promote brands and used celebrities or persons of knowledge to create excitement and interest in products, both established and new. The advertising aspects of branding create new values for the product and the manufacturer. New images and connections can attract consumers to associate quality with the product; they will often pay higher prices to acquire the branded items like Gucci bags or **Coco Chanel** couture. At the same time, higher prices have also led retailers to create their own generic brands that are not supported by such advertising campaigns, but can still create the same connections with consumers.

Further Reading: Hill, Daniel Delis. *Advertising to the American Woman, 1900–1999.* Columbus: Ohio State University Press, 2002; Klein, Naomi. *No LOGO: Taking Aim at the Brand Bullies.* New York: Picador, 2002; Peiss, Kathy. *Hope in a Jar: The Making of America's Beauty Culture.* New York: Metropolitan Books, 1998; Quart, Alissa. *Branded: The Buying and Selling of Teenagers.* New York: Basic Books, 2004.

Richard D. Driver

BROWN, BOBBI

Bobbi Brown (1957–) is a professional makeup artist and CEO of Bobbi Brown **Cosmetics** who is best known for her approach to enhancing a woman's natural beauty rather than masking it. Her philosophy has always been that women want to look and feel like themselves, only prettier. Bobbi Brown Cosmetics is one of several makeup lines created by makeup artists. Brown's line is distinctive because of Brown herself. She frequently appears in stores and the media, representing her products and teaching women to be their own makeup artists.

After earning a college degree in theatrical makeup from Emerson College, Brown went to New York in 1980 to begin her career. In the early years, she freelanced and gradually moved up the industry ladder, working on editorial spreads for such magazines as *Glamour, YM,* and ***Vogue*** with such renowned fashion models as Brooke Shields and Naomi Campbell. By the late 1980s, Brown became frustrated with the makeup products currently available to her. The trend in '80s makeup was extreme, with the heavy use of bright color on the eyes, cheeks, and lips. She was unable to create her signature **natural look** without extensive mixing and blending to achieve the desired muted tones. Through an unexpected encounter in 1990, Brown found a chemist at Kiehl's pharmacy who was able to make wearable lipstick colors to her specifications. She started with a limited number of 10 shades and debuted the product as Bobbi Brown Essentials at Bergdorf Goodman in New York City in 1991. The lipsticks were an instant success. One hundred were sold the first day, which was what Brown had hoped to sell in the first month. (All 10 shades are still carried in the line.)

By 1993, Bobbi Brown cosmetics were being carried by Neiman Marcus, then by other high-end department stores such as Bloomingdale's, Saks Fifth Avenue, and Nordstrom. After appearances on *Oprah* and the

Makeup artist Bobbi Brown, 2007. (AP Photo/Adam Rountree)

Today show, the line went international, debuting in London in 1994. In 1995, Bobbi Brown Cosmetics was sold to **Estée Lauder** Companies, but Brown retains control of the line. By 2008, the brand was available in over 450 locations throughout Europe, Asia, and Latin America. Brown continues to expand her television audience. In 1997, she was given a monthly slot on the *Today* show as its beauty editor. She frequently appears on the E! and Style networks, and in 2007 she debuted on the **QVC** shopping channel. According to QVC, Brown set a 20-year record for a one-hour beauty launch. The Bobbi Brown philosophy of natural beauty makeup is complemented by her dedication to instructing women on how to be their own makeup experts. Her principles of beauty include advice on healthy living, skin care, and makeup application. She has written five books on the art of makeup.

Further Reading: Galant, Debra. "The Makeup Maven of Montclair." *New York Times,* February 16, 2003; Gaudoin, Tina. "Read her Lips." *Times* (London), September 24, 2005; Schindelheim, Athena. "How I Did It: Bobbi Brown, Founder and CEO, Bobbi Brown Cosmetics." *Inc. Magazine,* November 2007.

Mary Thomasine Harkins

C

CALVIN KLEIN (1942–)

Calvin Klein became one of the most successful fashion **designers** by using edgy and sexually provocative marketing to sell his products to ordinary people. The first to recognize the opportunity to sell men's underwear as a fashion item, he consistently relied on simple designs and luxurious fabrics in all of his clothing lines. Klein also started the designer jeans craze of the 1980s.

Klein, born in 1942 in New York City; he studied at the Fashion Institute of Technology but never earned a degree. He essentially learned the clothing business by spending five years as a designer in the New York City garment industry. Eager to break out on his own, Klein collaborated with an old friend, Barry Schwartz, to form Calvin Klein, Inc., on December 28, 1967. Schwartz provided the financing and received half of the business, while Klein contributed his creative skills.

Klein revealed his first collection to buyers in March 1968. The entire set, aimed at women, consisted of six coats and three dresses. The buyer for Bonwit Teller, a high-end retailer, was impressed by the purity of Klein's lines and simplicity of the designs. She decided to take the risk of using Klein's designs as the centerpiece for the Miss Bonwit salon in 1968. The move gave Klein enormous exposure and helped ensure the success of his company.

In the next few years, Klein's styles evolved from coats and suits to sportswear. Yet he continued to produce simple pieces in luxurious fabrics, commonly using the color of chocolate brown. He did not venture into a wide use of color until the 1974 collection. Klein's signature coat, the pea coat, always made it into the collection. In 1973, Klein cemented his reputation as a designer of considerable note by winning the first of three Coty American Fashion Critics Awards. By this time, Calvin Klein products could be found in over 1,000 stores.

Klein and Schwartz wanted to expand their business but they decided upon an unusual growth strategy. Knowing that if people could not have it, then they would want it even more, the two men decided to reduce the number of places where Calvin Klein could be found. They cut the number of locations by half in 1974. They aimed to sell in only 300 of the most elite stores by 1976, while also raising the quality of the fabric used in the products. Klein stopped using polyester entirely.

At the same time, Klein and Schwartz decided to license the use of the Calvin Klein name to clothing manufacturers. Licensing had just become a new stream of revenue for designers in the 1970s. Without start-up costs and enormous

> "I don't hardly sell anything. There is no way to advertise jeans today by trying to push the jeans and make them interesting; it's been done. The only way to advertise is by not focusing on the product. Some people feel that what we're doing makes no sense, that it's just a waste of money. But it's working. My attitude is 'if you want to sell jeans, don't talk about them.'"
>
> *Calvin Klein*
>
> Source: "Interview: Calvin Klein." *Playboy,* May 1984. http://www.playboy.com/articles/playboy-interview-calvin-klein/index.html.

financial risks, licensing proved an efficient and cost-effective way for the designer to expand his empire quickly. The Klein company completed its first licensing deal with the furrier Alixandre. The logic was that if Klein was designing evening-wear, he had to give his customers something to wear on top of the gowns and dresses. Deals quickly followed with Omega for belts, Mespo for umbrellas, and Vogue Butterick for patterns. This growth and diversity took the company from being Calvin Klein Ltd. to being Calvin Klein Industries.

In 1974, Klein printed his logo on t-shirts for the use and amusement of staffers at his company. He could not imagine anyone wearing his name, but the logo soon became in hot demand. It eventually appeared on shirts, jeans, and underwear, making Klein the first company to combine brand **advertising** with style. The Calvin Klein name eventually became so iconic that it was featured in a joke about underwear in the 1985 **film** *Back to the Future."*

Calvin Klein jeans became the brand that led the designer jeans craze of the late 1970s and 1980s. More than 20,000 pairs were sold right out of the gate in 1978. To support the image of Calvin Klein jeans, the company embarked on its first advertising campaign. Klein advertisements would become famous for pushing the edge of acceptability. The first Klein billboard in Times Square featured model Patti Hansen in a sexual and highly controversial pose. In 1980, sexually provocative advertisements featuring 15-year-old actress Brooke Shields were created by long-time fashion photographer Richard Avedon. Shields famously said in a commercial, "Do you know what comes between me and my Calvins? Nothing." In the week following the debut of the advertisements, the company sold 400,000 pairs of jeans. The Calvin Klein image—edgy, clever, sexual, and usually controversial—was born.

Klein believed that a designer who designed for men should do everything for them. Men's underwear had long been a staple product that was sold three to a pack, typically at a promotional price. In 1982, Klein began selling boxer shorts, bikinis, and t-shirts in Bloomingdale's. The store was considered the best testing ground for new men's items. Realizing that women purchased most men's underwear, Klein aimed its advertisements at women. The strategy proved enormously successful as posters featuring former Olympic pole-vaulter Tim Hintinaus reclining in nothing but his Calvins were stolen from bus shelters across the country.

In 1984, Klein began selling women's underwear. Klein based his idea of modern underwear for women on men's designs. In the collection, he included briefs, bikinis, string bikinis, and boxer shorts, all with a fly. The company originally projected sales of $18 million to $20 million for the first year. Ultimately, underwear racked up sales of $70 million in 1984, based in part on typically sexy Calvin Klein advertising.

Klein sold his company to Phillips-Van Heusen in early 2003. The 700-person subsidiary is headed by Paul Thomas Murry and had revenues of more than $5 billion in 2007. The founder, who initially remained as creative director, no longer has any involvement with the firm bearing his name.

Further Reading: Gaines, Steven, and Sharon Churcher. *Obsession: The Lives and Times of Calvin Klein.* New York: Avon Books, 1995; Marsh, Lisa. *The House of Klein: Fashion, Controversy, and a Business Obsession.* Hoboken, NJ: Wiley, 2003; Weber, Bruce. *Calvin Klein Jeans.* New York: Condé Nast, 1991.

Caryn E. Neumann

CELLULITE

One of the most common beauty concerns for women is the development of cellulite. Cellulite refers to the dimpled appearance of the skin on the hips, thighs, and buttocks. Until the 1980s, excess weight was the focus of ads for weight loss and diet products. Increasingly afterward, it has become common to see ads referring to flab, bulges, or excess fat. Liposuction and the removal of cellulite are a result of this trend. Cellulite is more common in women because of the way fat is stored and distributed in women's bodies. It is not harmful to the health of the afflicted individual, but treatment for cellulite is in high demand due to its effect on one's overall appearance. The treatment for cellulite is costly, generally ineffective, and in some cases can be detrimental to the consumer's overall health.

Cellulite occurs in people of all races and, though it is more common in women, it can also occur in men. Genetics, gender, skin thickness, age, and the percentage of body fat can all influence the appearance and severity of cellulite. The dimpled appearance is caused by fat deposits beneath the skin. Many treatments for cellulite have been written about and promoted due to the desire to have smooth skin. Methylxanthines are chemicals that are present in caffeine and are often used in cellulite creams. These are known for their ability to break down fat stores, but such creams do not provide the high concentrations of the chemicals that would be necessary for any significant fat removal. Massage treatments can also be used to treat cellulite. These treatments provide a temporary decrease in the appearance of cellulite by redistributing fat. Massage treatments are often very expensive and require multiple treatments to maintain results. Therapies using lasers and lights have also been approved by the **U.S. Food and Drug Administration** (FDA), some in combination with massage therapy. These treatments are even more costly than massage. Mesotherapy, for example, involves injecting drugs directly into the skin, but this is controversial and is not widely available. Natural treatments such as special cellulite diets claim to reduce inflammation and improve circulation in order to change the appearance of the skin. Eating a healthy diet can also decrease fluid retention, which can in turn decrease inflammation.

Taking a combination of dietary supplements can also boost metabolism, improve overall circulation, and break down fat stores. Some salons also offer herbal body wraps as a treatment for cellulite that works by detoxifying the body.

None of these treatments has been proven effective at eliminating cellulite. It is possible to improve the appearance, but these effects are temporary. Liposuction can actually make cellulite worse and is not a recommended treatment. Eating a healthy diet and participating in regular exercise is promoted as the best way to prevent and decrease the appearance of cellulite.

Further Reading: Bordo, Susan. *Unbearable Weight: Feminism, Western Culture, and the Body.* Los Angeles: University of California Press, 1993; MedicineNet. "Cellulite." http://www.medicinenet.com; *Cellulite*; WebMd. http://www.webmd.com.

Krystal A. Humphreys

CHANEL, COCO (1883–1971)

Chanel was a French fashion pioneer of the 20th century. She was a leader of haute couture (high fashion) who focused on simplicity and elegance in women's apparel. Inspired by men's clothing, Chanel reworked the construction to have sports clothes for women enter the fashion lexicon. Some of her unique contributions to contemporary fashion are jersey outfits, cardigan suits, pleated skirts, the blazer, and the turtleneck sweater. A staple of every woman's closet, the little black dress was another of her trademark contributions. Her signature fragrance, Chanel No. 5, is still highly coveted today. The iconic Chanel quilted leather bags are huge sellers. Her impact on the world of fashion made her the only designer listed in *TIME* magazine's 100 most influential people of the 20th century.

Early Years

Gabrielle Chanel was born on August 19, 1883 in the French town of Saumur. The second oldest of six children, Chanel was born in a poorhouse. When Chanel was 12, her mother died, leaving her father to place her in a Catholic orphanage. The nuns there taught her how to sew. After she left the orphanage at age 18, she worked for a tailor. She soon met millionaire Etienne Balsan, who introduced her to a world of luxury and wealth, including riding horses. One of her earliest design inspirations was the riding jacket. For a brief time, Chanel worked as a café singer, where she adopted the name Coco.

Beginning as a milliner in 1908, Chanel's hats received notoriety after actresses began wearing them. She opened her first clothing shop in Paris in 1913. That same year, she fell in love with Boy Capel, the best friend of her former beau. He supported her next venture in Deauville, where she sold sportswear and sweaters for women. Her first couture shop opened in Biarritz in 1915. The American market had taken notice of her designs, especially the jersey dresses, which evoked a comfortable, loose fitting silhouette. The popularity of her jersey designs prompted **Vogue** magazine in 1917 to dub the Chanel brand "the Jersey House."

Building her Empire

Chanel enjoyed an aristocratic and cultured worldly clientele, including the future British Queen mother. Russian influences in her clothes were inspired by her new love, Grand Duke Dimitri Pavlovitch, grandson of Czar Alexander II. The collection had tunics, peasant blouses, and embroidered dresses. During this time, she developed one of her signature items, a coat whose lining matched the dress fabric worn underneath it. In 1921, she began selling perfume under the name Chanel No. 5, her lucky number. The bottle shape and **packaging** were her ideas. It was the first time a couturier put her name on a scent. Chanel also contributed to the Garçonne look of France, known as the flapper look in the United States. It was characterized by a short, bob hairstyle worn under a cloche hat, and a boyish appearance accentuated by higher hemlines and straight-waist skirts. Chanel also designed and wore women's trousers, making them fashionable for the first time. The little black dress was introduced in 1926. Used in both her day and evening looks, the concept was a huge success. Chanel also designed costume jewelry, and made fake jewels fashionable and affordable. She reversed the rules when she began wearing large amounts of jewelry in the daytime, and hardly any at all for evening. Her first jewelry workshop opened in 1924. Chanel is best remembered for the long strings of faux pearls she designed.

Despite the Depression, Chanel continued to garner huge success. Working for Samuel Goldwyn in Hollywood in 1931 and 1932 made her two million dollars. She designed wardrobes for the biggest starlets of the day, including Greta Garbo and Marlene Dietrich. Chanel's clothing was form fitting, accentuated by shoulder pads, with longer hemlines and frills around cuffs and collars. She also designed black velvet capes that were worn with berets. Her use of decorative bows, and the popular combination of black paired with white, were other contributions.

In 1932, Chanel introduced a diamond jewelry collection, sponsored by the International Diamond Guild. Collaborating with boyfriend and jewelry designer Paul Iribe, their collection had three design themes: feathers, stars, and knots. The necklaces were known for their lack of clasps, and were made to drape around the neck. After France's declaration of war against the Nazis in 1939, Chanel closed her fashion house. She remained in Paris after the Germans seized the city, living at the Ritz Hotel until the city was liberated in 1944. She then lived in Switzerland for the next 10 years.

Return to the World of Fashion

Chanel did not design clothes in the 1940s, but did continue to sell her perfume. Of her comeback in 1953, at the age of 70, Chanel said that she wanted to bring back comfort and beauty to women's clothes. The collection that debuted the following year received negative press because the styles she showed were revivals of earlier decades. Undaunted, Chanel continued to design, and later collections proved successful. The woman's suit had a side pleat in the skirt, with braiding on the jacket. The Chanel suit became a classic: a collarless jacket with skirt that touched the knee. Her variations on the suit included tweed, pastel colors, and her continued use of jersey. In 1955, she introduced the first quilted leather handbag. Made of leather and jersey, it had a twisted shoulder strap of leather and chain. She also returned to designing costume jewelry.

In 1964, she designed sailor pants and trouser suits. A musical production about her, *Coco,* debuted on Broadway in 1969, with Katharine Hepburn playing the lead. In 1970, she began selling Chanel perfume No. 19, a fragrance that appealed to a new generation of admirers. She passed away in Paris on January 10, 1971, at the age of 87.

After her death the company flourished with continued commitment to its perfume line. Chanel No. 5 was re-established as the exclusive fragrance for the fashion savvy. Chanel's fashion line was reinvigorated with the addition of Karl Lagerfeld as its chief designer in 1983. The company has remained successful by marketing its designs as classic pieces of simplistic elegance. Branching out into cosmetics, jewelry, shoes, and accessories, the Chanel brand upholds Coco's desire to dress the modern woman in comfort and impeccable style.

Further Reading: De La Haye, Amy, and Shelley Tobin. *Chanel: The Couturiere at Work.* New York: Overlook Press, 1994; Lewis, Jone Johnson. *Coco Chanel.* About.com: Women's History. http://womenshistory.about.com/od/chanelcoco/a/coco_chanel.htm. (Accessed May 12, 2009); Madsen, Axel. *Chanel: A Woman of her Own.* New York: Holt, 1990; Sischy, Ingrid. *Coco Chanel.* The 2009 Time 100. http://www.time.com/time/time 100/artists/profile/chanel.html. (Accessed May 12, 2009).

Corye Perez Beene

CHARM SCHOOLS

Charm schools are training facilities that teach their clients how to craft a pleasing personal appearance and a refined attitude. Historically, topics including etiquette, elocution, carriage, and personal grooming have been the subject of charm courses and instruction manuals.

Attending charm schools became a popular activity for young women and girls during the first half of the 20th century. Charm schools tutored clients in the etiquette, protocol, and customs that Americans associated with high-society culture and, as such, charm courses were viewed as an avenue for social promotion in the United States. While some schools operated as stand-alone private companies, charm classes were more frequently offered in a variety of other settings, including free lessons at local YWCA branches, the meetings of youth organizations, department store promotion events, and even employee training sessions in U.S. workplaces.

An example of popular 20th-century charm instruction can be found in the work of educator Charlotte Hawkins Brown. In 1902, Brown founded the Palmer Memorial Institute, an elite South Carolina boarding school for girls from the wealthiest black families across the nation. In addition to giving her students a rigorous high school education, Brown ran her female students through strenuous charm instruction. She taught these aspiring ladies etiquette, deportment, fashion, and manners in the hopes that such skills would better their lives. In one classroom exercise, Brown trained her pupils to balance a book on their head while walking—possibly the most famous activity associated with charm instruction—in order to guide her student's posture.

As well as formal charm classes, published guides also offered to teach the basics of female style, eloquence, beauty, and glamour. In addition to Brown's 1944 text, *The Correct Thing to Do, to Say, to Wear*, several other charm textbooks were published in the mid 20th century. These included model Barbara Watson's 1948 guide, *The Brandford Home Study Charm Course*, actress Anita Colby's 1952 text, *Anita Colby's Beauty Book,* and British personality Helen Hugh's 1955 manual *Glamour School*. Publications such as these focused on charm and beauty as a method for women to advance their lives. Reminding readers that such matters were "a passport to greater success," the *Beauty Fair Reference Guide* counseled readers on over 140 charm- and beauty-related subjects, including the selection of fashion accessories, methods of calorie-counting, cosmetic use, exercise, nail care, and deportment.

In addition to ordinary women, aspiring celebrities also used charm instruction to better their chances of success. In the 1950s, the leading British **film** studio Rank opened a charm school to guide actresses, including the star Diana Dors, on how to talk correctly, dress well, and behave in public. Similarly, in the 1960s, Detroit's Motown Records opened an in-house charm school run by image-builder Maxine Powell, who prepared music artists such as Martha Reed and Diana Ross for the glare of publicity.

Reflecting an emerging feminist agenda, many Americans began to view charm instruction as propagating an outdated model of femininity in the late 1960s and 1970s. As a result of these changes, traditional charm schools all but died out in latter decades of 20th century. However, in recent years, many components of charm school instruction have witnessed a rebirth in professional skills courses directed toward both men and women. For example, today, DeVore Carter Communications, a New York City company specializing in professional preparedness, teaches its clients competencies such as visual poise and vocal dynamics in order to help businesspeople to succeed in the 21st-century marketplace.

Further Reading: Brumberg, Joan Jacobs. *The Body Project: An Intimate History of American Girls*. New York: Vintage Books, 1997; Davidson, Tina. "'A Woman's Rights to Charm and Beauty': Maintaining the Feminine Ideal in the Canadian Women's Army Corps." *Atlantis,* 26 no. 1 (2001): 45–54; Gundle, Stephen. *Glamour: A History*. Oxford: Oxford University Press, 2008; McAndrew, Jennifer Malia. *All American Beauty: The Experiences of African American, European American, and Japanese American Women with Beauty Culture in the Mid-Twentieth Century United States*. PhD diss., University of Maryland, 2008; Peiss, Kathy. *Hope in a Jar: The Making of America's Beauty Culture*. New York: Metropolitan Books, 1998.

Malia McAndrew

COSMETICS

Cosmetics are consumer products that are used to beautify, clean, or protect the body. Cosmetics can be used on any part of the body, but they are most frequently applied to the face. The term *makeup* has become synonymous with cosmetics

Woman putting on her lipstick in a park with union station behind her, Washington, D.C., 1943. (Courtesy of Library of Congress)

because such formulations are often applied to enhance one's physical exterior. Cosmetics have played a significant role in female culture in the United States since the 19th century, when an identifiable cosmetic industry arose.

The 19th Century

During much of the 19th century, creams, lotions, tonics, and other cosmetic preparations were primarily produced and consumed in the home. Initially, these homemade concoctions were based on formulas found in popular advice books or derived from family-held recipes. By mid-century, cosmetics were popularly prized for their ability to soften the skin, protect against sunburn, and remove freckles. By the late 19th century, many American females were also grinding chalk to make face powder and using beets to give their cheeks a rouge glow. While a home-grown U.S. cosmetics trade prospered, many Americans viewed commercially produced cosmetic preparations with much skepticism and caution. They feared that commercially produced cosmetics were unsafe and could harm their health.

In addition to health concerns, many 19th-century Americans disapproved of cosmetic use for moral reasons. Inspired by the attitudes and beliefs of the Victorian era, these individuals referred to cosmetics as paint and questioned the virtues of those who applied it. Such objections were based upon the belief that a person's core moral character would manifest itself directly in the body's physical form. Under this line of reasoning, blemishes, for example, were not understood as a superficial skin condition, but were rather believed to be the result of personal moral failings. Persons who engaged in illicit sexual activity, it was thought, would develop skin conditions as a result of their sinful actions. The use of cosmetics, therefore, was taboo because it was seen as a ruse to cover up a lack of honesty, piety, frugality, or sexual purity. If pimples were the result of sinful behavior, using cosmetics to cover them up was similarly disdained. Indeed, before the 20th century, cosmetics were most frequently associated with sex workers and actors, persons who, it was believed, had an interest in masking their true identity in order to present an altered public persona.

Early 20th Century

During the early 20th century, several factors helped to popularize commercially produced cosmetics and change the stigmatization associated with their use. The Pure Food and Drug Act of 1906 allowed the federal government to regulate the cosmetics industry and crack down on faulty marketing practices. This legislation gave traction to the emerging cosmetic industry because it mandated that producers provide correct ingredient information for their goods, thereby discouraging inaccurate product labeling and the use of harmful chemicals in cosmetic preparations. The growth of national markets and the emergence of mass consumer cultures in the early 20th century were among the most important factors leading to the widespread acceptance of cosmetic use in the United States. With heightened national production capabilities and the development of a professional **advertising** industry, 20th-century producers were able to send positive messages about cosmetic consumption to a wide array of Americans. During the 1910s and 1920s, the number of advertisements for cosmetics in popular magazines ballooned. Ads featured in *The Ladies Home Journal, Good Housekeeping,* and other popular women's magazines helped to raise the public visibility of commercial beauty products and familiarize Americans with their use. Following the advent of the radio, in the 1920s, cosmetics manufacturers also began to market their products heavily through the airwaves. Commercial advertisements extolled the safety, effectiveness, and desirability of mass-produced cosmetic preparations.

Female Entrepreneurs

Female entrepreneurs played important roles in the growth of the cosmetics industry during the early 20th century. Women such as Sarah Breedlove (**Madam C. J. Walker**), Florence Nightingale Graham (**Elizabeth Arden**), Chaja Rubinstein (**Helena Rubinstein**), and Josephine Esther Mentzer Lauter (**Estée Lauder**) helped to create a national cosmetics industry that was not only headed by women, but that employed many female workers as well. Sarah Breedlove created the Madame C. J. Walker **Manufacturing** Company in 1906, and in 1918 her company began to sell an array of cosmetic products for African American women, including four shades of face powder, cold cream, and cleansing cream. Earning over a quarter of a million dollars that year, Walker vociferously fought back against critics who derided her industry as undesirable. Walker contended that the sale of her products offered African American females respectable employment and lucrative incomes at a time when employers were remiss to offer women of any color high-paying jobs. The fact that Walker drew large profits throughout World War I, a time of great public rationing, points to the solidification of the cosmetics industry in the early 20th-century United States.

The 1920s

The consumerist ethos that emerged during this era changed the most basic ways in which Americans related to, understood, and used their outward physical appearance. During the first decades of the 20th century, ordinary Americans began to use consumer goods as avenues for the expression of the inner self. The mass availability of cheap cosmetics allowed the American female to easily try on various makeup styles and the public personas associated with each look. By the 1920s, the Victorian mores that shunned cosmetic use had given way to the impulses of the modern girl, whose cosmetic preferences helped redefine the boundaries of womanhood. Alongside loosening sexual mores and changing clothing styles, cosmetic use was a staple feature of the era's popular flapper look.

It was in this atmosphere of change that the aspiring saleswoman Josephine Esther Mentzer Lauter learned her craft. Starting in 1924, Lauter worked at New Way Laboratories in Manhattan, a cosmetics manufacturing and distributing business owned by her uncle. At New Way Laboratories, Lauter became an expert at applying lip color, cleansing oils, powder, eye shadow, freckle remover, and cold creams on the faces of potential consumers. In 1933, she renamed herself **Estée Lauder** and began her own home-based cosmetics business. Rather than in the gregarious years of the roaring 1920s, Lauder launched her business during the Great Depression, when one out of four Americans was unemployed. However, as Lauder aptly realized, a national depression could be good for the cosmetics industry. In part because of the many economic problems people faced, Americans used inexpensive commercial pleasures, such as movie tickets, records, alcohol, and cosmetics, to boost their mood. Lauder grew her business by promising women both a new look and a new feeling about themselves. Attempting to briefly turn her clients' thoughts away from their economic woes, she offered them what she called "confidence-building beauty" through cosmetics.

1930s Hollywood

Another cultural factor that led to the mainstream acceptance of cosmetics use in the 1930s was its visibility in U.S. cinema. **Film** brought images of self-assured, sexually confident, and glamorous women to the masses of Americans living through the anything-but-glamorous realities of life during the Great Depression. Due to the popularity of cinema, fashionable clothing, cigarettes, and cosmetics became associated with a modern lifestyle. As a result, many American women demanded access to the look they saw on the silver screen. After applying cosmetics to the faces of Hollywood stars, including Judy Garland and Bette Davis, the Polish immigrant Maximilian Faktorowicz (**Max Factor**) was able to popularize his cosmetic line among young women. Max Factor cosmetics were popular among women in many immigrant households; for them, cosmetics use was not only glamorous, but also a way to solidify their identity as Americans. Max Factor advertisements regularly appeared in the Mexican American publication *La Opinión,* which was targeted to first- and second-generation Americans. In addition to film stars, many American women of different backgrounds learned how to stylize their bodies by mimicking the actresses they watched on television beginning in the 1940s. Taken together, print, film, radio, and television advertising were popular mediums that pushed cosmetics use into the mainstream of American culture during the first half of the 20th century.

Post–World War II Decades

By the mid-20th century, the targets of cosmetic marketing widened further. Cosmetic advertisements began to appear in new periodicals such as *Seventeen* and *Charm*; these were directed toward female adolescents and girls. The postwar era also saw increased marketing of cosmetic products to American men. However, while cosmetics use grew during the second half of the 20th century, its acceptance was never universal. Indeed, during the 1960s and 1970s, many American women rejected makeup use outright. Opponents of the cosmetic industry argued that producers and advertisers encouraged women to adopt unattainable standards of beauty. Indeed, many feminists cited cosmetics as a troublesome part of the larger male-dominated economy that manipulated women into a passive consumer role. The cosmetics industry, they argued, focused women's attention on making themselves into perennial objects of male desire.

Despite these critiques, the sale and use of cosmetics continued to increase during the second half of the 20th century. Between 1955 and 1965, U.S. **retail** sales for all cosmetic and toiletry items rose from $1.2 billion to $2.9 billion and the market came to be dominated by a handful of large international corporations. An early industry leader, Estée Lauder is exemplary of this trend. Between 1958 and 1965, the company's sales rose from $1 million to $14 million dollars. To expand their markets further during the later decades of the 20th century, Estée Lauder and other major cosmetic companies targeted multiple consumer groups simultaneously. For example, in 1968, Estée Lauder introduced its Clinique brand, a line the company developed to court women in their 20s who were interested in medically sound cosmetic preparations. Just over a decade later, in 1979, the company created its Prescriptives brand, which was marketed as a high-tech line of

"Today the possibility of transformation through cosmetics is often belittled as a delusion, 'hope in a jar' that only masks the fact of women's oppression. In truth, women knew then—as they do now-precisely what they were buying. Again and again they reported their delight in beautifying—in the sensuous creams and tiny compacts, the riot of colors, the mastery of makeup skills, the touch of hands, the sharing of knowledge and advice. Indeed, the pleasures of fantasy and desire were an integral part of the product—and these included not only dreams of romance and marriage, but also the modern yearning to take part in public culture."

Kathy Peiss, historian

Source: Peiss, Kathy. *Hope in a Jar: The Making of America's Beauty Culture*. New York: Metropolitan Books, 1998, 6.

skin care treatments. Prescriptives was aimed at consumers who were older than the Clinique buyer but younger than the purchasers of traditional Estée Lauder products. Again sensing an opening in the market, Estée Lauder introduced its Origins brand of cosmetics in 1990, a line of botanical-based products for both women and men. In this way, Estée Lauder and like-minded cosmetic companies sought to saturate the market with competing brands during the second half of the 20th century. Started as small enterprise created by a first-generation American woman in the 1920s, Estée Lauder, Inc., had grown into a four-billion-dollar corporation in 1990 and employed over 15,000 people. Indeed, the mass scale of the cosmetics industry was one of its defining features at the century's end. By the late 1990s, seven global corporations, including L'Oréal, **Procter and Gamble**, Unilever, Shiseido, Estée Lauder, **Avon**, and Johnson & Johnson accounted for almost half of all cosmetics revenues in the world.

Further Reading: Banner, Lois. *American Beauty.* New York: Knopf, 1983; Bundles, A'Lelia. *On Her Own Ground: The Life and Times of Madam C. J. Walker.* New York: Scribner, 2002; Kohen, Nancy. "Estée Lauder: Self-Definition at the Modern Cosmetics Market." In *Beauty and Business: Commerce, Gender, and Culture in Modern America,* ed. Philip Scranton, pp. 217–53. New York: Routledge, 2000; Peiss, Kathy. *Hope in a Jar: The Making of America's Beauty Culture.* New York: Metropolitan Books, 1998; Ruiz, Vicki. "'Star Struck': Acculturation, Adolescence, and Mexican American Women, 1920–1950." In *Unequal Sisters: An Inclusive Reader in US Women's History,* ed. Vicki Ruiz, pp. 346–61. New York: Routledge, 2007.

Malia McAndrew

COSMETIC SURGERY

Cosmetic surgery is an invasive medical practice that was developed mainly in the late 19th century. According to the American Society of Aesthetic and Plastic Surgery, over 10 million people had cosmetic surgery in 2008 in the United States alone. This is an overall increase of 446 percent since 1997. The term cosmetic surgery (from Greek *kosmetikós,* "adornment") can mean either plastic (from Greek *plastikos,* "fit for molding") surgery, to restore or repair body parts, or aesthetic surgery, which refers to a body part being made over surgically to appear more beautiful. The medical field of cosmetic surgery has evolved from the expertise gained in the field of *reconstructive surgery,* focusing on patients with physical problems or deformities present at birth, such as cleft syndrome, caused by accidents, or related to illnesses such as syphilis or breast cancer (mastectomy and lumpectomy). The 10 million people in the United States who underwent cosmetic surgery in 2008 were not those who were either born with deformities or developed deformities due to accidents or illnesses; rather, this figure exclusively counts those people who wanted to improve their appearance on their own account and for aesthetic purposes only. Worldwide, the International Association for Aesthetic and Plastic Surgery estimates an increase in cosmetic surgery of about 15–20 percent each year since 2004.

Precedents

The first part of the body to be altered surgically for aesthetic purposes was the nose. Even today, rhinoplasty remains one of the top five cosmetic surgeries. In 2008, there were 152,434 such procedures performed in the United States. Rhinoplasty dates back to 600 B.C.E., when it was performed by the Indian surgeon Sushruta, and the tradition of the Ayurveda Indian aesthetic surgery. The *Sushruta Samhita,* a Sanskrit text, suggests a procedure for restoring a "nose that had been cut off" (as a result of trauma or injury) with the use of a pedicle flap of skin taken from the cheek. The first Western manual of plastic surgery in which the procedure of the flap graft used to replace a missing nose is described dates to the Italian Renaissance. Physician Gaspare Tagliacozzi included such a description in his *De curtorum chirurgia* (1597). Tagliacozzi, who pioneered the method of nasal reconstruction in which a flap from the upper arm is gradually transferred to the nose, expressed his ethics as a physician as follows: "restore, repair, and make whole those parts of the face which nature has given but which fortune has taken away." He further pointed out that the most important principle for the restoration of a nose was symmetry, not just to "delight the eye" but to "help the mind of the afflicted." This is one very important early example of the attempt to address and change an individual's state of mind through a surgical intervention. The view that being unhappy about one's body image may produce unhappiness of the mind, described as body dysmorphic disorder in today's *Diagnostic and Statistical Manual,* is at the forefront of the cosmetic surgery revolution of the late 19th and early 20th centuries, and coincides with the invention of psychotherapy around the same time period. However, the impression an individual has about her own appearance that feeds the desire for surgically altering her body did not come out of nowhere. Indeed, it has been fueled by the science of physiognomy, in circulation since antiquity, which tries to read the body's appearance in relation to the character. Most notably, the Swiss pastor Johann Kaspar Lavater produced a doctrine of physiognomy in the late 18th century that spelled out an objectifying reading of character traits by classifying "the visible signs of invisible powers." In the 19th century, such knowledge was easily co-opted for racist discourses and biological determinism by such anthropologists as the Italian Cesare Lombroso, who believed that southerners were more prone to becoming criminals than northerners due to their physical appearance. Another guiding idea of 19th century ethnology was the similarity of the Jewish nose to the African nose. Again, the nose became of utmost concern to Jewish people, who started having cosmetic surgery in order to pass as non-Jewish Europeans. Anti-Semitism and other racist discourses are thus deeply rooted in the tradition of physiognomy.

20th Century

By the late 19th and early 20th century, cosmetic surgery had became a common practice, allowing people to express and realize their desire to look like the norm within their culture, or to rid themselves of what was often referred to as an inferiority complex. With this, the possibility of looking better than others came into the picture as well. In 1921, the first Miss America pageant tried to evaluate and objectively classify American female beauty. Despite the controversy that the nose job of the 1920s actress and comedienne Fanny Brice had stirred, such early celebrity **makeovers** helped to engrave the image of the perfect and famous face into the cultural imagination even more. Even outside of such issues of body image, the two world wars produced an unprecedented number of facial injuries that were met with new reconstructive surgical methods, helping to rapidly develop this medical field, which had been organized formally by the American Society of Plastic and Reconstructive Surgeons (ASPRS) since 1931. After World War II, the United States witnessed a significant growth in cosmetic surgery. In 1949, about 15,000 people had had cosmetic surgery in the United States; by 1969, that number had risen to about a half million. Women became particularly concerned with aging. The common face lift was seen to help them feel better about themselves and their world rather than changing society's image of beauty.

Contemporary Trends

Women have had 90–95 percent of all cosmetic surgery procedures carried out since the 1970s. In 2008, the top five surgical interventions for women were breast augmentation, liposuction, eyelid surgery, abdominoplasty, and breast reduction. In summary, these procedures express a desire to look more feminine, to eliminate the traces of childbirth or motherhood, to pass as Western, and to slim one's figure to appear healthy and fit. Such makeovers are still often described as an expression of a desire to match one's inside to the outside, according to the old rules of physiognomy. Many women report that they feel more sexual, young, healthy, and beautiful in their hearts than they appear, and are seeking to express such feelings through cosmetic surgery—not to alter themselves, but to reveal their real selves. The idea that a more beautiful appearance brings more success in life has long been proven. In today's Western culture, people are surrounded by and immersed in the idea of cosmetic surgery, makeover's quintessential expression, via reality television makeover shows (e.g., *Extreme Makeover*), computer games (e.g., *Sims*), and imaging technology that mathematically calculates an ideal self. However, from 2007 to 2008, the American Society for Aesthetic Plastic Surgery (ASAPS) noticed a 12 percent decrease in overall cosmetic surgery procedures (11 percent decrease for women and 21 percent for men). This is possibly a sign that noninvasive procedures such as **Botox** have become an even faster fix, or simply that Americans have become oversaturated with images of ideal beauty.

Further Reading: Elliott, Anthony. *Making the Cut: How Cosmetic Surgery is Transforming Our Lives.* London: Reaktion Books, 2008; Gilman, Sander L. *Making the Body Beautiful: A Cultural History of Aesthetic Surgery.* Princeton, NJ: Princeton University Press, 1999; Haiken, Elizabeth. *Venus Envy: A History of Cosmetic Surgery.* Baltimore, MD: Johns Hopkins University Press, 1997; Jones, Meredith. *Skintight: An Anatomy of Cosmetic Surgery.* New York: Berg, 2008; Kuczynski, Alex. *Beauty Junkies: Inside our $15 Billion Obsession with Cosmetic Surgery.* New York: Doubleday, 2006; May, Elaine Tyler. *Homeward Bound:*

American Families in the Cold War Era. New York: Basic Books, 1988; Wegenstein, Bernadette. *The Cosmetic Gaze: Body Modification and the Construction of Beauty.* Cambridge, MA: MIT Press, 2010.

Bernadette Wegenstein

COSMOPOLITAN

Cosmopolitan magazine, originally named *The Cosmopolitan,* was launched in 1886 as a general-interest family magazine by Schlicht and Field Publishers. It changed publishers several times and eventually enjoyed success as a leading publisher of both serialized novels and short stories. The 1950s saw the rise of inexpensive paperbacks and television, and circulation declined for magazines like *The Cosmopolitan.* The magazine industry shifted from a focus on general-interest magazines to special-interest magazines aimed at specific populations.

In 1965, the Hearst Company, then publishers of *The Cosmopolitan,* were about to stop production of the magazine. At the time, Helen Gurley Brown was attempting to find a publisher for a brand new type of magazine for the modern woman. Brown was best known at the time for her bestselling novel, *Sex and the Single Girl,* a book that celebrated the single life of young women, and she wanted to launch a magazine that spoke to the women who had made her book a bestseller: young professional women trying to find their place in the modern world. The Hearst Company received a proposal from Brown and opted to turn the magazine over to her rather than cease production completely. Brown took over as the new editor, transforming *The Cosmopolitan* into *Cosmopolitan,* the magazine people recognize today. In the mid '60s, however, a magazine for young single women that talked openly about sex and encouraged them to enjoy themselves as men did was considered shocking.

One of Brown's first editorial decisions was to print a cover story about the birth control pill with the headline, "The new pill that makes women more responsive." The headline promoted the idea that women would enjoy themselves more sexually if they did not have to worry about pregnancy. *Cosmopolitan* continued to print provocative articles and, in April 1972, the magazine featured a nearly nude centerfold of a minor actor, Burt Reynolds. The picture created a scandal, but also helped to push both *Cosmopolitan* and Burt Reynolds to the center of American popular culture.

Cosmopolitan, often referred to as *Cosmo,* remains a women's fashion and beauty magazine that emphasizes a woman's right to control her own sexuality and physical beauty. The magazine runs articles on current fashions, women's health, beauty tips, celebrity gossip, and sex. Each magazine features at least one *Cosmo* quiz on topics from finding out what kind of girl you are to how to tell if your man is cheating. The magazine has dedicated readers who are often referred to as *Cosmo* girls.

Feminist scholars have celebrated the magazine as upholding a vision of women living life on their own terms, but it has also drawn criticism for promoting unrealistic body images and for emphasizing male sexual pleasure over that of women. *Cosmopolitan* also drew criticism for running an article in the 1990s that told women they didn't need to be concerned about contracting HIV through heterosexual sex and for dismissive comments that Brown made about sexual harassment in the workplace. Brown was eventually forced out of the editor position in 1996.

Cosmo's covers continue to feature young attractive models and always contain at least one headline about sex. Some stores still consider it a racy magazine and sell it behind plastic flaps that cover the model and the headlines. *Cosmopolitan* publishes 58 international editions, is printed in 34 languages, and is distributed in more than 100 countries.

Further Reading: Scanlon, Jennifer. *Bad Girls Go Everywhere: The Life of Helen Gurley Brown.* New York: Oxford University Press, 2009; Valverde, Mariana. "The Class Struggles of the Cosmo Girl and the Ms. Woman." *Heresies,* 5 (1985): 78–82.

Kym Neck

COVERGIRL

CoverGirl is a **cosmetics** company that was founded by the Noxzema Chemical Company in 1958. Originally a line of only six products in the vein of the company's cleansers and toners, CoverGirl has become one of the largest and most recognizable cosmetics companies in the industry. Named for the especially highly regarded models who grace the covers of magazines, CoverGirl markets to the middle class at mid- to low-priced cosmetics in drug stores, rather than high-end cosmetic counters in department stores, through numerous celebrity endorsements, ubiquitous advertisements, and television sponsorships. **Procter and Gamble** acquired CoverGirl in 1989, and CoverGirl has become the best-selling line of face makeup in the nation. "Easy, breezy, beautiful" CoverGirl markets itself as a promoter of fresh-faced, natural beauty.

CoverGirl began with "medicated face makeup" in both liquid and pressed powder form, in three shades. Other early products included tube makeup and brush-on blushes in multiple shades. Now the company boasts a huge range of products, including face makeup, eye makeup, lipstick and lip liner, and nail polish. A far cry from their original two forms of face makeup, CoverGirl now sells more than a dozen different kinds of foundation, catering to all kinds of different needs, from oil-absorbing powders for acne-prone skin or moisturizing makeup for dry skin to wrinkle reducers and sunscreen-enhanced products. They have a similarly wide range of eye makeup, with a huge selection of mascaras for volume or length or curl or all three, eye shadows in every imaginable color, and both pencil and liquid eyeliners.

In addition to being a prominent retailer in the beauty industry, CoverGirl is also a pop culture icon thanks to its celebrity endorsements and television sponsorships. Christie Brinkley became the face of CoverGirl in 1976 and set off an explosion in the company's popularity. Brinkley remained under contract with CoverGirl for 20 years, and this remains the longest contract in modeling history. Many of the world's top models have served as CoverGirl spokesmodels over the years, including Molly Sims, Tyra Banks, Niki Taylor, and Cheryl Tiegs. In recent years, however, CoverGirl has turned to actresses, singers, and athletes to represent their products. Newer spokesmodels include actresses Drew Barrymore and Keri Russell, singers Faith Hill, Brandy, and Rhianna, and gymnasts Shawn Johnson, Natasia Liukin, and Alicia Sacramone. The newest addition is comedian Ellen Degeneres, lauded as a perfect example of the company's commitment to both inner and outer beauty. The company also promotes its image through sponsorship of the popular television show *America's Next Top Model,* hosted by former CoverGirl Tyra Banks. As part of her winnings, each season's winner receives a contract with CoverGirl and becomes a spokesmodel.

Further Reading: CoverGirl. http://www.covergirl.com; Foltz, Kim. "All About/Cover Girls; The Look That Sells is both Girl-Next-Door and Celebrity." *New York Times,* May 24, 1992; Peiss, Kathy. *Hope in a Jar: The Making of America's Beauty Culture.* New York: Metropolitan Books, 1998.

Abigail Mitchell

D

DANDRUFF

Dandruff is the shedding of the scalp's epidermal cells, something that affects most people in various degrees. The skin of the scalp constantly sheds, but when the scalp's dead cells shed at a rapid rate, large grey-white clumps appear on the top of the scalp and become visible. Manufacturers of shampoos and conditioners have produced an array of safe and unsafe over-the-counter products that have been sold under both the banner of beauty and medicine to eliminate or prevent dandruff.

Mild forms of dandruff are the most common and are easily treated by washing the hair more frequently, but more serious conditions also produce similar kinds of itching and flakes. Seborrheic dermatitis, for example, is often difficult to distinguish from dandruff, but it is treated with a prescription drug. People with oily scalps more easily produce yeast and thus tend to suffer most from seborrheic dermatitis, dandruff, and *Pityrosporum ovale,* which leads to scalp irritation and scaling. The yeast is rare among children, but its prevalence tends to increase with age. Males are also more likely than females to experience dandruff, probably because of the yet-unclear effect of androgen hormones. More severe dandruff may also indicate a fungal infection or another dermatological disorder such as psoriasis, a skin disease that must be treated by a dermatologist and that can occur on other parts of the body than the scalp.

Treatments

For individuals who do not find relief from shampooing, drug products may help. Mild dandruff is typically treated with popular over-the-counter shampoos such as Selsun Blue or the aptly named Head and Shoulders. In 1990, the **U.S. Food and Drug Administration** (FDA) banned 27 unsafe or ineffective ingredients commonly found in dandruff shampoos. There are currently five ingredients that the FDA has determined to be safe and effective, including coal tar, pyrithione zinc, sulfur, selenium sulfide, and salicylic acid. However, not all problems with these ingredients have been eliminated. Coal tar not only leaves an orange tint that often lingers after the shampoo has been used, especially in light-colored or dyed hair, but one form of treated bituminous coal increases sensitivity to sunlight, and long-term use is associated with skin cancer. Products that include coal tar advise its use only for a short-term basis.

Further Reading: Cook, Alan, ed. *Skin Disorders Sourcebook.* Detroit, MI: Omnigraphics, 1997; Engasser, Pat, John Gray, and Steve Sheil. *Dandruff and the Sensitive Scalp.* London: Royal Society of Medicine, 2004; Hingley, Audrey. "OTC Options: Controlling Dandruff." http://pinch.com/skin/docs/FDA-OTC-Dandruff-options.

Caryn E. Neumann

DERMATOLOGY

Dermatology, a medical specialization that deals with skin care, emerged from the study of venereal diseases. The first schools of dermatology were established in 18th-century France and early dermatologists specialized, for example, in the treatment of diseases such as syphilis. In the United States, the link between sexual disease and skin disorders such as lesions continued to shape the direction of the profession. Indeed, American medical journals such as *The Archives of Dermatology and Syphilology,* first published in 1870, reflect the degree to which the treatment of sexual disease and skin ailments were inextricably bound. Victorian assumptions that one's complexion was a reflection of virtue would lead medical professionals and laypeople to incorrectly conclude that skin disorders such as **acne** were a result of immoral behavior, particularly sexual deviance, a notion that would linger well into the 20th century.

Regardless of its cultural implications, blemishes and other imperfections have encouraged generations of Americans to seek some kind of help. However, in the 20th century an emerging beauty industry created competition for dermatologists, who relied on their medical stature to carve out a distinct niche. Many working-class Americans would never dream of seeking a specialist for treating skin disorders like acne. However, by the 1920s and '30s men and women, especially youths, sought to improve their complexions with store-bought products such as Pond's Extract or Lily Face Wash. They also frequented beauticians, who were often trained in hair and skin care, were more familiar to their patrons, and were less costly than dermatologists. Above all else, home remedies continued to persist and meant that rather than setting up an appointment with a doctor, do-it-yourselfers might simply cut off a troublesome wart, bleach skin to temper the tone, or spend hours in front of a mirror picking and squeezing.

Throughout the 20th and into the 21st century, dermatologists have continued to warn against non–medical professionals who may not understand the underlying cause of a particular skin ailment. Dermatologists undergo specific training in skin disorders, cancers, and diseases, as well as issues that relate to aging and other cosmetic conditions. These professionals also use topical and systemic medications, surgery, and **cosmetic surgery**, as well as therapies using lights and lasers. There are several subspecialties in dermatology, including venereology, the specialty that treats sexually transmitted diseases, and phlebology, which deals with the venous system. To be sure, acne remains one of the most common complaints that dermatologists deal with, yet dermatitis or eczema, a red rash or recurring irritable area of the skin, is also a common ailment that has many different causes and follows many different patterns. Stress can actually cause dermatitis or make it worse by suppressing the normal immune response, while hand dermatitis results from external contact with household chemicals and cleaning agents. Psoriasis is another common rash and tends to be genetic as well as influenced by many environmental factors. It can range in severity, and some people may even need to be hospitalized for treatment. Finally, skin cancer, now considered an epidemic, is the most serious skin disorder. Techniques like mole-mapping can be used to keep track of skin abnormalities to closely monitor atypical moles, but frequent visits to a dermatologist are now routine for many Americans.

Cosmetic Dermatology

Along with increasing health concerns, cosmetic dermatology, the branch of dermatology that specializes in aesthetic issues, is growing, but not without controversy. Cosmetic dermatologists deal with the treatment of whatever society deems to be common skin flaws. While worries over acne jumpstarted the development of cosmetic dermatology in the early 20th century, an ever-beauty-conscious consuming public has made the specialization part of mainstream popular culture, including reality shows. Less invasive treatments are designed to deal, for example, with age spots, which are brown patches of skin associated with sun exposure that appear as a person matures. Age spots are harmless but are an aesthetic concern. Similarly, birthmarks, though usually harmless, sometimes cause skin problems and require treatment or removal. Moles are round, brown spots on the skin. They can develop over time or may be present at birth. Though usually harmless, they can develop into skin cancer and must be closely monitored. Many people choose to have them removed due to cosmetic concerns. Rosacea is a skin affliction characterized by facial redness that usually affects fair-skinned adults and can be treated with either topical or oral medications.

These skin flaws and their cultural implications change over time as a result of evolving standards of beauty. These conditions are all completely harmless to one's overall health, but, like **cosmetics**, the treatment of them is meant to enhance one's overall physical appearance in order to meet certain (and ever-changing) beauty standards. For example, wrinkling of the skin is a perfectly natural part of the aging process, yet it fuels the growth of a rich array of procedures to mitigate the effect of sun exposure, smoking, and **dieting** that can exacerbate the wrinkling effect. Cosmetic dermatologists have long prescribed or recommended products to deal with wrinkles, but in recent years the use of injectable products like **Botox** has become common. Botox is a surgical procedure in which the toxic protein botulinum is injected into the skin in small doses in order to improve the skin's texture and appearance. It is sold commercially under the names Botox, Dysport, and Myobloc. The use of these products has become the most popular cosmetic procedure that dermatologists perform.

Dermatology is currently considered one of the more lucrative medical specializations, but it still fails to keep up with demand. It was noted in 2008 that there were approximately 10,500 dermatologists in the United States, but health and beauty patients have outpaced the number of available physicians. These numbers could be changing quickly because the specialty offers a much more controllable lifestyle for medical professionals. Dermatologists don't need to carry beepers, have weekends off, and the salary can almost reach that earned by a general surgeon. With increasing demands for cosmetic treatments coupled with growing concerns over skin cancer and other health issues, dermatology seems headed toward a two-tier industry that leaves frustrated patients at times waiting longer for skin cancer checks than for Botox injections. Cosmetic dermatology patients typically have money to spend and, in contrast to those requiring cancer screenings, they do not need to negotiate the bureaucracy of insurance companies. Physicians can spend 10 minutes checking a patient's skin for melanoma and be reimbursed $60–$90, or they can make $500 spending the same amount of time administering the latest anti-aging miracle. Research in 2008 found that patients with real medical needs often waited longer than those scheduling a cosmetic procedure. Some dermatologists have embraced the division that now seems almost inherent in the profession and even have different offices and answering services, further bifurcating their medical practice. Patients seeking cosmetic treatments find themselves in a luxurious spa-like atmosphere, while they are faced with the more clinical, cattle-car setting when dealing with a medical condition. In fact, some dermatologists have even opened businesses in shopping malls and provide Botox injections as if they were just another trendy fashion, even though the field of dermatology has long sought to define itself as distinct from the business of beauty.

Further Reading: Bisaccia, Emil, Liliana Saap, Razan Kadry, and Dwight Scarborough. "Exploring Aesthetic Interventions: Non-Invasive Procedures in Cosmetic Dermatology." *Skin and Aging.* http://www.skinandaging.com; Brumberg, Joan Jacobs. *The Body Project: An Intimate History of American Girls.* New York: Vintage, 1998; Einstein Medical. "Common Skin Flaws." *DocShop.* http://www.docshop.com/education/dermatology; Oakley, Amanda. "A-Z Index." *DermNet NZ.* http://dermnetnz.org; Richtel, Matt. "Young Doctors and Wish Lists: No Weekend Calls, No Beepers." *New York Times,* January 7, 2004; Singer, Natasha. "Botox Appointments Faster Than for Moles, Study Find." *New York Times,* August 29, 2007; Singer, Natasha. "The Price of Beauty: As Doctors Cater to Looks, Skin Patients Wait." *New York Times,* July 26, 2008; The Skin Care Center. http://www.dermatology.org.

Krystal A. Humphreys

DESIGNERS

Paris, France, has been the center of the fashion world for centuries, and any fashion designer desiring fame and fortune went there. Parisian fashion gained its foothold on history during the reign of Louis XIV, "The Sun King," in the 17th century. Skilled tailors spent hundreds of hours clothing the many courtiers as they flew through a flurry of outfits for various occasions throughout the day. This kept those at court so occupied with fashion that they had little time to cause any trouble for the king and he was free to do as he pleased. This French tradition of being at the forefront of fashion is less related to political machinations in today's world, but it is no less integral to those with the power and prestige to indulge in such luxuries.

19th-Century Founders of Haute Couture

Charles Worth (1826–95), an Englishman, is considered to be the father of *haute couture,* literally *high sewing* or *high fashion*. He moved to Paris in 1845. Although there was no established fashion house system at that time, the legacy of Louis XIV was still strong. Worth rose quickly through the ranks of society and became the couturier for Empress Eugenie in the 1860s. By the 1870s, Worth's designs were featured prominently in the **fashion magazines** of the day and he soon became a household name among the wealthy elite. Although Worth died in 1895, the House of Worth would flourish under his descendants until 1952 when his great-grandson would finally retire and close the house for good.

Following closely on the heels of Worth was Paul Poiret (1879–1944). He was a young, French fashion sensation who joined the House of Worth in 1901 before

French designer Yves Saint Laurent, center, with models, all wearing his safari-style designs, outside his Rive Gauche boutique in London, 1969. (AP Photo/FILE)

expanding into his own establishment in 1903. In 1911, he launched the world's first total lifestyle fashion offering, including perfume and makeup lines named after his eldest daughter, Rosine. This was followed by a decorative arts line named after his other daughter, Martine. Poiret was most famous for his use of harem pants and the slim, narrow-hemmed gowns called hobble skirts. He embraced Art Nouveau and the trend of Orientalism in all of his designs. He designed clothing meant to be worn without corsets and petticoats, something not done since the Renaissance. His designs were simple and relied more heavily on draping than tailoring, taking the costumes of Japan, Ancient Greece, and the Middle East as his inspirations. Poiret was called the King of Fashion and *Le Magnifique*; he is credited for being fashion's first modernist and for bringing the art of couture into the 20th century.

One designer who really took advantage of this bourgeoning modernism was **Coco Chanel** (1883–1971). Chanel rose from poverty to become of one the preeminent designers in history; her name still resonates strongly with consumers today. Chanel opened her first shop in Paris in 1913 and sold a small line of hats and women's garments made out of jersey knit fabric. Although she chose jersey for its practical cost, she also found that it draped well and was easy to work with, following in Poiret's footsteps of simple, modern garments. Chanel quickly established a loyal clientele and by 1919, at the age of 32, she had founded the House of Chanel and enjoyed a worldwide following. Chanel continued to design through the 1930s and created signature pieces such as the little black dress. In 1939, however, she closed her house when France declared war on Germany, signaling the beginning of World War II. She returned to fashion in 1953, partially in response to Christian Dior's New Look, which she found to be unsuitable for postwar women used to working out of the home. Chanel continued her devotion to practical designs crafted from classic textiles and the Chanel suit soon became a status symbol for women everywhere. Chanel also produced a full range of accessories and a large perfume line, the most famous of which is Chanel No. 5. Designer Karl Lagerfeld (1938–) took control of the house in 1983 and has continued to be a major force in modern fashion.

A contemporary of Chanel was Elsa Schiaparelli (1890–1973). Despite a cordial business relationship and recommendations from Poiret, Schiaparelli struggled in her early years as a Paris couturier. It was not until she began a knitwear line that was very heavily influenced by Surrealism that she began to gain the notice of the fashion industry and the buying public. Known for her whimsical items such as a hat shaped like a shoe and a dress decorated with the image of a giant red lobster, Schiaparelli also created a perfume called Shocking that was sold in a vibrant pink bottle in the shape of a woman's torso. But Schiaparelli could not adapt to the postwar fashion trends, and she closed her house for good in 1956. During the heyday of her career, Schiaparelli was hailed as a genius and created a legacy of fun and whimsy in fashion design that is still important in today's industry, paving the way for other avant-garde designers such as Paco Rabanne (1934–), Issey Miyake (1938–), Comme des Garçons (Rei Kawakubo, 1942–), Jean-Paul Gautier (1952–), and Christian Lacroix (1951–), among others.

Christian Dior (1905–57) began his career in design in 1935 as an illustrator and assistant. He opened his own house in 1946 and launched his very first collection in the spring of 1947. He called it the New Look, as it was a departure from wartime rationing, and it made him an instant success. The New Look featured softly rounded shoulders, a narrow corseted waist, and a full, sweeping skirt supported by stiff petticoats. He also paired his wasp-waisted torso silhouette with a narrow pencil skirt, always focusing on a highly feminine shape that borrowed nothing from the boxy looks associated with the Depression and prewar eras. He enjoyed historical references and trompe-l'oeil details. Dior also created parallel accessories lines of handbags, shoes, stockings, jewelry, and perfume, mostly licensing out his name and designs to other manufacturers. In 1948, he was the first designer to create licensing agreements, something that is ubiquitous today. Dior died in 1957, just 10 years after the launch of his groundbreaking line, but the House of Dior remains a thriving business today.

One of Dior's most trusted associates was Yves Saint Laurent (1936–2008), who took over the House of Dior in 1957. But Saint Laurent's styles were considered too revolutionary and dramatic for the house and, in 1963, he left to form his own company. Considered one of the most influential designers of the 20th century, Saint Laurent created such innovative looks as Le Smoking, which combined menswear with graceful femininity for an androgynous look that would remain popular through the 1960s and beyond, as well as his Mondrian dresses that used the geometric paintings of the Dutch artist as the main decorative element on simple tent dresses. Saint Laurent officially retired from fashion in 2002, although he remained very active both in his own house and the industry in general until his death in June 2008.

Paris has never lost the spotlight as the fashion center of the world, but during World War II when most of France was occupied by the Nazis, consumers were forced to look elsewhere and the way was cleared for designers from the United States, the United Kingdom, and beyond to step up and keep the industry running. New York City, London, Los Angeles, and later, Milan all became areas of fashion industry focus. Coming out of the wartime era of design were names like Claire MacCardell (1905–58), a pioneering American designer of women's sportswear, and Charles James (1906–78), an Englishman living in New York City who created elegant and structural gowns like the Four Leaf Clover dress. Balenciaga (1895–1972) was a Spanish designer who rose to prominence in the wartime era and redefined the fashion ideal in the 1960s with his sleek and far-thinking tunic dresses.

Contemporary Trends

Today, fashion does not rely on a single silhouette or on a single designer. Fashion design superstars exist in their own realms of style. Choosing to address fashion to the young was a new angle introduced in the 1960s. Previously, high fashion had been the purview of socialites and ladies of wealth and rank. Young women proved to be an audience ready to take part in the fashion system; they desired a look that was different from what their mothers wore. Vivienne Westwood (1941–) made her mark on fashion in the London-born punk movement and has moved into the fashion mainstream with a focus on a young and edgy target market. Betsey Johnson (1942–) and Mary Quant (1934–) also became involved in grassroots social movements of the 1960s and 1970s, and created youth-oriented fashion lines that remain popular today.

In the 21st century, becoming a designer is a completely different act than it was in the days of Chanel and Dior. Although training and apprenticeship are still an important part of the industry, many designers are able to gain public notice by a number of original means. With the advent of MTV (Music Television) in 1981, new designers had a larger platform upon which to display their creations through the music video. As the **Internet** gained popularity through the 1990s, ideas and designs would be disseminated instantly. The use of blogs, Internet video (YouTube), and online boutique Web sites (www.etsy.com) have made it possible for a designer to become personally accessible to potential customers the world over. The television reality show *Project Runway* and its many spin-offs have also changed the course of fashion careers. Previously unknown designers can suddenly be launched into stardom by the show's judges, who are established quantities in the industry, such as Michael Kors (1959–) and Tim Gunn (1953–).

Fashion has never lost its status as social symbol, but the language of fashion has changed. In the current industry, the personal expression of style and a focus on specific target markets are integral to any 21st-century designer's success. Fashion is no longer dominated by a single look or label, but as it did in the 17th century, the industry relies on consumers willing to indulge their inner courtiers and participate in the flurry of fashion.

Other designers who have had an impact on the fashion industry include Azzedine Alaïa (1940–), Giorgio Armani (1934–), Laura Ashley (1925–85), Pierre Balmain (1914–82), Geoffrey Beene (1927–2004), Dana Buchman (1987–), Pierre Cardin (1922–), Oleg Cassini (1913–2006), Liz Claiborne (1929–2007), Andre Courrèges (1923–), Oscar de la Renta (1932–), Jacques Fath (1912–54), Mariano Fortuny (1871–1949), John Galliano (1960–), Rudy Gernreich (1922–85), Hubert du Givenchy (1927–), Madame Grès (1903–93), Halston (Roy Halston Frowick, 1932–90), Edith Head (1897–1981), Norma Kamali (1945–), Donna Karan (1948–), **Calvin Klein** (1942–), René Lacoste (1904–96), Jeanne Lanvin (1867–1946), Ralph Lauren (1939–), Bob Mackie (1940–), Jessica McClintock (1930–), Isaac Mizrahi (1961–), Thierry Mugler (1948–), Todd Oldham (1961–), Jean Patou (1880–1936), Emilio Pucci (1914–92), Zandra Rhodes (1940–), Sonia Rykiel (1930–), Anna Sui (1955–), Ellen Tracy (Linda Allard, 1940–), Madeleine Vionnet (1876–1975), Diane von Furstenberg (1946–), Emanuel Ungaro (1933–), Gianni Versace (1946–97), Louis Vuitton (Marc Jacobs, 1963–), and Vera Wang (1949–).

Further Reading: Callan, Georgina O'Hara. *The Thames and Hudson Dictionary of Fashion and Fashion Designers.* London: Thames & Hudson, 1998; Coleman, Elizabeth Ann. *The Opulent Era: Fashions of Worth, Doucet, and Pingat.* Brooklyn: Brooklyn Museum, 1989. Exhibition catalog; De Marly, Diana. *Worth: Father of Haute Couture,* 2nd ed. New York: Holmes & Meier, 1990; Deslandres, Yvonne. *Poiret: Paul Poiret, 1879–1944.* New York: Rizzoli, 1987; Golbin, Pamela. *Fashion Designers.* New York: Watson-Guptill Publications, 2001; Kellogg, Ann, Amy T. Peterson, Stefani Bay, and Natalie Swindell. *In an Influential Fashion: An Encyclopedia of Nineteenth- and Twentieth-Century Fashion Designers and Retailers Who Transformed Dress.* Westport, CT: Greenwood Press, 2002; Milbank, Caroline Rennolds. *Couture: The Great Fashion Designers.* London: Thames & Hudson, 1985; Poiret, Paul. *My First Fifty Years.* Translated by Stephen Haden Guest. London: Victor Gollancz, 1931; Steele, Valerie. *Paris Fashion: A Cultural History.* New York: Oxford University Press, 1988; Troy, Nancy J. *Couture Culture: A Study in Modern Art and Fashion.* Cambridge, MA: MIT Press, 2003.

Sara M. Harvey

DIETING

Today, dieting is a multibillion dollar business and counting calories is an American pastime. Dieting is usually a practice that involves ingesting food in a regulated fashion to achieve or to maintain a goal weight, but it can also involve pills, procedures, and other lifestyle choices. Some people also diet in order to gain weight. For example, athletes often attempt to gain weight to bulk up or to move into a different weight class. In addition, individuals who suffer from anorexia nervosa or starvation are usually given diets in order to regain optimal levels of body fat, muscle, and essential nutrients. Weight-loss diets restrict the intake of certain foods in order to reduce body weight. This is the most common form of dieting, and its popularity can be seen in the number of weight-loss books, programs, and structured diet clubs that are available. Dieting to lose weight did not become popular until the late 1800s. For the average American, neither excess of food nor a sedentary lifestyle was often perceived as a problem. It is generally assumed that, until recently, emphasis was placed on a person's spiritual value rather than on aesthetics, so the need to be thin was not a dominant concern; however, there have been a number of contributing factors to this shift, including the ever-changing social and cultural perception of beauty and style.

Fashion Change and Body Type

The ideal woman of the 19th century invoked a maternal rather than sensual sense of self, and clothing tended to accentuate the fullness of her figure. Fashion trends, however, profoundly shaped what society viewed as the ideal womanly figure. For instance, the use of the corset to make one's waist appear small while enhancing the bust and the hips was the norm throughout the Victorian era. With the rise of the fashion industry, women increasingly began to purchase ready-made clothes. Instead of having clothes tailored to their body, they began to tailor their body to fit the clothes. In the 1920s, a more athletic and boyish ideal image of feminine style made popular the svelte figure of the flapper, as well as some first dieting books published in the teens. By the 1950s, quasi-Victorian hourglass figures were the ideal standards for Hollywood glamour girls, Barbie, and the girl next door. Since the 1960s, fashions that revealed more skin or body contour gave rise to waifs like Twiggy, a British model blamed (incorrectly) for originating the female obsession with thinness.

Counting Calories and Other Trends and Icons

When calories were discovered in the early 20th century, the war against fat became scientific. This helped to shape trends in fashion and the image of beauty, and produced a litany of weight-loss plans. Some diet programs have a greater effect on culture and eating habits than others. These diets usually focus on the scientific reasons for why losing weight is difficult. One of the most well known diet groups is Weight Watchers, which provides participants with structured diet plans, as well as support from other dieters. Weight Watchers was created in the 1960s, and remains so popular today that many restaurants have specific Weight Watchers sections on their menus. In the program, calorie-counting is replaced with a system of points designed to make dieting easier. At each level of the plan, the participant is allowed a certain number of points per day to spend on whatever they choose. The philosophy behind Weight Watchers is giving people a support system in which they can cut calories by cutting down portion sizes. Weight Watchers removes the scientific element of weight loss by eliminating calorie-counting, at least in name.

In the 1970s and '80s, new icons became to shape the direction of the dieting industry. Richard Simmons, for example, emerged as a motivational and somewhat flamboyant fitness instructor. Simmons was dissatisfied with fad diets and dedicated himself to spreading a message of healthy eating and exercise to change people's lives. His career spawned a successful fitness studio, a series of aerobics videos, countless television appearances and advertisements, and made him into a fitness icon. The Jenny Craig program was created in 1983 by Jenny Craig, and is a system that focuses on weight loss, weight management, and nutrition. The program combines nutrition, through meal plans and prepackaged foods, with fitness and counseling to help clients lose weight. The company has had numerous celebrity endorsements over the years, including Kirstie Alley, Valerie Bertinelli, and Queen Latifah.

During the early years of the 21st century, the oh-so-popular Atkins diet essentially began the low-carbohydrate craze that swept the United States. Dr. Robert Atkins's first book was published in 1972, but it did not become popular until the early 2000s. After he died in 2003, it lost popularity, but the brand name is still used to sell low-carb products. The Atkins Nutritional Approach, the diet's official title, centers on the science behind weight loss. It insists that one can lose weight not by eating less, but by eating the right foods to scientifically trick one's body into burning fat. The Atkins diet claims that the main problem leading to obesity is the overconsumption of refined carbohydrates like sugar, flour, and high-fructose corn syrup. The diet also emphasizes the danger of transaturated fats. The Atkins diet therefore involves the restriction of carbohydrates in order to force the body to burn stored fat. The Atkins diet has become so popular that low-carb products are sold in grocery stores and some restaurant menus include low-carb sections.

Extreme Measures and Criticism

Counting calories and regulating food intake has not been the only means of dieting. In the late 19th and early 20th century, early diet pills were rumored to contain tapeworms that, once ingested, would assist the dieter in losing weight. By the 1950s, doctors were prescribing diet pills that contained amphetamines. Amphetamines were used during World War II to keep soldiers alert, but had the added benefit of appetite suppression. However, many patients developed substance abuse problems and doctors stopped prescribing the pills. Today, weight loss pills claim to increase metabolism or aid in appetite suppression through herbal supplementation like green tea and additives like ephedra. Some pills, like the drug Alli, are used to block the absorption of fat from foods, but must be taken in combination with a healthy diet. However, the greatest concerns come from the popularity of extreme diets and fasting.

Since the 1960s, feminist criticism of seemingly unhealthy, super-thin fashion models has urged women to ignore trends that called for an ideal body shape and size most women find unattainable. This argument continues into the present day with media attention focused on models like Kate Moss and celebrities like Lindsay Lohan who are deemed anorexic due to their small size and are criticized as poor role models for impressionable young women. A particular concern is that when dieting is taken to the extreme, eating disorders can develop. Anorexia nervosa affects mostly girls and young women who feel pressure to conform to a certain body image presented by society. People with the disorder have an intense fear of gaining weight. Though the focus is on stress surrounding food intake, anorexia is also a way for people to feel more in control of life. There is no single cause of anorexia, but culture, family history, and stressful life changes can all play a role. Although less attention has been paid to men, similar trends have also shaped cultural ideas of male beauty. By the late 1970s, the athletic, muscular male body became the ideal and encouraged men to embrace a range of fitness programs and diet crazes that include dangerously unhealthy products and practices that have long been associated primarily with women and girls.

> "I have been invited to hang out at a birthday sleepover. . . . After a light dinner, the girls move to the living room, where they spontaneously begin painting toenails. . . . Almost as soon as her toes are done, one girl, willowy as a reed, hops on the stationary bike and shouts, 'I'm going to work off my dinner!' A few others jump up and begin clamoring for a turn. For the next hour, the girls climb on and off the bike, making sure to announce the number of calories they are burning with the regularity of train conductors. They are nine years old."
>
> *Rachel Simmons, author*
>
> Source: Simmons, Rachel. *Odd Girl Out: The Hidden Culture of Aggression in Girls.* San Diego: Harcourt, 2002, 155–56.

Further Reading: Alli. http://www.myalli.com; Atkins, Robert. *Dr. Atkins' New Diet Revolution.* New York: M. Evans, 2003; Bordo, Susan. *The Male Body: A New Look at Men in Public and in Private.* New York: Farrar, Straus and Giroux, 1999; Bordo, Susan. *Unbearable Weight: Feminism, Western Culture, and the Body.* Los Angeles: University of California Press, 1993; Brumberg, Joan Jacobs. *Fasting Girls: The History of Anorexia Nervosa.* New York: Vintage, 2000; Chenoune, Farid. *Hidden Underneath: A History of Lingerie.* New York: Assouline Publishing, 2005; Fields, Jill. *An Intimate Affair: Women, Lingerie, and Sexuality.* Los Angeles: University of California Press, 2007; Jacks, Matt. "The History of Dieting." *The History of Dot Net.* http://thehistoryof.net/the-history-of-dieting.html; Jenny Craig. http://www.jennycraig.com; Maurer, Donna, and Jeffery Sobal, eds. *Weighty Issues: Fatness and Thinness as Social Problems.* Piscataway, NJ: Aldine Transaction, 1999; Moore, Pamela. *Building Bodies.* New Brunswick, NJ: Rutgers University Press, 1997; Richard Simmons.com. http://www.richardsimmons.com; Stinson, Kandi. *Women and Dieting Culture: Inside a Commercial Weight Loss Group.* New Brunswick, NJ: Rutgers University Press, 2001; U.S. Department of Health and Human Services. "Anorexia Nervosa." *Women's Health.* http://womenshealth.gov; Vigilla, Hubert. A Short History of Diet Pills and Weight Loss Drugs Part One. February 11, 2008. Docshop. com. http://www.docshop.com/2008/02/11/a-short-history-of-diet-pills-and-weight-loss-drugs-part-one/; Wann, Marilyn. *Fat? So!: Because You Don't Have to Apologize for Your Size*. Berkeley, CA: Ten Speed Press, 1999; Weight Watchers International. "How Weight Watchers Works." *Weight Watchers*. http://www.weightwatchers.com.

Krystal A. Humphreys

DISPLAY

In the beauty industry, retailers use display booths and stands to demonstrate and advertise products and methods of use. Display stands are most prominent in large **retail** outlets where trained beauty product professionals apply and illustrate how products can be used and what immediate effects are available to the consumer. These professionals are also a component of the retail displays, indicating via their own use how a product can be applied and maintained in an ideal environment and for long periods of time (throughout the work day or longer in some cases).

At the core, display stands incorporate the **branding** and **packaging** aspects of the beauty industry into a one-stop mechanism for the consumer to test and evaluate the product before purchasing or using it on his own. Some displays, like those for lipstick applicators and perfume and cologne sprays, do not require the aid of a beauty professional or salesperson, allowing the consumer to test the product for use without the hassle or concern of a pressured buying environment.

Perfume and cologne stands often retain a professional to indicate what brands are popular or feature similar scents to a discontinued line of products. These salespersons also promote similarly branded lotions and care products that feature the scents of popular perfumes and colognes, often in gift sets for seasonal purchases and holidays. Brands such as **Calvin Klein** or Kenneth Cole feature gift sets for women and men, with the latter incorporating lotions and aftershaves into the collections and brands of the scented products. Increasingly, free samples of product and brand lines are also offered, to better familiarize the consumer with the variety of a manufacturer's offerings.

Displays often require the attention and aid of a professional who can demonstrate how the manufacturer or company intends the product to be used via demonstration or a makeover for the consumer. **Makeovers** demonstrate the talents of professionals employed at the counter and the positive benefits that derive from using the products applied, but also force consumers to experience products that they are generally disinterested in using. Consumers may not follow these procedures for personal and private use, but the application by retail professionals should follow the **advertising** and marketing campaigns that attracted the consumer to inquire about the use of a product and its benefits. The ideal application by cosmetic professionals allows consumers to select and test a variety of products to match their individual traits with the right product or brand of products. Product campaigns can give consumers expectations of products that may not be fulfilled. In that case, makeovers may demonstrate an appearance that is unattainable based on the specifics of each consumer, before considering the costs associated with purchasing an entire brand or line of products.

Beauty product professionals and salespersons may be employed by the retailer where the display is located, but are often trained by the manufacturer and provide information about further product use to the customer. Displays also allow various manufacturers and producers to compete for consumers in large retail spaces. Often, display stands and product counters are adjacent to competitors selling similar products and brands. Consumers may engage the help of various counter clerks and professionals to find the product they are most comfortable applying and wearing.

Some retail outlets, like superstore chains, do not require trained salespersons or professionals, instead they stock the products in displays that indicate use and promote marketability. Other manufacturers dispense with the use of displays in retail outlets altogether, hiring salespersons and trained professionals to sell the product directly to the consumers in their home. The advent of online advertising and marketing gives a new outlet and point-of-interest for manufacturers and consumers to interact and test product interest and use. With the **Internet**, professionals are dispensed with for the direct interaction between the manufacturer and consumer in an interactive market. Internet tools also allow manufacturers and advertisers to demonstrate the wide diversity of brands and products.

Displays provide retailers with point-of-sale devices to market and advertise the products and brands inherent to the **cosmetics** industry. Furthermore, the displays in a store give consumers an opportunity to test and examine the products for sale with and without the help of a sales associate. These facets give the cosmetics industry an outlet to determine what products and brands are popular, but displays also demonstrate an image and look that the consumer should desire and emulate with the aid of the products on display.

Further Reading: Bordo, Susan. *The Male Body: A Look at Men in Public and in Private.* New York: Farrar, Straus and Giroux, 1999; Peiss, Kathy. *Hope in a Jar: The Making of America's Beauty Culture.* New York: Metropolitan Books, 1998; Quart, Alissa. *Branded: The Buying and Selling of Teenagers.* New York: Basic Books, 2004.

Richard D. Driver

DOVE'S CAMPAIGN FOR REAL BEAUTY

The personal care company Dove, a subsidiary of parent corporation Unilever, launched the Campaign for Real Beauty in 2004 with a stated mission to widen the definition of beauty. In tandem with this **advertising** campaign, Dove markets products such as lotion, body wash, deodorant, firming cream, shampoo, and conditioner for skin and hair; it has also created the Dove Self-Esteem Fund, the Dove Global Study, and the U.S. Dove Report with the goal of putting perfect media images of beauty into perspective and revealing the artifice of touched-up perfection on television and in magazines.

One aim of the Dove campaign is to cut through what the campaign refers to as "a world of hype and stereotypes" by portraying real women in advertising in lieu of professional models. Real women of varying height, weight, and ethnicity appear wearing only **undergarments** in print ads for products such as the Dove Firming line, which includes a body wash, lotion, and **cellulite** gel-cream, all of which serve to reduce the appearance of cellulite. The purpose of using real women in advertisements, according to Dove, is to provoke debate about dominant beauty ideals. A video on the Campaign for Real Beauty Web site entitled Evolution **Film** also sends the message that contemporary beauty ideals are distorted. The video, which contains no dialogue, portrays the process of applying makeup, hair product, and then computer alterations to the face of a model, which is then used as an advertisement on a billboard. As part of the campaign, this video suggests that the unrealistic beauty ideals created by such images are damaging to women's self-esteem.

Self-esteem is the primary concern of another of the campaign's projects, the Dove Self-Esteem Fund. The Dove campaign states that beauty pressures make it hard for girls to keep up, resulting in low self-esteem and introversion; thus, the goal of the fund is to create change and to educate girls about a wider definition of beauty. A primary recipient of funding in the United States is the Girl Scouts of the USA, and specifically a venture called *uniquely ME!* that uses activity booklets, exercises, and hands-on activities to build self-esteem in girls ages 8–14 in the United States and Puerto Rico. The concerns of the program include recognizing one's strengths and best attributes, the power of positive thinking, and the effects of relationships and stress. The Dove Self-Esteem Fund cites statistics that suggest an increase in self-esteem problems in girls and young women, which the campaign links to distorted beauty ideals that are reinforced by the media.

More recently, the Dove Campaign for Real Beauty has included a Pro-Age line, which stresses the message that "beauty has no age limit" with commercials depicting artfully posed nude women, often with gray hair or wrinkles, and the tag line, "too old to be in an anti-aging ad," followed by, "but this isn't anti-age, this is pro-age." This line is accompanied by products such as pro-age body lotion, hand cream, and face care. The Dove campaign's message of female empowerment has been very successful as a marketing tool, garnering positive attention from mainstream media sources, but it has also been critiqued by some as hypocritical for promoting inner beauty and pro-aging while marketing products that reduce blemishes and signs of aging.

Further Reading: Bordo, Susan. *Unbearable Weight.* Berkeley: University of California Press, 1997; Dove's Campaign For Real Beauty. http://www.dove.us/#/cfrb/; Wolf, Naomi. *The Beauty Myth.* New York: William Morrow and Company, 1991.

Laura Harrison

DR. 90210

Dr. 90210 is a popular documentary-style reality television program that premiered on the E! network in 2004 in the United States. It has recently completed its sixth season. The show follows the lives of cosmetic surgeons, including their personal and professional lives. *Dr. 90210* is often credited with playing a large role in increasing the popularity of **cosmetic surgery**. The program lays bare the often hidden world of cosmetic surgery, allowing viewers to see the entire process, from consultations, to surgery, to recovery, to the end results. It educates viewers about cosmetic surgery, including the types of procedures and reasonable outcomes. The actual surgery is televised and quite graphic. However, critics note that the show only superficially addresses the risks and costs of the procedures.

The namesake of *Dr. 90210* is Dr. Robert Rey. He specializes in transumbilical breast augmentation (TUBA), which is a scarless procedure. He is not a board-certified cosmetic surgeon. He serves publicly as an expert on cosmetic surgery in a wide variety of media contexts, including *The Today Show, Dr. Phil, The Early Show,* and *The View* and also as a commentator for the Oscars, Emmys, and Golden Globes.

The show focuses greatly on Dr. Rey's personal life. He was born in Brazil and brought to the United States by missionaries. Dr. Rey says that he has achieved the American dream, coming from poverty in Brazil to become a successful cosmetic surgeon with an idyllic home and family, including wife Hayley Rey and two children. Both Robert and Hayley Rey admit to having cosmetic surgery. Both had previous careers in the entertainment business.

While the show primarily follows the life of Dr. Rey, it also shows a variety of other cosmetic physicians in personal and professional settings, including Jason Diamond, Richard Ellenborgen, Raj Kanodia, Will Kirby, Robert Kotler, Linda Li, Gary Motykie, Steven Svehlak, and Daniel Yamini, among others. This adds more drama to the program by incorporating a wider variety of personal situations and crises. In addition, these surgeons and Dr. Rey expose the viewer to a large variety of surgical procedures, including vaginal rejuvenation, breast reconstruction, nose jobs, face lifts, liposuction, tummy tucks, cosmetic **dermatology**, penile implants, and hymen reconstruction. Viewers see different approaches to the same procedure, such as various methods and degrees of performing facelifts or augmenting breasts. This amount of education about cosmetic surgery was not easily attainable for the average patient prior to *Dr. 90210*.

Further Reading: Gilman, Sander L. *Making the Body Beautiful: A Cultural History of Aesthetic Surgery.* Princeton, NJ: Princeton University Press, 1990; Haiken, Elizabeth. *Venus Envy: A History of Cosmetic Surgery.* Baltimore, MD: Johns Hopkins University Press, 1997; Heinricy, Shana. "The Cutting Room: Gendered American Dreams on Plastic Surgery TV." In *How Real is Reality TV? The Role of Representation in Reality Television,* ed. David S. Escoffery, pp. 149–66. Jefferson, NC: McFarland, 2006.

Shana Heinricy

E

EBONY

Ebony, first published on November 1, 1945, is a monthly magazine that chronicles the social, political, economic, and cultural activities of people of African descent in the United States and abroad. Founded by John H. Johnson, *Ebony* was influenced by the popular *Life* magazine—a mainstream publication that used a distinctly photojournalist style to capture scenes of American life and culture. Anticipating the end of World War II, Johnson suspected the climate would be "ripe for a Black picture magazine," and that young soldiers returning from war, as well as war-weary black communities, would be looking for a more entertaining counterpart to Johnson's newsy *Negro Digest.*

At its prime, *Ebony*'s readership increased from 125,000 an issue to more than 9 million an issue: dealing with topics related to social justice and economic empowerment, and proclaiming themselves to be the "earliest and most passionate defenders of Black beauty." From its earliest days in publication, *Ebony* had a clearly defined mission to promote the fascinating "Black rainbow" of beauty and confront white America's disregard for beauty that challenged Eurocentrism. Johnson was a strong proponent of the political maxim that black is beautiful, and understood that *Ebony* could play a major role in challenging historically exclusionary paradigms. Johnson believed that despite their exclusion, there were thousands of African American women who could become icons of beauty. Stressing the importance of using black models, Johnson Publications and *Ebony* had a major influence on the **advertising** industry. A savvy businessman, Johnson's belief in the importance of the use of models with whom his readers could identify in advertisements not only proved a significant business principle, but also helped open the doors of the fashion industry for black models. Ads featuring black models, including the Johnson Company's own line of beauty products, Fashion Fair **Cosmetics**, became prominent and permanent fixtures in *Ebony.*

Johnson Publications and *Ebony* were principal agitators and advocates for civil rights and black empowerment. Encouraged by the promise of a shifting racial climate in the United States, Johnson believed that *Ebony* would create new opportunities. As his vision evolved, Johnson developed a threefold philosophy for *Ebony*—it would emphasize the positive aspects of black life, highlight the achievements and make blacks proud of themselves, and create a windbreak that would allow diversion from the problems of the day. Focusing on the "total Black experience," *Ebony*'s purpose was to showcase black achievement and highlight a progressive and cultured black society. *Ebony* has been criticized for its contributions toward developing a bourgeois aesthetic and cultivating a politic of respectability.

Though without much of the social and political cache of its zenith, *Ebony* maintains its threefold philosophy and continues, along with its sister publication, *Jet*, to be the leading African American monthly magazine. Johnson served as CEO of the Johnson Publishing Company before naming his daughter, Linda Johnson Rice, as his successor; however, until his death in 2005, Johnson remained as chairman and publisher.

Further Reading: "Corporate Biography of John H. Johnson." http://www.johnson publishing.com; Johnson, John H., and Lerone Bennett Jr. *Succeeding against the Odds.* New York: Warner Books, 1989.

Danica C. Tisdale

ELIZABETH ARDEN. *SEE* ARDEN, ELIZABETH

ENDORSEMENTS OF PRODUCTS, CELEBRITY

Many people are familiar with the ubiquitous Wheaties box with its rotating pictures of star athletes or the titillating ads featuring nothing coming between a pubescent Brooke Shields and her Calvins. Using celebrity images to market products has become a heavily used, stealthily applied concept to win over consumers, to change and solidify beauty norms, and ultimately to create and form a market for all types of goods and products. In the 19th century, celebrity status may have existed in the form of Queen Victoria selling purity and imperial might on a bar of soap—by the postwar period, however, celebrities had taken on a different significance, a different character and, indeed, a different social and economic class. The power of a celebrity endorsement of a product is both implicit and explicit—the assumption is that the celebrity is one the public admires and aspires to be and uses the product he is selling. Thus, to be like Mike, that is, like basketball legend Michael Jordan, the message is often that the actual use, consumption, or ownership of the product can bring one a little closer to his celebrity. In the beauty industry, celebrity endorsements take things one step further by having celebrities presumably use and testify to the efficacy of a product. They are stars, they are beautiful, in part because of the products they use. The consumer then has the possibility of achieving that same beauty by purchasing and following the regime of her favorite celebrity.

Makeup

Makeup companies and artists have had long-standing relationships with actresses because they may work together on a project. **Max Factor**, a pioneer in movie makeup, used his relationships with such stars as Jean Harlow, Clara Bow, Bette Davis, Joan Crawford, Claudia Colbert, and Judy Garland to sell his line of **cosmetics**. Max Factor was one of the first to use his connections with movie studios and with studio starlets to sell his products. He even appeared in cameos in the films—bringing a new type of beauty reality to beautiful fiction. Not only

Cashing in on the 2008 presidential election. (Courtesy of Julie Willett)

was he a pioneer in **advertising** campaigns and in the popularizing of celebrity products for the common consumer, but Max Factor also understood the fairytale associations between what people saw on the screen, on the pages, in the glossies, and what women hoped to appear to be.

Other companies such as Maybelline (Kristin Davis, Zhang Ziyi, Jessica Alba, and Christy Turlington), **CoverGirl** (Rihanna, Drew Barrymore, Ellen Degeneres, and Queen Latifah), and L'Oréal (Beyoncé Knowles, Andie McDowell, and Diane Keaton) have followed suit. Even higher-end makeup companies, such as Kinerase (Courtney Cox Arquette), **Estée Lauder** (Elizabeth Hurley and Gwyneth Paltrow), **Elizabeth Arden** (Catherine Zeta-Jones), **Coco Chanel** (Nicole Kidman and Keira Knightly), Christian Dior (Charlize Theron), and SKII (Cate Blanchett) use celebrity images and endorsements. Celebrities are not only endorsing products, they are making their own—Britney Spears, Jennifer Lopez, Mariah Carey, Gwen Stefani, Iman, Cindy Crawford, David and Victoria Beckham, Victoria Jackson all have their names on perfumes, cosmetics, or skin care lines. The message is simple—one can be beautiful if one uses the same products as these celebrities.

Hair Care

The hair care industry also understood the power of the celebrity endorsement in the name brand familiarity and the marketing of styling products and shampoos. In the mid 1980s, actress Kelly LeBrock made the slogan "Don't hate me because I'm beautiful" famous for Pantene. Her shiny, smooth, and fabulously coiffed locks were the envy of many women—and they were available to all, with the purchase of a bottle of Pantene. Maria Menounos, an entertainment journalist who began her career on Entertainment Tonight, is Pantene's latest spokeswoman—making a celebrity of someone whose job is to talk to celebrities. L'Oréal (Andie Mac-Dowell and Eva Longoria) and Garnier Nutrisse (Sarah Jessica Parker and Katie Holmes) have featured actresses who use their hair color products. Most recently, David Babaii created a line of eco- and animal-friendly hair products with actress Kate Hudson. The tag line for his products? "Tested on Kate, not on animals." There are also examples of celebrity-endorsed and celebrity-developed products. Both Jessica Simpson and Paris Hilton have their own lines of hair extensions.

Supermodels and Actresses

The rise of the supermodel—among the greats, Cindy Crawford, Claudia Schiffer, Naomi Campbell, and Kate Moss—in the 1980s and 1990s brought a different kind of celebrity endorsement to the beauty industry. While models had certainly been the faces for advertisements of the beauty industry since its inception, by the 1980s, supermodels were no longer nameless, beautiful faces. The women brought their own style, sensibility, and name recognition to the products and the brand name.

By the 1990s, however, supermodels gave way to actress-turned-models. Beauty magazines like **Vogue**, *Elle, Vanity Fair,* and *Women's Wear Daily* began to feature actresses as well as models on their covers. Perhaps in reaction to the two-dimensional characters that models often portrayed, actresses now talked about lifestyles, incorporating their professional careers with their roles as mothers, wives, and as women. Rather than presenting a perfect image to emulate, celebrities spoke candidly about their own flaws and weaknesses. There may be no greater example than ProActiv, a skin care and **acne** line that has received endorsements from Jessica Simpson, Sean P. Diddy Combs, Vanessa L. Williams, Britney Spears, Alyssa Milano, Julianne Hough, Jennifer Love Hewitt, and Serena Williams—to name some. These celebrities talked about their insecurities, their beauty problems, and their final remedy through the product. Their skin flaws were the consumer's skin flaws and their solution could be the consumer's solution.

Related to beauty products are exercise regimens, fitness equipment, and meal plans. Gwyneth Paltrow, Jennifer Aniston, Madonna, and Courtney Cox helped make Pilates, yoga, and *budokon* popular. These may not have been official endorsements, but as actresses talked about their own nutrition and exercise routines, women used their testimonials to explore new forms of exercise. Chuck Norris and Christie Brinkley are both paid spokespeople for the Total Gym. They host an infomercial and claim to be users themselves. Whoopi Goldberg was both a client and spokesperson for LA Weight Loss; Kirstie Alley, Valerie Bertinelli, and Queen Latifah joined and lost weight with Jenny Craig; and Jenny McCarthy became an official spokeswoman for Weight Watchers in 2006.

Recent Trends

The fashion industry, which has long exploited its relationships with starlets (think Audrey Hepburn and Givenchy), now hires stylists and public relations firms to entice celebrities to wear the newest couture from their newest lines. Whereas it had frequently been the practice of the past to have wardrobe **designers** make and select gowns for the stars of their films for awards shows such as the Oscars, celebrities are now being sent designer dresses from established and new fashion houses alike. With the plethora of awards shows, television appearances, and print photographs, newer designers have gained recognition through the celebrity endorsement of having their gowns worn by A-list actresses. Elie Saab, for example, became one of the most sought-after designers when Halle Berry wore his gown when she became the first African American woman to win the Oscar in the best actress category for her work in *Monster's Ball* (2002). Eva Longoria used the opportunity of hosting the ALMA Awards to feature Latino designers like Angel Sanchez. Most recently, when Michelle Obama appeared on *The View* in a $148 White House/Black Market sheath, the dress virtually sold out overnight. This is proof positive that celebrity endorsement, whether intentional or not, is a powerful marketing tool.

Further Reading: Berry, Bonnie. *Beauty Bias: Discrimination and Social Power.* Santa Barbara, CA: Praeger, 2007; Corner, John, and Dick Pels. *Media and the Restyling of Politics: Consumerism, Celebrity and Cynicism.* London: Sage Publications, 2003; Lahusen, Christian. *The Rhetoric of Moral Protest: Public Campaigns, Celebrity Endorsement, and Political Mobilization.* New York: Walter de Gruyter, 1996; Marshall, P. David, ed. *The Celebrity Culture Reader.* New York: Routledge, 2006; McGracken, Grant. *Culture and Consumption II: Markets, Meaning, and Brand Management.* Bloomington: Indiana University Press, 2005; Norr, Serena. "The Power of Celebrity Endorsements." *Tea and Coffee Trade Journal,* 179 no. 4 (2007): 44; Pringle, Hamish. *Celebrity Sells.* Hoboken, NJ: Wiley, 2004; Rosenblatt, Ira. "At Issue: The Lawful Use of Celebrity Endorsements." *San Fernando Valley Business Journal,* 11 no. 20 (2006): 43; Segrave, Kerry. *Endorsements in Advertising: A Social History.* Jefferson, NC: McFarland, 2005.

Aliza S. Wong

ESTÉE LAUDER

Estée Lauder (1908–2004) was known for her belief that all women can be beautiful. Like the other grande dames of the **cosmetics** industry, Lauder gained entrance to the cosmetics business through skin care products. Her company's global reputation was built on brands such as cosmetic line Clinique, and Aramis, her first specialty fragrance line for men. Lauder's marketing philosophy is based on product loyalty in specialty niches that recognize the diversity of women's demographics. Marketing a wide variety of cosmetics, fragrances, and clothing lines, Lauder remains one of the more diverse beauty corporations. The Lauder product lines project an image of high-class society, thus accessing the snob appeal inherent in purchasing.

Cosmetics entrepreneur Estée Lauder at the Estée Lauder Companies, Inc., headquarters on Fifth Avenue, in New York City, 1988. (AP Photo/Susan Ragan)

Early Life and Marketing Philosophy

Born Josephine Esther Mentzer, of Hungarian and Czech parents, Lauder was raised in Queens, New York. Starting as a skin product salesgirl and selling her uncle John Schotz's creations (legend says out of a restaurant's kitchen), Lauder learned about selling methods and the power of the personal touch between women. She also understood that presentation, and especially limited color choices, can be used effectively to guide public purchasing power. She finished high school and in 1930 married a son of Austrian immigrants, Joseph Lauder. Her professional name became Estée, a take on her nickname, Esty, and her husband's last name.

Lauder helped popularize the free gift or sampling marketing strategy to attract and retain customers; in today's customer base, free samples are frequently used as trial or travel cosmetics by women. Gift with a purchase is another very successful marketing ploy, which expanded the range of products bought by customers in the Lauder product lines. Knowing that women share their experiences with friends and family, Lauder accessed word-of-mouth **advertising** of her products through these sharing and personal touch strategies. Like other beauty corporations, Lauder employed the services of face models, which helped the product lines to gain customer recognition; this was a precursor of the supermodel brand recognition strategy. Her use of signature colors, blue for the Lauder brand and light green for Clinique cosmetics, reflected her understanding of the totality of many women's home environment decorating schemes: blue and green would coordinate with most bathrooms.

The Company

Lauder and her husband expanded the sales business to beauty salons and hotels, founding the Estée Lauder Company in 1946 with $50,000. The first Estée Lauder brand products were Super Rich All Purpose Crème, Crème Pack, Cleansing Oil, and Skin Lotion. In 1948, her talent for sales led to a counter at Saks Fifth Avenue, then to Nieman Marcus in 1950, and thereafter to contracts with other high-end department stores. The company's first international store counter was at Harrods in London in 1960, followed rapidly by contracts in Central America, Australia, France, Belgium, Germany, and Japan. Over the next three decades, the Lauder Companies expanded further by establishing their own **manufacturing** plants and research and development facilities, and finally establishing business contracts in the USSR (1973) and China (1993).

Specialty Niches

Capitalizing on the idea of product niches, Clinique was introduced in 1967 with its neutral green **packaging** and asexual advertising presentation; it became a favored choice among professional women. It was dermatologist tested, hypoallergenic, and fragrance free, which also appealed to the health-conscious clientele. The Prescriptives brand, using color authority and individualized products, followed in 1979. Tapping the interest in natural products, Origins Natural Resources, launched in 1990, touts "age-old remedies from nature" in skin care, makeup, and bath/body products. Because of its ownership of widely diverse cosmetics lines and brands, the Lauder corporate holdings have marketed across a range of clientele; many of their products, sold under various names, vary mainly in packaging, marketing focus and price, rather than ingredients. The Estée Lauder brand's main competitors seem to be product lines within the company's own holdings.

Company Legacies

Among the famous Lauder products are Youth Dew, a bath oil/skin perfume first introduced in 1953, and Aramis, a fragrance and grooming line for men, introduced in 1965. Besides Aramis, the Lauder company markets more than 70 fragrances, including White Linen (1978) and Beautiful (1985). Broad ranging acquisitions have followed in the last two decades as the company diversified its offerings in licensing ventures such as Thomas Hilfiger (1993) and online sales of its various brands and product lines beginning in 1996. Lauder continues to acquire high-end brands in specialty niches; M.A.C., the makeup artist brand in 1994–98 was followed by **Bobbi Brown** in 1997, **Aveda** (hair care) in 1997, Stila Cosmetics in 1999, and Jo Malone in 2000.

Today, the Estée Lauder brand is seen as a classic and continues to seek ways to lure the new under-40 clientele without alienating its loyal base. Besides acquiring high-end specialty niches, Lauder's tradition of sampling may also be accessing young women, inviting them to join the beauty routine culture of their elders. The company's skin care products continue to underpin the corporation's economic well-being. Marketing strategy follows Lauder's tradition of ground-breaking approaches and keeping up with the image of the times; it spends approximately $65 million per year on promotion.

The Estée Lauder Company surpassed $1 billion in sales in 1985, $2 billion in 1991, and $5 billion by 2003. In 2008, the company's global sales exceeded $6.4 billion annually; it controlled 45 percent of prestige cosmetics in the United States and nearly 20 percent in Europe and Australia. The Estée Lauder Company stock has been public since the year of Lauder's retirement in 1995; however, the Estée Lauder empire remains a family affair today, 77 percent run by direct descendants of Estée and Joseph Lauder. Lauder granddaughters Aerin and Jane are senior vice presidents of the Lauder and Clinique brands, respectively.

The Lauder empire continues to support many philanthropic organizations, including contributions to restoring the Palace of Versailles and building playgrounds in New York's Central Park. The company today declares that it conducts no animal testing on its products, unless required by law. It also maintains statements on global citizenship, reduction of the impact of product manufacturing on the environment, and its philanthropic interests.

At the same time, controversy has surrounded the company despite its philanthropic efforts. For example, during the Campaign for Safe Cosmetics in California in 2005, the company lobbied against efforts to implement a regulatory framework for the use of chemicals in beauty products that would require companies to report all toxic ingredients used in their products.

Further Reading: Begoun, Paula. *Don't Go to the Cosmetics Counter Without Me.* Seattle, WA: Beginning Press, 2003; Estée Lauder Company. http://www.elcompanies.com. (Accessed September 4, 2008); Gavenas, Mary Lisa. *Color Stories: Behind the Scenes of America's Billion-Dollar Beauty Industry.* New York: Simon & Schuster, 2002; King, Elizabeth. "Magna Cum Lauder." *Australian,* April 10, 2003. http://www.lexisnexis.com/us/lnacademic. (Accessed October 15, 2008); Peiss, Kathy. *Hope in a Jar: The Making of America's Beauty Culture.* New York: Metropolitan Books, 1998.

Christina Ashby-Martin

EXTREME MAKEOVER

Extreme Makeover (ABC, 2002–7) was a reality TV makeover program, where subjects who considered themselves to be ugly submitted a videotape that detailed their facial and bodily flaws in hopes of being flown to Hollywood for an extensive makeover. Because *Extreme Makeover* capitalized on rewarding those people whose stories of suffering and hardship were the bleakest, it has often been compared to *Queen for a Day,* a radio and TV program that began in the 1950s and featured ordinary housewives who had experienced financial hardships telling their sad stories in exchange for gifts and prizes.

The *extreme* of *Extreme Makeover* came from the fact that both male and female subjects received upward of 10 different plastic surgery procedures (including tummy tucks, breast enhancements, chin implants, facial recontouring, rhinoplasties, brow lifts, and face lifts), cosmetic dentistry, physical training, and hair and wardrobe restyling. All of these costly interventions were given to participants for free. During the course of their extreme **makeovers**, subjects experienced their transformations in isolation periods of roughly six to eight weeks, each episode ending with an elaborate reveal ceremony that reunited the makeover recipient with his or her always enthusiastic family and friends. Reveal moments were often staged as red-carpet events, and subjects frequently spoke of feeling like a celebrity.

Though all participants underwent major surgical procedures, screen time devoted to healing was relatively nonexistent. As a consequence, *Extreme Makeover* generated considerable attention, drawing criticism for its often gratuitous depiction of plastic surgery as virtually a pain-free, cost-free, and consequence-free aesthetic choice, here represented as a necessary form of wellness surgery. Recipients, roughly 75 percent of whom were women, spoke with gratitude about their makeovers, suggesting that they were now worthy of both love and heterosexual romance in ways that their former appearance (and consequent low self-esteem) had blocked.

The show on occasion also drew praise for the manner in which it allowed subjects to proactively claim conventional articulations of beauty and thus to capitalize on the cultural currency attaching to beautiful faces and bodies. Subjects on the show very often spoke of their transformations as the best thing they had ever experienced, a dream come true, or the release of a real self. Although these experiences have clearly been edited by the show's producers for dramatic effect, the feelings of joy and relief seemed to resonate with a wider viewing audience.

Extreme Makeover initially aired to high ratings and gave rise to two spin-off programs: *Extreme Makeover: Home Edition* and *Extreme Makeover: Wedding Edition,* both on ABC. *Extreme Makeover* also led the crest of other reality TV plastic surgery makeover programs, including *The Swan* (Fox), *I Want a Famous Face* (MTV), *Brand New You* (BBC), **Dr. 90210** (E!), and *Miami Slice* (Bravo). It continues to air in the United States on the Style Network as well as on cable outlets across the world in such countries as Australia, Spain, Bulgaria, Canada, Croatia, Mexico, Norway, and the Philippines.

Further Reading: Deery, June. "Trading Faces: The Makeover Show as Prime-Time 'Infomercial.'" *Feminist Media Studies,* 4 no. 2 (2004): 211–14; Heyes, Cressida J. "Cosmetic Surgery and the Televisual Makeover: A Foucauldian Feminist Reading." *Feminist Media Studies,* 7 no. 1 (2007): 17–32; Pitts-Taylor, Victoria. *Surgery Junkies: Wellness and Pathology in Cosmetic Culture.* New Brunswick, NJ: Rutgers, 2007; Weber, Brenda R. "Beauty, Desire, and Anxiety: The Economy of Sameness on ABC's *Extreme Makeover."* *Genders,* 41 (2005). http://www.genders.org.

Brenda R. Weber

F

FACTOR, MAX. *SEE* **MAX FACTOR**

FASHION MAGAZINES

Women the world over look to fashion magazines to guide them in their clothing, accessories, and makeup choices. Illustrated periodicals related to fashion and style began to circulate soon after the invention of the movable type press in the 15th century. Part gossip, part news, clothing was not the main focus of these pamphlets, but it was an important component that attracted women seeking to emulate the styles of the upper classes. By the 17th and 18th centuries, pamphlets depicting court fashions were common throughout France. It would not be until the mid 19th century that magazines devoted to fashion appeared. Early fashion magazines depicted haute couture coming out of Paris with illustrated plates. Some of the finest magazines featured hand-tinted lithographs. The drawback of this was twofold, however: First, the magazines took time to produce and even longer to distribute, often coming to subscribers several months or even years after the fashion originated. Second, the illustrations showed the ideal fashionable silhouette, often depicting anatomically impossible bodies. Early fashion magazines were published in gazette style as an inexpensive weekly newspaper. Colored plates could be included or could be purchased at an additional cost. Early catalogs also doubled as fashion magazines, **advertising** the latest styles and trends and detailing textiles, trims, and accessories.

The 19th Century

Some of the best known fashion magazines of the 19th century come from the United States. Being so far removed from Paris, fashionable American women were desperate to find out about the latest styles; *Godey's Lady's Book* was established in 1830 to fill that need. In addition to fashion illustrations, *Godey's Lady's Book* included poetry and current events articles as well as sheet music and patterns for needlework designs and clothing. Many thought that this magazine would not last to the end of its first year, but it continued to be a popular monthly source for fashion and other information for American woman until it stopped being published in 1878. *Godey's Lady's Book* was especially influential in the American South during the Civil War when the Confederate states were blockaded and cut off from the rest of the world. Women were known to walk miles to a friend or relative's house to look at an issue of *Godey's* that was many months out of date.

Harper's Bazaar

Harper's Bazaar was the first American magazine devoted specifically to fashion. It debuted in 1867 as a weekly gazette with a mix of fashion illustrations, colored plates, and reports on what society's elite was wearing. In 1901, *Harper's Bazaar* moved to a monthly magazine style. Early issues prominently featured the designs of Charles Fredrick Worth, an English designer working in Paris who has been called the father of haute couture. Paul Poiret, another extremely influential designer in the late 19th and early 20th centuries, knew the value of the American customer and appeared regularly in *Harper's Bazaar* and an upstart magazine called **Vogue**. *Harper's Bazaar* is still being published today and is still ranked among one of the best fashion magazines in the world. It is not only available in the United States, but rather has sister titles published throughout the world in such expectedly fashionable places like the United Kingdom, Hong Kong, Japan, Singapore, and Latin America; at the same time, the magazine publishes native-language versions in countries not known for being at the forefront of style such as Bulgaria, Kazakhstan, and the Czech Republic.

Vogue

Vogue is the single best-known fashion magazine title in the world. It was first produced as a weekly gazette in 1892. Originally, *Vogue* was akin to *Godey's Lady's Book* in that it contained not only fashion information and illustrations but book, theater, art, and music reviews, tips on etiquette, and reports on society. Like other magazines of the time, *Vogue* included clothing patterns and patterns for needlework and other handicrafts. But unlike many other gazettes, *Vogue* also included information about men and children's clothing, as well as reports on ready-made clothing found in various shops and tips for budget-minded consumers. In 1909, 17 years after the initial publication, *Vogue* was bought by Condé Montrose Nast, a lawyer and publicist from St. Louis, Missouri. Although *Vogue* was still successful, despite being neglected by the previous owners, Nast sought to create a magazine that would be the premier source for fashion and society news. In today's market, *Vogue,* and its Web presence www.style.com, is the most trusted source for fashion, but also has a strong impact on journalism and culture in general. *Vogue* is published around the world and includes many imprints such as *Teen Vogue, British Vogue, Vogue China*, and *Vogue Italia,* along with versions for Australia, Portugal, Japan, Switzerland, Mexico, Russia, and many others. *Vogue* also offers **men's magazines:** *Men's Vogue* in the United States, *Vogue Hommes International* out of Paris, and *L'uomo Vogue* in Italy. *Vogue* produces home and decorative style versions of its magazine. *Vogue Patterns* is no longer owned by the parent company, but is licensed to Butterick, which once ran its own fashion magazine called *The Delineator: A Journal of Fashion, Culture, and Fine Arts,* published from 1873–1937.

Lasting Trends

As fashion magazines began to crop up all over, various titles sought to establish themselves in their own niche. *Vogue* made itself fashion forward and avant-garde, often employing highly artistic and often scandalous photo layouts. The photography of Annie Leibovitz is renowned for being beautiful and sensational. Other magazines have not been so lucky. Former *Vogue* editor Grace Mirabella founded her own fashion magazine called *Mirabella*. It was intended to be a less opulent, less elitist magazine targeted toward the average smart woman. Lasting from 1989 until 2000, *Mirabella* lost ground to other titles such as *Elle,* which targeted the same demographic and was published by the same parent company. With the launch of Oprah Winfrey's *O* magazine, *Mirabella* officially ceased production. Before closing, *Mirabella* had suffered a loss of consumer confidence and became the target of media ridicule.

Elle, on the other hand, took a more lighthearted approach to fashion and style, but without seeming frivolous. Focusing on college-aged and young career women with attention not only to fashion but also to health and entertainment, *Elle* secured its niche. Begun in Paris in 1945, *Elle* was a breath of fresh air for the war-ravaged country and ordinary women were drawn to it. *Elle* expanded into an American production in 1985, with native-language versions in Brazil, China, Korea, Norway, Italy, and many other countries. In today's market, *Elle* is considered second only to *Vogue.*

Like *Mirabella, Mademoiselle* began to lose its edge in the 21st century. Founded in 1935, *Mademoiselle* featured short stories and articles as well as fashion, but it was not able to keep up with the ever-changing youthful style and shuttered production in 2001. The employees and features were absorbed by *Glamour,* a title published by *Vogue*'s Condé Nast. *Glamour* focuses not only on fashion and makeup, but also on celebrity style and news. *Marie Claire* is experiencing a renaissance of interest among young customers. With a focus on lifestyle as well as fashion, this publication is gaining a larger following among college-aged women who want a magazine that speaks to them and does not take itself too seriously.

The merging of lifestyle and fashion is a major trend in women's magazines. **Cosmopolitan** is the best known of these hybrids, offering health tips, high fashion layouts, and sexual advice. *Cosmopolitan* is owned by the Hearst Corporation, the same parent company as *Redbook, Marie Claire, Town and Country, Good Housekeeping,* and *Harper's Bazaar.* Each of these titles covers a separate age group and interest market, tackling topics as diverse as high fashion and homemaking. Very small niche magazines are also popular, such as *FRUiTS,* which solely covers the youth style in the Harajuku district of Japan. Oprah Winfrey's *O* strives to recreate her television show in print, where she talks about health, celebrity news, current events, and style, and to reach a diverse market of women young and old, single and married, career women and homemakers. This broad appeal makes *O* unique in the fashion magazine world, but its connection to an international icon creates an almost entirely new subgenre. No other magazine has managed to incorporate all of these elements into one successful magazine. Without Oprah Winfrey's driving force, it might not be possible.

The new frontier of all magazines, fashion or otherwise, is the **Internet**. Companies are faced with the dilemma of how to allocate money, features, and other resources between their print and online divisions. All major magazines have Web sites to support their product and promote subscriptions. Many magazines also carry blogs and special features not available in the magazine. Subscribers are often given special access to these features, to help bridge the audience gap between magazine subscribers and those interested in online content. To keep an edge in an ever-changing market, fashion magazines need to be able to compete in an online arena.

When fashion magazines first became available, information could take months or even years to reach the consumer. In the 21st century, fashion information can be instantaneously uploaded to a blog, a Web site, or YouTube. Before the fashion show is even over, images of the first pieces can be seen and commented on by millions. Many popular magazines that have lost revenue and closed since the turn of the 21st century have failed because they could not negotiate the ever-changing face of the fashion magazine market. Only those publications that can stay nimble and current and navigate this new fashion world will succeed.

Further Reading: Angeletti, Norberto, and Alberto Olivia. *In Vogue: The Illustrated History of the World's Most Famous Fashion Magazine.* New York: Rizzoli International Publications, 2006; National Cloak and Suit Co. *Women's Fashions of the Early 1900s: An Unabridged Republication of New York Fashions, 1909.* Mineola, NY: Dover Publications, 1992; Tortora, Phyllis, and Keith Eubank. *Survey of Historic Costume: A History of Western Dress,* 3rd ed. New York: Fairchild Publications, 2005.

Sara M. Harvey

FAT FARMS

Fat farms are weight loss retreats/**spas** that put participants through rigorous fitness regimens in order to lose weight rapidly. They work by combining bootcamp-style fitness with starvation-level nutrition and use controversial treatments such as colonics. These farms originally catered to wealthy women, often celebrities, who wanted to lose weight quickly for a movie role or for an event such as a wedding. Over time, the trend filtered down to the upper and middle classes of women who could both afford the high-priced retreats and had the time to devote to them. Fat farms provided short-term weight loss, but upon returning to one's regular lifestyle, weight was often regained. By the 1970s, fat farms were no longer as popular due to an increasing focus on healthy diets and long-term weight management rather than rapid weight loss.

Similarly, in the '60s and '70s, children's fat camps began to be popular. Since the 1920s, society began to focus more on beauty than on health. Young girls wanted to become fashionably thin and were frequent fat campers. Like fat farms for adults, these camps had very restrictive diets. With the emergence of second-wave **feminism**, fat camps became less popular. Mothers and other women who were influential in children's lives began encouraging girls to focus on what they could do with their lives rather than on how they looked. Additionally, like fat farms, most campers quickly regained the weight when they returned to their everyday lives.

Today's fat camps and the more appropriately named weight loss spas focus more on teaching young people and adults healthy life habits that promote weight loss and healthy weight management. These healthy life habits include a more scientific approach to eating in which one focuses on the body's needs and combines healthy eating with a more active lifestyle.

Further Reading: Fat Camps? http://www.fatcampsinfo.com/history_of_fat_camps.html; Green Mountain at Fox Run. http://www.fitwoman.com/fat-farm.htm.

Krystal A. Humphreys

FEMINISM

Though the beauty industry is largely a product of the 20th century, since its advent, it has become a major point of contention and debate among feminists. Interestingly, the key to the growth of the American beauty industry has been the involvement of women as consumers, creators, and icons. As **Naomi Wolf** demonstrated in her 1991 book *The Beauty Myth,* however, the influence of the beauty industry on its consumers has been directly connected to the social construction of ideal beauty as the purpose of womanhood. Following the influence of American theater makeup, as well as the rise of photography, American women increasingly sought an ideal appearance through **cosmetics**. Female leadership in the cosmetics industry was central to the success of the business, because women centered consumerism on other women in a search for ideal beauty. As historian Kathy Peiss explained, women in the early beauty industry reacted to the lack of access to **retail** markets for women by turning to home-based methods such as demonstrations and door-to-door sales in order to cater to female customers. This method of direct marketing gave women such as **Madam C. J. Walker** and **Helena Rubinstein** access to wealth and market power traditionally denied to women. The beauty industry quickly transformed from a face paint mixed by a druggist to a cultural rite of passage for American girls. Through the 1940s and 1950s, the rise of **advertising** and mass media meant uncontrolled growth in the beauty industry. What started as a cottage industry became a symbol of cultural and national identity, attached frequently to notions of success, freedom, acceptability, and modernity.

That the beauty industry was created and maintained by women is clear. For feminists, however, the question is whether the beauty industry is a harmful, objectifying creation or a source of strength and independence for women. This beauty dilemma is one of the most contentious debates in American feminisms. Feminist opinions about the beauty industry, however, are as varied as feminism itself. Feminisms prevalent in the 1960s, such as radical feminism and liberal feminism, were critical of the beauty industry and its reliance on patriarchal definitions of beauty. In the 1980s, the key debate among feminists was about the history and rationale of the beauty industry as a path to independence for women, while the 1990s beauty dilemma was marked by a debate among feminists about the cultural role that beauty media played in America. Twenty-first-century feminisms—including third-wave, postmodern feminisms, and the debates about body led by transgender and fat activists—continue to bring up a myriad of issues related

"OUR BODIES MAKE US WORRY"

Graffiti painted on a Cornell University building, 1995.

Source: Brumberg, Joan Jacobs. *The Body Project: An Intimate History of American Girls.* New York: Random House, 1997, Photo Insert 60.

to the beauty industry. In each of these phases, there was also concentration on the collusion of the beauty industry and racism. Authors including bell hooks, Maxine Hong Kingston, and Toni Morrison have written on the interlocking aspects of race, beauty, and the middle-class white paradigm of the beauty industry. Throughout these growing debates about the power of the beauty industry, the industry itself has grown to include over one billion dollars in profits annually in the United States alone.

Often termed *second wave,* the feminists in the 1960s and 1970s saw the beauty industry as a challenge to sex equality. Of particular interest to second-wave feminists was the power of the beauty industry to hold women to patriarchal standards of sexuality and acceptability. Betty Friedan, founding president of the National Organization for Women, wrote in her groundbreaking 1963 book *The Feminine Mystique,* that the beauty industry used advertisements to oppress women by perpetuating stereotypical myths about appearance and sex appeal. Feminist leaders increasingly called on American women to refuse to wear makeup, perfume, or brassieres in an attempt to highlight the ways in which the beauty industry was holding women hostage to beauty, and to an untenable patriarchal system that demanded women be attractive before they could be successful. At the same time, the *black is beautiful* movement developed as part of civil rights activism in the United States, encouraging black American women to stop straightening their hair, wearing makeup, and lightening their skin. The result was a schism in the women's movement of the 1960s and 1970s. While radical feminists protested **beauty pageants**, liberal feminists increasingly saw cosmetics and fashion as essential to women's success in the workplace. Black American feminists embracing the black is beautiful movement were increasingly stereotyped as radicals of the civil rights movement, and in many ways excluded from feminist movements. It has been noted that radical feminists were portrayed as an unfeminine fringe that marginalized activists and reinforced beauty industry standards. Liberal feminists such as Gloria Steinem and Betty Friedan, for example, sought advertising investments from cosmetics companies for the magazine *Ms.* (founded in 1972) under the argument that that tactful advertisements from companies founded and owned by women were inherently feminist. The marginalization of radical feminists led to the creation of a modern lesbian rights movement in the United States, but the stereotype of radical feminists as unattractive and unfeminine (and possibly lesbian) became part of the American social system.

By the end of the 1970s and the early 1980s, feminism began to shift considerably. Powerful women in the United States and abroad emerged on the international stage, and these women were powerful with cosmetics and while attractive. Feminist women of color, however, argued that attractiveness was still being measured in white, middle-class terms. In particular, the acceptability of black women with braids, Afros, or other nonwhite **hairstyles** led to a renewed culture war over beauty and hair. It has been noted that this debate was so rancorous that schools across the country banned inappropriate hairstyles such as cornrows and dreadlocks. Oprah Winfrey, who made her network television debut in 1986, devoted an entire program to the debate about hair and discussed her own decisions to straighten her hair—it would become a recurring theme on the program. Meanwhile, as radical white feminists continued to argue that the beauty industry was inherently oppressive, other white feminists rationalized the beauty industry as a form of women's empowerment. Feminists, wrote Rita Freedman in her 1985 book *Beauty Bound,* should "regard looking pretty as part of the feminist mandate to project confidence, to utilize assets, and to feel good about oneself" (231). These feminists argued that the tools offered by the beauty industry were to be used as a path to power, not seen as a tool of oppression to be refused. Despite these many debates about the beauty industry in feminist circles, the industry grew exponentially in the 1980s.

The 1990s saw a major revival of interest in the beauty industry among white American feminists. This revival was caused by the publication of two books: Naomi Wolf's *The Beauty Myth* (1991) and Camille Paglia's *Sexual Personae* (1991). Wolf and Paglia, both feminists who attended Yale University, presented two completely different views of the power of the beauty industry. In *The Beauty Myth,* Wolf argued that the entire notion that beauty equaled liberation was false and constructed by the industry itself as a marketing tool. According to Wolf, the beauty industry co-opted second-wave feminism by convincing women that attractiveness and stereotypical beauty were the path to liberation. Paglia, however, presented an entirely different view of the beauty industry. In *Sexual Personae,* she argued that human history was the story of men's drive to control nature—which Paglia stated was inherently feminine. According to Paglia, the result was that the whole of Western civilization was the result of men's control of women's nature. Wolf and Paglia were almost immediately juxtaposed in the American press, and their inflammatory debate splashed across the American media. Paglia stated that Wolf "owed everything to the hair," while Wolf referred to Paglia as "the most dutiful of patriarchal daughters."

Though the debate between Wolf and Paglia caught the attention of the media, and of many white feminists, for feminist women of color the debates about the beauty industry continued to expand. Black American writers and activists such as Angela Davis and bell hooks increasingly sought to critique the role of the beauty industry in reifying racism and the fetishism of women of color. Hooks, in her essay "Selling Hot Pussy" (1992) criticized the beauty industry for its reliance on women of color that conformed to white beauty standards in features such as straight hair and lighter skin. At the same time, women of color attacked the continued distortion of Asian, indigenous, and biracial women in the beauty industry. Feminist scholars Elaine Kim and Yen Le Espiritu wrote strident critiques of Asian women as exotic others in beauty media, and specifically on the portrayal of Asian women in beauty media as either promiscuous "dragon ladies" or chaste and diminutive "china dolls." Paula Gunn Allen's *The Sacred Hoop* (1992) explored the history of colonization among indigenous women and positioned the beauty industry as a part of the continued oppression of native women by the myths of colonialism.

The debates about beauty, sexuality, and feminism that ignited in the 1990s led to new forms of feminism in the 21st century. Led by the zine revolution and popular press magazines such as *Bust* and *Bitch,* third-wave feminists believe strongly that the use of cosmetics, fragrances, or fashion can be separated from individual identity. Third-wave feminism is especially influenced by transgender activism and activists who trouble the very notion of the beauty industry as a feminine industry. Multicultural feminism, which continues to develop as a critique of white feminism, relies on the work of hooks, Allen, and others to build an inclusive critique of racism in beauty media. Another growing field of feminism in the 21st century is fat-positive feminism. Fat-positive feminists focus on the beauty industry as a system that portrays fatness as inherently ugly and unattractive, therefore creating an unrealistic and oppressive stereotype for women. Between and among these feminisms are women and girls themselves, who have highly individual opinions about the body, attractiveness, and the beauty industry.

The beauty industry is more prevalent in the lives of 21st century Americans than ever before. From advertising, to television series such as **Extreme Makeover** and *Tim Gunn's Guide to Style,* to the rise of celebrity in American culture, Americans are more aware of beauty standards, products, and stereotypes than ever before. That feminists will have something to say about beauty in the 21st century is certain. What those feminists will say, however, is as varied as the people who shop in the beauty aisle.

Further Reading: Baumgardner, Jennifer, and Amy Richards. *Manifesta: Young Women, Feminism, and the Future.* New York: Farrar, Straus and Giroux, 2000; Cheng, Anne Anlin. "Wounded Beauty: An Exploratory Essay on Race, Feminism, and the Aesthetic Question." *Tulsa Studies in Women's Literature,* 19 no. 2 (2000): 191–217; Davis, Flora. *Moving the Mountain: The Women's Movement in America since 1960.* New York: Simon & Schuster, 1991; Espiritu, Yen Le. *Asian American Women and Men: Labor, Laws, and Love.* New York: Rowman and Littlefield, 2007; Freedman, Rita. *Beauty Bound.* Lexington, MA: Lexington Books, 1986; Friedan, Betty. *The Feminine Mystique.* New York: Dell, 1963; hooks, bell. "Selling Hot Pussy: Representations of Black Female Sexuality in the Cultural Marketplace." In *Black Looks: Race and Representation,* pp. 61–77. Cambridge, MA: South End Press, 1992; Kolmar, Wendy K., and Frances Bartkowski. *Feminist Theory: A Reader,* 2nd ed. Boston: McGraw Hill, 2005; Paglia, Camille. *Sexual Personae: Art and Decadence from Nefertiti to Emily Dickinson.* New York: Vintage, 1991; Peiss, Kathy. *Hope in a Jar: The Making of America's Beauty Culture.* New York: Metropolitan Books, 1998; Wann, Marilyn. *FAT! SO?: Because You Don't Have to Apologize for Your Size.* San Francisco, CA: Ten Speed Press, 1999; Wolf, Naomi. *The Beauty Myth: How Images of Beauty are Used against Women.* New York: Harper, 1991.

Amber R. Clifford

FDA. *SEE* **U.S. FOOD AND DRUG ADMINISTRATION.**

FILM

The world of makeup was transformed by the rise of film as popular entertainment. The original black and white films presented actors with stark, dramatically emphasized faces, using the same techniques and makeup made popular on the live stage. With black and white, the vivid contrast between dark and light, shadow and radiance helped to sharpen actors' features, to heighten their facial expressions, and to whitewash any number of flaws through the thick cover of blue- or green-tinted makeup. As early black and white film stock did not register a wide range of colors—the red spectrum, for example, often appeared black and dark grey on film—actors, who often applied their own makeup for scenes, compensated by using green- and blue-toned makeup to bring a more natural appearance to their albeit shades of grey complexions. With the introduction of Technicolor and panchromatic film, the world of cinema opened itself to a rainbow of colors and makeup techniques and film **cosmetics** were allowed a new palette of shades and hues with which to experiment.

Max Factor

One of the first makeup artists to experiment successfully with the wide range of colors now available to costume **designers** and cosmeticians, **Max Factor** is known for having revolutionized movie makeup. Working skillfully with different combinations of chemicals and even inventing his own line of products designed at first for film but later marketed to a wider public, Max Factor changed the ways in which film, cosmetics, and the skillful application of powder, rouge, and lipstick could transform a woman into a screen siren. He is credited with coining the term *makeup,* based on the phrase "to make up one's face." Born in Poland, Max Factor was apprenticed to a pharmacist at the age of eight and soon discovered he had an extraordinary talent for understanding the chemistry of cosmetics. He was discovered in Moscow, where he opened a store in the suburbs and was subsequently appointed the official cosmetician to the Russian Royal ballet. Max Factor and his family immigrated to the United States in 1904. At the St. Louis World Fair in 1904, Max Factor found his first public by selling the rouges and creams he had developed earlier in Russia. In 1914, he developed a foundation for actors that would not crack, cake, or crepe under the harsh studio lights and he became a highly sought-after makeup artist in the film industry soon afterward. His makeup was a thinner greasepaint made in 12 shades in cream form and packaged in jars, unlike the thick stick greasepaints used in the theater. His makeup technique was dramatic but real, beautiful but natural. He enhanced the best features of the face while keeping women unique, interesting, and strong.

During the 1920s and 1930s, the golden years of filmmaking, Max Factor became intimately associated with the world of movie stars. He worked with iconic beauties such as Claudette Colbert, Judy Garland, Joan Crawford, Bette Davis, and Jean Harlow. Max Factor invented some of the most influential and iconic looks for actresses—he created the first false eyelashes for silent film star Phyllis Haver; rosebud lips and the Cupid's bow lip style in the 1920s; and the hunter's bow lips for Joan Crawford in the 1930s. Max Factor was not only a skilled chemist, a makeup artist, and a charismatic character; he was also a savvy businessman. He maximized his relationship with the most popular movie stars of the day, achieving celebrity status by making up celebrities. His close and intimate friendships with the movers and shakers at the movie studios allowed him to make cameo appearances in some of the most popular films of the day. His move from behind the scenes to the maximum visibility in front of the camera made him a familiar brand name, brought him a new marketability, and introduced him to a plethora of celebrities who could endorse and help him sell his cosmetic breakthroughs. Many of Max Factor's celebrity clients appeared, at no cost, in beautiful full-page, color magazine ads to promote Max Factor cosmetics.

Max Factor became a household name because he brought glamour and beauty to the stars—and he understood that if he marketed his own line of products, he could convince the wider public that he could do the same for them. His numerous cosmetic innovations were often created for the screen first, firsthand testimony to their efficacy, before they were introduced to the public. Some of his inventions included the first motion picture makeup in 1914; lip gloss, originally developed for the screen, in 1932; Pan-Cake Makeup, forerunner of all modern cake makeups, in 1937; Tru Color Lipstick, the first smear-proof lipstick in 1940; Pan-Stik Makeup in 1948; Erace, the original cover-up cosmetic, in 1954; and the first waterproof makeup in 1971. Max Factor was the first to realize the lengths to which women would go to emulate their favorite divas. He marketed his products not only to flatter individual stars, for example, in creating shades specifically for the actresses: Platinum for Jean Harlow, Special Medium for Joan Crawford, and Dark for Claudette Colbert; but he also allowed the average woman to identify with and ultimately purchase the desired look of her idol. He developed the color harmony principles of makeup—enticing millions of women to have their colors done to enhance natural hair, eye, and skin coloring with complementary makeup colors. In 1935, he opened the Max Factor Makeup Salon in Los Angeles, bringing movie magic into the reality of the everyday world. One did not have to be an actress to have access to Max Factor's expertise; one just needed an appointment. Max Factor & Company became a multigenerational, international cosmetics giant before it was sold for $500 million dollars in 1973.

Movie Studios

Certainly, the popularity of the moving pictures brought a new form of celebrity to the wider public. Actors and actresses who make film so varied, interesting, and entertaining became the new idols and icons for the masses. The increasing availability and accessibility of the cinema meant that singular models of beauty and aesthetics were becoming more standardized, more uniform, more hegemonic as larger and larger audiences were bombarded with examples of what beauty looked like. Movie studios took great care in choosing and grooming their actors and actresses—studios often had direct and final control over the creation of the image and reputation of its corps of actors. Studios changed the names of their young stars, required them to conform to rigorous diets and exercise regimes, even physically changed their appearances in order to make them more attractive, more appealing, and in many ways, more mainstream to their mainstream audiences. The young actress Judy Garland, for example, was forced to take a variety of drugs, including amphetamines, to attain and maintain the more svelte and streamlined figure popular at the time. For the film *Meet Me in St. Louis* (1944), director Vincente Minelli requested that makeup artist Dorothy Ponedel beautify Garland for the movie. Ponedel took dramatic measures to refine Garland's features, including extending and reshaping her eyebrows, changing her hairline through plucking, modifying her lip line, and removing her nose discs (rubberized disks used to reshape the nose). Movie studios implicitly understood the impact of beauty on their viewing public and spent copious amounts of money to keep Hollywood beautiful.

Stars and Celebrities

The influence of movie stars and celebrities on the definitions of beauty and glamour are undeniable. Marlene Dietrich sold her beauty secrets by endorsing Lux Soap and Woodbury Cold Cream. Audrey Hepburn became the picture of elegance, and women wanted to emulate her Givenchy-garbed gamine beauty. Elizabeth Taylor helped to popularize the extended lash line of the Cleopatra cat-eye. Sophia Loren brought a new, raw sexuality and sensuality to the voluptuous hourglass figure and brunette became the new sexy. Bo Derek made braids alluring when she stepped out of the ocean onto the beach to the delight of Dudley Moore. Julia Roberts revitalized hooker chic when she played a prostitute with a heart of gold, complete with a fashion montage. Most recently, the onslaught of incredibly skinny, lollipop-headed (so called because their heads appear so big on their thin-as-stick bodies) actresses, on average a size 0 or a size 2, has made the diet and fitness industry one of the fastest and most profitable enterprises in the modern period. The glamorous, but ultimately unrealistic, images presented on film often have a negative impact. Women are especially affected by this phenomenon as the model of beauty does not reflect the average appearance of women in society. Since the 1960s, the number of cases of eating disorders among girls under the age of 10 has doubled. New studies show that more than 80 percent of 10-year-old girls have already dieted.

Beauty Space and Culture

Film has the power to transport and transform the viewer—often by reflecting the very intimacy and power of space and community. The 1980s and 1990s saw the popularity of films that not only put beauty on screen but also put the making of beauty, the unifying cultural space of beauty parlors and barbershops, directly into the language of popular media. With films like Herbert Ross's *Steel Magnolias* (1989), which framed the relationship between a mother and daughter within a larger family of strong, independent southern women whose sharp, cutting, and caring repartee permeated the local beauty shop, and Rob Lekutic's hit *Legally Blonde* (2001), in which Reese Witherspoon's Elle Woods's friendship with a manicurist and her extensive firsthand knowledge of beauty salon techniques give her the winning edge in the difficult defense of a fellow sorority sister accused of murder—beauty parlors, the friendships made within them, the relationships occasioned by this public yet intimate space came to the forefront of American cinema. In 2002, Tim Story brought another dimension to the depiction of space and community in his film, *Barber Shop,* by placing his story about brotherhood, economics, racism, and community squarely in an African American barbershop. For the men and women in the movie, the barbershop represented a gathering place, an intimate space, a safe domain in which the elements of home and community could be combined. In 2005, Billie Woodruff directed *Beauty Shop,* a film headed by Queen Latifah, who played a woman who finds independence, respect, and her own voice in the ownership of her own beauty parlor. In a film that celebrates girl power and the strength that feeling confident and looking good can offer, the beauty parlor itself, the very space, becomes its own living and breathing character—providing a place for diversity, racial harmony, economic opportunity, and the appreciation of individual beauty.

Often, film describes an idealized beauty, space, and community, but it may do so by making promises it cannot keep. Some of the most evocative films describe the fairy godmother–like transformations of women, from ignorance to knowledge, from frumpy to beautiful, from abhorred to desired, all in under two hours and all for the price of admission. Most recently, the very popular *Princess Diaries* performs the ultimate makeover on a young woman who is deemed a nerd because of her bad hair and glasses. Several makeup artists, a temperamental hairstylist, contact lenses, and a few spa treatments later, Hollywood transforms Anne Hathaway, and she is instantly depicted as beautiful, poised, elegant—the lost princess. From the Disney cartoon, *Cinderella,* where the fairy godmother bibbidy-bobbidy-boos the poor Cinderella from servant girl to unrecognizable princess save for her glass slipper; to *My Fair Lady* where Eliza Doolittle is transformed from curbstone flower girl to Hungarian princess; to *Pretty Woman* where Julia Roberts goes from hooking on Hollywood Boulevard to crying tears of joy at the opening of the San Francisco opera in a red Eugene Alexander designer gown and $250,000 ruby and diamond jewels—film has offered women the ultimate makeover.

See also: Barbers and Barbershops; Makeup Artists, Celebrity

Further Reading: Basinger, Jeanine. *The Star Machine.* New York: Knopf, 2007; Basten, Fred E. *Max Factor: The Man Who Changed the Faces of the World.* New York: Arcade Publishing, 2008; Basten, Fred E., Robert Salvatore, and Paul Kaufman. *Max Factor's Hollywood: Glamour, Movies, Make-Up.* Toronto: Stoddart, 1995; Frank, Gerald. *Judy.* Da Capo Press, 1999; Gomery, Douglas. *Shared Pleasures: A History of Movie Presentation in the United States.* Madison: University of Wisconsin, 1992; Hozic, Aida. *Hollyworld: Space, Power and Fantasy in the American Economy.* Ithaca, NY: Cornell University Press, 2002; Jewell, Richard. *The Golden Age of Cinema: Hollywood, 1929–1945.* Malden, MA: Blackwell, 2007; Riordan, Teresa. *Inventing Beauty: A History of the Innovations that Have*

Made Us Beautiful. New York: Broadway, 2004; Sennett, Robert. *Hollywood Hoopla: Creating Stars and Selling Movies in the Golden Age of Hollywood.* New York: Watson-Guptill, 1999; Stokes, Melvin and Richard Maltby, ed. *Hollywood Abroad: Audiences and Cultural Exchange.* London: British Film Institute, 2008.

Aliza S. Wong

FOCUS GROUPS

Many beauty industry manufacturers and distributors use focus groups to help determine whether their product is appealing, delivers its intended material, and elicits the desired consumer response. Such groups help the maker determine whether they have gotten it right. While some may be volunteer groups assembled through **advertising**, others are paid as test groups of regular women or men.

Many industry experts know the marketing value of connecting with their consumer directly and emotionally; if they do not, the potential client will not buy or continue buying their products. Many efforts of the beauty industry involve the direct marketing of perceptions; therefore, focus groups are essential whenever a company decides to update or change a product with which consumers are familiar, or to market a new product line. These groups can save manufacturers millions of dollars in wasted effort or failed product lines.

Beauty companies often conduct multiple focus groups in varied locations and varied climates to ensure the diversity of the population and conditions under which their product is being tested. Through these diverse groups, the company may be able to fine-tune its targeted audience and advertisement campaigns. **Packaging** changes are one area where focus groups are especially important; changing company logos or familiar package shapes and colors can be disastrous if the consumer no longer recognizes the product and feels more comfortable staying with her favorite.

Focus groups are also used within the industry, or by outsiders, to access information on how the industry is affecting people's lives. They can be used to determine health risks, facility usage, diversity, and psychological effects, among many other topics. Marketers, lobbyists, industry interest groups, and health professionals may all use focus groups as a way to build informational databases on various aspects of the beauty industry. The information may determine the future directions of product ingredients, specialty consumers, safety, and product trends.

Some groups masquerading as focus groups are actually product demonstrations or sales meetings that may be gathering product/consumer information, but whose main purpose is actually to directly sell the product at that time.

Further Reading: Beyer, Alisa Marie. "Marketing Matters: The Beauty of Focus Groups." *GCI Magazine,* January 10, 2008. http://www.gcimagazine.com; Gavenas, Mary Lisa. *Color Stories: Behind the Scenes of America's Billion-Dollar Beauty Industry.* New York: Simon & Schuster, 2002; Lieberman, Alexis, and Diana Harris. "Acknowledging Adult Bias." *Health Promotion Practice,* September 15, 2006. http://hpp.sagepub.com/cgi/content/absttract/8/2/205. (Accessed May 19, 2009).

Christina Ashby-Martin

G

GENTLEMEN'S QUARTERLY (GQ)

Gentlemen's Quarterly (GQ) has been in existence for more than half a century. The magazine, originally owned by the publishers of *Esquire* (f. 1933) was launched in 1957, under the editorial direction of Everett Mattlin. This new publication, an upmarket venture intended to whet the consumer appetites of fashion-conscious men of style and provide a broad range of lifestyle advice to its decidedly prosperous readers, emerged out of some specific developments dating back to the 1920s and 1930s.

The first of these related to the creation of trade magazines, one of which lent *Gentlemen's Quarterly* its title, that provided retailers with pictures and descriptions of the latest trends in American menswear. These publications, which had other evocative titles like *Club and Campus, The Etonian,* and *Gifts for a Gentleman,* were fairly straightforward ventures intended to help retailers generate consumer interest in men's suits, shirts, and hats. The other development occurred in 1931, when the publishers David Smart and William Hobart Weintraub, along with the editor Arnold Gingrich (the founders of *Esquire*) launched *Apparel Arts*—a quarterly journal similar in form to *Fortune,* created by Henry Luce in 1930, and the direct and immediate predecessor to *Gentlemen's Quarterly*—that included not only fashion features but some editorial items, mostly related to men's style and the clothing trade. After Smart, Weintraub, and Gingrich launched *Esquire* in 1933, *Apparel Arts* continued to be published as a fashion supplement directed primarily at men's **retail** stores until it was replaced by *Gentlemen's Quarterly* in 1957.

The title *Gentlemen's Quarterly* first appeared, alongside that of *Apparel Arts,* on the cover of the summer 1957 issue. The magazine's shift in focus was reflected more precisely in its new subtitle, "The Fashion Magazine for Men," which replaced the more market-oriented "The Fashion Magazine for Men's Stores" and hinted at the projected broader appeal of the new publication. The abbreviated version of the title, *GQ,* by which the magazine is now formally known, first appeared on the cover of the fall 1957 issue. In its first few years, *GQ* remained primarily concerned with reporting recent fashion trends and bringing style to its readers. By the early 1960s, however, the magazine's focus began to shift, with an increased amount of emphasis on lifestyle issues: features on travel, **film**, interior decorating, college life, and automobiles, as well as fiction by established and emerging authors became standard fare for the magazine's upmarket subscribers. By the 1960s, the magazine departed from an exclusive reliance on models wearing the most recent trends for cover images and began to publish photographic portraits of celebrities from the world of theater, film, television, and politics, including President John F. Kennedy (March 1962).

Despite these nods in the direction of lifestyle writing, the magazine remained primarily devoted to fashion through the 1970s. Under the leadership of S. I. Newhouse Jr., the publishing conglomerate Condé Nast acquired *GQ* from *Esquire* in the early 1980s, a move that ultimately led to an intense competition for readers between the two publications. With Art Cooper at the editorial helm from 1983 until 2003, *GQ* was transformed into a general men's magazine, focusing on celebrity and political journalism, food and diet features, and financial advice for an affluent readership in the age range of 25–39 years. It was during this period, as well, that *GQ* went international, launching a United Kingdom edition in 1988.

By the 1990s, *GQ,* as one of the venerable old-timers of the men's magazine market, faced increasing competition from young upstarts like *FHM* (f. 1985), *Maxim* (f. 1995), and *Details* (f. 2000), all of which promulgated a more irreverent, hipper, and youthful style of masculinity and relied, increasingly, on images of scantily clad women to draw in readers who identified themselves as heterosexuals and who also happened to be interested in fashion and men's lifestyle issues. Under the editorial leadership of Jim Nelson, who replaced Cooper in 2003, the magazine has shifted its focus once again to younger readers (18–30 years old) with an interest in both a more informal, man-on-the street style of dress, an edgier aesthetic, and an emphasis on popular culture, including a heavy dose of material on female celebrities. These changes have led to an increase in readership, with subscriptions approaching one million and a general readership somewhere between four and five million. The magazine has also gone digital with www.gq.com where up-to-date features on fashion and grooming; stories on celebrities, sex, sports, and cars; and images of beautiful women are a click away for subscribers.

See also: Magazines, Men's; *Men's Health*; Metrosexuals

Further Reading: Benwell, Bethan. *Masculinity and Men's Lifestyle Magazines.* Oxford: Blackwell, 2003; Collier, Richard. "The New Man: Fact or Fad?" *Achilles Heel: The Radical Men's Magazine,* 14 (Winter 1992/1993). http://www.achillesheel.freeuk.com/article14_9.html; Jackson, Peter, Nick Stevenson, and Kate Brooks. *Making Sense of Men's Magazines.* Cambridge: Polity Press, 2001; Law, Cheryl, and Magdala Peixoto Labre. "Cultural Standards of Attractiveness: A Thirty-Year Look at Changes in Male Images in Magazines." *Journalism and Mass Communications Quarterly,* 79 no. 3 (2002): 697–711.

Paul R. Deslandes

GLOBAL MARKETS, U.S. TRENDS IN

Since the international fanfare of **Max Factor** and movie makeup in the 1920s and '30s and the early global growth of beauty giant **Avon** in the 1950s, the American beauty industry has become one of the pioneering leaders in the international **cosmetics** market. From the early 1920s, **Max Factor** understood the importance of selling an international image to a larger global market, and to that end, Max Factor demonstrated his genius by using his cinematic connections and close relationships with actresses while he applied their makeup for filming. He named certain products after specific international beauty icons, and asked them for their endorsements. At a time when the cinema served as the conduit between continents and cultures, Max Factor hit upon the most widely recognized faces and used them as a marketing tool for his products. By 1949, Max Factor had convinced Mexican-born Hollywood actor Ricardo Montalban to serve as one of his spokespeople as the line broke into the Spanish-speaking markets.

An American Look

As the cosmetics industry continued to grow, companies such as **Avon** recognized not only the utility and marketability of certain stars' looks, but also of wider cultural/ethnic/national sensibilities. The selling of a

Vietnamese hairdresser trainee practices using a mannequin head in front of a hair salon in Hanoi, Vietnam, 2009. (AP Photo/Chitose Suzuki)

stereotypical American fresh-facedness, of naiveté, hope, and freedom became attractive in the post–World War II period. While the French projected a sophisticated, haute couture look, the Italians developed a sensual, earthy Sophia Loren va-va-voom, and the Americans sold health, vitality, youth, and innocence. The wholesome, all-American, Caucasian girl next door look became highly sought after and cosmetics companies realized there was a market, not only in cosmetics, but also in beauty products, that could sustain that **natural look** for as long as possible. Cosmetics companies could sell this new look, via cinema, glossy magazines, and television as part of a larger cultural industry.

Global Celebrities

Global market research specialist Euromonitor has shown that millions of generation X- and Y-ers, as well as more mature adults, are looking up to celebrities and fashion icons and the brands that surround them in a hope of emulating some of their cool status and exciting lifestyle, in spite of the credit crunch. Whatever

"Fashion may be a language spoken everywhere, but it is never a universal language. It was, and remains, profoundly local, deeply vernacular."

Jean Allman, historian

Source: Allman, Jean, ed. *Fashioning Africa: Power and the Politics of Dress*. Bloomington: Indiana University Press, 2004, 6.

the reasons for this trend, the following of this fad by the creators of these brands is a clever way to maintain a foothold in the changeable and fickle global market. Euromonitor believes that in the midst of economic recession, cocooning customers are only keener to immerse themselves in the fairytale world of celebrity, with all the aspirations this entails. Celebrity endorsement has certainly provided a fairytale-like success for the U.S. beauty industry, allowing it further global triumph.

Rappers, singers, models, actors, and actresses are queuing up to join forces with fragrance and fashion houses to help raise a global profile and ensure steady growth for the U.S. beauty market. Stars such as Gwen Stefani, Jennifer Lopez, Snoop Dogg, Jay-Z, P. Diddy, Britney Spears, Sarah Jessica Parker, and Kanye West are wielding incredible influence on the global marketplace with their clothing lines, **perfumes and fragrances**, and lifestyle products. Certainly, there are both financial and popular gains for celebrities when they endorse certain products. A report by Euromonitor titled "The Impact of Celebrities on Consumer Lifestyles" argues that people of all ages can be targeted through icon-led marketing. However, the use of these celebrity endorsements is not only a way to convince the consumer of the legitimacy of the product; it also helps to magnify the product beyond simply a self-help, self-improvement promise. The beauty industry no longer desires to simply sell a well-made product; it promises an image, credibility, and the possibility of star power.

New Imperialism

With this in mind, cosmetics companies are marching toward continued global market success through the use of a more universal aesthetic that has been codified by mass and popular culture and the cosmetics industry. The emergence of a global beauty industry was interconnected with the growth of mass production and a more international **labor** market in the second half of the 19th century. The connection between economics, beauty, and hygiene became even more pronounced as government embarking on New Imperialism found new justifications for the old tradition of colonization. In certain parts of Africa, indigenous peoples were described as savage, barbaric, dirty, disgusting—and the British Empire sold soap, endorsed by Queen Victoria, to cleanse away the heathen and make the native bright, shiny, and new. Soap was one of the first products to become truly global. The influence of other national imperatives—the selling of the British Empire to its own people, the independence of the single woman in France, the embracing of Western aesthetic norms in Shanghai—made Americanization an uneven process, a heterogeneous, transnational phenomenon.

The rise of the modern girl, as demonstrated by the academic research group that wrote "The Modern Girl around the World: A Research Agenda and Preliminary Findings" (2005), became a mark of defining femininity, racializing beauty, engendering politics, and exploring sexuality. The creation of the modern girl and her cosmopolitan look, whether culturally defined as *garçonne, xiaojie, neue Frauen,* or flapper, was not unidirectional, singularly defined, or homogeneous in makeup. As the article describes, the fashioning of the modern girl, can be envisioned "as a gendered and radicalized formation that is web-like, comprised of multi-directional citations: mutual, though non-equivalent, influences and circuits of exchange connecting disparate parts of the world." Perhaps the first identity to be commodified into a global package, the modern girl could be Chinese, German, French, Senegalese, African American—but she was recognizable because of the amalgamation of multiple colonial, national, racial, and gendered traits. Those characteristics were sold via newsprint and glossy magazines. Toothpaste and tooth-whitening formulas; lightening products for the skin; girdles and **undergarments** to produce a lithe, svelte form; and deodorants and perfumes to mask body odor—the same products were produced by the same multinationals, but marketed to the modern girls of each nation and colonial experience.

Unilever was one of the first multinationals to ask its board to examine the possibilities of a global market for the beauty industry in 1950. World War II had opened up new horizons for businesses, mass culture, and the exchange of goods and information. Those companies that had established themselves as a global commodity were most able to take their corporations in different directions, accessing diverse markets and offering new products. Although certain concessions had to be made to be competitive in the global market—changing skin tones, hair colors, cultural preferences—those that invested in tweaking their products for individual markets experienced dramatic success. By 1970, Helene Curtis products were sold in over 100 different countries.

Asian Markets

The United States did not look only toward Europe as a viable market place; it also examined the possibilities in Asia, particularly in Japan, as the American government had a heavy hand in reconstructing postwar Japanese society. The Barbie doll, with its blue eyes and blonde hair, was one of the first American successes in the Japanese market. Although earlier prototypes made in Japan had what some call more Asian eyes, ultimately, it was the classic all-American Caucasian Barbie that won the hearts of Japanese females and introduced them to a new definition of beauty based on American standards. In the 1980s, when Michael Jackson had reached the pinnacle of his career as the king of pop, Japanese fans took adoration to the extreme when they made Jackson's distinctly African American look into their new It look. **Tanning** solutions, **permanents**, and **Afro** wigs became popular in Japan as the youth sought to emulate their idol. Most recently, No Doubt band member Gwen Stefani, inspired by her travels in Japan and by the carefully and whimsically constructed fashions of Japan's Harajuku girls, made the look popular in the United States and consequently returned the fad back to Japan and the rest of the world with her clothing line, Harajuku Lovers.

Foreign Companies

Even foreign companies are banking on American conceptions and models of beauty and freshness. Coty, a company founded in Paris by Francois Coty in 1904, has achieved huge global success through acquisitions and licensing partnerships. Coty worked with *Sex and the City* New York icon Sarah Jessica Parker to create a line of feminine, fashion-forward fragrances; with Latino actress/singer Jennifer Lopez, because her international appeal has created an incredibly loyal fan base that provides an almost guaranteed market for her perfumes; and with **hip hop** diva Kimora Lee Simmons, whose perfumes are described as embodying a type of hip hop, urban sophistication marked by the glam and bling of the B-girl all grown up. Coty is currently working with five-time Grammy Award–winning country singer, Faith Hill, who is portrayed as an all-American beauty, debuting her perfume, an olfactory sensation that will represent in a bottle her ability to juggle her different roles as a woman—singer and entertainer, mother, wife, American. While certainly these celebrity endorsements help to sell products, these famous women are also used as models for understanding and personifying the myriad possibilities of American multicultural beauty. Not only are American companies such as **CoverGirl** and Maybelline making the diversity of American beauty a commodity that can be applied with the brush of a wand or a swipe of lipstick; European, Asian, and multinational companies are also banking on the wide range of American archetypes in cultural beauty, from **hip hop** to country, from New York to Miami to California, to sell their products. The American beauty industry has not only economically infiltrated the international cosmetics market: the very nature of Americanness and the American aesthetic has permeated the international lines.

Internet

The American beauty industry is experiencing one of the most interesting phases, with the ongoing and growing demand for celebrity endorsements, technological and medical advances, the cultural imperative of having multimedia sources of information, and the overwhelming desire to look more beautiful, appear younger, and get longer-lasting results more quickly. The **Internet** has provided a new marketplace for cosmetics companies, drugstores, and beauty stores such as Sephora, beauty.com, and drugstore.com. New Web sites such as bellasugar.com, Beauty at style.com, beautyaddict.blogspot.com, afrobella.com, and beautysnob.com bring the discussion of beauty out of the realm of stylists, makeup artists, and celebrities into the voices of real women. Even youtube.com has tutorials on how to apply makeup, such as those by Michelle Phan, who has over 100,000 subscribers. These sites have transformed the beauty industry and made not only the products but also the looks global. So intrigued was the Dove company with the findings of a 2005 Unilever survey of 3,200 women that revealed that only 2 percent of females would call themselves beautiful that it started a new campaign in which real women defined real beauty on their own terms. The campaign, which began in Europe, has spread to the United States. On a Dove Web site (www.campaignforrealbeauty.com) women are asked to define what is beautiful—freckles, wrinkles, pregnancy, straight hair, curly hair, underweight, overweight. With taglines such as, "Oversized or Outstanding?" women are encouraged to vote for their favorite ads. The Internet has proved a powerful tool in both globalizing and diversifying notions of beauty.

See also: Advertising; Dove's Campaign for Real Beauty; Endorsements of Products, Celebrity; Film

Further Reading: Allen, Margaret. *Selling Dreams: Inside the Beauty Business.* New York: Simon & Schuster, 1981; Banet-Weiser, Sarah. *The Most Beautiful Girl in the World: Beauty Pageants and National Identity.* Berkeley: University of California Press, 1999; Barlow, Tani E., Madeleine Yue Dong, Uta G. Poiger, Priti Ramamurthy, Lynn M. Thomas, and Alys Eve Weinbaum. "The Modern Girl around the World: A Research Agenda and Preliminary Findings." *Gender & History,* 17 no. 2 (2005): 245–94; Burke, Timothy. *Lifebuoy Men, Lux Women: Commodification, Consumption, and Cleanliness in Modern Zimbabwe.* Durham, NC: Duke University Press, 1996; "Developing Cosmetics for an International Market." *Drug & Cosmetic Industry,* May 1982, 38–41, 108; Hamermesh, D. S., and J. F. Biddle. "Beauty and the Labor Market." *American Economic Review,* 84 (1994): 1174–94; Jermyn, Deborah. "'Death of the Girl Next Door': Celebrity, Femininity, and Tragedy in the Murder of Jill Dando." *Feminist Media Studies,* 1 no. 3 (2001): 343–59; Jones, Geoffrey. "Blonde and Blue-Eyed? Globalizing Beauty, c. 1945–c. 1980," *Economic History Review,* 61 no. 1 (2008): 125–54; Jones, Geoffrey. *Multinationals and Global Capitalism: Multinationals and Global Capitalism from the Nineteenth to the Twenty-First Century.* Oxford: Oxford University Press, 2005; Peiss, Kathy. "Educating the Eye of the Beholder—American Cosmetics Abroad." *Daedalus,* 131 no. 4 (2002): 101–9; Peiss, Kathy. *Hope in a Jar: The Making of America's Beauty Culture.* New York: Metropolitan Books, 1998; "The Impact of Celebrities on Consumer Lifestyle." *Euromonitor International,* December 2008. http://www.euromonitor.com.

Kate Brinton and Aliza S. Wong

GROOMING, MALE

The preoccupation with male grooming, most closely associated with the modern phenomenon of the metrosexual and his fastidious rituals of hair and skin care and physical fitness, is not simply the product of late-20th-century consumer culture.

Men have been obsessed with their physical appearance for centuries. In the ancient Egyptian world, for example, men practiced a rigorous health and beauty regimen that included the use of skin conditioners and moisturizers as well as the application of **cosmetics** to the eyes, lips, and cheeks. The obsession with skin care was also reflected in the Roman penchant for elaborate bathing rituals that included, along with the use of ointments and oils to replenish and restore vitality to the skin, the practice of bathing in mud. Makeup on the eyes and cheeks, as well as the use of hair dyes, were common features of the male grooming regimen in Rome by the first century C.E.

In medieval Europe, the Christian church generally frowned upon the extravagant adornment of the male body and issued injunctions against the wearing of wigs and the use of facial powders and paints. During the reign of Elizabeth I in England (1558–1603), however, the preoccupation with male physical appearance seems to have come to the fore once again. During this era, men used rosemary water on their hair, sage to whiten their teeth, and elderflower ointments to moisturize their skin. They also resorted to a lead- and arsenic-based powder to whiten their complexions and applied rouge made from geranium petals to pink their cheeks. These early precedents point to the complex nature of the history of male grooming.

Male grooming in North America predates the arrival of European settlers and was a common feature of the indigenous cultures of the New World. By the 18th century, the European fascination with male wigs held considerable sway in the American colonies of the British and reflected a preoccupation with a trend that served to not only mark status but also reinforce specific standards of attractiveness. The concern with covering the head in a fashionable manner affected all segments of society, including slaves, who fashioned wigs from animal hair and plant fibers and used them both as standard accessories and as a mechanism for changing their appearance, particularly when they were on the run. While never as elaborate as equivalent French fashions, wigs of this nature point to the role that male vanity and grooming have played in the larger history of physical appearance.

Men's Hair

Since the 19th century, men have been obsessed with three specific areas of grooming: hair, the beard, and the male physique. Historically, hair (and more particularly the lack of hair) has proven to be an obsession for men. In the 19th century, Native Americans in the southwest used, among other techniques, an ointment of yucca and chili pepper oil to encourage hair growth and prevent male pattern **baldness**. Cowboys, during the era of westward expansion, lined up at medicine shows to purchase a whole array of snake oil products thought to prevent hair loss. Similarly, purveyors of patent medicines in this period offered remedies for baldness in the pages of numerous periodical publications such as *Harper's Weekly*. Products like Scalpine, created by patent medicine entrepreneur H. H. Warner in the 1880s as one of his Log Cabin remedies, promised to cure a host of scalp disorders, counteract baldness, and prevent the premature growth of gray hair.

Concerns about baldness and premature graying remained pressing concerns in the 20th century. For most, relief from these afflictions was frequently found through the use of hair dyes or the wearing of a hairpiece. Despite the fact that they were frequently stigmatized and often the subject of humor, more than 350,000 men were wearing toupees by the end of the 1950s. By the 1960s, the quest for a remedy for baldness led to the development of several products based on the so-called Helsinki formula, a corn derivative identified as polysorbate 60 that was said to encourage hair growth. While its success was open to scientific questioning, this development led to new research that resulted in the discovery, by the pharmaceutical giant Upjohn, of minoxidil, an effective restorative. By the 1970s, new semipermanent hairpieces like the Micro-Lock wig were being marketed and the first hair implants, using artificial fibers and infection-producing techniques, were being offered to men willing to shell out more than $1,000 for the procedure. Upjohn continued to offer pharmaceutical solutions to men interested in encouraging hair growth by launching Rogaine in 1988. New advancements in the 1980s also led to the development of a broad range of hair transplantation techniques that offered new hope, and in some instances a broad range of medical and aesthetic complications, to millions of balding men.

While worries about hair loss have certainly provided the impetus for one particular male grooming ritual, concerns about the cutting and styling of hair have inspired another. Barbershops have been a prominent feature of urban and rural landscapes for generations. Barbers, responsible for shaving the face, trimming beards, and cutting hair, were found in ancient history. In the premodern world, they provided aesthetic services while also performing medical functions as dentists, bloodletters, and surgeons. Despite criticisms of men who paid excessive attention to their physical appearance, mid-19th-century barbers in rural villages, smaller towns, and large urban settings offered a variety of aesthetic services to their clients. Most men went to barbers for haircuts, shaves, and beard and mustache trimming. Their shops, however, were also places where clients could sample a broad range of beautifying techniques and products, including face washes, colognes, and concoctions intended to hide gray hair.

In the antebellum period, a number of freed African American men served, especially in urban areas, as barbers for a largely white clientele. These men often achieved an impressive level of financial independence and social prominence in their local communities. By the 1880s, these African American barbers were displaced by white competitors, drawn primarily from German and Italian immigrant communities. By the 20th century, African American barbers were catering increasingly to an exclusively black clientele, providing specialized services and creating, within their shops, an important public space for men organized around the rituals and practices of grooming.

Since the end of World War II, men's hair care has changed dramatically. Despite a brief penchant among American men for longer hair and elaborate beards, sideburns, and mustaches in the 1840s and 1850s and then again in the countercultural 1960s and 1970s (the era of the **natural look**), the general trend in the 19th and 20th centuries has been toward closely cropped short hair and minimal facial hair. Since the 1960s, the prominence of the barbershop as the institution of male grooming has been challenged by the rise of the unisex hairdresser and, more recently, by the emergence of the upscale salon and spa catering to both female and male customers, especially those men most closely associated with the rise of **metrosexuals**.

Beards and Shaving

The growth of facial hair and, perhaps more importantly, the ritual of shaving, have always functioned as important rites of passage for adolescent boys in a diverse range of cultures. Prior to the emergence of self-shaving in the late 19th century, most men had their beards shaved by servants or barbers. The straight-edge razor was the preferred instrument and remained prominent until the introduction of the safety razor in the 1880s. This period also witnessed the proliferation of a broad range of shaving paraphernalia and products like shaving soaps and soothing homemade washes such as cherry laurel water. In the 1890s, King Camp Gillette revolutionized shaving with the invention of the disposable razor blade. By 1905, Gillette had emerged as the undisputed leader in the shaving industry, selling close to 100,000 razors and 125,000 blades annually and expanding into European markets. In part, Gillette's successes were brought about by inventive **advertising** campaigns that appealed to middle-class notions of self-sufficiency and used portraits of famous self-starters like Andrew Carnegie and Horatio Alger, or idealized, and frequently clean-shaven, images of baseball players and soldiers. The technology of men's shaving was altered in the 1960s and 1970s by the introduction first of the plastic disposable razor, intended to be used only once or twice, and then by the widespread marketing of electric shavers.

The shaving industry was not just affected by innovations in razors and blades. By the 1920s, producers were capitalizing on shaving consumers by offering men new, and highly masculinized, toiletries that were intended to ease the rigors of shaving and improve appearance. New lines of lotions, powders, and moisturizers like Florian, introduced in 1929 by beauty industry entrepreneur Carl Weeks, were routinely advertised in prominent **men's magazines** like *Fortune* (f. 1930) and *Esquire* (f. 1933). Since World War II, when military men embraced fastidious grooming habits in order to meet the military expectations of short hair, a clean shave, and pressed and polished clothes and shoes, the men's shaving industry and the market for attendant skincare products has expanded dramatically. From this point on, men became big consumers of aftershave products, skin lotions, and deodorants in order to live up to new standards of male cleanliness. By the late 1950s, female cosmetics companies began to develop lines specifically directed at men. This commercialization of men's appearance has led to further significant developments since the 1960s. By the 1980s, cosmetics companies were seeking to further encourage men to use products previously thought to be reserved exclusively for women. Clinique, by the mid 1980s, began marketing skin care products specifically to men by giving key products like exfoliating masks new masculine-sounding names like Scruffing Lotion. The products, increasingly advertised in a growing number of men's magazines like **Gentlemen's Quarterly (GQ)** were, by the late 20th century, becoming more common accessories for men interested in achieving their best possible appearance. This emphasis on skin care, which grew out of the shaving industry, also led to a new valorization of the hairless male body as a symbol of youthfulness and a general sign of cleanliness. Since the 1980s, when the hirsute look of the '70s epitomized by Burt Reynolds's 1972 centerfold spread in **Cosmopolitan** was replaced by a hairless ideal, men have been shaving and **waxing** their chests, back, buttocks, and, in some instances, even arms and legs.

Building Better Bodies

The final area of men's grooming relates to the maintenance and improvement of the body's general appearance. While concerns about, for example, the fineness of a man's leg appeared in considerations of masculine appearance in the 18th century, the preoccupation with an athletic and trim body was, primarily, an invention of the 19th century. Concepts of muscular Christianity, borrowed in part from Britain, predominated in discussions of the male body in antebellum America. The muscular Christian, who trained his body through moderate exercise and appropriate games, was expected to achieve physical fitness as a general sign of moral and spiritual health. While some men in this period, like Diamond Jim Brady (1856–1917) and President William Howard Taft (1857–1930), embraced corpulence as a sign of prosperity, most middle-class American men, by the late 19th and early 20th centuries, began to eschew fatness as a sign of foreignness and lower social status. Indeed, it was during this period that many men came to groom their bodies, as they groomed their hair and beards, through sports like football, baseball, and track and field and, increasingly, through physical culture exercises and bodybuilding, promoted most notably by Bernarr Adolphus Macfadden (1868–1955). Macfadden, as a proponent of physical culture, promoted healthy diets, regular exercise, and the acquisition of muscle through his magazine *Physical Culture* (f. 1899).

This physical culture craze, despite a recent rise in general obesity rates, has continued unabated for the past century, and informed, in rather profound ways, concepts about the ideal male body. In 1939, the well-built muscular body was celebrated as an ideal worthy of admiration and reward with the creation of the Mr. America contest. This idealization of the

"[T]he athletic, muscular male body that Calvin [Klein] plastered all over buildings, magazines, and subway stops has become an aesthetic norm, for straights and well as gays. 'No pecs, no sex,' is how trendy Barton gym sells itself: 'My motto is not "be healthy"; it's "Look better naked,"' Barton says. The notion has even made its way into the most determinedly heterosexual of contexts, a Rob Reiner film. In *Sleepless in Seattle,* Tom Hanks's character, who hasn't been on a date in fifteen years, asks his friend (played by Rob) what women are looking for nowadays. 'Pecs and cute butt,' his friend replied. 'You can't even turn on the news nowadays without hearing about how some babe thought some guy's butt was cute. Who the first woman to say this was I don't know, but somehow it caught on.' Should we tell Rob that it wasn't a woman who started the craze for men's butts?"

Susan Bordo, philosopher

Source: Bordo, Susan. *The Male Body: A New Look at Men in Public and in Private.* New York: Farrar, Straus and Giroux, 1999, 185.

muscular body was further promoted through the work of Harvard psychologist William Herbert Sheldon who, in work published in 1940, valorized the positive physical and emotional traits of the V-shaped mesomorph. This emphasis on fitness led, by the 1950s, to large-scale efforts to promote physical education as a means of improving national efficiency and health. While this preoccupation with the cultivation of a muscular body seemed to fall off somewhat in the 1960s and 1970s, concerns about fitness never disappeared entirely. In the late 1960s and 1970s, running as a form of exercise experienced something of a boom as sedentary men sought to improve their health and their body image through aerobic activity. The 1970s also witnessed an increase in the sale of exercise equipment and the formation of health clubs, intended to provide people with an opportunity to retain or reclaim a youthful appearance and strive for individual physical perfection. Since the 1980s, the impossibly chiseled muscular body, complete with perfect pectoral muscles, well-developed biceps, and the rock-hard abdominal six-pack has been the ideal that many men have struggled to achieve through the consumption of dietary supplements, long hours at the gym, and, in some cases, liposuction, pectoral implants, and the use of steroids. Concerns with the grooming of the body have also led, since the Reagan era, to the creation of a broad range of fitness magazines, such as ***Men's Health*** (f. 1987), concerned with providing male readers with how-to advice about achieving the perfectly sculpted body.

See also: Barbers and Barbershops; Models, Male; Wigs and Hairpieces

Further Reading: Bordo, Susan. *The Male Body: A New Look at Men in Public and in Private.* New York: Farrar, Straus and Giroux, 1999; Harris-Lacewell, Melissa Victoria. *Barbershops, Bibles and BET: Everyday Talk and Black Political Thought.* Princeton, NJ: Princeton University Press, 2004; Luciano, Lynne. *Looking Good: Male Body Image in Modern America.* New York: Hill and Wang, 2001; Peiss, Kathy. *Hope in a Jar: The Making of America's Beauty Culture.* New York: Metropolitan Books, 1998; Pinfold, Michael John. "'I'm Sick of Shaving Every Morning': or, The Cultural Implications of 'Male' Facial Presentation." *Journal of Mundane Behavior,* 1 no. 1 (2000): 75–88; Rauser, Amelia. "Hair, Authenticity, and the Self-Made Macaroni." *Eighteenth-Century Studies,* 38 no. 1 (2004): 101–17; White, Carolyn L. *American Artifacts of Personal Adornment, 1680–1820: A Guide to Identification and Interpretation.* Lanham, MD: AltaMira Press, 2005; Willett, Julie A. *Permanent Waves: The Making of the American Beauty Shop.* New York: New York University Press, 2000.

Paul R. Deslandes

H

HAIR CARE PRODUCTS

Since ancient times, natural and formulated substances have been used to care for and style hair. Products were designed as cleansers, treatments to regrow or remove hair, styling elements like stiffening agents, or beautifiers imparting shine, curl, or color. From shredded vegetables, to bear grease, to Dippity-do, hair care products run the gamut through shampoos, conditioners, stylers, and colorizers.

The hair product with the longest history is likely henna. Made from a flowering plant native to warm regions, its leaves are dried, ground, and mixed with an acidic substance, producing a natural dye. When used on hair, it imparts shine and a warm brown/auburn color. Believed to have been first used in ancient Egypt, henna has experienced a resurgence over the years and remains in wide use today. Other natural and ancient hair products include ancient Egyptians' use of shredded lettuce placed on the head to encourage hair growth or regrowth. Also recorded is Cleopatra's use of a gel made from bear grease to control her hair, while her contemporaries, besides using henna, also used cow's blood, oil, and crushed tadpoles to recolor graying hair. In ancient Rome, people used a mixture of natural materials to cover gray hair that included ashes, boiled walnut shells, and earthworms.

Today, the hair product industry is a multibillion-dollar worldwide industry. Because the products are used on humans, they are also widely regulated for safety. In the United States, products are monitored by the **U.S. Food and Drug Administration** (FDA).

Shampoos

The name for a product to wash out the buildup of natural oils from the hair, the word *shampoo* actually comes from the Indian word *chāmpo* (or Hindu *champoo*), which means "massage." The word was brought into English use in the mid-to-late 1800s, when colonial India introduced the practice of therapeutic scalp massage to Great Britain.

Ancient Egyptians, Native Americans, and Native Latin Americans record some of the earliest substances used to cleanse the hair, made by accessing the substance saponin from soapwort and soapberry plants. Those cultures without plants containing saponin found other similar substances to formulate a soaplike product; in Africa, mixtures of clay and fragrant oils were used, while Ancient Romans combined animal fat with ashes to cleanse their hair.

In the Western world, soap was generally used to wash both the hair and the entire body. British **hairdressers** at the turn of the 20th century developed a mixture of soap, water, and fragrant herbs that was less harsh than straight soap, and applied it to their clients' hair in a massaging technique. Soon both the mixture and the process became known as a shampoo. The first commercially available cleansing shampoo was created in Germany in the 1890s. In the United States, by the early 1900s, shampoo was available in several name brands. Some of the earliest to be mass marketed came out in the 1930s and included Wella (established 1880) and Breck (established 1930).

While these early shampoos contained soap, modern shampoos often use a synthetic surfactant as a base for their formulas. Chemistry continues to evolve and shampoo manufacturers continue to research new ways for shampoos to impart shine and improve hair condition. In fact, one product, Neutrogena, specializes in the removal of residue left by other hair products, and advertisers use a slogan advising customers to use Neutrogena once a month so that their regular hair product choices work better. New markets have emerged in recent years with renewed interest in natural or organic ingredients, and expanded into a variety of hair textures, including products specifically formulated for African Americans' needs.

Shampoo comes in many product forms, including solid (usually a bar), liquid, gel, or powder. A very wide variety of shampoo products exists today, from those available at grocery and drug stores, to beauty supply stores catering to professional hair dressers, and through salons. Paul Mitchell's products, originally available only through salons, still carry the warning label that their guarantee is only valid if bought via a salon professional.

Shampoo products are formulated for a wide variety of hair types, including the Short and Sassy, and Long and Silky brands, as well as for fine, coarse, oily, dry, or damaged, all with their special ingredients to cleanse and improve hair. Touted as medicated shampoos, Head and Shoulders (owned by **Procter and Gamble**) and Selsun Blue (owned by Abbott Laboratories) are widely available shampoos for dry, itchy, and flaking scalp conditions, also known as **dandruff**.

Shampoos and their product identifications have made their way into popular culture references. Clairol products have long capitalized on pop culture trends, with Long and Silky drawing on the culture of jeans and long hair trends of the 1970s; recent **advertising** campaigns for their Herbal Essence Organics line referenced the "yes, Yes, YES" lines from the **film** *When Harry Met Sally* (1989) as a "Totally Organic Experience" to boost their sales.

Conditioner

Conditioner is a hair product that is generally used to restore moisture and shine following a shampoo. It is also called cream rinse. Conditioners first appeared commercially in the 1950s as a way to reduce tangles and dryness after shampooing hair. Older home recipes range from oils, such as olive oil—a historical favorite—through organic mayonnaise combining both oils and eggs, to the beer/

raw egg concoction. Commercial products range from deep conditioners specially formulated for occasional use and to restore damaged or dry hair, such as Wella's Kolestral, and hot oil treatments, to daily treatments often referred to as *crème rinse,* and the leave-in variety of conditioners, which blur the lines between conditioners and styling agents. In addition, herbal oils have also become a recent consumer favorite, often mixed with daily conditioners to impart both their essential oils and their scent.

Conditioners are marketed in tandem with specific shampoo and styling products, to create a line where they are touted as working best. They are advertised as being formulated to work together, thus also ensuring that when one in the line runs out, the customer will buy more of the same in order to remain in line.

Color

Products that change the color of the hair have been used for centuries, both to cover gray hair and appear to restore a previous natural color or to completely change the color of a person's hair. Early experimentation with human-made concoctions and procedures for hair coloring were sometimes toxic to the user. In ancient Rome, when lighter hair became fashionable, women who experimented with harsh bleaching mixtures experienced partial or total hair loss. In the second century, Claudius Galen, renowned physician and researcher in the Roman Empire, described the use of a combination of lead oxide and slaked lime to color hair black. The chemical reaction that occurred when these elements combined with human hair formed sulfur and allowed the lead to penetrate the shaft of the hair. This process is what some hair color products are still based on today. In Elizabethan England, in order to mimic their queen, men and women used a red coloring agent for the hair that contained sulfur and caused physical illness. Although they were successful in attaining color change in the hair, early hair coloring attempts involved chemicals that were toxic to human health and life. In 1907 a French chemist, Eugene Schuller, is credited with developing the first commercial hair color product that was safe for human use. The company he founded became L'Oréal.

Temporary colors that fade or wash out over time can be found in various forms, including rinses, shampoos, gels, sprays, and foams. Temporary hair color does not penetrate the shaft of the hair and thus can generally be removed with repeated shampoos. If the hair shaft is damaged in any way from over-dryness or previous permanent color, temporary color can permanently penetrate the hair shaft and become semipermanent or permanent. Henna hair coloring is still used today as a temporary colorizer, available both in pure powder form and in natural product mixtures. Other temporary dyes are widely marketed as less damaging to hair than permanent coloring, and are even lauded as conditioning agents.

There are various levels of temporary coloring. Most dyeing agents fade over time, and therefore even those marketed as permanent are not really permanent. Clairol's products have been categorized into four levels that exemplify the differences: *permanent*—those which retain their color beyond 28 shampoos;

demi-permanent—through 28 shampoos; *semipermanent,* the natural coloring agents; and touch-up and highlighting products. The temporary categories of coloring agents might best be described as blending dyes, as they are meant to blend away the appearance of gray hair, enhance natural color, or disguise graying through highlighting and touch-up products. These dyes have to be regularly reapplied in order to maintain coverage.

Permanent hair color does penetrate the hair shaft through a chemical reaction with the hair. During this reaction, which generally occurs simultaneously, ammonia is used to open the hair shaft, peroxide to remove existing color, and a pigment is deposited on the open shaft. The chemical process is then neutralized, and a conditioning agent is applied to restore the appearance of health and shine. Hair bleach is generally hydrogen peroxide, which is used to lighten or remove all pigment from the hair, and is frequently used prior to changing dark hair to very light hair color, such as black to blonde.

The products extensively marketed as permanent are simply those that change the existing hair color, and must be reapplied as hair grows or as the dye fades. Both temporary and permanent hair color, in reality, have about the same staying power in terms of numbers of shampoos or weeks of wear; they differ mainly in the harshness of the chemical process used. Permanent coloring cannot wash out; it must be allowed to grow out or be covered with another dye job. Permanent coloring agents are developed for a wide variety of hair color ranges and highlighting combinations, as well as for men and for ethnic hair types, to which Clairol's Textures and Tones is targeted. Included in the permanent category are also mustache- and beard-dyeing products.

In an uncertain category of hair coloring is the recent use of home recipes such as Kool-Aid and food coloring to achieve startling colorations in modern punk styles, spike formations, and vivid streaks. The Kool-Aid trend has led to some mainstream commercial products that have been willing to invest in developing the hot colors sought by current consumers. Use of these products often requires the removal of prior hair color through bleaching in order to attain the most heightened final color. Hair salon professionals have also pursued this new market through their offerings of highlighting streaks and more vivid and made-to-order color combinations.

Methods of dyeing or bleaching hair have been demonstrated in popular released films for decades. Ginger Rogers demonstrated touching up roots for her bleached blond hair in the 1930s, while many recent films and TV shows, such as *The Fugitive* and *NCIS,* have included the changing of hair color as part of a disguise. Hair color has also been extensively used, as well as style, to define a person's character or grouping in society.

Styling Products

Styling products fall into three main categories: fixatives (hairspray and gels), smoothers (pomades and gels), and texture agents (relaxers, straighteners, and curlers).

Hairspray is a fixative product that is sprayed in a mist on a completed hairstyle to hold it in place or is used during the styling process. The first hairspray became available commercially in the United States in the 1920s, but the product was not widely commercially successful until aerosol technology was used with it in the 1940s. Styles then came to rely on the mixture of lacquer and alcohol to achieve new dimensions. The popular **bouffant** styles of the 1950s and 1960s relied on liberal use of hairspray and many were held in place for a week and then washed, restyled, and sprayed for the following week. In the 1970s, when **hairstyles** became more soft and supple, hairspray use declined, though smoothing agents like gels and conditioners replaced them. The industry was regulated in the 1970s when it was determined that aerosol hairspray released environmentally toxic chlorofluorocarbons (CFCs) into the atmosphere. Manufacturers found alternate mechanisms for the spray function, including manual pumps and alternative propellants, although CFCs are still used in hairspray production in some countries.

Hair gel is a jelly-like fixative product that is used on wet or dry hair to help create a style and thereafter to hold a style in place. Mousse is a very similar product in a foam delivery form. Hair gels vary in delivery systems, from spray form to jelly consistency and everything in between. Sometimes referred to as setting gels, products like Dippity-do, by Gillette and now owned by White Rain, were very popular in the 1950s and 1960s and were applied to wet hair, before rolling the hair on curlers, and their setting quality would hold the style in place after the hair dried. Still extensively used in various forms today, gel and mousse products are often used as alternatives to hair spray by both men and women. Products like L.A. Look are unisex, while those that target curling may be considered more gender specific. Various weights of hair gel are available, from light style to hold down flyaways, to curl sets like Shirley Temple ringlets, to heavy sets that often contain added waxlike ingredients capable of stiffening hairstyles such as Mohawks.

Pomades are those products that give a wet look to hair and are most frequently used to relax or smooth down coarse or very curly hair. Marketed often to Latin men or African Americans, products such as Brylcreem (1928), "a little dab will do ya," Murray's Hair Dressing Pomade (1925), and Royal Crown are still available at some consumer locations, but also have found a continuing market through **Internet** sales. Many of these types of products contain petrolatum and mineral oil as their primary ingredients. Highly reminiscent of ancient hair oiling techniques, these types of products easily reference the continuity of hair grooming interests and product ingredients that people have used over millennia.

Texture

Straighteners/ relaxers are chemicals applied to the hair to make the texture or appearance of curly hair smoother. Pomades (usually derived from grease) were the earliest forms of this and offered a temporary smooth appearance by slicking the hair to the head. More permanent straightening solutions came when oil was applied to the hair followed by an iron or hot comb; this created a straight look until the hair came in contact with water or high humidity. In the mid 1800s, chemical straighteners were released that frequently contained very harsh chemicals, including lye, and offered a more permanently smooth result. Around the turn of the 20th century, **Madam C. J. Walker** became a well-known entrepreneur who formulated, advertised, and sold a variety of **hair straightening** products for African Americans. Scientific advances have resulted in today's hair straightening products, which are much less harsh and more effective at achieving permanently smooth hair.

A permanent wave is a combination of curlers and chemicals applied to the hair to change the texture but instead of changing curly hair to straight, it makes straight hair curly. Available at hair salons, as well as through home products like Ogilvie's Home Perm, **permanents** have frequently been the butt of jokes when their results don't match the intent. Quite damaging to hair, both straightening and waving products today attempt to mitigate their damage by conditioning the hair with separate procedures after the curling or straightening agents have been washed away. Many of the conditioners mentioned in various shampoo/crème rinse combinations target hair that is damaged or dry due to permanents and straighteners.

Further Reading: Clairol. http://www.clairol.com; Fewster, Sarah. "The Past, Present, and Future of Looking Good." *Science World,* 60 no. 6 (2003): 12; Helmenstine, Anne Marie. "Hair Color Chemistry Bleaching & Dyeing." About.com. http://www.chemistry.about.com/cs/howthingswork/a/aa101203a.htm; Herbal Essences. http://www.herbalessences.com; Just For Men. http://www.justformen.com; L'Oréal. http://www.loreal.com; Murray's. http://www.murrayspomade.com; Sherrow, Victoria. *Hair: A Cultural History.* Westport, CT: Greenwood Press, 2006; Viegas, Jennifer. "Ancient Hair Dye Worked at Nano-Level." *Discovery News,* October 2, 2006; Walker, Susannah. *Style and Status: Selling Beauty to African American Women, 1920–1975.* Lexington: University of Kentucky Press, 2007.

Lauren P. Steiner and Christina Ashby-Martin

HAIRDRESSERS

Hairdressers and stylists, also known as beauticians, beauty operators, barbers, and cosmetologists, tout the creation of style, in contrast to barbers who have traditionally been associated with cutting hair that has grown too long. Hairdressers typically possess high-level skills that include cutting, perking, straightening, coloring, finishing, and sometimes braiding and weaving. In a nod to the history of barbering, some hairdressers catering exclusively to men are still identified as barbers and have embraced many of the techniques more commonly identified with women's fashion trends. Men's hairdressers also design facial hair shapes and are experienced with shaving techniques as well. Increasing interest in **male grooming** since the 1990s has provided additional business opportunities and thereby a relatively recent rise of a new generation of skilled barbers whose services are less distinct from hairdressing.

Precedents

While barbering is one of the oldest professions in the world, ladies' hairdressing only became a common pursuit in the 19th century as public hair care establishments opened for women. Archeologists have found haircutting tools that date back to 30,000 B.C.E. However, the introduction of **hairstyles** dates to the ancient Egyptians, who developed hairdressing tools and techniques around 6000 B.C.E. These ancient hairdressers served men, while women created their own hairstyles in private spaces. Over the next centuries, few hairdressers would specialize in men's hair care. The popularity of hairdressing is instead linked with the development of late 19th and early technological innovations such as hair dye, dryers, and thermal and chemical methods designed to permanently wave or straighten hair, as well as various concoctions to make hair grow and look more lustrous.

African American Hairdressers

African American entrepreneur **Madam C. J. Walker** and **Annie Turnbo Malone** were unique trendsetters in the early 20th century, creating a niche for African women as beauty consumers, workers, and entrepreneurs. In the United States, hairdressers historically have largely served women and, thus, transformations in women's social, cultural, and economic roles have fueled the growth of the profession. In the early 20th century, Walker Agents sold products door to door, and emphasis on pampering customers and rags-to-riches stories appealed to middle- and working-class women longing to have their hair professionally styled. The flapper of the 1920s and her willingness to adopt a range of male prerogatives, including short hair, encouraged women to frequent barbershops—a social taboo. Barbershop patrons were not thrilled with the female intrusion. The cultural ambivalence women faced in barbershops, coupled with permanent wave machines and the proliferation of Hollywood-inspired trends in length, color, and texture created a female business niche and the beauty shop became an iconic American institution.

Segmented Market

The golden age of the independently owned and operated beauty shop came in the 1950s and '60s, and offered even women with children at home a unique opportunity to find a creative way to earn a living and engage in entrepreneurial pursuits, thanks to increases in women's purchasing power and leisure time. However, since the 1970s, many hairstylists have shifted from sole proprietors to working for corporate-owned salons.

The American hair salon remains highly fragmented. Regis Corporation, begun in 1922, is the largest owner and franchiser of hair salons in the world, with over 10,000 salons in North America and the United Kingdom. It operates the chains Supercuts, Master Cuts, Trade Secret, Regis Hairstylists, and Smart Style. The success of the company is rooted in its decision in the 1960s to open salons in shopping malls. Yet, Regis only holds a two-percent share of the U.S. market. Such large corporate chains created new problems and opportunities for hairdressers. Today, many salons do not require an appointment; they tend to be less personal in service, and often have management policies that can challenge an individual hairstylist's pace and creativity. At the same time, they often offer more benefits than the independent shop and allow hairdressers to pick up and start again—moving place to place—with no strings attached. Women generally own and operate hair salons. The smaller salons typically employ five hairdressers, while some work for themselves renting booths or simply operating a small shop in or adjacent to their homes. While larger salons may employ a receptionist and shampoo crew along with a greater number of hairstylists, owner-operator shops may mean the hairdressers take care of all business and customer needs.

Training

The first school of cosmetology opened in the late 1890s to train students, primarily women, in the burgeoning profession. Today, modern schools of cosmetology teach cutting, dyeing, washing, setting, perking, and straightening, and some also teach how to lengthen hair with extensions. Even after passing courses and becoming licensed, salons often train new employees to follow their own particular techniques and decorum; thus, many highly trained cosmetology graduates start out in the role of apprentice such as the shampoo girl who is also expected to sweep hair or bring clients magazines and refreshments. Although each state requires a certain number of hours to be licensed, generations of hairstylists have worked in an underground economy, cutting hair in parks, tenements, and factory bathrooms with or without official license or training.

Relationship with Customers

Hairdressing is one of the few professions where the employees exercise enormous power over the owner of the business. African American hairdressers, for example, had such unique business opportunities, sometimes being the only black-owned business in a town or community, that their status and economic independence offered them paths into politics and community leadership. In turn, African American women long viewed hairdressing as a particularly unique occupation, since so much of black **labor** was associated with the least desirable service for white customers/employers. The personal nature of the business encourages connections between clients and hairdressers, with the result that customers are loyal to the hairdressers and not to the business that employs them. This relationship allows hairdressers to be unusually mobile, moving from shop to shop and taking their clients with them or establishing their own businesses. Often known as the poor woman's psychologist, the hairdresser has been a stock character in films ranging from Dolly Parton's small-town socialite Trudy in *Steel Magnolias* (1989) to Queen Latifah's starring role in the film *Beauty Shop* (2005), and their interaction with clients that sometimes spans a lifespan cannot be overstated. Not just a sympathetic ear, hairdressers are confidantes, often knowing secrets about their clients unbeknownst to their own families. Because loyalty to one's hairdresser spans decades, stylists often grow old with their customers, and it is no surprise then that hairdressers are often asked to style their clients in hospitals, nursing homes, and funeral homes.

Gender Stereotypes and the Shop Floor

At the same time, the gossipy hairdressers of **film** and fiction project an image that is less than professional and has been the bane of the industry leaders, who have often sought to push out irregulars. Often, rules against gossip are coupled with dress codes, and the image of the dimwitted hairdresser prevails in popular culture. Although women dominate the industry, the most famous hairdressers tend to be men, in part because they more easily meet prevailing notions of professionalism that long privileged men regardless of occupation. Female clients have often suggested that male stylists know what men like or have admitted that flirtation is often a perk. Men who chose hairdressing as a profession, however, are venturing into a career that has been feminized in the public's mind. As a result, male hairdressers have long been stereotyped as gay. The stereotyping has undoubtedly limited the number of males who pursue a hairdressing career; however, men looking for work spaces that tolerate sexual and gender identities often find hairdressing rewarding, personally and professionally. Female hairstylist have long complained about the attention men receive in salons, but have also embraced them as a valuable part of their work culture; as hair salons attract increasing numbers of male clients, some of the gender dynamics that seemed tilted in favor of men can be muted.

Concerns

Regardless of gender dynamics, the work can be far from glamorous. Satisfying customers when it comes to personal looks can be challenging; listening to problems while maintaining a diplomatic mien can also be part of the daily experience. The work can also be hazardous. Products used to change hair color and texture affect the workers who apply them day in and day out. Hair spray and perms to curl and straighten hair have long been cited as health hazards. Standing on one's feet and holding a dryer or using the same hand to repeatedly cut or curl is linked to carpal tunnel syndrome. Perhaps most problematic are the wages and the widespread lack of health insurance that means many with or without children to support still struggle to earn a living wage.

See also: Barbers and Barbershops

Further Reading: Blackwelder, Julia Kirk. *Styling Jim Crow: African American Beauty Training during Segregation.* College Station: Texas A&M University Press, 2003; Bristol, Douglas. *Knights of the Razor: Black Barbers in Slavery and Freedom.* Baltimore: Johns Hopkins University Press, 2009; Gill, Tiffany M. *Beauty Shop Politics: African American Women's Activism in the Beauty Industry.* Champaign: University of Illinois Press, 2009; Gordon, Michael. *Hair Heroes.* New York: Bumble and Bumble, 2002; Lister, Maurice. *Men's Hairdressing: Traditional and Modern Barbering.* London: Thomson Learning, 2004; Peiss, Kathy. *Hope in a Jar: The Making of America's Beauty Culture.* New York:

Metropolitan Books, 1998; Plitt, Jane R. *Martha Matilda Harper and the American Dream: How One Woman Changed the Face of American Business.* Syracuse, NY: Syracuse University Press, 2000; Schroder, David. *Engagement in the Mirror: Hairdressers and Their Work.* San Francisco, CA: R&E Associates, 1978; Walker, Susannah. *Selling Beauty to African American Women, 1920–1975.* Lexington: University Press of Kentucky, 2007; Willett, Julie A. *Permanent Waves: The Making of the American Beauty Shop.* New York: New York University Press, 2000.

Caryn E. Neumann

Contestant shows off her hairstyle during the Patron Tequila Hair Competition and Martini Revue in Manchester, New Hampshire, 2006. (AP Photo/Jim Cole)

HAIR SHOWS

Hair shows are **trade shows** that focus on hair design and products and are held regionally, nationally, and internationally. Generally only open to hair professionals (cosmetology students, barbers, hairstylists, and salon professionals), they feature competitions, product and technique demonstrations, business seminars, hair runway shows, sales, and opportunities for professional development. Organized by trade associations and sponsored by styling product vendors, trade show displays represent a significant investment by vendors seeking to market new or emerging products. As with other trade shows, hair shows include numerous demonstrations, sampling, and competition opportunities for hair care professionals.

While many trade fairs are being presented virtually or online, none yet approach the large-scale productions and elaborate settings of the live hair shows. Online sources are currently used as **advertising** sites for the content and locations of hair shows and also act as marketing sources for products and techniques demonstrated at the hair shows. Bonika Shears's Web site http://www.bonika.com lists 28 hair shows, classes, and symposia where the company's products may be found. The site also includes listings of shows geared toward nonwhite audiences and clients.

One of the largest live hair shows, the International Beauty and Barber Show, draws 50,000–70,000 international attendees to New York and is credited with being the first to launch the hairstyle trends of **the bob**, marcel, kiss curl, and pageboy.

Others large shows include America's Beauty Show in Chicago and HairWorld, which holds annual events in the United States and Europe featuring Olympic-style international individual and team competitions. Several shows are geared specifically to African American hair professionals, including the American Health and Beauty Aids Institute (AHBAI), Proud Lady Beauty Show, and the Bronner Bros. International Hair Show. One of the most esteemed and exclusive hair shows on an international scale is the Intercoiffure Mondial World Congress, which is held in cities around the globe and is by invitation only. In 2002, international hair product company Wella sponsored "the first hair show in the Middle East" in Dubai.

While little is known about the larger history and development of the hair show, the first on record is the International Hair Show, held in New York in 1917. However, the Bronner Bros. hair product company, based in the Atlanta, Georgia, area credits itself with inventing the concept, and holding its first event in Atlanta with 300 attendees in 1947.

Competitions

Competitions held in conjunction with hair shows vary widely and include hair cutting, hairstyling, manicuring, nail sculpturing, and pedicuring. Often categorized by level of experience, from long-time professional to student, competitions are limited by entry fees and include prizes of money, trophies, and/or photographs of winning works featured in trade publications and online. The category called fantasy hair and nail competitions can be the most visually interesting, with styles that defy gravity and include a variety of colors, patterns, and objects.

Platform Artist

A platform artist demonstrates a hair service on a platform or stage at a hair show. Effective platform artists are usually experienced hairstylists representing an individual product line or company and combine public speaking and theatrics with the ability to cut or style hair.

Specialized Hair Shows

A specialized hair show is specifically geared toward certain types of styles. The World Natural Hair Show in Atlanta, organized by Braids, Weaves & Things, Inc., beginning in 1999, was founded by Taliah Waajid. It specializes in nonchemical approaches to hair treatments and includes demonstrations of Waajid's hair-braiding techniques.

Other, less product-oriented hair shows include the religiously themed In the Beginning God Created! in Rock Hill, South Carolina, or the International Fantasy Hair Show in New England. The latter specializes in architectural constructions made from hair, Styrofoam, fake flora, or other accessories, hosts a competition with prize money, and also acts as a fundraiser—in 2009, money was raised for the New Hampshire Food Bank.

A hair show was the subject of a 2004 narrative **film** called *Hair Show* starring Mo'Nique and made by UrbanWorks Entertainment. A competition was also televised during HairWorld: The Pursuit of Excellence, which portrayed the HairWorld Championship (also known as the battle of the bouffants) on the Public Broadcasting Service (PBS) in 2007.

Further Reading: Beautybarbershow.com. http://www.beautybarbershow.com; Bonika Shears. http://www.bonika.com; Brubach, Holly. "Hair-Raising." *New York Times Magazine,* April 13, 1997, 57; Chun, Rene. "Really Big Hair Show." *New York,* March 25, 1996, 29 no. 12: 24; Ford, Tamara. "Salvation in Style: Rock Hill Women Create Hair Show to Deliver God's Message." *The Herald* (Rock Hill, SC), June 16, 2007; Naturalhairshow.com. http://www.naturalhairshow.com; "New York City's Largest Events." *Crain's New York Business,* March 2, 2009; Sherrow, Victoria. *Hair: A Cultural History.* Westport, CT: Greenwood Press, 2006; Thomas, Chandra R. "Cuttingedge," *Atlanta,* September 2007, 47 no. 5: 158–63; "Tremendous Tresses Shown Off at Hair Show." Associated Press, April 28, 2009. http://www.wftv.com. (Accessed May 11, 2009).

Lauren P. Steiner

HAIR STRAIGHTENING

In Western culture, long, straight hair has traditionally epitomized both feminine beauty and sexual desirability. This aesthetic continues to shape how women of other cultures process and style their hair. Although concerns related to self-worth, success, and attractiveness affect both genders, women of all backgrounds have felt greater pressure to maintain a socially acceptable appearance. This was especially the case for African American women, whose femininity and sexual identity were often measured by the length and texture of their hair.

Unable to straighten their hair during slavery, black women covered it with scarves, kerchiefs, and straw hats to protect their scalp from the scorching sun. Inside plantation homes, domestic workers wore tight braids and cornrows inspired by traditional African hairdos. Since hair was considered the most telling feature of African ancestry, mixed-race African Americans relied on straight hair and fair skin to find jobs and protect them from harassment. In response to racially and culturally biased assumptions about black hair, white-owned companies during the antebellum years marketed hair straightening products to free black women in the North. These products advised black women to wash their hair and apply a hair straightening solution before using a garment type iron to flatten it out. Such techniques only damaged the hair, further leaving behind burned scalps and often permanent hair loss. Slave or free, African Americans recognized the impact straight hair had in signifying freedom, economic opportunity, and social status.

These concerns influenced the styling decisions of black women into the 20th century. With the rise of new beauty standards and commercial **hair care products**, black women used a host of styling techniques, including wrapping, waving, straightening, and hair pieces. While each allowed black women greater styling versatility, hair straightening had the most controversial appeal. At a time when many black women had trouble growing thick healthy hair due to scalp diseases, stress, and harsh chemical treatments, hair straightening with the use of the hot comb and later lye-based relaxers placed additional strains on fragile tresses.

The best-known styling tool for straightening black hair, the hot comb, was sold by department stores as early as the 1870s. A reconfiguration of earlier metal combs made by the French, black **hairdressers** perfected its use by sectioning the hair, applying heated oils, and moving the heated comb often from a stovetop or other heated chamber from the base of the scalp to the ends of the hair before reversing the process. While not the original inventor of the straightening comb, beauty culture pioneer **Madam C. J. Walker** popularized its use with her introduction of the shampoo-press-and-curl method of straightening hair, which later became the foundation of black hairdressing. She and other beauty experts such as **Annie Turnbo Malone** were among the first to use heated pressing irons and metal hair rollers; however, they insisted that such techniques were not an attempt to imitate white beauty standards, but rather to offer black women a chance to create and meet their own beauty ideals.

At a time when millions migrated to urban areas seeking social and economic opportunity, African Americans straightened their hair as a sign of upward mobility and acclimation into modern America. This included black men who were no less influenced by prevailing notions of beauty. With the use of tonics, pomades, and homemade kits, black men also experimented with hair straightening. In an attempt to look hip and stay in touch with urban trends, some applied large amounts of hair pomade and water to hair before going to bed wearing a wave cap, while others tried the cold soap wave, a process in which shampoo was left in the hair and later tied down with a cloth, or do-rag, to produce sleek waves. Others sought more permanent solutions with the congolene, or conk for short. Made of potatoes, eggs, and lye, the conk was designed to straighten the hair for longer periods of time, the effects of which were no less damaging. Burning the scalp and often permanently damaging the hair follicles, the conk was made popular by entertainers of the early 20th century, including Cab Calloway, Nat King Cole, Little Richard, and Nation of Islam leader Malcolm X.

By the mid 20th century, both white- and black-owned companies introduced the first permanent relaxers. These chemical-based products, almost all of which contained lye, promised straightened tresses for longer periods in place of heated combs. Despite their growing popularity, relaxers required additional maintenance, with touch-ups done every four to eight weeks plus the cost of professional application or supplies. By the late 1960s, many African American women favored natural styles over straightened hair. With the natural style, such as the **Afro**, they embraced their African heritage and growing identification with the politics of Black Power.

Whether temporary or permanent, the practice of hair straightening elicited widespread debate and public discussion across the black community. In some circles, straightened hair symbolized modernity and middle-class status, while others equated it with self-hatred and shame. Black civic leaders often took sides on the issue, castigating women who opted to straighten their hair in favor of

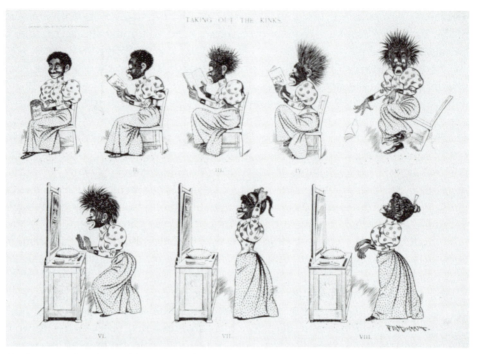

Caricature showing African American woman taking kinks out of her hair after reading a hair-raising ghost story, 1895. (Courtesy of Library of Congress)

trying to look white. Such feelings of inadequacy were often rooted in negative messages given to black women about their hair in the media and popular culture. Print advertisements often urged black women to straighten their hair to gain social acceptance in an attempt to adopt a standard of beauty that was difficult if not impossible to achieve. This was especially the case for poor rural women who with less access to hair salons or the money for their services, continued to rely on the time-honored practices of wrapping, braiding or tying down the hair with colorful scarves for a more polished look.

In the midst of ever-changing images of beauty in the 21st century, hair straightening remains a popular styling option for women of all backgrounds continuing to define mainstream ideals of beauty and success.

Further Reading: Blackwelder, Julia Kirk. *Styling Jim Crow: African American Beauty Training during Segregation.* College Station: Texas A&M University Press, 2003; Bundles, A'lelia. *On Her Own Ground: The Life and Times of Madam C. J. Walker.* New York: Washington Square Press, 2001; Byrd, Ayana D., and Lori L. Tharps. *Hair Story: Untangling the Roots of Black Hair in America.* New York: St. Martin's Griffin, 2001; Rooks, Noliwe M. *Hair Raising: Beauty, Culture, and African American Women.* New Brunswick, NJ: Rutgers University Press, 1996.

De Anna J. Reese

HAIRSTYLES

Hairstyles are rich with meaning and inextricably bound to a larger political economy that has profoundly shaped the cultural landscape as well the beauty industry. A multitude of industries and institutions are devoted exclusively to hairstyle processes, products, and accessories. Hairstyles have made peoples' careers, cost them their jobs, and, at times, even threatened their lives. Entire generations and subcultures have been defined in terms of their hair, creating a folklore devoted to the implications of hair. Length, shape, color, and texture challenge, distort, and reassert stages of the lifecycle as well as notions of gender, race, and respectability.

Actress Farrah Fawcett with her iconic mane, 1977. (AP Photo)

Precedents

Since ancient times, people have been arranging hair for practical, decorative, and deeply symbolic purposes. Some hair was kept long and fastened in a band or cropped short to allow ease of movement and unobstructed vision, while more elaborate styles often held certain significance and status. In ancient Egypt, both men and women cut their hair very short or shaved their heads to stay cool, and the nobles wore heavy wigs in ceremonial and public appearances. In Asia, the heads of men were shaved, leaving a line to which horsehair was sometimes added in braids, signifying submission. Several ancient cultures shaved the heads of slaves. In Africa, men and women developed complex styles using natural substances to stiffen and color the hair, which were time consuming and lasted for several weeks. Cultures in Africa, China, and the Americas developed certain styles for young women that signified that they were unmarried or pregnant. In some cultures, wild, unkempt styles came to signify insanity.

Religions continue to inform the meaning of hair. Jewish religious law contains specific guidelines for personal appearance and the manner in which hair should be worn. Men are to keep their heads covered with a yarmulke or skullcap.

In addition, they are forbidden to shave with a razor and, as a result, many wear beards. Jewish Orthodox men wear their hair short with long sidelocks. Jewish law also requires Orthodox married women to keep their hair covered for modesty and many wear wigs on top of their hair. Muslim women and men often believe in concealing hair in public with turbans and veils. Dreadlocks are divided into individual sections and treated with one of several methods (backcombing, braiding, hand rolling, or allowing hair to naturally separate into individual "locks" on its own). They can vary in width, compactness, and length, resulting in different types of styles. Popular with men and women regardless of religion or culture, they are most readily identified with followers of the Rastafarian movement, which traces its earliest references to the Bible.

Style and Social Movements

Many hairstyles of the 20th century reflect the ebb and flow of social and cultural change. In the 1920s, when women bobbed their hair en masse, it captured the rebellious spirit of a new generation of women, who asserted a right to an array of male prerogatives that ranged from cycling to smoking. **The bob**, a short cut just below the earlobe with layers up the back, was first attributed to a popular vaudeville dancer, Irene Castle. Variations evolved that included layered hair around the face, a blunt cut line at the back of the hair, and curls, whether around the face, all over, or in finger waves. Because the bob was a drastic departure from very long styles worn previously, its rise in popularity during the Roaring Twenties coincided with women gaining the right to vote and cropped skirt lengths. A longer version of the bob, called a pageboy, was popular among women in the 1950s, and is commonly associated with Uma Thurman's character in the 1994 **film** *Pulp Fiction*. Variations of the bob were seen in the 1960s with the work of celebrity hairdresser **Vidal Sassoon** and the style of actresses Nancy Kwan, Mia Farrow, and British model Twiggy.

For men, however, short hair has long been standard. The crew cut is generally a man's hairstyle and is closely and evenly cropped all over. Crew cuts and barbershops were part of coming-of-age social rituals for generations of American men. The short style came from an aerodynamic haircut worn by members of the Yale rowing crew in the early 1900s. The hair is cut in graduated lengths with the longest hair at the hairline and the shortest at the crown. The hair on the sides and back of the head is usually tapered. The clean style was adopted by the United States Armed Forces during World War II and later became a popular style for civilian men of the 1950s. Variations of the style are the buzz cut (evenly short all over) and the flattop (crown to hairline is cut to resemble a flat plane). In contrast, generations of male rebels that included zoot-suiters, hipsters, rock and rollers, Hippies, and bikers have made long hair a symbol of male defiance.

"Castro Valley Man Killed his 20-year-old Son after a Row about the Boy's Long Hair and [his] 'Negative Attitude toward Society.'" *San Francisco Chronicle*, April 14, 1971.

Poodle Cuts and Bouffants

Some of the most iconic hairstyles of the century emerged in the 1950s and '60s when cold war containment produced both acquiescence and rebellion that defined the looks of an era. Most of the hairstyles demanded perms, hairspray, elaborate backcombing techniques in which hair is teased to stand off the head, and above all else the hands of a skillful hairdresser. The poodle cut is short and uniformly curled, named after the then popular breed of dogs, whose coat was tightly curled and carefully clipped. A famous wearer of the poodle was Lucille Ball, whose closely cropped red curls inspired many imitators. By the early 1960s, Jackie Kennedy's **bouffant** was the height of glamour and involved the hair being set in rollers, dried, backcombed (and then the surface hairs brushed smooth and held in place with hairspray to create big hair. Women often had standing appointments at beauty shops so they could have their bouffant style redone every week. Between appointments, they would cover their new do with a scarf to protect it and while they may have had it touched it up daily, it was not washed until they went back to the salon the following week. Last but not least, the beehive, which reached the height of its popularity in the mid 1960s, is a version of the bouffant and requires the same setting and teasing process, but features a complex arranging of the hair on top of the head in a large dome shape, resembling a beehive. Because of its gravity-defying structure, it required generous amounts of teasing and hair spray, and some women even used hairpieces to add height and volume to their beehives.

Ponytails

To be sure, there have been some styles that emerged with the baby boom generation that required just a quick bush. Ponytails went hand-in-hand with saddle shoes and poodle skirts and invoked youthful simplicity with flirtation. The informal style consists simply of gathering long hair together in a fastener, such that it resembles a horse's tail that can be placed at the nape of the neck, higher toward the crown on the head, or on either side of the head. The style of two evenly spaced ponytails is called *pigtails* and brings to mind the *Brady Bunch*'s littlest blonde, Cindy, as well as a litany of tennis stars. Both versions remain popular and are often a work-out must, but even on adult women, ponytails and pigtails invoke a sense of girlish play and innocence.

The 1970s

By the 1970s, the **natural look** seemed a departure from a generation of women who still frequented old-fashioned beauty shops for a weekly wash and set. Nevertheless the latest looks still required a host of products and at least an occasional appointment with a hairstylist. Although singer Cher's waist-length hair was the envy of many girls swearing off haircuts altogether, it would not be long before Farah Fawcett's California tan, sun-streaked feathered layers and unforgettable pin-up smile made the Farah with highlights and wings one of the most asked-for styles of the late 1970s. Striking a different aesthetic, another American sweetheart, Olympic skating champion Dorothy Hamill's short and sassy brunette wedge also filled the pages of many yearbooks. Seventies styles, like earlier trends, never completely disappear. The Shag, for example, involved cutting many layers that impart volume in the crown and become wispy around the face and neck, was first introduced in the 1970s and is associated with actress Florence Henderson, but in the 1990s, thanks to television star Jennifer Aniston, the look was updated and known simply as the Rachel after her character on the hit show *Friends*.

One of the most controversial styles from the late 1960s and '70s was the **Afro**. Playing with hair texture has long been cast as tampering with racial identity and politics. Like flappers who embraced boyish style, white women who frizzed their hair were often caught in racial metaphors that suggested that their character and hair were a bit wild. Straightening hair, however, also invoked social comment. At times, the style was condemned as a form of self denial. African American women and men have long debated the meaning of processing or pressing hair straight that often goes beyond simplistic notions of assimilation. Much of these debates, however, came to a head in the late 1960s as the Afro became increasingly popular. For men and women with very tight natural curls or straight hair, an Afro style can be achieved by braiding the hair and then separating it using a tool called a *pick*. The pick is a narrow comb with long and widely spaced teeth. The style rose in popularity as part of the Black Freedom movement in the late 1960s, and the hairstyle symbolized a shift from the demands of the civil rights era to the rise of Black Power. By the late 1960s, Barbara Streisand emulated the look with a bubble perm and by the 1970s, Afro wigs could be bought and sold like any other fashion accessory.

Hair and Pop Culture since the Late 20th Century

When it came to big hair, the 1980s inspired some of the most audacious styles. MTV had a profound influence on youth culture. Many styles that were popular, for example, in the streets of London made their way to Middle America thanks to music videos. The late 1970s punk movement was defined by its in-your-face music and style. Mohawks and other vertical hairdos were held with mousse and gel and were often dyed outrageous colors or bleached blonde to give bands ranging from The Sex Pistols to A Flock of Seagulls their signature look. At the same time, homegrown hair bands like Bon Jovi and Poison touted perms and highlights along with good-old American rock 'n' roll. There were also rockabilly conks worn by The Stray Cats that emulated Elvis's earlier borrowing from black culture, and the king of pop Michael Jackson along with soulful Lionel Richie who inspired a generation of Jheri curls. The fashion trends of the 1980s seemed suddenly subdued with rise of Kurt Cobain and the popularity of the unwashed, unkempt look of grunge. In addition, rapper Tupac Shakur made a shaved head the epitome of the new cool. B-boy cuts involved razoring and shaving techniques that touted corporate logos and designs, giving a whole new meaning to shorn hair. Post-punk music and youth cultures continue to invoke everything from Goth and its romanticizing of the macabre, jet-black hair, makeup, and clothes to more androgynous fringe bangs of emo's (coming from the word emotional) ethos that embraces self-mutilation (cutting), depression, and at times suicide—trends that reinvigorate age-old concerns over the youth of today. More mainstream is the influence of metrosexuality that came of age with fashion icon and English footballer David Beckham, whose spiky fin cut paved the way for a range of men's hair fashion that have often been decidedly short but stylish, demanding products and skills that seem a far cry from the old-fashioned barbershop. Today, hairstyles, whether from the soccer pitch or music videos, continue to reveal connections between commerce and culture as well as politics and style.

See also: Afro; Barbers and Barbershops; Beauty Shops and Salons; Bed Head; Bouffant; Hair Care Products; Hairdressers; Hair Shows; Hair Straightening; Metrosexuals

Further Readings: Almog, O. "From Blorit to Ponytail: Israeli Culture Reflected in Popular Hairstyles." *Israel Studies,* 8 no. 2 (2003): 82. Religion and Philosophy Collection, Ipswich, MA; "Braids through the Ages." *Essence,* May 1998, 32; Bryer, Robin. *The History of Hair: Fashion and Fantasy down the Ages.* London: Philip Wilson Publishers, 2003; Buchman, Rachel. "The Search for Good Hair: Styling Black Womanhood in America." *WORLD & I,* February 2001, 190–99; Byrd, Ayana D., and Lori L. Tharps. *Hair Story: Untangling the Roots of Black Hair in America.* New York: St. Martin's Griffin, 2001; Corson, Richard. *Fashions in Hair: The First Five Thousand Years,* 3rd ed. London: Peter Owen Ltd., 2000; Cox, Caroline, and Lee Widdows. *Hair and Fashion.* London: Victoria and Albert Museum, 2005; "The Elizabethan Face of Fashion." *Renaissance,* 4 no. 2 (1999): 42–48; "History of Hairdressing." http://www.queensnewyork.com/history/hair.html. (Accessed December 8, 2008.); Kroll, Jennifer. "Mad for Fads." *Weekly Reader,* March 2, 2001, 28–31; Schiff, Judith Ann. "John Hay Whitney: Philanthropist, Film Producer, and Father of the Crew Cut." *Old Yale,* April 2002; Sellers, Ruth. "Hairstory." *History Magazine,* December 2001–January 2002, 47–49.

Lauren P. Steiner and Julie Willett

HAIRSTYLISTS, CELEBRITY

Hairstylists have always held an intimate and fabled position in the creation and maintenance of female charm and beauty. The role of the hairstylist as magic worker, beauty artist, and perhaps even more importantly, as confidante, friend, and advisor, who constructs the safe haven in which women can be transformed into their idealized selves, has been mythologized in **film**, on television, and in magazines and newspapers. By the 1950s and '60s, some male **hairdressers** were as famous as the icons whose hair they styled. One known simply as Alexandre de Paris had clients including Elizabeth Taylor and Sophia Loren. Kenneth Battelle, better known as Mr. Kenneth, became internationally known for Jackie Kennedy's **bouffant** and made the cover of *Glamour* magazine, while West Coast playboy Gene Shacove, who once boasted that hairdressing was a "license to touch married women," was the inspiration for the 1975 **film** *Shampoo* starring Warren Beatty as the motorcycle-riding hairdresser who seduced much of his female clientele.

"I don't know what happens, they just smell so good in the chair; I can't resist. I had this insatiable appetite for new women. Hairdressers are lucky; they have a license to touch married women."

Gene Shacove, celebrity hairstylist

Source: Gordon, Michael. *Hair Heroes.* New York: Bubble and Bubble Press, 2002, 59.

Coupled with the continued aggressive **advertising** and public relations campaigns, many in the beauty industry, but perhaps most prominently the hairstylist, achieved a celebrated status that continues today.

Vidal Sassoon

One of the best-known celebrity hairstylists today is arguably the great **Vidal Sassoon**, a British hairdresser who rose to fame in the 1960s. Sassoon, born in 1928 and as skilled a business person as he was a hairstylist, rose to fame when the geometric bob cut he created in 1963 made him a household name. Sassoon was also known for his wash-and-wear perm, but his modernist edge, his ability to create geometric shapes, to create lacquer-like shine with very few products, and his precision and dedication to pushing the industry forward set him apart from his peers. His incredible talent, coupled with his business acumen, changed the hair industry forever. Sassoon was one of the first to envision the beauty and hair industry as a multimillion dollar industry. He had a short-lived television show called *Your New Day with Vidal Sassoon* in the mid 1970s, and has also authored several books. Perhaps most well known is a line of professional products he introduced in 1973. In the early 1980s, Sassoon sold his **manufacturing** name to **Procter and Gamble**, which sold his products in mainstream markets across the United States. Now, his salons, schools, and products may be found globally.

Paul Mitchell

Vidal Sassoon not only helped to create the new hair care industry; he was also mentor and teacher to many other stylists who would rise to fame in his wake. Paul Mitchell, born in Scotland in 1936, was the son of a hairstylist mother who entered beauty school at age 16. After winning numerous competitions, he joined Vidal Sassoon in the 1960s and became one of the most sought-after and popular hairstylists in London. Gambling on his fame and reputation, Paul Mitchell left Vidal Sassoon in 1966 to open salons in the United States, where he achieved even more celebrated acclaim. Although he was well respected and famed for his styles and cuts, Mitchell soon achieved celebrity status when, in 1980, he joined with business partner John Paul DeJoria to launch a professional hair care system. The centerpiece of this system was a revolutionary new styling tool, a sculpting lotion. The lotion was soon joined by other styling products, shampoos, and conditioners. The 2008 Adam Sandler film *You Don't Mess with the Zohan* played on Mitchell's fame when aspiring hairstylist Zohan (Sandler) seeks to work for the best, Paul Mitchell. In 1989, Mitchell died of pancreatic cancer.

John Frieda

British stylist John Frieda also followed in Sassoon's footsteps in the late 1960s. Frieda got his start at a London salon owned by one of Sassoon's protégés, Leonard Lewis. He quickly became Lewis's top assistant, which also brought him much attention. While Sassoon certainly had some famous clients that made his famous haircuts even more popular (Nancy Kwan, for example, wore a Vidal Sassoon bob in the movie, *The Wild Affair,* in 1963 and inspired tens of thousands of women to seek the same, sleek angular bob cut), Frieda used the celebrity connection to even greater advantage. Frieda began to develop a celebrity clientele of his own—including Diana Ross and Jacqueline Kennedy Onassis. Similar to Sassoon, he developed a signature haircut that was featured in the popular television series, *The Avengers*. Perhaps Frieda's most famous client was Lady Diana Spencer, later known as Princess Diana. Frieda also developed a line of professional products, a risky venture as Sassoon was the only previous example of this kind of entrepreneurship. He introduced the Frizz-Ease serum in 1990 in his newly opened New York salon. Because of a small marketing budget, Frieda did much of the publicity himself, which also brought personal attention to the stylist. Frizz-Ease continues to be one of his more popular products along with the Sheer Blond line first introduced in 1998.

Sally Hershberger, Chris McMillan, and Ken Paves

In 1999, John Frieda opened a salon with Sally Hershberger, a well-known celebrity hairstylist, most famous for creating Meg Ryan's signature shag. Hershberger now works independently and has developed not only a line of **hair care products**, but also her own clothing label. Many other celebrity stylists developed name recognition because of a well-loved, and copiously emulated, hairstyle. For example, Chris McMillan was an unknown stylist until he cut Jennifer Aniston's hair for the hit show *Friends*. The Rachel helped McMillan gain a following—not only did women want Rachel Green's haircut, but they also now sought out the hairstylist himself. McMillan currently also styles Lindsay Lohan and Kate Walsh, has appeared on the *Oprah Show,* and blogs on www.huffingtonpost.com. Ken Paves—whose clients include Jessica Simpson and Eva Longoria—is not only an in-demand stylist, but also has his own products—including hair extensions—which his celebrity clients help to sell. He has also been a fixture in the tabloids, often pictured with his clients at his salon or out on the town.

Television Personalities

Some stylists, like Jose Eber, Kim Vo, and Jonathan Antin, are as known for their personalities as they are for their hair. All three have appeared on television shows dedicated to the art, and business, of hairstyling. Eber, long time stylist to Jaclyn Smith, has appeared on a hairstylist Bravo TV contestant/reality show she hosts, *Shear Genius*. Vo is co-host with Smith and has also appeared on various entertainment and style shows, offering tips, opinions, and **makeovers**. *Shear Genius* follows 14 hairstylists vying for a cash prize and name recognition. Indeed, Bravo TV's *Tabatha's Salon Takeover* features Tabatha Coffey, a former contestant on *Shear Genius,* who gives floundering hair salons a makeover. Bravo TV, capitalizing on America's fascination with celebrity hairstylists, has been aggressive at the forefront of beauty television. Its show, *Blow Out,* followed hairstylist Jonathan Antin as he struggled to start his own high-end salon. The Style Network, an entire network devoted only to style and beauty, has also been concentrating much of its programming on hairstylists. Peter Ishkhans, a celebrity stylist whose cuts are "mindful of balance and form," hosted a popular show titled *Peter Perfect,* in which he would give failing businesses, and their staff, makeovers. Oprah Winfrey has dedicated entire episodes to celebrity hairstylists. Although many of these stylists gained fame because of their celebrity clients, many have become celebrities in their own right and their status as pop icons is evidenced in their appearances in tabloid magazines and in popular curiosity about their lives outside of the salons.

See also: Hair Care Products; Hairdressers; Hairstyles

Further Readings: Eakin, Julie Sinclair. *Salons and Spas: The Architecture of Beauty.* Beverly, MA: Rockport Publishers, 2007; Fishman, Diane, and Marsha Powell. *Vidal Sassoon: Fifty Years Ahead.* New York: Rizzoli, 1993; Frieda, John. *Hair Care.* Seattle, WA: Bay Books, 1983; Frieda, John. *John Frieda Precision Styling System.* Darien, CT: Zotos International, 1989; Gordon, Michael. *Hair Heroes.* New York: Bumble and Bumble, 2002; Riley-Katz, Anne. "Cold Cuts: Reality Show has Stylists Trading Places." *Los Angeles Business Journal,* 28 no. 44 (2006): 3; Sassoon, Vidal. *Cutting Hair the Vidal Sassoon Way.* Oxford: Butterworth-Heinemann, 1984; Sassoon, Vidal, Gerald Battle Welch, Luca P. Marighetti, Werner Moller. *Vidal Sassoon and the Bauhaus.* New York: Distributed Art Publications, 1994; Simon, Diane. *Hair: Public, Political, Extremely Personal.* New York: Thomas Dunne Books, 2000; York, Emily Bryson. "Salon Savvy: John Paul DeJoria is Keeping the Spirit of Paul Mitchell Alive in Maintaining the Core Values of the Company they Founded in 1980." *Los Angeles Business Journal,* 28 no. 42 (2006): 27.

Aliza S. Wong

HEALTH AND SAFETY

Since 1938, the **U.S. Food and Drug Administration** (FDA) has regulated the safety, rather than the efficacy, of cosmetic products. The regulation of **cosmetics**, ensuring some measure of safety to its users, was the result of problems caused by cosmetics, from redness and swelling to blindness, paralysis, and death.

In the late 19th century, women who wore cosmetics did so discretely. Those who did so wore little makeup, applied it lightly, and produced it themselves. Receipt books contained practical information on cooking, soap production, and mustard plasters, as well as recipes for beauty powders and skin lotions. Lead and mercury, widely recognized as hazardous, appeared in recipes, which often delineated the long-term effects, from graying gums to trembling limbs, and then included them in the ingredient list. Because women at that time typically made their own cosmetics, they were well aware of what they were putting on their faces.

In the early 20th century, most notably in the interwar years, cosmetics shifted from small, individual preparations to mass manufacture. In the process, women lost their intimate knowledge of what went into each product. A lack of ingredient lists compounded the difficulty. At the same time, more women began to wear more makeup. The look required a heavy use of powder, lipstick, and eye products. As women wore more makeup, the problems multiplied. In addition to the persistence of lead and mercury in products, coal tar dyes and other new chemicals were present.

Manufacturers, cosmetologists, **hairdressers**, and physicians read and were aware of potential problems; the public was not always aware. Many in the former group knew that powders made from crushed rice or talc often irritated the skin. The more women persisted in applying these products, the more pronounced their allergic reaction became. Contact dermatitis, an allergic reaction enhanced by repeated use, was a frequent diagnosis. The challenge for physicians was determining whether their patients wore makeup. Some women applied it such that it was not obvious to the (male) naked eye; others feared physician disapproval; and still others regarded it as such a basic part of their routine that it failed to register as a possible problem. At other times, the physician needed to be more thoughtful. In one case in the 1920s, a male patient had a rash on his lips with no obvious cause. Eventually it was deduced that his girlfriend's lipstick provoked the reaction. In another case in the 1930s, a woman had weakness of limbs, nausea, and fever of indeterminate origins. As the hospitalized patient began to improve, she suffered a relapse. Questioning revealed that she felt so good that she had asked a friend to bring some makeup to her, including the offending product, a face powder with mercury. Discontinuing use of said product solved the problem, although not without argument from the patient, who preferred this product.

Cosmetologists had a personal as well as professional interest in the safety of the products and devices used. These women wanted satisfied and safe clients. The quest for colored or permanently waved hair had its hazards. A permanent wave required the application of chemicals and heat. Some people suffered burns from the combination of the chemicals and the heat used to set the waves. Other women's scalps burned from the machine around which the hair was entwined. In most cases, the cause was not improper use of the many-tentacled machine, but too much of one or another ingredient in the potion applied to the hair.

Hair and lash dyes derived from coal tar (aniline dyes) were both effective and problematic. Prior to 1938, articles in the medical and beauty literature warned about the danger of these dyes. One such product, Lash Lure, an eyebrow and eyeliner product, relied on a coal tar derivative for its staying power. Several women were blinded after using this product. Less severe reactions included nausea, paralysis (temporary or permanent), swelling (often localized), redness, and irritation.

Two other types of products caused similar health problems. The first was depilatories, used to remove unwanted hair. As with dyes, the stronger the chemical, the stronger its impact. One depilatory, Koremlu, relied on thallium acetate, an ingredient commonly found in rat poison, at quite high and varying levels.

The product effectively removed unwanted facial hair, and occasionally wanted hair as well. Many women reacted poorly to Koremlu, and one died from a staph infection when the thallium acetate entered her bloodstream.

The second dangerous product, for most of the 20th century, was nail polish. Resin and nitrocellulose, used to hold the color, were common allergens. So, too, were some of the dyes for the shades of polish. Reactions to nail polish included swollen fingers, detached nails, itchy fingers and hands, and redness. Women who bit their fingernails or placed their fingers in their mouths occasionally had rashes on their face and lips. One woman had an unusual case: contact dermatitis on her ear. It emerged that her husband snored quite loudly; to combat the noise she slept with a finger stuck in each ear.

Nail polish, and its matching accessory, lipstick, provided many of the health and safety problems in the mid-to-late 20th century. In both products, the ingredient used to hold or create the color was sometimes not the safest one available. In the case of a lipstick by Guerlain, a French company, in 1941 the federal government ordered the lipsticks recalled, melted down into a molten wax mass and shipped back to France. In the case of nail polish, most companies gradually omitted the allergens.

During World War II, some unusual problems popped up in the manufacture of cosmetics, or cosmetic **packaging**, because of the exigencies of war. Despite limitations, the U.S. government felt it vitally important that some cosmetics still be produced to help boost morale. Although limited in terms of color, perfumes, and other essentials, women bought makeup. No new health problems arose, only the expected: common allergens led to allergic reactions. With the war's end, many of these problems disappeared as manufacturers returned to their original formulations.

As nail polish ingredients continued to change in the 20th century, some concerns remained and others disappeared. As early as the 1930s, nail polish created problems. Although manufacturers were aware of the problems posed by polish, they did not alter their formularies. By the 1980s, health concerns had changed. Some consumers were worried about acetone in nail polish remover. A harsh yet effective chemical, acetone was a possible carcinogen. Others worried about the health and safety of the nail technicians, recent female Asian immigrants, who inhaled the fumes of polish, primer, and other products for many hours each day as they gave manicures. Nail technicians, unlike hairdressers, are neither regulated nor licensed, so safety measures are ad hoc. These concerns extended to patrons of **nail salons**, who feared infection from unsterilized tools, exposed skin and unclean water for foot and hand baths.

The federal government has had limited impact with the cosmetics market. In 1938, a revised food and drug act brought cosmetics under the jurisdiction of the FDA. Among other policies, this new legislation demanded an ingredients list of all products. There were some loopholes in this law, most notably allowing for the continued use of coal tars in hair dyes, despite their known hazards. Implementation of this law, slated to take effect in 1939, was postponed to 1941 because of World War II. From the consumer perspective, the FDA's concern is not whether

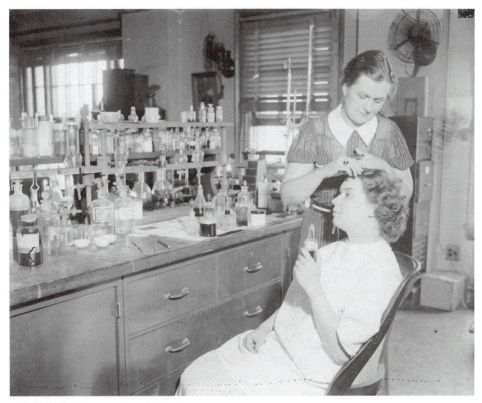

Testing hair dye for the U.S. Department of Agriculture, Washington, D.C., 1937. (Courtesy of Library of Congress)

a product works but whether it is harmful. A lipstick that does not actually last all day, as Hazel Bishop claimed hers did in the early 1950s, was not cause for FDA investigation. A lipstick that caused serious reaction, with multiple reports of swollen lips, a swollen esophagus, or blotchy skin, would be different. From the beautician's perspective, the regulations did little to protect the people applying the product. As concern mounted in the 1980s, there was little done to protect these workers. Fans, face masks, and other devices have been implemented, and some nail product is free of acetone, parabens (now banned by the European Union), and other potentially hazardous ingredients.

See also: Animal Rights

Further Reading: Environmental Working Group's Skin Deep: Cosmetic Safety Database. http://www.cosmeticsdatabase.com; Hilts, Philip. *Protecting America's Health: The FDA, Business, and One Hundred Years of Regulation.* Charlotte: University of North Carolina Press, 2004; Kay, Gwen. *Dying to Be Beautiful: The Fight for Safe Cosmetics.* Columbus: Ohio State University Press, 2005; Peiss, Kathy. *Hope in a Jar: The Making of America's Beauty Culture.* New York: Metropolitan Books, 1998; Riordan, Teresa. *Inventing Beauty: A History of the Innovations that Have Made Us Beautiful.* New York: Broadway Books,

2004; Willett, Julie. *Permanent Waves: The Making of the American Beauty Shop*. New York: New York University Press, 2000.

Gwen Kay

HIP HOP

In the 1970s, a new type of groove called hip hop that relied on rhythm, technology, and poetry became the music of choice within African American and Latino communities in New York City, particularly in the Bronx. Borrowing from African American, West African, and Caribbean forms of musical expression, hip hop artists would combine the flavor of rhythmic phrasing, percussion breaks, and melodic sampling to create dance hits that were often politically charged and socially relevant. Using large stereo systems, DJs would manipulate turntables, intertwining, overplaying, and undercoating beats over which artists could rap and slam. As the art form became increasingly popular and recognized as a new form of giving voice to marginalized communities, DJs, MCs, word stylists, and singers would perform at neighborhood block parties, using call and response chants, involving the people into the work itself. Break-dancers found their role in the performances early, inventing body flows, freezes, power moves, top rocks, and down rocks in time to the syncopation and the complications of the music. B-boys and B-girls became permanent fixtures and new personalities in the formation of youth identity among many African Americans and Latinos.

Emerging from hip hop was a distinct style of dress, of aesthetic, of swagger. Although more mainstream and traditional critics called this new art form noise, a degeneration of youth, and delinquent, others praised the music as finally speaking the truth to the social, economic, and political realities of oppressed and marginalized communities. For those who found voice in hip hop, the hip hop look became a part of owning the identity. Although certain garments, **hairstyles**, and makeup were considered hip hop cool, the aesthetics of hip hop became much more associated with an attitude, a gangsta reputation, a street cred. It was not until hip hop became part of the MTV generation, with music videos and documentaries introducing an underground movement into a wider, whiter mass and popular culture that the term hip hop became a **branding** that could be sold to a much broader market.

Fashion Trends

Hip hop artists such as Grandmaster Flash and the Furious Five, Sister Souljah, the Sugar Hill Gang, LL Cool J, Public Enemy, Dr. Dre, Notorious B.I.G., Roxanne Shante, and Tupac Shakur wielded unprecedented power and influence in American youth culture. Distinct and talented artists, together they helped to give an edge, a particular flavor to a subversively political urbanity. Just as the messages about inequality, racism, and prejudice in America were communicated loud and clear through hip hop, so too were the clothes and aesthetic bold, bright, and bombastic. Hip hop fashion harmonized with the attitudes and expressions of hip hop culture—at times outrageous, many times in your face, and at all times creative. In the 1980s, as hip hop moved from the streets onto the television screen and radios, boom boxes, and stereo systems everywhere, name brands such as Timberland, Adidas, Nike, Le Coq Sportif, Carhhart, and Kangol sold themselves as outfitters to B-boys and B-girls. For men, tracksuits, bomber jackets, sneakers with phat laces, Clarks shoes, harem pants, low-rise jeans, and leather work boots became identified with the male swagger of the new culture. Hairstyles ranged from dreadlocks to hi-top fades, braids to Afros. Accessorized with large eyeglasses, nameplates, bold

"My brother Andy [director of public relations for Tommy Jeans] brought me a bunch of hip-hop groups. He said, 'Tommy, these groups are very hip. And they love your clothes. Let's dress them.' So we dressed Snoop Doggy Dogg for *Saturday Night Live*. And all of a sudden these hip young groups from Harlem and the Bronx started singing about my clothes. And I thought it was cool. A lot of people, uptight Wall Street people, said 'What do you think about all of *these* hip-hoppers wearing your clothes?' I said, 'I think it's pretty great.' That got back to the hip-hoppers and I think I looked as if I was embracing them. Which was true. So I began surrounding myself with street people to get more of a grip on it."

Tommy Hilfiger

Source: "Interview: Tommy Hilfiger." *Playboy,* October, 1997. http://www.playboy.com/articles/tommy-hilfiger-interview/index.html.

belt buckles, big gold rings, heavy gold chains, and blinged-out pendants, hip hop fashion for males was in control and on **display**.

Although many saw hip hop as a predominantly male genre, many female artists demanded a place in the new world and a mic to express their views. Women such as Missy Elliot, Queen Latifah, Left Eye Lopez of TLC, MC Lyte, and Salt-N-Pepa rapped their way into starring roles in the hip hop and rap worlds. Inspired by black nationalism in the late 1980s, many of these female artists adapted their look to the political movement, dressing in the red, black, and green of the pan-African flag, wearing kente cloth head wraps, and playing with the stereotypes of male and female clothing. In her video, "The Rain (Supa Dupa Fly)," Missy Elliot pushed the definitions of masculine and feminine with various outfits of baggy overalls, black leather, sci-fi shiny blown-up pleather, and track suits. Some female artists wore what male hip hop artists wore—baggy jeans, work boots, and jerseys, but with makeup and flair. At the same time, other women such as Lil' Kim and Foxy Brown used sexuality as part of their modus operandi, donning tight, glamorous, and sexy outfits that celebrated their curves and played on their roles as women who controlled their own desires and the satisfaction of those needs. While the outfits often manipulated ideas of gender, makeup tended to be feminine, sexy, and sensual. Haloed by a multiplicity of hairstyles, from weaves to braids, from short to long, from curls to straight, women often had glossy, dark lips; long, luscious lashes; and glowing, lustrous skin. Blinged out in nameplate necklaces, oversized gold doorknocker and hoop earrings, and large shiny rocked rings, hip hop females played with the nuances of gender and sexuality.

Critiques

In juxtaposition with these strong female figures, however, were the women cast in the music videos of primarily male artists. Cultural critics and feminists decried the objectification of women in these videos, often scantily clad, sexually posed, and derogatorily depicted, as sustaining and perpetuating the patriarchal, hyper-sexualized stereotypes of African American males in the black community. Many male artists referred to women as *ho* and *bitch,* and described cases of physical abuse, rape, and psychological violence in the song lyrics. Accused of being misogynistic, hip hop culture has been heavily criticized for exacerbating male/female power relations and advocating male dominance and violence toward women.

Designers and Artists

As the hip hop movement became increasingly visible and popularized by MTV, hip hop artists defined the parameters and limits of the art form and soon realized the potential of their influence on youth culture. While many hip hop artists wore **designers** such as Tommy Hilfiger, Nautica, and Polo Ralph Lauren in the 1990s, other artists ventured out of the music industry into the fashion and beauty world. Sean Diddy Combs, to whom the term *ghetto fabulous* is commonly attributed, was one of the first producer/performers to use his image and reputation to sell his own brand of clothing. Sean John earned critical and commercial success, taking hip hop from the streets into couture. Russell Simmons, producer and cofounder of hip hop label Def Jam and brother of Rev. Joseph Simmons (also known as Run of Run-DMC), created the Phat Farm clothing line. Simmons's now ex-wife, Kimora Lee Simmons, took the Phat Farm line one step further, expanding into women and children's fashion and offering hip hop fashion-forward fabulous clothing to the wider American public. Jay-Z and Damon Dash started Rocawear, 50 Cent runs G-Unit Clothing, Kanye West is slated to debut Pastelle, and Eve relaunched her Fetish clothing line in 2008. Female hip hop artists have also been involved in the makeup industry. Queen Latifah is a spokesmodel for **CoverGirl**; Kimora Lee Simmons has started her own makeup line, KLS **Cosmetics;** and Lil' Kim, Missy Elliot, and Eve all represented the M.A.C. Viva Glam series.

Global Influences

Hip hop fashion and beauty has also had a strong international influence. In Italy, southern youths and young Arabs living in Rome have appropriated the art form, the mode of dress, and the lifestyle as a way to communicate their own dissatisfaction with Italian politics and society. Hip hop artists in France have found voice through poetry and beat as the country struggles with racial integration, anti-Arab racism, and nationalism. In Japan, where hip hop was part of an underground club scene, the art form has become part of the mainstream as Japanese hip hop stars have made their own albums, speaking their own poetry, telling their own stories. Throngs of youth crowd record stores looking for the latest albums by such artists as Schadaraparr, Rhymester, King Giddra, and Hime. Beyond the music, the fashion has hit the streets of Tokyo as well—more than 300 stores selling hip hop clothing have been doing fast business with Japanese youth.

Further Reading: Asante, M. K. *It's Bigger than Hip Hop: The Rise of the Post-Hip-Hop Generation.* New York: St. Martin's, 2008; Chang, Jeff, and D. J. Kool Herc. *Can't Stop Won't Stop: A History of the Hip-Hop Generation.* New York: Picador, 2005; Condry, Ian. *HIP-HOP Japan.* Durham, NC: Duke University Press, 2006; Condry, Ian "Yellow B-Boys, Black Culture, and Hip-Hop in Japan: Toward a Transnational Cultural Politics of Race." *Positions,* 15 no. 3 (2007): 637–71; George, Nelson. *Hip Hop America.* New York: Penguin, 2005; Kitwana, Bakari. *Why White Kids Love Hip Hop: Wankstas, Wiggers, Wannabes, and the New Reality of Race in America.* New York: Basic Civitas, 2006; Oliver, Richard, and Tim Leffel. *Hip-Hop, Inc.: Success Strategies of the Rap Moguls.* Cambridge, MA: Da Capo, 2006; Rose, Tricia. *The Hip Hop Wars: What We Talk about When We Talk about Hip Hop—And why it Matters.* New York: Basic Civitas, 2008; Rosen, Jody. "A Rolling Shout Out to Hip Hop History." *New York Times,* February 12, 2007. http://www.nytimes.com/2006/02/12/arts/music/12rose.html?pagewanted=1&_r=1; Watkins, S. Craig. *Hip Hop Matters: Politics, Pop Culture, and the Struggle for the Soul of a Movement.* Boston: Beacon Press, 2006; Wood, Joe. "The Yellow Negro." *Transition,* 73 (1997): 40–67.

Aliza S. Wong

HOW TO LOOK GOOD NAKED

How to Look Good Naked (United Kingdom, Channel 4, 2006; United States, Lifetime, 2008) is a reality program first begun in Britain, where it was hosted by Gok Wan, and then modified in the United States, where it is hosted by Carson Kresley (the fashion stylist from **Queer Eye for the Straight Guy**). In both versions of the program, the hosts encourage women who are insecure about their bodies to undergo a perception revolution where a woman's eyes can be reeducated to appreciate her actual size. This modified form of seeing, the show argues, will allow a woman to lay claim to greater self-confidence and consequent beauty.

Both Wok and Kresley lead women through various perception modification exercises that include asking a female subject to strip down to her underwear and slowly categorize her perceived body flaws. Quite often, women will comment on how much they hate the size of their hips or thighs. In the American version, Kresley then leads the female subject to a lineup of women, all with the same flaw that the subject perceives in herself. He then asks the makeover subject to insert herself into the continuum of women. She invariably misidentifies herself, believing she is worse than she is by putting herself at the bad or large extreme of the continuum rather than at the good or thin end. In another exercise, subjects are asked to look at three female figures walking down the street, their faces obscured. One woman is dressed casually, another sophisticated, the third messy. In each case, the makeover subject selects the woman in more expensive, sophisticated clothing as being thinnest and most attractive. Kresley reveals at the end of this exercise that each of the women being examined was actually one woman dressed three different ways, all to underscore that clothes help to shape perception.

Given the importance of clothing for such altered perceptions, it is somewhat ironic that the show bills itself as *How to Look Good Naked*. Both the British and American version of the show make good on the claim of looking good naked by ending each makeover episode with a photo shoot in which the formerly in-secure makeover subjects now flaunts her curvy body while nude. *How to Look Good Naked* has been hailed by television critics as well as by Oprah Winfrey as a positive antimakeover show, since it does not feature plastic surgery or weight loss and seems to advocate that women embrace themselves at whatever size they may be. Popular appeal has been strong, and *How to Look Good Naked*'s premiere on Lifetime had the network's largest ratings event in its 24-year history.

The show's perception alteration exercises, however, work to reinforce a notion that big is bad, so women on this show learn that they aren't as large as they be-lieved, but bad, fat, ugly, and unkempt are still shameful categories to be avoided. *How to Look Good Naked*'s premise suggests that women (and, indeed, it targets only women) are essentially skewed in their perceptive abilities, and they cannot find happiness in an image-obsessed world until their pathologized way of seeing is reeducated by the respective male host.

Further Reading: Weber, Brenda R. "Makeover as Takeover: Scenes of Affective Domi-nation on Makeover TV." *Configurations,* 15 no. 1 (2008): 77–100; Weber, Brenda R. *Makeover TV: Selfhood, Citizenship, and Celebrity.* Durham, NC: Duke University Press, 2009.

Brenda R. Weber

INFOMERCIALS

Infomercials are television commercials that sell products using programming imitative of noncommercial television shows. They can run anywhere from one minute to one hour, with the standard length being just under 30 minutes. Originally shown between the hours of 2 A.M. and 6 A.M., as a network's alternative to signing off, infomercials can now be viewed on numerous channels 24 hours a day.

Infomercials, also called paid programming, are characterized by more in-depth information about a product than the viewer receives in a typical television advertisement. Many infomercials try to conceal their commercial interests, and structure their programming to resemble talk shows or other programs. Some are developed around narrative storylines, and many feature celebrity endorsements and interviews concerning the product. Infomercials are considered direct response marketing, and feature several short segments within the larger structure that invite the customer to call and place an order right away. They often rely on tactics such as limited-time offers, exclusivity of TV sales, and emphasizing the revolutionary qualities of their products in order to make sales. In addition to celebrity endorsements, personal testimonials are common, as are recommendations from scientists and experts in the field. Most tend to be repetitive, interspersing the broader content of narrative and testimonial with catchphrases and lists of the product's attributes.

Infomercials burgeoned in the 1980s, after the Federal Communications Commission eased restrictions on television commercial programming. While early infomercials were usually limited to late night screening, stations are finding it increasingly lucrative to show infomercials at all hours of the day. In 2008, much of infomercial spending took place in the morning and daytime hours. In addition to the option of buying products directly from a phone number given in the infomercial, customers are increasingly turning to Web sites that deal specifically in merchandise shown on infomercials. Web sites such as www.infomercials-tv.com and www.isawitontv.info sell huge ranges of products, from exercise and health products to electronics and household goods, all of which are featured in infomercials on a wide variety of channels.

The beauty industry has found a market in infomercials, especially for personal care products and exercise equipment, which benefit from personal testimonials and demonstrations. Unlike traditional retailers, which rely solely on displays and **packaging** to advertise, infomercials provide before and after footage, step-by-step instructions with models on the use of the product, and interviews with customers asserting the life-altering capabilities of the product. A vast number of beauty and health products that use infomercials also use celebrity endorsements, with the celebrity's exceptional beauty as further testament to the product's revolutionary effectiveness.

See also: Endorsements of Products, Celebrity

Further Reading: Bruno, Richard. *A Quick and Easy Guide to the World of Infomercials.* Miami, FL: Hawksbill, 1992; Direct Marketing Association. http://www.the-dma.org; Direct Marketing News. http://www.dmnews.com; Elcoff, Alvin. *Direct Marketing through Broadcast Media.* Lincolnwood, IL: NTC Business Books, 1995; Evans, Craig Roberts. *Marketing Channels: Infomercials and the Future of Televised Marketing.* Upper Saddle River, NJ: Prentice Hall, 1993; Hope, Wayne, and Rosser Johnson. "What is an Infomercial?" *Advertising and Society Review,* 5 no. 2 (2004); Stern, Remy. *But Wait . . . There's More! Tighten Your Abs, Make Millions, and Learn How the $100 Billion Infomercial Industry Sold Us Everything but the Kitchen Sink.* New York: Collins Business, 2009.

Abigail Mitchell

INTERNET

The World Wide Web, accessed through the Internet, is home to retailers from every possible area, and the beauty industry is no exception. Consumers not only have the chance to buy beauty products from the Web sites of stores where they are available, but they can also purchase them directly from the companies that manufacture them. Many online retailers specialize in beauty products, including www.beauty.com and www.ibeauty.com.

Online Advertising

The **advertising** market has been completely revolutionized by the Internet. While print, television, and radio advertising is still prevalent, online advertising is securing an ever increasing segment of the market. A huge number of Web sites use advertising to pay for their costs and earn a profit, and as a result advertisers are able to cater their material to the readership of specific Web sites. Beauty industry retailers can pinpoint women and men of various ages for their products, and provide them with a quick link to a purchasing opportunity.

The World Wide Web also serves as a host to numerous sites dispensing information regarding beauty. Sites such as www.beautytipsonline.com and www.freebeautytips.org provide how-to guides, makeup tips and tricks, and beauty regimens. While they are not direct retailers, sites like these and others frequently recommend products to their readers, who in the same manner which they found the information, can easily click to find the manufacturer of the product or a retailer that sells it.

Further Reading: Moss, Gloria, Rod Gunn, and Krzysztof Kubacki. "Success and Failures of the Mirroring Principle: The Case of Angling and Beauty Websites." *International Journal of Consumer Studies,* 31 no. 3 (2007): 248–57; Schaefer, Kayleen. "Beauty

Blogs Come of Age: Swag, Please." *New York Times,* January 31, 2008; Schell, Bernadette H., and Bob Tedeschi. "E-Commerce Report; When Beauty is More than a Click Deep." *New York Times,* October 1, 2007; Zukin, Sharon. *Point of Purchase: How Shopping Changed American Culture.* New York: Routledge, 2005. See esp. chap. 9, "The Zen Internet Shopping."

Abigail Mitchell

J

JOHNSON PRODUCTS

George Ellis Johnson, born in Richton, Mississippi in 1927, founded the Johnson Products Company in Chicago in 1954. Johnson had worked as a chemist for the Fuller **cosmetics** company for 10 years before starting his own business with 500 dollars in borrowed money. The company represented part of a larger trend of growth in the **African American beauty industry** after World War II and fit into a longstanding tradition of black-owned beauty businesses that included the Poro Company of **Annie Turnbo Malone**, the **Madam C. J. Walker Manufacturing** Company, and Sara Washington's Apex Company. Johnson Products was different from these businesses in that it focused, initially, on the male hair care market and on chemical straightening products that were safer and easier for customers to use at home.

Johnson's first product was Ultra Wave, a chemical hair relaxer for men. Ultra Sheen, a chemical relaxer designed for women, came out in 1957 and helped to revolutionize the African American female hair care industry. Before the 1960s, black women had almost exclusively straightened their hair using oils and heated metal pressing combs. Chemical straighteners (commercial and homemade) had always been too harsh, causing longer hair to break and turning black hair red; in addition, they were generally considered socially inappropriate for women to use. By the 1970s, chemical relaxers for women were commonplace in the African American beauty market. Johnson Products also innovated by developing **Afro** Sheen, a line of products designed in the 1960s to care for unprocessed hair, and by introducing Gentle Treatment, the first no-lye relaxer on the market, in 1981. Johnson Products was also a prolific advertiser in black magazines like *Ebony*, notably using innovative and original appeals to black pride in advertisements for Afro Sheen in the late 1960s and early 1970s.

Johnson Products was the first African American business to be listed on the New York Stock Exchange in 1973, but, like many black-owned beauty enterprises in this period, it faced increasing competition from white-owned firms. The company confronted additional problems in 1975 when the Federal Trade Commission forced Johnson Products to sign a consent decree admitting that the lye (or sodium hydroxide) in Ultra Sheen could cause hair to fall out and irritate skin, and mandating warning labels on **packaging**. White-owned companies that produced relaxers did not, to George Johnson's chagrin, have to put similar labeling on packaging until several years later. In 1993, the Miami-based, white-owned Ivax Corporation absorbed the Johnson Products Company, retaining the brand name, product lines, and Chicago headquarters. Carson Inc. bought Johnson Products in 1998, and L'Oréal bought Carson in 2000. This time, L'Oréal replaced the Johnson brand with their own, but moved its entire African American hair and cosmetics line to the Johnson Products building in Chicago in 2002. However, Johnson Products brands continue to be produced. In 2001, the Department of Justice ordered L'Oréal to divest its interest in the Ultra Sheen and Gentle Treatment brands. Wella bought the interest in these lines and continued to manufacture them after **Procter and Gamble** bought that company in 2003.

See also: African American Beauty Industry

Further Reading: Craig, Maxine B. *Ain't I a Beauty Queen? Black Women, Beauty, and the Politics of Race.* New York: Oxford University Press, 2002; Johnson Products. "Johnson Products Heritage." http://www.johnsonproducts.com/heritage.html; Walker, Susannah. *Style and Status: Selling Beauty to African American Women, 1920–1975.* Lexington: University Press of Kentucky, 2007; Weems, Robert E. *Desegregating the Dollar: African American Consumerism in the Twentieth Century.* New York: New York University Press, 1998.

Susannah Walker

K

KLEIN, CALVIN. *SEE* CALVIN KLEIN

L

LABOR

The fashion industry's association with a world of glamour and haute couture has been contrasted with the issues of sweatshop labor, including child labor, unregulated factories, below subsistence-level wages, and forced labor. This dichotomous view of work and production in the beauty industry becomes even more complex when not only **manufacturing**, but also beauty sales and services, are considered. Returning to the racks piles of clothing left carelessly on dressing rooms floors, manicuring nails of someone who is suspicious of one's culture and language, or owning one's own salon creates complex work cultures that can tout rewarding autonomous entrepreneurial niches as well as a host of problems typical of service occupations that involves pleasing both managers and picky customers. Since the birth of the fashion and beauty industry in the 19th century, the production and sales of goods and services reflect an often precarious balance between worker opportunity and exploitation.

From Dressmaker to Garment Worker

Some of the contradictions that shape labor and fashion reflect the invisibility of 19th-century female entrepreneurs and mistress craftswomen in the dressmaking and millinery trades. Since men have commonly been associated with the marketplace and women with domestic production, female dressmaking and millinery have often been ignored or forgotten. By the midcentury, an emerging middle class afforded the growth of the men's ready-made clothing industry, although some men continued to frequent tailors for a custom-made fit. According to labor historians, Victorian fashions for women were still fitted to the individual and provided a means of creative labor for women more commonly associated with skilled male occupations. Female artisans in dressmaking, for example, cut patterns, tailor-fit dresses, and owned their own shops. In part, their market niche reflected gendered assumptions that female attire with all of its ornate ruffles and bows needed a feminine touch. It has been noted that unlike the less-skilled, less-respected seamstresses, dressmakers not only designed and produced ladies garments, but also acted as ambassadors of the fashion industry whose savvy in the business helped to placate and balance contemporary mores with fashion trends that seemed frivolous and potentially harmful to female virtue.

Better known and far more notorious is the sweatshop labor that also had its roots in 19th-century America. Both centralized factories and outwork (piecework assembled at home and outside the factory) reflected the subdivision of labor and deskilling that defined industrial production and worker exploitation. At the same time, many of the women who manufactured the latest fads and fashions of the early 20th century also consumed and produced apparel and accessories for their own use. Whether it was sewing together scraps from the shop floor, skimping on meals to pay for a new hat, or frequenting secondhand shops, working-class women embraced what has been called *putting on style*. It has been shown how the desire to consume a bit of glamour often reserved for middle-class ladies inspired working-girls to embrace labor organizations as they collectively pushed for the time, money, and well-being needed to enjoy fancy dresses, French heels, and other cheap amusements.

In the early 20th century, labor activism was on the rise and female garment workers were at the forefront in cities like New York. The Triangle Shirtwaist Company's management policies were indicative of the kind of disregard for worker safety that seemed ubiquitous in the garment industry. In an effort to secure greater managerial control of the labor process, employers often locked doors to prevent workers from stepping out on the job. Such draconian polices were all too tragically revealed to the public at large when 114 young workers at the Triangle Shirtwaist Company who were unable to escape the burning factory either jumped multiple stories to their deaths or succumbed to the inferno. As a result, the International Ladies Garment Workers Union (ILGW) gained widespread sympathy, along with the institution of better working conditions and wages, shorter days, and some of the first factory inspection laws in the country. It has been noted that The Triangle Shirtwaist Fire of 1911 acted as a catalyst for anti-sweatshop campaigns; these campaigns would reemerge in the 1990s.

Outsourcing

The golden age of American manufacturing and working-class wages would begin to wane in the late 1960s and 1970s and lead manufacturers to intensify their efforts to secure cheap labor. Some manufacturers followed the path of 1920s textile mills that moved to anti-union strongholds in the Carolinas; although this time the search led them across the Sunbelt south—from Virginia south to Florida and west across Texas to southern California. The Sunbelt provided plenty of cheap (often immigrant) labor and an anti-union sentiment that was pervasive. However, as companies discovered cheaper parts of the country, they also found cheaper labor costs across the globe, especially in developing countries where minimum wages, safety regulations, and worker rights were far and few between. While manufacturers generally found the cheap labor and lax regulations they were searching for, stories of worker exploitation and violence eventually attracted the attention of the media that brought public focus and outrage to bear on the working conditions typical of some of America's best-known consumer goods— Nike shoes and Levi's jeans. One of the most famous scandals of the 1990s involved all-American talk show host Kathy Lee Gifford's Walmart line of clothing that turned out to be produced using illegal sweatshop labor in New York as well as the product of child labor in Honduras. More headlines attacked Nike apparel

Boss waving his fist at female employee in a sweatshop (clothing factory). Illustration in *Frank Leslie's Illustrated Newspaper,* **November 3, 1888, 188. (Courtesy of Library of Congress)**

that had been sewn in factories in Pakistan by children who made as little as six cents an hour.

Forced Labor

While examples of forced illegal immigrant labor have surfaced in, for example, El Monte, California, a producer of garments sold in Target, Sears, and Nordstrom's, prison labor has become increasingly popular since the early 1980s. During the 1990s, the United States prison population doubled to around two million, earning the country the dubious distinction of having the largest prison population in the world, and making accessible to American manufacturers another cheap source of labor. Prison labor is typically identified with the post-Reconstruction South (late 19th century), where newly freed slaves confronted a criminal justice system determined to undermine their freedom and civil rights and a convict leasing system that ruthlessly exploited their labor. The resurgence of prison labor in

"On July 1, 2000, the MPLU [Missouri Prisoners Labor Union] initiated an international boycott of the products made by Colgate Palmolive because the company did not back up MPLU's demand that the state of Missouri establish a minimum wage for all Missouri workers, abolish forced labor, and condemn executions. In a letter to Colgate, which hires Missouri prisoners, the MPLU noted: 'We realize that your company did not put us in prison. This is a matter of Colgate-Palmolive reaping immense profits for our incarceration and as the largest single consumer block you have a social obligation to us. The situation I am outlining is the same argument organized labor has used to oppose sweatshop labor employed by Kathy Lee Gifford, Nike, etc. I would also like to add that we are not asking for anything from society except that we be treated in a fair manner as defined by the United States Constitution and numerous legal cases. We are not advocating for a cushy life style but simply a fair days pay for a fair days work and a safe, non-abusive work environment.'"

Vijay Prasad, historian

Source: Prashad, Vijay. *Keeping Up with Dow Joneses: Debt, Prison, Workfare.* Cambridge, MA: South End Press, 2003, 107–8.

the 1980s and 1990s (that also saw the reemergence of the chain gang) once again made use of a prison population that was disproportionately African American (as well as Latino) and extraordinarily low wages. This time out, however, the use of labor was not confined to a relatively small number of jobs—often in agricultural, mining, or railroad construction. Companies today are made up of a number of different products and the beauty industry is well represented: Nordstrom's, **Revlon**, Macy's, Pierre Cardin, Eddie Bauer, and Victoria's Secret (to name a few) have benefited from prison labor either directly or through one of their subsidiary companies.

Service Occupations

While the most problematic labor experiences often reflect their invisibility and a production process hidden away in sweatshops or distant factories, service workers often endure unhealthy and poorly paid working conditions despite their face-to-face interaction with the customer in commercial spaces like department stores, beauty shops, **nail salons**, and **spas** where labor and consumption are intimately linked. Like the production of apparel, service workers not only face long hours and low wages, but also the unruly customers whose demands often have no bounds. Hairstylists have long dealt with customers who hate their new do or complain that they don't look like the supermodel they long to emulate. But they also face long hours on their feet, harsh chemicals, and problems like carpal tunnel syndrome. **Retail** sales workers, whether located at the upscale department store or the local discount retailer, often complain about customers who leave merchandise on the floor and treat them like maids. At nail salons, the harsh-smelling substances used to produce fake talons and elaborate **nail art** are often hard to ignore, even for the casual passerby. So, too, is the imagery of the nail tech wearing a mask bent over the manicure table with coworkers in assembly-line fashion. Language barriers further complicate these relationships and have accompanied the proliferation of

Asian-owned nail salons, along with a level of cultural suspicion and racism that further exacerbates relations between patron and worker.

Yet those same difficult-to-manage customers also shape the work culture in unexpected ways that can make life easier for a variety of different service workers and create unexpected opportunities. Some saleswomen in department stores in the early 20th century successfully managed a supportive work culture by cultivating a loyal clientele that afforded them the ability to negotiate management's demands or, if need be, to take their customers elsewhere. The beauty industry offers workers a unique degree of intimacy and social interaction that profoundly shapes day-to-day experiences, and especially those who apply hands-on service doing nails or giving facials can provide touch and conversation that customers look forward to as much as the final product. Such loyalties have often been particularly important in hair salons, where a customer's loyalty can span a lifecycle, and where workers are offered an entrepreneurial niche that is often hard to find in other occupations. In both the early and late 20th century, African Americans, along with some of the newest of immigrants, have also created occupations as well as products and businesses that have redefined the beauty industry. From **cosmetics** to hair products, they have made their operations into some of the most successful business models. To be sure, beauty service work is a segmented industry and that complicates the more romantic image of the hairstylist chatting away with clientele. Yet the beauty industry encourages touch and social interaction not typically found in other service occupations such as fast food. While the hands of the hairstylist or nail tech can be dismissed and abused, their skills and sympathetic ear are hard to replace and often afford a unique opportunity for the kind of creative labor and entrepreneurial pursuits reminiscent of 19th-century dressmaking shops.

Further Reading: Ehrenreich, Barbara. *Nickel and Dimed: On (Not) Getting By in America.* New York: Holt, 2002; Enstad, Nan. *Ladies of Labor, Girls of Adventure: Working Women, Popular Culture and Labor Politics at the turn of the Twentieth Century.* Columbia, NY: Columbia University Press, 1999; Fields, Jill. *An Intimate Affair: Women, Lingerie, and Sexuality.* Berkeley: University of California Press, 2007; Gamber, Wendy. *The Millinery and Dressmaking Trades, 1860–1930.* Urbana: University of Illinois Press, 1997; Han, Jeong woo. "Eye To Eye, Nail To Nail: Body and Identity in Korean Nail Salon Workers in New York City." PhD diss., New School for Social Research, 2004; Kang, Miliann. *The Managed Hand: Race, Gender, and the Body in Beauty Service Work.* Berkeley: University of California Press, 2010; Klein, Naomi. *No Logo.* New York: Picador Press, 2000; Porter-Benson, Susan. *Counter Cultures: Saleswomen, Managers, Customers in American Department Stores, 1890–1940.* Urbana: University of Illinois Press, 1986; Peiss, Kathy. *Hope in a Jar: The Making of America's Beauty Culture.* New York: Metropolitan, 1998; Prashad, Vijay. *Keeping Up with Dow Joneses: Debt, Prison, Workfare.* Boston: South End Press, 2003; Walker, Susannah. *Style and Status: Selling Beauty to African American Women, 1920–1975.* Lexington: University Press of Kentucky, 2007; Willett, Julie. "'Hands across the Table': A Short History of Manicurists in the Twentieth Century." *Journal of Women's History,* 17 no. 3 (2005): 59–80; Willett, Julie. *Permanent Waves: The Making of the American Beauty Shop.* New York: New York University Press, 2000.

Julie Willett

LATINA BEAUTY INDUSTRY

The Latina beauty industry includes hair care, cosmetics, and fragrance products and services. The industry includes mainstream brands and Latina-owned companies that target U.S.-born and immigrant Latinas as consumers. The American beauty industry may target marketing toward U.S. Latinas in English or Spanish. U.S.-born and immigrant Latinas are also business owners and employees of the Latina beauty industry.

Latina Identity Defined

Latinas are women of Latin American heritage. Latinas are a racial mix of indigenous, Spanish or other European, and African roots. Depending on regional lineage and family histories, Latina phenotypes represent a wide range reflecting indigenous, mestiza (mixed Spanish/indigenous), European, or African features. Latina skin tones and hair colors vary from light and blonde to medium tan and brown to black and in various combinations. Hair textures vary widely among Latinas from straight to curly, thick to thin. Latinas born in the United States may be predominantly English speakers or bilinguals whose lives are shaped by various degrees of Latina and Latino cultural traditions and values. Latina immigrants in the United States may be predominantly Spanish speakers with strong ethnic cultural ties. The Latina beauty industry includes women from Spain and Latin America.

Hairstylist and entrepreneur Silvia Castro at her West Texas business, Casa Capelli Salon, 2009. (Courtesy of Julie Willett)

Latina and Latino Market

Latinas and Latinos represent the fastest growing population in the United States. Estimates for 2006 report a Latina and Latino total population of over 44 million. Those of Mexican heritage represent 28 million. Puerto Ricans, Central Americans, and South Americans reflect an estimated 3.9 million, 3.3 million, and 2.4 million of the U.S. population, respectively.

Latina and Latino purchasing power reached $700 billion in 2007 and is expected to reach $1 trillion by 2010. Marketing research findings conclude that Latinas make 75 percent of the product-purchasing decisions for their households. Latinas spend 27 percent more on **cosmetics** and 43 percent more on fragrances than general consumers. Additionally, Latinas are found to be 37 percent more likely to spend $300 a year on cosmetics and 43 percent more on fragrances than general consumers. Latinas purchase 10 percent more premium hair care, 86 percent more hair color, and more of every different type of hair care product than the general consumer.

Latina studies scholars agree that cultural upbringing, gender socialization, and the influences of Latina representation in American popular culture help to explain their beauty product consumption and usage. Latinas learn culturally specific and class-specific ideals of femininity from their mothers, peers, and the mass media. Latina subjects describe preening and being presentable in public, whether or not one leaves the house, as a source of pride and empowerment. The hypersexualized, spitfire images embraced by Latina movie stars and celebrities further influence the kinds of beauty products Latina adolescents and young adults favor.

Recognizing the Latina consumer growth potential, U.S. cosmetics companies target Latinas with specific products and multicultural **advertising**. Mainstream brands such as Unilever, JossClaude Products, **Estée Lauder**, **Revlon**, Maybelline, **CoverGirl**, and L'Oréal have created new product lines for women of color and have selected women of color celebrities and models to promote products in multimedia outlets.

Unilever initiated an advertising campaign in 2005 geared toward the Spanish-speaking Latina audience by working with programs on the Spanish station Telemundo to incorporate segments on beauty featuring Unilever products. JossClaude released Formula Latina in 2004, a line of hair products for U.S. Latinas. According to JossClaude surveys, frizz and shine are the top two concerns of Latinas, which their products aim to address. JossClaude admit that their products would suit women of any ethnic/racial background.

Beginning in the 1990s, mainstream cosmetic brands such as Revlon and Maybelline have attempted to meet the needs of Latinas and women of color by adding more colors of foundations, concealers, and powders and hiring Latina and Spanish celebrities, including Penelope Cruz, Salma Hayek, Jennifer Lopez, and Eva Mendes as spokeswomen. Additional colors and shades reflect the light-to-medium skin tones and not the dark skin tones common among Latinas with more indigenous and African features. Darker foundations tend to be more challenging to create because of the added opacity and heavy textures caused by increases in pigment. Thus, darker-skinned women continue to have significantly fewer cosmetic color choices.

Critics contend that the mainstream beauty industry has failed to sustain a successful product line for Latinas and women of color. The three challenges for mainstream brands are in the areas of product development, **retail** strategy, and advertising. Another point of critique is that beauty industry spokeswomen reflect the light-skinned to moderately tan Latinas with more European features, a look that some in the industry describe as the universal appeal.

Producers, Entrepreneurs, and Advocates

Latinas and women of color have opened their own businesses in the beauty industry and produced their own lines of cosmetics to address the lack of choices offered by mainstream brands. Latinas also act as advocates in support of Latina and Latino beauty industry professionals and students and the broader Latina and Latino community.

Zalia Cosmetics is Latina-owned and released its line of multicultural color cosmetics for Latinas in 2001, offering a selection of foundations, concealers, and powders in olive and yellow tones. Founder and president Monica Ramirez launched Zalia at shopping malls in Miami, Los Angeles, Dallas, and New York. Three percent of Zalia's profits go to organizations that service Latinas and entrepreneurs.

The success of Jennifer Lopez's Glow is one example of ethnic fragrance marketing. Along with a significant advertising campaign, Lopez's own popularity and the ubiquitous coverage of her romances in magazines and entertainment news at the time of Glow's launch in 2005 is said to have facilitated its success.

Latinas are also owners and employees of small businesses affiliated with the beauty industry. Out of every 10 businesses, 1 is Latina or Latino owned. Latina-owned businesses represent 35 percent of the 2 million Latina- or Latino-owned businesses registered in the United States; the number increased by 121 percent between 1997 and 2006. Research on Latina-owned beauty parlors demonstrates the role that these small businesses, particularly Latina beauty parlors, play in providing support to, educating, and empowering Latina communities regarding personal and public health issues.

The National Latino Cosmetology Association (NLCA), a nonprofit founded by CEO Julie Zepeda in 2006, supports and promotes the businesses and careers of cosmetologists, estheticians, nail technicians, massage therapists, barbers, and beauty industry students. Beyond professional support, the NLCA supports the development of natural products and eco-friendly **packaging**.

Health and Safety

Latinas are the subject of public health concerns related to the beauty industry. Shampoos, lotions, hair dyes, fragrances, and makeup contain chemicals linked to breast cancer, reproductive problems such as birth defects, and other illnesses.

The use of toxic chemicals in U.S. beauty products is traced back to the inception of the industry in the mid 1800s. Today, only 10 percent of all chemical ingredients used in beauty products are regulated by the **U.S. Food and Drug Administration**. In the United States, companies are not required to list chemicals used in their beauty products.

Chemicals of concern include coal tar, often used in permanent hair dyes; formaldehyde and sodium lauryl sulfate, often used in shampoos, conditioners, and shower gels; lead acetate, often used in red lipstick; nanoparticles, often used in sunblock lotions and anti-wrinkle creams; parabens, often used in underarm deodorants; and phthalates, often found in nail polish.

Some products popular among Latinas contain the highest levels of toxic chemicals. These include Vaseline Intensive Care Lotion—Aloe and Naturals, Revlon ColorStay Overtime Liquid Lipcolor in Ultimate Wine, and OPI Classic Shades Nail Lacquer in OPI Red. Neurotoxins are also found in red and wine lip colors made by L'Oréal, Christian Dior, and CoverGirl. People in occupations affiliated with the beauty industry are at a higher risk of exposure to hazardous chemicals. For instance, breast cancer rates for cosmetologists in Los Angeles County are nearly twice that of the general population, and cosmetology is a popular occupation among Latinas.

The Campaign for Safe Cosmetics, initiated in 2002, is a collaboration of organizations including the Breast Cancer Fund, the National Black Environmental Justice Network, Women's Voices for the Earth, and the Environmental Working Group calling for national and state-level legislation and corporate accountability to ensure consumers are informed of all chemicals used in beauty products. The campaign also publishes reports and fact sheets to inform women of the toxic chemicals found in specific beauty products, as well as their negative health impacts.

One legislative outcome of the efforts of the Campaign for Safe Cosmetics is the passage of Senate Bill 484 in California (CA SB 484), also known as the Safe Cosmetics Act of 2005. CA SB 484 implements a regulatory framework for the use of chemicals in beauty products and mandates that companies report all toxic ingredients used in their products beginning in fall 2008. Companies that lobbied against CA SB 484 included **Estée Lauder**, L'Oréal, **Procter and Gamble**, **Avon**, **Mary Kay Cosmetics**, Neutrogena, and Johnson & Johnson, many of whom actively promote products for Latinas and other women of color. A similar California bill to outlaw the use of lead in lipstick was defeated in June 2008.

See also: Health and Safety

Further Reading: Alvarez, Julia. *Once Upon a Quinceanera: Coming of Age in the USA.* New York: Viking Adult Press, 2007; Breast Cancer Fund. "Cosmetics Popular With Latinas Linked to Cancer, Other Serious Health Problems." August 10, 2005. http://www.breastcancerfund.org; The Campaign for Safe Cosmetics. "Unmasked: 10 Ugly Truths Behind the Myth of Cosmetic Safety." http://www.safecosmetics.org; Center for Women's Business Research. "Firms Owned by Women of Color Outpace All Firms in Growth in Numbers: Yet Revenues and Employment are Lower than Average." February 20, 2007. http://www.nfwbo.org; Delgado, Melvin. "Role of Latina-owned

Beauty Parlors in a Latino Community." *Social Work,* 42 no. 5 (1997): 445–53; De Lourdes Sobrino, Maria, and contributor Mirna Medina. *Thriving Latina Entrepreneurs in America.* El Monte, CA: Academic Learning Company LLC, 2007; Malkan, Stacy. *Not Just a Pretty Face: The Ugly Side of the Beauty Industry.* British Columbia: New Society Publishers, 2007; Mendible, Myra. *From Bananas to Buttocks: The Latina Body in Popular Film and Culture.* Austin: University of Texas Press, 2007; Molinary, Rosie. *Hijas Americanas: Beauty, Body Image and Growing Up Latina.* Berkeley, CA: Seal Press, 2007; Peiss, Kathy. "Making Faces: The Cosmetics Industry and the Cultural Construction of Gender, 1890–1930." In *Unequal Sisters: A Multicultural Reader in U.S. Women's History,* ed. Vicki Ruiz and Ellen Carol DuBois, pp. 324–45. New York: Routledge Press, 2000; Ruiz, Vicki, and Virgina Sanchez Korrol, eds. *Latina Legacies: Identity, Biography, Community.* New York: Oxford University Press, 2005.

Perlita Dicochea

LAUDER, ESTÉE. *SEE* ESTÉE LAUDER

M

MAGAZINES, MEN'S

Magazines for American men, dealing variously with topics as diverse as politics, health and fitness, fashion and other aspects of consumerism, sexual health and performance, and travel, can be traced back to the 18th century. Since the 1980s and 1990s, magazines directed at men with a range of interests and sexual identities have expanded dramatically.

The 18th Century

The English *Gentleman's Magazine,* a publication aimed at an educated male audience, was first published in London by Edward Cave in 1731. Functioning as a monthly digest of political affairs (including colonial developments), a compendium of literary and artistic production, and a summary of sporting news, this magazine was regularly perused by men on both sides of the Atlantic. Colonial subjects in North America also had recourse to a broad range of other publications. The 18th century (in both the pre- and postrevolutionary periods) witnessed the publication of at least 100 magazines, most of which were rather short-lived. The *American Magazine and Historical Chronicle,* a periodical focusing on moral essays, literary extracts, poems, and historical topics was published in Boston in 1743–46. Beginning in 1732 (until 1757), Benjamin Franklin began to publish his highly popular *Poor Richard's Almanack* and, in 1741, the decidedly utilitarian *General Magazine and Historical Chronicle for all the British Plantations in America.* Mostly masculine and upper class in orientation, publications of this sort represent the first important stage in the development of the American men's magazine.

The 19th Century

The 19th century ushered in dramatic changes in both printing techniques and audiences. As literacy rates rose, due in part to an increase in public education, magazines directed at more diverse groups began to appear with far greater frequency. In the years following the American Civil War, a shift in magazine content occurred. Whereas in the 18th and early 19th centuries the focus was primarily on the dissemination of helpful information, enlightenment, and education, in the years after 1860 magazine publishers turned more toward entertainment and amusement. They also, however, began to tap into a more segmented market that was slowly beginning to recognize the connection between magazine consumption and personal identities. Class distinctions were highlighted, for some, by the types of magazines one purchased and read. *Scribner's* (f. 1887), for example, was directed at an upper-class and genteel readership, while *McClure's* (f. 1893) and *Munsey's Magazine* (f. 1889), with 15- and 10-cent cover prices, respectively, were directed at a much broader reading public. These new and much cheaper magazines, which kept their subscription costs down by selling photoengraved illustrated advertisements, purveyed images of men (in advertisements for sports and shaving equipment, hair tonics, and exercise regimens) that offered a new vision of an athletic and dynamic manhood and were embraced by an eager consuming public.

With the growing popularity of the illustrated magazine, pioneered in the United Kingdom by Herbert Ingram in his *Illustrated London News* in 1842 and popularized in the United States by the publishers of *Leslie's Weekly* (f. 1852) and *Harper's Weekly* (f. 1857), came a new opportunity for those interested in reaching an exclusively male readership. These mass-produced, widely distributed, and visually stimulating publications fed an increasing appetite for up-to-date information and weekly or monthly installments of easily digested entertainment. The advent of the modern magazine market also brought about a number of highly specialized magazines that provided boys and men with an opportunity to embrace particular masculine identities. Boys were treated to a broad range of publications that were intended to cater to their particular interests. In 1865, for example, *The Little Corporal,* a magazine with a military theme and concerned with fighting evil and wrong and emphasizing all that was good, true, and beautiful, began a 10-year run of entertaining boys with stories of martial heroism and purveying helpful advice. By the end of the century, however, magazines directed at boys and men began to focus less on narratives of heroism and the self-made man and more on physical appearance.

At the fore of this development were publications dealing primarily with bodily improvement and the new physical culture craze, a development founded in part to counteract both the negative consequences of urbanization and the perceived degeneration of American racial stock. Bernarr Adolphus Macfadden (1868–1955), considered by many to be the American father of physical culture, began this particular form of magazine publishing in England, where he launched, in 1898, the magazine *Physical Development*. In 1899, he introduced what was to be become the most successful of the American magazines on the topic, *Physical Culture*. Containing articles on muscle development, diet, exercise, and bodily and facial appearance more generally, *Physical Culture* served as a prototype for a new form of men's literature that would come to play a major role in 20th century magazine markets. As a complicated cultural product (that was as much about visual stimulation as it was about the provision of written advice), this magazine functioned not only as a vehicle for the transmission of ideas about physical culture but also as a titillating and homoerotically charged text for same-sex desiring men in the early decades of the 20th century.

The 20th Century

This emphasis on physical appearance was also seen in several other notable men's publications in the 1920s and 1930s. MacFadden built on the success of *Physical Culture* by creating several pulp magazines that provided readers with opportunities to tell their own stories. Among the most significant of these were *True Story* (f. 1919) and *True Romances* (f. 1923). By the 1930s, the commercial viability of the men's magazine became readily apparent to entrepreneurs like Arnold Gingrich who founded, in 1933, *Esquire,* an oversized, glossy magazine for men that focused on style and heterosexual titillation in the form of scantily clad female models. As the magazine matured, it became more literary in orientation, publishing the works of Ernest Hemingway, William Faulkner, and John Steinbeck. It also began, in the 1940s and '50s, to focus on providing general lifestyle information in the form of fashion features; book, **film**, and music reviews; and satirical humor, often relating to politics and other contemporary events. While the audience for *Esquire* was decidedly upmarket, working-class men were also catered to in a number of pulp (and later glossy) adventure magazines that burst onto the scene beginning in the 1930s. Focusing in their first incarnations on Wild West stories, encounters with the indigenous peoples of African and Latin American lands, and the conquest of nature, magazines like *True* (f. 1937) were transformed in the postwar period into publications that entertained readers with stories of rapacious Nazis and dangerous Communists, often depicted as direct threats to American womanhood. African American men (and to a certain extent women) were provided with their own lifestyle magazine with the founding, by John H. Johnson, of **Ebony** in 1945.

The most notable postwar development in men's magazine production undoubtedly occurred in 1953, when Hugh Hefner first published his now infamous *Playboy.* Intended as both a celebration of female beauty and a lifestyle guide for urban men, the magazine met with almost immediate success. The first issue featured Marilyn Monroe as centerfold and began a tradition, quickly followed in subsequent issues, of providing not just sexually explicit, but still tasteful, images, but also advice on interior design, cocktails, dress, and physical appearance. The focus was on creating an image of manhood and a masculine lifestyle that appealed to the wealthy, heterosexual, and driven urban sophisticate. In his opening editorial for the first issue of the magazine, Hefner defined the playboy as an urban pleasure seeker, not an outdoorsy adventurer: "WE like our apartment. We enjoy mixing up cocktails, and an *hors d'oeuvre* or two, putting a little mood music on the phonograph, and inviting in a female acquaintance for a quiet discussion on Picasso, Nietzsche, jazz, sex." Like *Esquire,* the emphasis on helping to develop the whole man led Hefner and his staff to also place a high premium on publishing literary items that might appeal to educated readers by writers as diverse as Ian Fleming and, more recently, Margaret Atwood.

The men's magazine was not confined exclusively, in the postwar period, to men who identified with *Playboy*'s heterosexual ethos. Borrowing from the work of physical culturists like MacFadden, photographers catering to a queer market began to produce physique magazines for consumption by same-sex desiring men. Most notable were perhaps the efforts of Bob Mizer, who began, in 1945, to offer homoerotic photographs to customers through the catalogue that he produced for his Athletic Model Guild. In 1951, he began publishing the magazine *Physique Pictorial,* which included images of well-developed and nearly naked physique models, as well as erotic drawings by artists such as Tom of Finland. To avoid prosecution under the 1873 Comstock Act, which policed the trafficking of obscene images, *Physical Pictorial* and other magazines like *Vim* (f. 1954) sought to evade detection by adhering, outwardly at least, to the traditionally sports-oriented and hypermasculine tone of other men's magazines.

The 1960s and 1970s witnessed the growth of the market for men's magazines and the products that companies like Gillette and Jockey advertised on their pages. A significant magazine from this period had begun life in the 1930s as *Apparel Arts.* In 1957, *Apparel Arts,* a glossy magazine that contained images of men's fashion, as well as fabric samples for men's clothes, was relaunched as **Gentlemen's Quarterly (GQ)**. Through the 1970s, this magazine focused principally on men's style and clothing. With its sale to the publishing conglomerate Condé Nast in the 1980s, however, the magazine began a shift that focused more on general lifestyle and cultural issues, thus putting it into direct competition with *Esquire.* This decade of change also witnessed the rise of several other magazines directed exclusively at male audiences, including *Details* (f. 2000) and the enormously popular health and fitness–oriented magazine **Men's Health** (f. 1987).

Recent Developments

The modern proliferation of men's magazines really began in the 1990s, as publishers began to tap into potentially lucrative youthful male audiences who viewed concerns about their physical appearance and grooming not as markers of femininity but as a prerogative of a new type of masculinity. Most notable among these magazines have been the so-called lad magazines. Frequently British in origin, these publications have often picked up where *Playboy* left off. **Maxim** (f. 1995), functions as an international magazine famous as much for its risqué (but non-nude) pictorial spreads of female actors, models, and rock stars as for its lifestyle advice to its target audience, 18–30-year-old men. Frequently aggressive in tone, magazines like *Maxim,* even as they focus on the attention to physical appearance most closely associated with the rise of the narcissistic and decidedly fashionable **metrosexuals**, have served to reinforce heterosexual desire; produce acquisitive consumer fantasies that often revolve around cars, tools, and other toys; and frequently separate straight men from gay men.

Consumer fantasies and the attention to physical appearance, combined with fairly superficial doses of gay, lesbian, bisexual, and transgender politics, have also figured prominently in the growth of magazines targeted explicitly at openly gay men. Most prominent among these publications has been the magazine *Out* (f. 1992), a lifestyle magazine that focuses on travel, fashion, culture, and physical fitness and appearance. It currently enjoys the largest circulation of any gay publication and reflects the diversity inherent, in the early 21st century, in the genre of the men's magazine.

See also: Grooming, Male; Models, Male

Further Reading: Benwell, Bethan. *Masculinity and Men's Lifestyle Magazines.* Malden, MA: Blackwell, 2003; Breazeale, Kenon. "In Spite of Women: *Esquire* Magazine and the Construction of the Male Consumer." *Signs: Journal of Women in Culture and Society,* 20 no. 1 (1994): 1–22; Crewe, Ben. *Representing Men: Cultural Production and Producers in the Men's Magazine Market.* Oxford: Berg, 2003; Fraterrigo, Elizabeth. "The Answer to Suburbia: Playboy's Urban Lifestyle." *Journal of Urban History,* 34 no. 5 (2008): 747–74; Jackson, Peter, Nick Stevenson, and Kate Brooks. *Making Sense of Men's Magazines.* Cambridge: Polity Press, 2001; Morgan, Tracy D. "Pages of Whiteness: Race, Physique Magazines, and the Emergence of Public Gay Culture." In *Queer Studies: A Lesbian, Gay, Bisexual, and Transgender Anthology,* ed. Brett Beemyn and Mickey Eliason. New York: New York University Press, 1996; Parfrey, Adam. *It's a Man's World: Men's Adventure Magazines, the Postwar Pulps.* Los Angeles, CA: Feral House, 2003; Pendergast, Tom. *Creating the Modern Man: American Magazines and Consumer Culture, 1900–1950.* Columbia: University of Missouri Press, 2000.

Paul R. Deslandes

MAGAZINES, WOMEN'S. *SEE COSMOPOLITAN*; FASHION MAGAZINES; *SEVENTEEN*; *VOGUE*

MAKEOVERS

A makeover is a transformation from an inadequate before to a superior after; it is often used to refer to a transformation in appearance. One can be made over or make over oneself. In the U.S. mythos, the makeover is often an element in the rags-to-riches story.

History

The makeover has been used as a device in **advertising**, magazines, films, and television shows. The first proper makeover has been traced to a special story on the "Made-Over Girl" in *Mademoiselle* magazine in 1936. An ordinary reader of the magazine, nurse Barbara Phillips, wrote to *Mademoiselle,* asking for advice on how to improve her looks. *Mademoiselle* took up the challenge of making Phillips into a beauty and showcased the makeover in the pages of its magazine, from inadequate before, through the transformation, and finally, into the glamorous after. If one ordinary reader could be transformed by the makeover, then the reader of the magazine could herself follow the instructions and become beautiful. In the 1970s and 1980s, the makeover reached its height as a popular feature in women's magazines. However, instead of featuring an ordinary reader, women's magazines at that time primarily featured models as makeover subjects. Makeovers still serve as features in women's magazines. Through the makeover, magazines have taught their readers how to consume, dress, and style themselves to look beautiful.

In the 1930s, makeovers were a staple of Hollywood fan magazines. In fact, the first recorded use of the word makeover was in a fan magazine in 1939. Fan magazine makeovers explicitly drew on the reader's identification with the movie star; in following the star's beauty practices, the fan could become like the admired star. Different stars represented different ideal types that readers aspired to be.

Even the stars themselves could be made over in the movies. Beginning with *Now, Voyager,* in 1942, the makeover has served as a plot device in films. In *Now, Voyager,* Bette Davis (playing Charlotte Vale) is transformed from an unhappy, frustrated, and unattractive girl/woman, to a strong, satisfied, and attractive woman through a makeover. More recently, films like *Pretty Woman* and *Miss Congeniality* used the makeover to enact and signal a transformation in their protagonists' identities. While the makeover serves as an element in Vivian Ward's (Julia Roberts) rags-to-riches Cinderella romance in *Pretty Woman,* it operates as a way of feminizing and humanizing Sandra Bullock's character (Gracie Hart) in *Miss Congeniality*. In all of these films, the makeover enhances the star's glamour.

The makeover moved to television in 1953 with *Glamour Girl,* a show in which four ordinary women competed for the chance to be made over by telling their sad stories. The woman with the saddest story won a day of beautification and pampering and then returned to the show to display her new look and outlook on the show the next day. In the 1980s and 1990s, the makeover reappeared on television in the form of short segments on various talk shows. In the 2000s, the makeover became the basis for a new genre of reality television, the makeover show (e.g., **Extreme Makeover**, *A Makeover Story,* **What Not to Wear**, *The Swan*). In these shows, real people (much like the ordinary reader) are transformed inside and out through formulaic, didactic makeovers.

Cultural and Political Meanings

The makeover rests on two different myths: Cinderella and Pygmalion. In the Cinderella tale, the stepdaughter's beauty is hidden by rags or made evident by beautiful clothes. Her beauty makes her special; the prince falls in love with her because she is beautiful. Her beauty also reflects her goodness. In the Pygmalion tale, a man carves himself the perfect woman out of stone and the goddess Venus brings her to life. In other words, man makes the beautiful woman. In both of these myths, the woman's value rests on her appearance, and her beauty enables her to marry a powerful man.

When women are valued for their appearance, the makeover offers a way for women to improve their value, both for themselves and in society. When women are defined by their appearance, the makeover offers a way for women to remake themselves. The makeover is seductive because it offers both the promise of being able to fashion oneself and the promise of being valued. Through making herself over, a woman can improve herself, win a (better) man, and marry, thus securing her social place and economic future.

The makeover promotes consumption. In the makeover, the body is objectified and analyzed, broken into pieces to be evaluated according to a particular ideal. Good aspects must be shown off; bad aspects must be hidden or fixed.

For instance, puffy eyes can be reduced with a special cream; difficult hair fixed with a particular serum; a heavy waist disguised by a dress with an empire waist; a nice figure shown off with a tailored dress. Beauty is not a whole, but the sum of malleable parts. For each problem, a product offers a solution. The makeover promises that beauty can be achieved through knowledgeable consumption and application.

While all makeovers can be seen as advertisements for the products featured, makeovers are often featured in advertisements themselves. Many advertisements use the iconic imagery of the makeover: the before and after images. Indeed, all advertisements can be regarded as after images, promising a new and better state of being for the price of the product. As with the star image in the magazine or the made-over girl, identification with the ideal image encourages consumption of the advertised product.

The makeover upholds and enforces cultural standards. First, it upholds beauty as the standard by which women are judged. Second, the makeover's promise that anyone could be beautiful results in the imperative for all women to become beautiful. If people can follow the advice, purchase the products, and learn how to apply them, there is nothing holding them back. The failure to be attractive is no longer a matter of luck, but a personal failure to make oneself over.

See also: Makeover Television

Further Reading: Berry, Sarah. *Screen Style: Fashion and Femininity in 1930s Hollywood.* Minneapolis: University of Minnesota Press, 2000; Braithwaite, Ann-Marie. "From Makeovers to Making Over: Bodies, Agency, and Popular Feminism in Women's Beauty Magazines." PhD diss., University of Rochester, 1998; Cassidy, Marsha. "The Cinderella Makeover: *Glamour Girl,* Television Misery Shows, and 1950s Femininity." In *The Great American Makeover: Television, History, Nation,* ed. Dana Heller. New York: Palgrave Macmillan, 2006; Fraser, Kathryn. "The Makeover and Other Consumerist Narratives." PhD diss., McGill University, 2002; Fraser, Kathryn. "'Now I am Ready to Tell How Bodies are Changed into Different Bodies. . .' Ovid, *The Metamorphoses.*" In *Makeover Television: Realities Remodelled,* ed. Dana Heller. London: I. B. Tauris, 2007; Heller, Dana. "Before: 'Things Just Keep Getting Better. . .'" In *The Great American Makeover,* ed. Dana Heller, pp. 1–7. New York: Palgrave Macmillan, 2006; Peiss, Kathy. *Hope in a Jar: The Making of America's Beauty Culture.* New York: Metropolitan Books, 1998; Peiss, Kathy. "Making Up, Making Over; Cosmetics, Consumer Culture and Women's Identity." In *The Sex of Things: Gender and Consumption in Historical Perspective,* ed. Victoria de Grazia and Ellen Furlough, pp. 311–36. Berkeley: University of California Press, 1996.

Yael D. Sherman

MAKEOVER TELEVISION

Makeover television, a subgenre of reality television, began in earnest in the United States in 2001 with *Trading Spaces* (a home decoration show) and soon spread to body and beauty renovations and a broader international audience. More than 250 makeover-centered shows, across 40 different network/cable sites and created by over 50 production companies are available for television audiences.

The genre can be loosely typified as including most forms of transformation-themed narratives. Although many shows overlap with each other in terms of strategy, outcome, and the kind of body that is altered, makeover TV's broad types include plastic surgery, through such programs as **Extreme Makeover**, *The Swan*, **Dr. 90210**, *Miami Slice, Brand New You,* and *I Want a Famous Face*; noninvasive but often medicalized changes (where subjects can receive liposuction, **Botox**, chemical dermabrasion, or LASIK eyesight correction) in such shows as *10 Years Younger* or *Style by Jury*; style/wardrobe overhauls in such programs as **What Not to Wear, Queer Eye for the Straight Guy**, *Tim Gunn's Guide to Style, How Do I Look?* and *Style Her Famous*; weight loss, in such shows as *The Biggest Loser, The Craze,* and *Shaq's Big Challenge*; lifestyle and parenting style, in such shows as *Supernanny, Shalom in the Home, Honey We're Killing the Kids, Real You Real Simple,* and *Maxed Out*; car and truck renovations, as featured in programming such as *Pimp My Ride, Trick My Truck, Overhaulin',* and *Monster Garage*; and, of course, the staple of home improvement and design programming, in such shows as *Extreme Makeover: Home Edition, Trading Spaces, While You Were Out, Carter Can, Toolbelt Diva,* and *Greenovate*.

As a genre, makeover programs are widely produced in the United Kingdom and the United States, and many countries purchase makeover programming for directing airing or modification. Though produced in the United States, for instance, both *The Swan* and *Extreme Makeover* have been sold in more than 50 international media markets, including in Latvia, Malaysia, Australia, Croatia, and Finland. The weight-loss program *The Biggest Loser* is now an international franchise, with nationalized weight-reduction programs in Australia, Germany, Brazil, the United Kingdom, India, and more.

Makeover TV's immense focus on the body—whether that body be the actual human body or its symbolic referent in kids, dogs, houses, or cars—highlights the social meaning of size and shape and underscores larger investments attached to the body as a signifier of mores and values. One thing insistently iterated through makeover TV, for instance, is the idea that it is precisely because the body is itself so intrinsically malleable—able to take on different shapes or sizes as a consequence of diet, exercise, surgery, or demolition—that there exists so much social pressure for the body to conform to dominant body ideals.

In specific relation to the physical body, even if human forms were incapable of going up and down in weight, muscle mass, or quantity of **cellulite**, people would still have dominant body ideals. Yet, these normative codes of perfect bodies as they exist for both men and women would be more a matter of an abstract desire rather than an achievable reality. With the advent of ever-increasing aesthetic procedures, both surgical and noninvasive, there has been a consequent shift in how these body and beauty ideals are perceived. What once might have been considered the domain of the few—exceptional beauty—is now considered a requisite and attainable feature of modern living, an appearance-based dividend purchasable through credit cards and second mortgages.

Indeed, in this new domain where idealized bodies can be shopped for, there is a consequent rise in the expectation that people are remiss if they do not invest resources of time, money, and energy in body work. Such an attitude is made intelligible through the makeover's tacit ultimatum: if one can change, one should; if one refuses to change, one deserves the consequences. One of these consequences is an increased degree of social shaming, a public referendum that associates the obese or ugly body (or, as one program aptly puts it, *The Ugliest House on the Block*) as morally corrupt and the thin, stylish, and beautiful body as prerequisite to the highest ideals: happiness, confidence, well-being, and lovability. For women, appearance of both body and home have long marked a prerequisite standard of values, where class mobility and feelings of personal worth correlate to beliefs about one's relative degree of conventional attractiveness. As expressed through the logic of makeover shows, a woman's beauty is meant to serve as an intermediary currency that will enable her to purchase other valued objectives— good mothering, sexual attention, an abstract kind of happiness, and even her womanhood, so that many women claim at the culmination of their transformations, "I'm me now!" As such, beauty promises the ultimate reward—celebratory subjectivity. Indeed, this promise is uttered through the system of equivalencies *Extreme Makeover* poses: beauty is health, beauty is confidence, beauty is happiness, beauty is romantic love, beauty is stability, beauty is prosperity, beauty is democracy, and, ultimately, beauty confers self-hood.

For men on television makeover shows that involve the changing body, the logic is similarly compelling. The ugly man has been blocked in his upward mobility. So, for instance, on *Extreme Makeover* or *10 Years Younger,* male makeover subjects bemoan their entry-level positions, complaining about the low-status and low-paying jobs they have been forced to work in because their appearance makes them too self-conscious to assume the masculine swagger that is part of hegemonic masculinity and workplace efficacy. For these male subjects, then, cosmetic procedures that correct their protruding ears, weak jaws, and jagged teeth help to create an image on the body and face that better coheres to what a male in a position of authority looks like. Just as with women on these shows, makeover TV suggests that both male and female participants have obligations to fulfill and embody preexisting notions about what signifies value. The makeover does not argue for doing battle with the world's larger expectations about idealized bodies and beauty; instead it suggests that to live life outside of social norms is so debilitating that it is better to cut away the body to enable disadvantaged subjects an equal shot at participating in a globalized economy predicated on free-market competition.

Makeover TV thus ostensibly offers a window into the world of democratization. An average person wishing for the beautiful/celebrity body is aided in the process by a well-meaning plastic surgeon; ostracized ugliness is brought into meritocracy through glamour. In advocating for such engagement with the free market through the currencies that beautiful faces and bodies afford, however, the ideal (and rarity) of living in a beautiful body remains perfectly intact. If it's possible for real people to become celebrities, this calls into question the exclusivity implied by celebrity. The question remains whether everyone can be physically beautiful. Since ideals are constructed around the logic of desiring what is statistically least possible, the more plastic surgery—or radical home renovation—brings beauty to the masses, the less beauty signifies as privilege. For beauty to mean anything, a good many other people in the world have to be unbeautiful. For celebrity to signify, most people have to be unknown.

What makeover television primarily specializes in, then, is not the stated intent of bringing new and meaningful lives to the meritorious ugly (a term conveniently and tacitly referencing the deserving poor), but rather the insistent message that people must be aware of and concerned about appearance. Whether they are scrutinized for freakish ugliness or admired for glamorous appearance, these shows assert that people are all objects of the gaze, intensely self-conscious, that there are seeing eyes (or cameras) on them at all time, even when those eyes are their own. In the land of makeover shows, whether before or after, one refrain rises above all others—self-improvement (understood almost ubiquitously as attaining a narrow form of physical beauty) requires a speedball mixture of desire and anxiety. In effect, the shows exploit the same bodily anxieties that fuel the psychic pain they ostensibly cure, offering makeover participants and home viewers a contradictory pairing—the despair of anxiety, the (promised) joy brought by beauty. To salve the wounds of this contradiction, on offer is a form of beauty-by-the-numbers that is narrow, formulaic, and dependent on the very cycles of anxiety and desire it promises to transcend.

And yet, the makeover is quite right in its assertions: it is much easier to live in a body or home that conforms to social codes that mark it as attractive; there is more currency attached to the beautiful or handsome body than to the obese, aberrant, or ugly body. And so, in claiming the body as its primary agent of entertainment and instruction, the relatively new medium of makeover TV manages to tap into larger desires and anxieties that have fueled our notions of identity, agency, and worth since ancient times.

See also: Makeovers

Further Reading: Heller, Dana, ed. *The Great American Makeover: Television, History, Nation.* New York: Palgrave Macmillan, 2006; Heller, Dana, ed. *Makeover Television: Realities Remodeled.* London: I. B. Tauris, 2007; Lewis, Tania, ed. *TV Transformations: Revealing the Makeover Show.* New York: Routledge, 2008; Weber, Brenda R. *Subject to Change: Becoming a Self on Makeover TV.* Durham, NC: Duke University Press, 2009.

Brenda R. Weber

MAKEUP ARTISTS, CELEBRITY

Although it was iconic hairstylist **Vidal Sassoon** who made the phrase "If you don't look good, we don't look good" famous, the sentiment can be equally and passionately applied to makeup artists as well. With the increased accessibility and popularity of the visual and image industry, the carefully made-up faces of movies stars, singers, performers, and celebrities of all genres became their calling cards. The makeup artists behind the scenes who transformed ordinary people into stars and ingénues, divas, and femmes fatales soon became highly sought-after masters of the craft.

Max Factor

Perhaps the first of the celebrity makeup artists is **Max Factor**, a man who revolutionized movie makeup and who changed the ways in which **film**, **cosmetics**, and the skillful application of powder, rouge, and lipstick can transform a woman into a screen siren. In 1914, Max Factor, a Polish immigrant, developed a foundation for actors that would not crack, cake, or crepe under the harsh studio lights, and he became a highly sought-after makeup artist in the film industry soon afterward. He invented lip gloss for the movies in 1914, and he is credited with coining the term *makeup*, based on the phrase "to make up one's face." During the golden years of filmmaking in the 1920s and 1930s, Max Factor became intimately associated with the world of movie makeup. He worked with iconic beauties and actresses such as Judy Garland, Joan Crawford, Bette Davis, and Jean Harlow. Max Factor invented some of the most influential looks for actresses—he created the first false eyelashes for silent film star Phyllis Haver; rosebud lips and the Cupid's bow lip style in the 1920s; and the hunter's bow lips for Joan Crawford in the 1930s. But it was Max Factor's idea to maximize his relationship with the most popular movie stars of the day that brought him celebrity status. His close and intimate friendships with the movie studios allowed him to appear in cameos in some of the most popular films of the day. His ability to move from behind the scenes to the front of the camera brought him a familiar brand name, a new marketability, and a plethora of celebrities who could endorse and help him sell his cosmetic breakthroughs. He was the first to realize the lengths to which women would go to emulate their favorite divas. He marketed his products not only to flatter individual stars, for example, creating shades specifically for the actresses—Platinum for Jean Harlow, Special Medium for Joan Crawford, and Dark for Claudette Colbert—but also to allow the average woman to identify with and ultimately purchase the look of the idol she desired to emulate.

Contemporary Artists

Many of the modern-day celebrity makeup artists find their beginnings in the entertainment industry. The everyday interactions with producers, actors, directors bring these people to the forefront. Charlie Green, a renowned makeup artist who has worked with celebrities such as Jewel, Tyra Banks, and Elizabeth Hurley and as a makeup artist with Heidi Klum on Bravo TV's *Project Runway*, has not only served as a commentator on VH1 shows such as *Best of . . .* and *Best Week Ever*, she was recently tapped as one of the co-hosts of Lifetime's *Blush: The Search for the Next Great Makeup Artist* along with Vanessa Marcil (cast as the "Most Beautiful Girl in the World" in 1994 by Prince). Stila Cosmetics, named after the individual style that everyone woman exudes, was founded by celebrity makeup artist Jeanine Lobell, who was encouraged by her celebrity clients to create the now multi-million dollar makeup line that was bought by **Estée Lauder** in 1999 and sold to Sun Capital Partners, Inc., in 2006. The makeup artist on the set of *ER*, where she met her husband, Anthony Edwards, Lobell has named some of her lipsticks after icons—a celebrity in her own right calling the lipsticks in her line after celebrities in their own right.

Other makeup artists have found fame after developing innovative and popular makeup lines. **Bobbi Brown** moved to New York to become a makeup artist. In 1991, she launched a line of lipsticks that are now sold, along with an entire cosmetics line, in over 400 stores and 20 countries internationally. Now a household name, Bobbi Brown is the exclusive beauty editor of *The Today Show* and a frequent guest on the E! Entertainment and Style channels. She is the author of *Bobbi Brown Beauty, Bobbi Brown Teenage Beauty,* and *Bobbi Brown Beauty Evolution.* Kevyn Aucoin, an American makeup artist who was discovered while he was volunteering his time and talent on models, became one of the highest-paid celebrity makeup artists of his time. His philosophy that makeup was simply a tool for a women's self-discovery became an inspirational mantra to supermodels, celebrities, and everyday women alike. He worked with such celebrity A-listers as Gwyneth Paltrow, Amber Valletta, Nicole Kidman, and Janet Jackson. After helping to create several makeup lines for other companies, most notably for Ultima II, he created the Kevyn Aucoin line with limited products, mascaras, brushes, lip glosses, and colors.

Pat McGrath, a British makeup artist who has been described as "the most influential make-up artist in the world" by *Vogue* magazine, was discovered while working with Edward Enninful, the fashion editor of *i-D* magazine, in the 1990s. She worked with **designers** such as Jil Sander, John Galliano, Prada, and Dolce and Gabbana. McGrath designed the Giorgio Armani cosmetics line in 1999. **Procter and Gamble** chose McGrath to become their new global creative-design director in 2004—where she now heads the cosmetics giants **CoverGirl** and Max Factor. Pat McGrath now also comments on various style shows on TV.

Further Reading: Aucoin, Kevyn. *Face Forward.* Boston: Little, Brown and Company, 2001; Aucoin, Kevyn. *Making Faces.* Boston: Little, Brown and Company, 1999; Basten, Fred E. *Max Factor: The Man Who Changed the Faces of the World*; Basten, Fred E., Robert Salvatore, and Paul Kaufman. *Max Factor's Hollywood: Glamour, Movies, Make-Up.* Toronto: Stoddart, 1995; Brown, Bobbi. *Bobbi Brown Beauty.* New York: Harper, 1998; Brown, Bobbi. *Bobbi Brown Living Beauty.* New York: Springboard, 2007; Lauder, Estée. *Estée.* New York: Rizzoli, 2009; Nars, Francois. *Makeup Your Mind.* Brooklyn, NY: Powerhouse Books, 2002; Riordan, Teresa. *Inventing Beauty: A History of the Innovations that Have Made Us Beautiful.* New York: Broadway, 2004; Woodhead, Lindy. *War Paint: Madame Helena Rubinstein and Miss Elizabeth Arden, Their Lives, Their Times, Their Rivalry.* Hoboken, NJ: Wiley, 2004.

Aliza S. Wong

MALONE, ANNIE TURNBO (1869–1957)

A pioneer of black beauty culture and the founder and president of Poro College in St. Louis, Annie Minnerva Turnbo Malone was one of the most successful black female entrepreneurs of the early 20th century. While her fame would later be eclipsed by that of her former student and business rival, **Madam C. J. Walker,** the significance of Malone and her business to the development of commercial black beauty culture and the economic independence it gave African American women made her a leader among her peers. The 10th of 11 children, Malone was born August 9, 1869, in Metropolis, Illinois. After losing both parents, Malone moved to Peoria, Illinois, where she lived with older siblings and by high school began to chemically experiment with solutions to straighten and enhance the texture of black hair. Despite setbacks from chronic illness during her teen years, Malone, dissatisfied with the hair-care remedies and styling techniques available to black women, introduced Wonderful Hair Grower, a product she claimed would make thin, dull, and sparse hair grow.

Black migration to urban areas, greater accessibility to store-bought goods, and the use of mass **advertising** made cities such as St. Louis and later Chicago ideal locations for beauty entrepreneurs like Malone to market their products and training. After years of perfecting her trademark product, the Wonderful Hair Grower, Malone relocated her business across the Mississippi to St. Louis in 1902. Inspired by her African heritage, Malone chose the name *Poro,* of West African origin, for its connection to organizations dedicated to the physical and spiritual enhancement of the body and spirit. With the rental of a small flat in downtown St. Louis, the center of the black commercial and residential district, Malone made plans to purchase a larger facility to accommodate her growing business. She also adopted effective marketing techniques with the use of newspaper advertisements, door-to-door demonstrations, lecture tours, and the later establishment of a beauty training college.

Devoted to training black women for careers in beauty culture and enhancing the cultural and civic life of the community, Poro College opened in 1918. The three-story building consisted of a factory and store for Poro hair and cosmetic products, a hairdressing school, dormitory, auditorium, and dining and committee rooms used for meetings, banquets, lectures, and entertainment. Taking in some of the largest revenues of any black business, Poro became one the city's most prominent institutions. A gifted businesswoman and philanthropist, Malone employed nearly 200 women locally, for whom she represented an example of leadership, grace, and personal achievement. With assistance from her then husband, Aaron E. Malone, Malone made generous donations to a host of black institutions, especially the St. Louis Colored Orphan's home, renamed the Annie Malone Children's Home in 1945. From 1900 until her death in 1957, the Poro business included 32 **beauty schools** and upwards of 75,000 beauty agents in the United States, Canada, South America, the Caribbean, and the Philippines. Such accomplishments distinguished Malone as one of the first women in the United States without inherited wealth to become a millionaire from her professional efforts.

See also: African American Beauty Industry

Further Reading: Byrd, Ayana D., and Lori L. Tharps. *Hair Story: Untangling the Roots of Black Hair in America.* New York: St. Martin's Griffin, 2001; Walker, Juliet. *The History of Black Business in America: Capitalism, Race, Entrepreneurship.* New York: Macmillan

Library Reference USA, 1998; Walker, Susannah. *Style and Status: Selling Beauty to African American Women, 1920–1975*. Lexington: University Press of Kentucky, 2007.

De Anna J. Reese

MANICURISTS AND NAIL TECHNICIANS

People who work at **nail salons** are usually called *manicurists*. But when it comes to more skilled manicurists engaged in some complicated and refined method of manicuring, they are often called *nail technicians*. Although manicurists have worked in barbershops and beauty salons since the early 20th century, they typically served only the well-to-do. However, by the 1990s, dramatic changes were plainly visible as Korean and Vietnamese women (and increasing numbers of men) came to dominate the nail industry, transforming the manicures and pedicures into a mass market phenomenon that caters to women and some men across class and race boundaries.

> "My manicurist at T & T Nails tends to me with a great deal more solicitude than does my doctor. When I show up for my biweekly appointment, her eyes light up, her lips to busy grinning to finish the noodles she's been nursing between customers. She waves me to her station, nodding happily and smoothing my hands with her own. . . . The Chinese Shops are everywhere and they are cheap."
>
> *Natasha, nail salon patron*
>
> Source: Willett, Julie. "Hands across the Table: A Short History of Manicurists in the Twentieth Century." *Journal of Women's History,* 17 no. 3 (2005): 73.

History

For most of the 20th century, work culture and popular culture have cast manicurists as the least-skilled and least-respected worker on the beauty shop floor. In films, the manicurists played the profoundly working-class, dimwitted gossip mongers who could not even do hair. In barbershops, the manicurist was often the only woman; she was hired and placed in the front window to attract a male clientele interested in something other than a shave and a haircut. In part, manicurists' assumed servitude reflected class distinctions that were often more abrupt than the divisions between **hairdressers** and their patrons. Until the very late 20th century, manicures were a luxury associated with society ladies and the country club set or a very special occasion. In the 1980s and '90s, nail salons began to appear everywhere, including working-class neighborhoods and business districts where now immigrant-owned and operated salons provided quick, inexpensive manis and pedis that could be had on the way home from work, during lunch, or while shopping. Nails salons also offered more than shape and color, but intricate designs and massages that pampered and pleased a new working- and middle-class clientele. Despite the democratization of the services, xenophobia and racism have often mitigated the intimacy of touch and conversation and thus potential relationships between the nail tech and patron, and thus prevented her from attaining status as a skilled artisan.

Contradictions in Body-Related Labor

Korean and Vietnamese women who work in nail salons tend to be recent im-migrants with limited English proficiency and job skills. Some of them are college graduates and were professionals in their homeland prior to immigration to the United States. In New York, for example, Korean manicurists often enter into a line of work that is at first entirely unfamiliar, since they were not only oblivious to the existence of nail salons but also could not have imagined providing pedi-cures could be a line of work. Korean culture generally looks disparagingly at nail salon work because it involves intimate physical contact with another person's body. Such body work is considered shameful and humiliating, as in the meta-phor "lowering oneself to cleanse another's feet sat on the throne-like pedicure chair." Polishing one's nails with colorful enamel also threatens the dictates of tradition. Despite the foreign terrain of nail work, immigrant women and men have managed to carve out a formidable wedge in the beauty industry through the establishment of nail salons. Immigrant manicurists have both creatively (volun-tary) and disgracefully (involuntary) come to participate in a body-related service sector in a foreign country.

The physical contact between manicurists and customers of diverse backgrounds evokes intense feelings among manicurists. Manicurists occupy an awkward po-sition straddling the requirements of their job and the cultural narratives about body-related **labor**. This *skinship*—serving their clients in close physical proxim-ity, touching their hands, feet, and often other parts of the body—contributes to the formation of relationships between manicurists and women of other ethnic identities. In an attempt to synthesize these conflicting relations, the concepts *eye to eye* and *nail to nail* reveal two dimensions of interaction between the immigrant manicurists and their clients that are not separate but overlap to form complex relationships.

Characteristics of Interaction with Customers

Eye to eye speaks to the relationship the manicurists build with their custom-ers at a human level, as they get acquainted. While working, women may share information with the clients about health, children, and family matters, de-pending on their English conversational abilities and their feelings about the depth of their mutual intimacy. Through conversational encounters with their clients, immigrant manicurists are able to ascertain knowledge about Ameri-cans and American culture. In their encounters with Americans from various ethnic backgrounds, manicurists also learn a lot about a range of customs and lifestyles.

Nail to nail refers to the relationship that exists between manicurists and clients based on the racial/ethnic hierarchy in the United States. This relation speaks to the differences and otherness between them as underscored by the performance of servicing the body. In the act of tending to the physical body of another, mani-curists experience conflicting and competing views over the meaning of nail work in terms of **labor** on another person's body and in terms of the different cultural meanings on specific body parts (nail, foot). The difficulty of assigning meaning to the experience of laboring on another person's body is particularly noticeable. The discrepancy between the manicuring body (manicurist) and the manicured body (client) is heightened in the process of gendered practices for the production of beauty. Some manicurists, for example, attempt to legitimize, compromise, or negotiate their work by using Christian concepts of service (cleaning the feet of others like Jesus), likening their job to that of a foot doctor, or defining themselves as nail artists, and adopting the Puritan work ethic. This speaks to the intense feelings they harbor toward their body labor. While manicurists on one hand may be economically empowered as the main breadwinners in the family, they, like many service workers, often hide behind their smile while on the job, masking feelings of anger, pain, and confusion to ensure that that manicured body of the customer is rested, refreshed, and adorned.

These dichotomies stem from the two different socioeconomic positions represented by these two groups of women, which has developed through the feminization of the service sector caused by global and national economic restructuring. In this process, first-world women sit in positions of power as wage earners who possess the means to consume beauty-related services, while third-world workers comprise the workforce in response to increased consumer demand. Through their work experience, represented by the aforementioned characteristics of interaction, manicurists learn about the nature of their role in the workplace and forge a new identity in line with the new social and cultural context of immigrant life.

Contests over the Use of Language

Contests over the use of language highlight underlying systems of power and control. Immigrant manicurists pose challenges to the status quo with the practice of talking about their customers to coworkers in their native language, or pretending not to understand English in order to avoid responding to a customer request that they believe is unreasonable. On the surface, these practices appear to be a means for the women to vent their frustrations or a strategy to avoid unreasonable demands. Deeper analysis, however, indicates that by using their own language, immigrant manicurists are engaging in a form of resistance that undermines the power dynamics of class and racial hierarchies, while at the same time allowing them to create a sense of solidarity among their cohorts.

Tips

For manicurists, tips are not only an important part of their income, but also a meaningful token that represents social relations and hierarchy. Clear differences in tipping emerge according to the race and class of the clientele and the location of the business. Such variations in tipping patterns by clientele are also important factors that influence identity and the nature of interactions between the manicurist and her customer.

The wage systems of different nail salons reflect an understanding of this variation in tipping patterns according to the race, class, and cultural background of customers. Manicurists working in some neighborhoods may be paid weekly, but almost half of their weekly income comes from tips and this justifies their lower wages to nail salon owners. In contrast, manicurists in other locales are paid weekly wages plus a commission because tips are rare and few, if any, and such a wage structure guarantees manicurists a somewhat stable and sufficient income. The commission, which is based on the number of customers served, also acts as a deterrent for manicurists who might otherwise turn away undesirable clients. This wage system entangled with tips and commissions reveals that the nail salon industry is not a free wage economy determined simply by supply and demand, but is instead shaped not only by class but by such other factors as race, ethnicity, and locality.

The sharply contrasting tipping patterns result in dissimilar service patterns. Service patterns are the outcome of what the entrepreneur believes to be the tipping habits of their respective clients, which in turn, are also influenced by the customers' sense of racial distance and bias against immigrants. In other words, tipping patterns, the quality of service being provided, and hierarchies of class and race are all intricately intertwined. It is hard to discern the primary factor at work in determining the sharp differences that exist according to race and class in the provision of services, namely, whether different tipping habits are a result of cultural patterns or whether perceived quality reinforces a sense of social distance between manicurists and customers.

Ranks Based on Skill Level

Manicurists are divided into three categories according to their skill level: most skilled, medium skilled, and novice. This classification figures importantly not only in hiring, but also in defining work positions and relationships among manicurists in a nail shop. It typically takes almost five years to rise from a novice to the best. Given the cultural meaning of nail work, the practice of ascribing skill levels to different classes of manicurists seems rather incongruous. The professional connotation attached to the concept of skill becomes inappropriate: skill is not counted as enhancing self-evaluations, and all manicurists are collectively dismissed as service workers, irrespective of skill level. Being skillful at nail work, therefore, is in itself unlikely to be a factor that dramatically alters the manicurists' sense of job satisfaction.

Like other aspects of the beauty industry, however, nail salons reflect a segmented industry. Often family owned, nail salons afford many immigrant women an entrepreneurial niche. Even the manicurist who never owns a business often develops a steady clientele with favorites who tip well and engage in meaningful conversations. In urban spaces noted for poor relationships that redraw race hierarchies and tensions, nail salons at times offer some interracial relationships that seem more tolerant and owe much to the touch of someone often deemed other. In more swank **spas**, admittedly less likely to employ Asian immigrants, manicurists who offer services work in luxurious locations at a slower pace; here, their skills and position are far from the bottom of the beauty chain.

See also: Nail Art

Further Reading: Han, Jeong woo. "Eye To Eye, Nail To Nail: Body and Identity in Korean Nail Salon Workers in New York City." PhD diss., New School for Social Research, 2004; Kang, Miliann. "The Managed Hand: The Commercialization of Bodies and Emotions in Korean Immigrant-Owned Nail Salons." *Gender & Society,* 17 (2003): 820–39; Lee, Jennifer. *Civility in the City: Blacks, Jews, and Koreans in Urban America.* Cambridge, MA: Harvard University Press, 2002; Willett, Julie. "'Hands across the Table': A Short History of Manicurists in the Twentieth Century." *Journal of Women's History,* 17 no. 3 (2005): 59–80.

Jeong woo Han

MANUFACTURING

The word *manufacture* means to make by hand, but long ago it lost that connotation, meaning now to create many goods as part of a large-scale operation. In the beauty and apparel industry, the manufacturing of products must be timed to coincide with specific seasons and created to appeal to the appropriate target market.

Timing is an important element in the manufacturing of any beauty product, including apparel. Within each year, there are seasons that demand different types of clothes and **cosmetics**. In the winter, warm clothing is necessary and, due to dry skin conditions caused by heaters and cold weather, people also tend to buy more moisturizers, lip balm, and other health-related cosmetics. In the summer, lightweight clothes and swimsuits are needed and sunscreens are required. Besides the temperature changes, colors are seasonal as well. Dark colors and deep jewel tones are popular for fall and winter, while in the spring and summer customers prefer lighter and sheer shades.

Apparel Industry

In the apparel-manufacturing world, the two main seasons are fall and spring. Clothing for fall is usually sold in stores beginning in July, although the actual fall season is quite some time away. Spring styles begin to be sold in stores as early as late December to coincide with a rush of holiday shoppers. The design and manufacturing of these items are done far in advance, often beginning a full calendar year before the projected date of sale. But fashion is a constantly changing market and manufacturing firms must maintain enough flexibility to keep up with consumer demand. A garment that is the wrong color or comes to market even just days too late can be completely unsalable.

Each garment sold in a **retail** store has a vast history behind it. First, the raw materials to make it are gathered: cotton, linen, wool, silk, polyester, nylon, acrylic, and rayon are commonly used textile fibers. The fibers are converted to yarns in a mill, going through a variety of processes that include carding, combing, bleaching, dyeing, crimping, stuffing, straightening, or any number of steps to create the desired look and feel in the finished yarn. Yarns are then sent to another plant to be woven into fabric. Looms of all kinds exist to facilitate various types of special weaves from a plain 1x1 weave to satin to jacquard, dobby, brocade, matelasse, and other specialty and pictorial weaves. Yarns can also be knit to achieve a fabric with natural stretch and a soft drape. The newly woven fabric is still considered unfinished and is known as greige or gray goods. Greige goods can then be bleached, dyed, printed, embossed, flocked, calendered, embroidered, pleated, or just starched with sizing before being sold to an apparel manufacturer to be made into clothing.

Apparel manufacturers have many fabric choices available to them in any given season, but there is always the option for custom orders. Most manufacturers work from a variety of sources including textile, trim, and notions vendors and companies that specialize in custom work. The goal of the manufacturer is to keep the cost of goods, that is, the price of the materials and **labor** that goes into each garment, in line with the intended price level of the garment, which is anywhere from budget (inexpensive) to designer (costly). Another challenge faced by manufacturers is not only to deliver a product on time, but to fabricate that product exactly to the desired quality and price point.

Manufacturers usually have a workforce of sewing operators and finishers in-house. They primarily work assembly-line style with individual operators responsible for a single step in the construction process. This allows for fast-paced and reasonably accurate work as each operator becomes an expert on his or her step in the process. For higher-end garments such as designer lines and men's fine suits, one sewing operator might be responsible for the entire garment from start to finish. Men's fine suits are some of the most labor-intensive items of clothing made. Men's shirts, however, are some of the least, due to standardized sizing of cuffs, collars, pockets, and sleeves. This allows for the mass production of these standard components and streamlines the process. Most women and children's wear, as well as men's sportswear, activewear, and intimate apparel, is created using the piecework system. Items such as children's sleepwear are tightly regulated and must be treated with a flame retardant. Strict rules also govern, for example, the use and type of closures on newborn and infant apparel as well as sizing. Manufacturers working in the children's clothing industry must be aware of the regulations surrounding their products.

Contractors are used for specialized work like creative endeavors such as beading and embroidery and more industrial needs such as pleating, covering buttons, and making belts. Contractors allow for manufacturers to utilize these more specialized services without employing a full-time employee that might not have work every day. The end result is a finished garment that is ready to be shipped to a retail outlet for purchase by the consumer.

Cosmetics Industry

In the cosmetics industry, the manufacturing process is more like that of a plant that makes food or drugs. Compounds are tested to ensure safety and quality.

The raw materials needed for cosmetics will vary widely depending on what kind of item is being made. Ingredients for lotion, lipstick, eye shadow, and concealer are all very different but have similar purposes. A base is the foundation for the product—in liquid, solid, gel, or powder form. For purely cosmetic items, the next most important factor is the pigment. Pigments are highly concentrated and closely monitored by government agencies to ensure that they are made from nontoxic, hypoallergenic ingredients. Some coloring agents that create a frosted look can make a lipstick very hard. Using real crushed pearl or mica gives a high-quality shimmering appearance to lipsticks and eye shadows, but these have to be handled carefully, as these ingredients are fragile and can be destroyed in the manufacturing process. Additives such as fragrance, flavoring agents, moisturizers, conditioners, and the like can also be included in the product. Often, these are considered a selling point, for example, making a lipstick longer wearing or with a moisturizing capability. In lotions, vitamins and specialty ingredients like collagen, green tea, shea butter, silk protein, and the like are what create market appeal.

Batches of each product can be made from small or sample scales up to quantities large enough to serve a multinational market. Many cosmetic manufacturers are also responding to a trend that demands smaller batches with higher quality made with organic and eco-friendly ingredients. With an ever-changing market, manufacturers of both fashion and cosmetics have to keep up with customer demand or risk losing their edge.

See also: U.S. Food and Drug Administration

Further Reading: Brown, Patty, and Janett Rice. *Ready-to-Wear Apparel Analysis.* Upper Saddle River, NJ: Pearson/Prentice Hall, 2001; Dracelos, M. D., and Zoe Diana. "Cosmetics." http://www.emedicine.com/derm/topic502.htm; Gavenas, Mary Lisa. *Color Stories: Behind the Scenes of America's Billion-Dollar Beauty Industry.* New York: Simon & Schuster, 2002; Glock, Ruth E., and Grace I. Kunz. *Apparel Manufacturing: Sewn Product Analysis,* 4th ed. Upper Saddle River, NJ: Pearson/Prentice Hall, 2005; Heil, Scott, and Terrance W. Peck, eds. *The Encyclopedia of American Industry,* 2nd ed. Detroit, MI: Gale Research, 1998; Peiss, Kathy. *Hope in a Jar: The Making of America's Beauty Culture.* New York: Metropolitan Books, 1998; U.S. Food and Drug Administration Center for Food Safely and Applied Nutrition (FDA/CFSAN). "Cosmetic Good Manufacturing Practice Guidelines." http://www.cfsan.fda.gov/~dms/cos-gmp.html.

Sara M. Harvey

MARY KAY COSMETICS

Mary Kay **Cosmetics** is a direct sales company specializing in beauty products, especially skin care and makeup. The company, begun in Dallas, Texas in 1963 by Mary Kay Ash, is known for its conservative corporate culture and the pink Cadillacs that the company offers as rewards for top sellers. The company operates through a multilevel system of marketing. Salespeople (almost all are women) make the bulk of their profits not through their own sales, but by recruiting other independent beauty consultants to serve on their sales team, whom they oversee as independent sales directors. The company sells products to consultants and directors at wholesale prices (traditionally half the market price) and the salespeople market those products through skin care classes, usually hosted by their friends, neighbors, and family members. Most consultants work irregular and infrequent hours selling Mary Kay products, and the majority of consultants cannot rely on their direct sales income alone.

Critics have compared the company to a pyramid scheme. Because sales directors and the corporation itself depend on the purchase of products at wholesale prices from new consultants, the corporate focus is on continually enlisting new recruits and encouraging them to buy large quantities of product to start up their businesses. Detractors suggest that assisting consultants in selling that product, so that they, too, will profit, is a secondary priority.

As founder, Mary Kay Ash served as the charismatic leader of the company for nearly four decades. She died in 2001, but the company continues to rely heavily on Ash's image and writings to motivate its sales force and recruit new consultants. Ash's autobiography, *Mary Kay,* first published in 1981, was a mixture of Christianity, self-help literature, and business advice, and it is offered as a motivational guide to new consultants. Ash urged her consultants to share her priorities of "God first, family second, career third." She promised that a well-managed career selling her cosmetics would make fulfillment of those priorities possible. According to company recruiting literature, Mary Kay Cosmetics offers a more supportive, flexible atmosphere for women than the traditional business world.

Mary Kay Ash, president of Mary Kay Cosmetics, in her Dallas, Texas office, 1982. (AP Photo)

The company motto promises that the priority is "enriching women's lives." Ash encouraged consultants to sell products through parties, a sales strategy perfected by Brownie Wise at Tupperware in the 1950s and 1960s. Mary Kay describes the parties as facials or skin care classes to emphasize the education and personalized attention that a beauty consultant can offer her customers. By conducting these events in the home of the consultants' friends or family members, the guests can encounter significant peer pressure to purchase products. The company has marketed its products as luxury items, priced higher than most drugstore cosmetics and skin care products. In 2007, the company boasted 2.4 billion dollars of wholesale sales.

Further Reading: Ash, Mary Kay. *Mary Kay.* 1st ed. New York: Harper and Row, 1981; Biggart, Nicole Woolsey. *Charismatic Capitalism: Direct Selling Organizations in America.* Chicago: University of Chicago Press, 1989; Fricke, Erika. "Sisterhood is Powderful: Inside the Feminine World of the Direct-Sales Industry." *Bitch,* 17 (Summer 2002): 44–49, 99; Underwood, Jim. *More than a Pink Cadillac: Mary Kay Inc.'s Nine Leadership Keys to Success.* New York: McGraw-Hill, 2003.

Beth Kreydatus

MAX FACTOR (C. 1877–1938)

Max Factor is best known for his invention of specialty **cosmetics** used in the early American **film** and television industries. Beginning with foundation products, his innovations expanded into the mass market. Factor also developed the concept that makeup used should match a person's coloring.

Early Years

Born Max Faktor in Lodz, Poland, he gained recognition as a wigmaker and makeup man for the Russian Imperial Ballet and the Grand Opera House. Immigrating to the United States in 1904 with his wife Lisa and their three children, his name was changed to Factor at Ellis Island. He found employment at the St. Louis World's Fair displaying his skin creams. When the film industry began to develop, Factor moved his family to Los Angeles around 1909, began his company, and became a distributor for theatrical makeup manufacturers Leichner and Miner. Thereafter, Factor started experimenting with his own products for movie actors.

Career and Innovations

Coining the term *makeup* to describe his inventions, Factor gained recognition with his innovative approach to traditional theatrical greasepaint. In 1914, he formulated greasepaint into a convenient tube for sanitary dispensing—a lighter formula specifically designed for film actors that would not crack when dry. Available in varying shades, Supreme Greasepaint was the forerunner of subsequent foundation products.

When actors began using his product in their social lives, Factor launched Society Make-up in the 1920s, and developed the color harmony principle of matching makeup shades to a person's coloring. His success in these endeavors won him a special Academy Award in 1928. Further innovations followed with Lip Gloss in 1930, Liquid Nail Enamel in 1934, and Pan-Cake Make-up in 1937 (adapted for color film). Hollywood stars were frequently used in his **advertising** campaigns and this resulted in huge returns. Pan-Cake Make-up was launched with color advertising and became one of the fastest- and best-selling makeup items in cosmetics history. It remains one of the most popular cake makeup products.

Besides foundation makeup products, Max Factor, Inc. also had a strong reputation in wig **manufacturing**, one of the areas of Factor's early reputation in Hollywood. The company thereafter expanded into clothing and perfume lines.

Legacies

Max Factor died at age 59 in 1938; his son Frank took over the name and expanded Max Factor and Company into the high fashion and international markets. The innovative quality of the company continued, and known products followed: Tru-Color Lipstick (smear proof) in 1940, Pan-Stick Make-up in 1948, Erace (concealer) in 1954. The company also had an Armed Forces Division that catered to servicemen's female dependents, advertised the American Look, and even produced its own newspaper, *Max Factor Country*. The company was run by family members until 1976; it became a subsidiary of **Revlon** in 1987 and was acquired by **Procter and Gamble** in 1991. In 2009, Max Factor pulled out of the U.S market, a reflection of the recession and competitive market.

See also: Endorsements of Products, Celebrity; Film; Makeup Artists, Celebrity

Further Reading: Gavenas, Mary Lisa. *Color Stories: Behind the Scenes of America's Billion-Dollar Beauty Industry.* New York: Simon & Schuster, 2002; Peiss, Kathy. *Hope in a Jar: The Making of America's Beauty Culture.* New York: Metropolitan Books, 1998; Procter and Gamble. http://www.pg.com/company/who_we_are/max_factor_history.jhtml. (Accessed August 4, 2008).

Christina Ashby-Martin

MAXIM

Maxim is a monthly men's magazine founded in 1995 that features articles about men's health, fashion, sports, consumer goods, and other male activities and men's culture. It is most readily identified with the rise of self-indulged, fashion-conscious **metrosexuals**. The magazine is also well known for its non-nude photography of female celebrities, models, musicians, and actresses, which can overshadow the magazine's features and articles that discuss the male beauty industry. *Maxim* competes for readers with other magazines like **Gentlemen's Quarterly (GQ)**, *Esquire*, and **Men's Health**, also focused on the male beauty industry but not distinguished by non-nude photography of women.

Maxim was first published in the United Kingdom in 1995 before being published in the United States and other countries. Unlike the American version, the British version features topless photography of women. The magazine is published by Dennis Publishing and is promoted alongside its sister magazines like music-focused *Blender*. *Maxim* is an industry leader in the United States, with a reported circulation of over 2 million readers. The magazine targets 18-to-30-year-old men and provides entertainment and advice on a variety of issues men face, including male beauty and health concerns. The male beauty industry is heavily advertised and marketed in *Maxim* and issues typically feature interviews with male celebrities and models. Interviewees also include actors, musicians, and politicians, and discussions often revolve around the celebrity and fashion industries, fitness and health regimes, and opinions on careers. There are also articles and reviews of new consumer goods like electronics and cars, and field reporting and columns on city life, subcultures, and films and television. Issues have also explored the nightlife of certain cities and included hot spots and places of interest for traveling men. Calendar-based articles are also featured, with information on elections and seasonal activities included when pertinent and relevant to men's culture.

The success of the magazine has led to its introduction in other markets outside the United Kingdom and the United States. *Maxim* is published in over 25 other countries, including countries in Europe, South America, and Asia. An official Web site was launched in 1999 and features pictures and content not available in the print issues. The Web site also includes collections of photographs from a majority of the women it has featured and exclusive videos and interviews. A satellite radio channel was launched with Sirius Satellite in 2005. The magazine has also expanded its brand name into other projects and products, with special products derived from the magazine's prominent features. The magazine routinely undertakes searches to find women to mark as the most attractive in a certain geographic area or profession.

The interviews and discussions contributed by women photographed for *Maxim* are also overshadowed by the near nudity of the photographs. Articles and interviews with women photographed concern their approaches to their careers, opinions on their appearance, and how they are portrayed in the media. The quotations chosen from interviews to accompany images of these women can also detract from the information about their chosen health and fitness regimes.

The near nudity of the women featured in *Maxim* has given the magazine its most notable feature, since the women photographed are as close to nudity as allowed. Some retailers, including chain Walmart, have deemed the magazine pornography and do not carry it in stores. Written content and advertisements have also caused retailers to stop carrying the magazine. The photography and some advertisements featured in the magazine have also led to allegations of sexist depictions of women from some groups. The success of the magazine due to its near-nude photography has spread to its sister magazines, with similar criticisms laid at *Blender* for featuring more sex-based photographs than information on music and music culture.

See also: Advertising; Magazines, Men's; Models, Male

Further Reading: Benwell, Bethan. *Masculinity and Men's Lifestyle Magazines.* Malden, MA: Blackwell, 2003; Crewe, Ben. *Representing Men: Cultural Production and Producers in the Men's Magazine Market.* Oxford: Berg, 2003; Jackson, Peter, Nick Stevenson, and Kate Brooks. *Making Sense of Men's Magazines.* Cambridge: Polity Press, 2001; Jha, Alok. "Lad Culture Corrupts Men as Much as it Debases Women." *Guardian,* March 30, 2006. http://www.guardian.co.uk/commentisfree/2006/mar/30/comment. prisonsandprobation. (Accessed December 7, 2008); *Maxim: Guys' Ultimate Guide.* http://www.maxim.com/. (Accessed December 7, 2008).

Richard D. Driver

MEN'S HEALTH

Men's Health was launched in 1987, under the editorial leadership of Mark Bricklin, as a general health and fitness magazine for American men. The president of Rodale Press, Robert Teufel, conceived of the magazine as a workout and healthy lifestyle magazine in keeping with the philosophy of its founding company. J. I. Rodale created Rodale Press in 1942 when he began to publish *Organic Farming and Gardening,* a magazine devoted to promoting sustainable food production, soil improvement, and natural living. In 1950, Rodale Press turned its attention more directly to health with the publication of *Prevention,* a magazine devoted to illness and disease prevention. Rodale Press remains a foremost publisher of health and wellness magazines with a diverse range of titles including *Women's Health* (f. 2005) and *Runner's World* (f. 1966).

Men's Health began life as an annual publication but, by 1988, had emerged as a quarterly. By 1994, the magazine was published 10 times a year with combined issues for January and February and July and August. From the beginning, the magazine focused on the ways in which men could enhance and improve their lives, and by extension the appearance of their faces and their bodies, through exercise and healthy living. The magazine, from its inception, has privileged expert knowledge and opinions, citing in its articles a range of scientific and medical studies authored by seasoned professionals and relying on credentialed nutritionists, sex therapists, and sport-science specialists in formulating advice for its readers. Almost from the magazine's inception, contributors to *Men's Health* have also presented readers with advice on a broad range of emotional issues, especially those related to stress relief. This multipronged approach to male wellness led to some great commercial successes in the 1990s. Over the course of this decade of dramatic expansion for the men's magazine market, the circulation figures for *Men's Health* grew from just under 500,000 in 1991 to nearly 1.7 million by 1999. The 1990s also witnessed the dramatic expansion of the magazine's readership with the introduction of a number of international editions; there are currently more than 30 international editions of the magazine available in a diverse range of countries including Australia, China, Croatia, India, and Turkey.

As *Men's Health* faced increasing competition at the beginning of the 21st century, its editors (most notably editor-in-chief David Zinczenko) sought to broaden the appeal of the magazine by expanding its content and incorporating a number of new features on careers, finances, family life, and personal grooming. This shift in focus was also reflected in covers for the magazine which, with Zinczenko at the helm, moved away from photographs of impossibly chiseled and shirtless physique models toward images of fully clothed celebrities and athletes. This attempt to create a more comprehensive lifestyle or how-to manual for men has had the effect of defining the *Men's Health* audience, in more highly articulated ways, as white, heterosexual, and educated. Like **Gentlemen's Quarterly (GQ)**, *Esquire,* and the so-called lads' magazines (**Maxim**, *FHM, Stuff*), *Men's Health* has also focused the attention of readers on matters of sexual performance and proficiency while providing them with titillating images (particularly in its online versions) of attractive women. This shift in content focus has not led to a decline in the number of items dealing explicitly with men's physical appearance. Features on creating highly defined pectoral or abdominal muscles still punctuate the pages of the magazine, alongside articles outlining the benefits of different facial creams, revitalizing eye gels, and exfoliators. Magazines like *Men's Health* and *GQ* have thus contributed to a broad range of impulses: on the one hand, they have privileged the traditional heterosexual gaze (encouraging men to view women as sex objects); on the other, they have been noted to have filled their pages with fashionable and attractive men who are viewed by male readers simultaneously as objects of envy and desire.

Despite these changes, *Men's Health* continues to take its mission to promote health and exercise seriously. In the 1990s, it lobbied U.S. Congress to pass legislation mandating that the week of Father's Day be designated National Men's Health Week and, in 2007, it inaugurated a FitSchools campaign to combat childhood obesity and encourage health and exercise awareness in the nation's schools.

See also: Magazines, Men's; Metrosexuals; Models, Male

Further Reading: Benwell, Bethan. *Masculinity and Men's Lifestyle Magazines.* Oxford: Blackwell, 2003; Crewe, Ben. *Representing Men: Cultural Production and Producers in the Men's Magazine Market.* Oxford: Berg, 2003; Jackson, Peter, Nick Stevenson, and Kate Brooks. *Making Sense of Men's Magazines.* Cambridge: Polity Press, 2001; Stibbe, Arran. "Health and the Social Construction of Masculinity in *Men's Health* Magazine." *Men and Masculinities,* 7 no. 1 (2004): 31–51.

Paul R. Deslandes

METROSEXUALS

The term metrosexual, which was first coined by British cultural critic Mark Simpson in a 1994 article for the *Independent* and in a 2002 discussion of the English soccer star David Beckham written for www.salon.com, burst onto the American scene with three specific developments in 2003: the publication of a *New York Times* article titled "Metrosexuals Come Out" on June 22, 2003; the airing of a VH1 documentary called *Totally Gay* in which metrosexuality was identified as an emerging trend; and the premiere, on July 15, 2003, of Bravo Television's smash hit *Queer Eye for the Straight Guy*. All three of these events elevated the status of this supposedly new version of American masculinity and prompted a national obsession with men's skin care and the general state of early-21st-century American manhood.

Defining the Metrosexual

The metrosexual is most commonly understood to be the consummate male consumer: narcissistic, preoccupied with physical appearances, and obsessed with urban culture. The creation, in part, of capitalist producers of men's clothing, skincare, and hair products; savvy hairstylists; and the media, the metrosexual is frequently characterized as the embodiment of a new form of feminized masculinity; a man thought to enjoy the pleasures of both female and male attention. The pleasure-seeking and fashion-obsessed metrosexual's desire to show off and be admired is also seen, by some, as a subversion of the traditional masculine gaze; a reversal of the historical male prerogative to travel freely through urban spaces in pursuit of the visual and sensual stimulation derived from viewing women, as objects of desire, in public places. While the general assumption is that the metrosexual is, in fact, a heterosexual who has embraced the aesthetic and consumerist sensibilities of gay men, this definition tends—according to some critics who see the metrosexual as being gay, straight, or bisexual—to be rather limiting.

Precedents of the 18th- and 19th Centuries

While the term metrosexual is a recent invention, the idea of the fashion-conscious and appearance-obsessed young man possesses a much longer history in Anglo-American history. In mid-18th-century England, the term macaroni was used to describe men whose interests in extravagant powdered wigs, continental fashions and mannerisms, and elaborate forms of dress were thought to exceed the bounds of propriety. Similarly, the word dandy also came to be used to describe middle-class men like George Bryan "Beau" Brummell (1778–1840) who, in the late 18th and early 19th centuries, aped the mannerisms and styles of the upper classes in Europe (most notably in Britain and France) and were known for their fastidiousness of dress and their obsession with appearance. These trends, which had their American counterparts, continued throughout the 19th century and culminated in the aesthetic movement, reflected most notably in the artistic poses and sartorial styles of people like the poet and playwright Oscar Wilde in Britain and the photographer Fred Holland Day, the architect Standford White, and even Mark Twain in the United States. These men, especially when they visited the western territories of the United States, might be negatively labeled as *dudes,* a term of ridicule usually applied to men who were criticized for their overly fussy forms of dress, speech, and, in some cases, gestures.

Precedents of the 20th Century

The precursors to the modern metrosexual are equally varied in the 20th century. By the 1920s and 1930s, the appearance-conscious fashionable man could be found in several distinctive places. The bachelor, who was a prominent feature of the urban landscape by the early 20th century, took special pride in his appearance, as did the gangster and the Chicano and African American zoot-suiter in the 1930s and 1940s. The image-conscious man also entered popular culture through literary characters like F. Scott Fitzgerald's Gatsby and advertisements, especially for products directed at fashionable men, such as Arrow shirts. In the more immediate past, authors like Charles Hix (a stylist and journalist who wrote for **Gentlemen's Quarterly [GQ]** and *Playboy*) set, in his 1978 book *Looking Good,* an impeccably outfitted stage for the modern metrosexual. Focusing on a masculine beauty regimen that included features on shaving, moisturizing, hair and beard care, and genital odor, Hix helped to establish, with this book, the current fixation with masculine attractiveness, a trend he furthered with the publication of *Dressing Right* (1979) and *Working Out* (1983). The current metrosexual emerged out of the commodification and marketing of this new masculine ideal, a trend that culminated in the publication, in 2003, of Michael Flocker's *The Metrosexual Guide to Style: A Handbook for the Modern Man.*

Reactions

The metrosexual's rise has not, however, been viewed in an entirely unproblematic manner. Almost as soon as the concept was popularized in 2003, attacks from a variety of different sectors emerged. Most critiques, generated by men and women alike, focused on the problems associated with the feminizing tendencies of the metrosexual. One female contributor to the online ESPN magazine *Page 2,* for example, expressed open reservations about the "icky dude who's in touch with his feminine side" and called for a "resurgence of masculinity." Reservations about the metrosexual also appeared in a variety of popular cultural forms in the years after 2003, including the animated television series *South Park;* marketing campaigns for Burger King and Old Spice aftershave; and films like *Talladega Nights* (2006). In all instances, the message was clear: reject metrosexuality (and by implication the feminine) for an essentialized version of a true man, identified by some as a *retrosexual.* This reactionary figure—identified as a man who is aggressively and virulently heterosexual, sports-obsessed, macho, and ultimately unconcerned with fashion, refined manners, or beauty regimens—points to just some of the ways in which the emergence of the metrosexual has forged yet another crisis of masculinity in modern American society.

See also: Magazines, Men's; *Maxim;* Men's Health

Further Reading: Blanchard, Mary Warner. *Oscar Wilde's America: Counterculture in the Gilded Age.* New Haven, CT: Yale University Press, 1998; Bordo, Susan. *The Male Body: A New Look at Men in Public and in Private.* New York: Farrar, Straus and Giroux, 1999; Coad, David. *Metrosexual: Gender, Sexuality, and Sport.* Albany: State University of New

York Press, 2008; Osgerby, Bill. *Playboys in Paradise: Masculinity, Youth Culture, and Leisure-Style in Modern America.* Oxford: Berg, 2001; Simpson, Mark. *Male Impersonators: Men Performing Masculinity.* New York: Routledge, 1994; Verma, Himanshu. *The Metrosexuals: Exploring the Unexplored.* New Delhi: Red Earth, 2004.

Paul R. Deslandes

MODELS, MALE

While the profession of the male fashion and underwear model is a relatively recent invention, men have served as models for centuries, primarily in artists' studios and academies. In the 18th and 19th centuries, formally trained artists regularly conducted studies of frequently nude, living models, both male and female. Artistic institutions, in this period, especially in European capitals like Paris and London, employed physically attractive models to teach students in life classes about the intricacies and aesthetic appeal of the human body. Generally humble in status and origins, many male models in these studios and academies held other jobs as soldiers, street boxers, or casual laborers.

Men in Advertising

The male model became increasingly important in the late 19th and early 20th centuries with the rise of two distinctive developments: the emergence of photography and the growth of a print **advertising** industry that came to rely, increasingly, on images of celebrities and attractive figures to sell products and produce consumer desires. With the rise of the print advertisement as a new form of visual culture came the emergence of new kinds of male celebrities noted for their physical beauty and their appeal to—especially—female consumers. This was nowhere more apparent than in the case of the Arrow Man, an advertising gimmick first introduced in 1905 by Cluett, Peabody, and Company, the manufacturer of the Arrow detachable shirt collar. The model for this advertisement, the lover of illustrator Joseph Christian Leyendecker, created a state of near mania when, during one month alone in the 1920s, he received some 17,000 fan letters containing marriage proposals, offers of sex, and even suicide threats.

Physique and Underwear Models

Another development in male modeling during this period came from a very different source—the fitness craze inaugurated by physical culture experts like Eugen Sandow (1867–1925) and Bernarr Adolphus Macfadden (1868–1955). Some men, naturally endowed with fine physiques and attractive faces and followers of the movement, were able to build careers for themselves as physical culture models and fitness experts. Among the most prominent of these men was the New York-based Tony Sansone who had a modeling and personal fitness career that spanned from 1923 until the 1960s. Born in 1905 to Sicilian immigrants, Sansone was a convert to physical culture by the age of 14 when he began to run in Brooklyn parks, do

Eugen Sandow, body builder, c. 1893.
(Courtesy of Library of Congress)

countless chin-ups, and practice acrobatics. By the 1920s, Sansone was posing as a model for sculptors connected to Gertrude Whitney Vanderbilt and posing for physical culture magazines and books. Known for his classical and statuesque beauty, Sansone quickly became a sensation, inspiring rhapsodic celebrations by Charles Atlas, himself a specimen of supreme physical fitness, who labeled him the most beautiful man in America. By the latter years of the decade, Sansone's success as a physical culturist led to his appearance in plays and films and to the sale of his image in popular magazines.

The 1930s and 1940s brought about several important shifts that had a direct bearing on the experiences of male models. With the growing popularity of magazines like *Esquire* (f. 1933), marketed directly to men, new opportunities for male models began to emerge. While some men began to earn decent incomes, in this period, as professional models, many advertisers relied on images of soldiers, as an idealized version of masculinity first celebrated in propaganda posters and advertisements for products like Ivory soap during World War I, and Hollywood actors to peddle a broad range of American goods.

In the 1950s, a staple of the modern male modeling industry—the underwear model—began to appear with some regularity in print advertisements. Spurred, in part, by the development of swimwear-inspired men's briefs, underwear companies like Cooper and Sons and Jockey International began to rely on images of men, stripped down to their underclothes, to sell these new products. While advertisements for underwear in the 1950s remained largely sanitized and asexual and most male models continued to wear conservative suits and sportswear in magazines, catalogues, and newspapers, this emphasis on the scantily-clad male body led to new possibilities for those men interested in pursuing a career before the camera. By the 1960s and the 1970s, the eroticization and commercialization of the nearly nude male body presented opportunities for emerging modeling stars like Tony Sanchez and Jack Scalia. This decade also witnessed a dramatic rise in the significance of a new kind of modeling agency that dictated the terms of modeling contracts more specifically and began to represent men with much greater frequency. According to one estimate, the growing importance of male modeling led, by 1978, to several top agencies in New York reporting that their men's divisions were now responsible for up to one-third of their annual income.

Recent Developments

Men's modeling was revolutionized in the 1980s as several companies, including **Calvin Klein**, began to rely on appealing images of well-developed and well-endowed men to sell products to both women and increasingly powerful gay male consumers. In 1983, at the very moment when Jockey International had revolutionized men's underwear sales by relying on revealing photographs of Baltimore Orioles pitcher Jim Palmer in skimpy (and often quite colorful) briefs, Calvin Klein plastered New York City buildings and buses with a Bruce Weber image of Olympic pole-vaulter Tom Hintinauss in white briefs. Since this campaign and others selling, most notably, male fragrances, male models have figured prominently in American culture as a new, and highly erotic, form of celebrity.

This celebration of the male body and face as a prominent feature of consumer culture in the United States continued in an unabated fashion in the 1990s as magazines like *GQ* (f. 1957) and *Men's Health* (f. 1987) celebrated the male form, relied on partially clothed images of men to sell products and increase subscriptions, and contributed further to the male model's meteoric rise. As their stars rose in the final decade of the 20th century, new male modeling icons emerged in magazines, in television advertisements, and on runways, including Mark Vanderloo and Marcus Schenkenberg. The popularity of male models has continued into the 21st century, fueled by the reality television craze, which has offered viewers titillating images of the male model in popular shows like *Manhunt: The Search for America's Most Gorgeous Male Model* (2004) and *Make Me a Supermodel* (2008).

See also Magazines, Men's

Further Reading: Bordo, Susan. *The Male Body: A New Look at Men in Public and in Private*. New York: Farrar, Straus, and Giroux, 1999; Hill, Daniel Delis. *Advertising to the American Woman, 1900–1999*. Columbus: Ohio State University Press, 2002; Hix, Charles (with Michael Taylor). *Male Model: The World Behind the Camera*. New York: St. Martin's, 1979; Luciano, Lynne. *Looking Good: Male Body Image in Modern America*. New York: Hill and Wang, 2001; Massey, John. *American Adonis: Tony Sansone, The First Male Physique Icon*. New York: Universe, 2004; Postle, Martin and William Vaughan. *The Artist's Model: From Etty to Spencer*. London: Merrell Holberton, 1999.

Paul R. Deslandes

MODELS AND MODELING

Models are generally divided into groups based on the type of work they do; the most common types of models are fashion, glamour, fine art, and body part models. While modeling has a reputation for consisting solely of tall, thin, exceptionally beautiful women, the industry actually encompasses both men and women with a huge range of body types and looks.

Fashion Models

The most famous type of model is undoubtedly the fashion model. Fashion models are hired to advertise clothing through print advertisements (editorial modeling) and to promote fashion **designers** in runway shows. Many fashion models succeed at both editorial and runway modeling, but it is not uncommon for them to specialize in one or the other, as they each have a slightly different set of requirements.

In terms of body type, fashion modeling is the most ruthless, especially for women. Female fashion models need to be both uncommonly tall and uncommonly thin; the average height of a female fashion model is 5 feet 10 inches with a weight of 110 pounds, while the average American woman is 5 feet 4 inches and weighs 160 pounds. Male fashion models are also taller and thinner than average: a typical male fashion model is 6 feet and 150 pounds, while the average American man is 5 feet 9 inches and 190 pounds.

Beauty is an important factor for fashion models, though not as much as it is for glamour models. For runway models in particular, beauty is less important than body type, well-defined bone structure, and ease in walking on the catwalk. Beauty is more important for editorial fashion modeling, as photographs present a closer view of the model than is found on the runway. In fact, many highly successful editorial fashion models also become engaged in glamour modeling, where beauty is paramount.

Glamour Models

Glamour modeling places an emphasis on the model instead of a product—most instances of glamour modeling do not feature a product for sale at all. Glamour modeling is almost exclusively a female profession; while there is a small market for male glamour models, some may argue the types of work given to men and women are not equivalent.

Female glamour models are mostly featured in **men's magazines**. The beauty and sexuality of the model are the main focus of the photograph, and many of the pictures feature short profiles about the model. One of the most recognizable instances of glamour modeling is swimsuit modeling, made famous by the hugely popular *Sports Illustrated* "Swimsuit Issue." Glamour modeling became popular in the United States in the first half of the 20th century with pinups and posters featuring scantily clad women, and today a huge range of men's magazines highlight glamour modeling. Nude glamour modeling is also a pervasive type of pornography, made famous by *Playboy* magazine.

While there are instances of male glamour modeling, it isn't nearly as omnipresent as female. Most male glamour modeling takes place in the handful of pornographic magazines targeted at women and gay men. Some mainstream women's magazines, such as ***Cosmopolitan***, feature semi-nude photographs of **male models**, but they are not as important a feature of content as the corresponding female models in men's magazines.

Other

While fashion and glamour models are the most common, there are many other types of models who do not fit the popular image of models and modeling. The original models posed for painters and other artists, and visual artists in the 21st century continue to hire models to pose for artistic work. Fine arts models come in virtually all shapes and sizes, and while nude images are common, they are distinguished from pornography based on the lack of emphasis on the sexuality of the model.

Many advertisements for accessories demand a close-up shot of a specific body part: for example a wrist and hand modeling a watch, or foot and lower leg displaying a shoe. While the part in question is usually especially elegant, the demands placed on the body as a whole are not nearly as stringent as for other types of modeling. Body part modeling is often an avenue to success, especially for petite models that do not fulfill the height requirements set forth by fashion modeling.

Fitness models are used to advertise exercise equipment and lifestyles, and this is the one area of modeling that is dominated by men, though both men and women participate. Fitness models have athletic physiques, with more muscle mass and definition than is customary for fashion or glamour modeling.

Another example of alternative body types in women's modeling is plus-size modeling. Any model wearing a dress size 8 or greater is considered plus size, though most plus-size models wear size 12–16. A high fashion runway model, on the other hand, usually wears a size 2. Plus-size modeling is most common in editorial fashion pages in magazines, as well as advertisements for specialty retailers such as Lane Bryant. There are almost no plus-size runway models, as runway work is usually limited to haute couture, the designers of which rarely work in plus sizes. While the body size standards for plus size models are different, the rest of the requirements still apply: plus size models must be beautiful, with clear skin and straight teeth, and extremely photogenic.

The most famous of all model types is the supermodel, the very highest echelon attainable for models. Supermodels are almost entirely female and gain celebrity status akin to Hollywood actors and rock stars. Supermodels also usually cross modeling boundaries, combining fashion and glamour modeling, and often including television commercials and even films.

"I like what Tyra Banks is doing on her show by portraying how beauty is such a constructed fantasy. I really like how she exposes young girls and women to the work that goes into creating one shot we see in magazines. I wish young women would look into mirrors and find the only judgment of appearance that matters is their own. For individual beauty, we should always be thankful."

Laila Haidarali, historian

Source: Shana Burg, A Thousand Never Evers. http://www.shanaburg.com/research2.php.Controversy and Criticism

The modeling industry is a frequent recipient of criticism from the public. Many argue that the bodies presented in **fashion magazines** create unrealistic expectations for young women, citing the rise of eating disorders in teenage girls and young women in recent decades.

The 2006 deaths of two models caused the public to look with an even sharper eye at the fashion industry and its demands on models. In August 2006, Uruguayan model Luisel Ramos died during a fashion show of a heart attack brought on by anorexia nervosa, and just a few months later anorexia also claimed the life of Brazilian model Ana Carolina Reston. Ramos's body mass index, a figure calculated from a person's height and weight, was well below starvation levels at the time of her death. In response to the public outcry, the administrators of the 2006 Madrid Fashion Week instigated new weight minimums for all its models, regulated by monitoring the models' body mass index. Italian designers followed suit later that year by signing a joint measure with the Italian government banning size 0 models from their catwalks.

Despite the frantic response to these tragic events, it is unclear whether the exceptional thinness of high fashion models will cease to be the trend. The ease of flattering a tall, thin body originally prompted the popularity of typical model sizes with haute couture designers, and it seems unlikely that they will suddenly abandon tradition. Many top designers have advocated the hiring of healthy models to the runways, but it is important to note that just because obscenely thin models may be banned, the models that remain are by no means indicative of the average bodies of women. Glamour models are a perfect example of a healthy figure that is still virtually unattainable for a majority of women. While glamour models are far more voluptuous and usually shorter than runway models, they are still much thinner and much more beautiful than the average woman.

While glamour models might not induce eating disorders in women the way high fashion models do, the pervasiveness of images of glamour models is often cited as the source for poor body image among women. Not only are they thinner than most women, the vast majority of photographs of glamour models are airbrushed, or altered with a computer, creating even more unrealistic expectations. Airbrushing is ubiquitous and far-reaching and not just used to erase the occasional blemish. It is also used to completely reshape the body of the model. Waists are whittled, legs are slimmed, and stomachs are flattened, all with the click of a mouse on a computer program. The images created leave the average woman feeling a sense of failure that she can't look like that, without realizing that in fact, no one looks like that, not even the model.

See also: Advertising

Further Reading: Cole, Louise, and Giles Vichers-Jones. *Professional Modeling.* London: New Holland Press, 2009; Haidarali, Laila. "Polishing Brown Diamonds: African American Women, Popular Magazines, and the Advent of Modeling in Early Postwar America." *Journal of Women's History,* 17 no. 1 (2005): 10–37; Haidarali, Laila. "'The Vampingest Vamp is a Brownskin': Colour, Sex, Beauty and African American Womanhood, 1920–1954." PhD diss., York University, 2007; Koda, Harold, and Kohle Yohannan. *The Model as Muse: Embodying Fashion.* New York: Metropolitan Museum of Art, 2009; Lenz, Bernie, and Ria Niccoli. *The New Complete Book of Fashion Modeling.* New York: Crown Publishers, 1982; Mears, Ashley, "Discipline of the Catwalk: Gender, Power, and Uncertainty in Fashion Modeling." *Ethnography,* 9 no. 4 (2008): 429–56; Snyder, Didiayer. *On Your Mark: An Insight Guide to Modeling,* Bloomington, IN: Author House, 2008.

Abigail Mitchell

NAIL ART

Nail art refers to decorative embellishments of fingernails, while nail art fashion includes designs, paintings on nails, and the length of fingernails. This tradition of decorative embellishments of female fingernails has lasted for over 6,000 years in one form or another. As foot binding and the desire for diminutive feet originated among elites and initially served as an indicator that a family could afford to remove a woman from active **labor** in ancient China (after 1300 C.E.), some noblewomen also grew their nails long for the same reason. At different times and cultures, these high-status displays, accompanied by the application of brightly colored varnish to the nails, illustrated the fact that these were hands that never had to toil. Unmarried women with polished long nails could expect a good marriage rather than a life as a servant. In ancient China, wealthy noblewomen had long nails painted with gold to signify their membership in the leisure class.

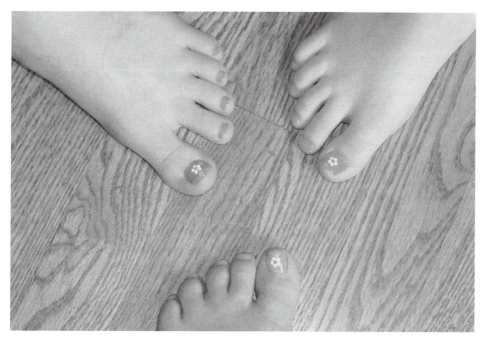

Mother and daughters admire their new pedicures, 2008. (Courtesy of Terri Merrigan)

Contemporary Trends

Neatly manicured nails would remain a sign of the leisure class throughout most of the 20th century and among many different cultures. However, like the use of **cosmetics**, brightly painted nails were often linked to artificiality and impropriety. Even as nail polish became a common beauty ritual, local five-and-dimes offered an array of choices for do-it-yourself applications that reserved a professional manicure for the wealthy.

In the past couple of decades, however, the fashion for long, painted fingernails has been amplified, along with the widespread growth of **nail salons** than now provide nail art as well as more traditional manicuring services. Nail salons offer a variation of designs for nails in which fancy patterns are added to the surface of the nails. This includes everything from a natural-looking French manicure to elaborate nail art of acrylic nail sculptures, stick-on rhinestones, hologram tips, and dangling nail jewelry for pierced nails. The list is endless, including themed nail art for holidays like Halloween or Christmas that only well-trained, highly skilled professionals are capable of mastering.

Nail salons label different nail styles with names such as Airbrush, French, Tropical, American, and Silk Wraps, in addition to the regular nail polish procedure. Almost every year, new nail fashions are added to the current repertoire of nail styles and, like the clothing industry, certain nail fashions go out of style to be replaced with new ones.

Nail Fashion and Identity

Women across spectrums of race, class, age, and ethnicity have their nails done. But different nail styles are popular among different groups of women. The variety of nail styles and fashions makes individual and group choices meaningful. White middle-class women in middle management and professional positions, on the whole, choose nail fashions characterized by short cuts and light polish with nails that are well kept and are markers of neatness, professionalism, and good grooming. The specific nail fashion of attaching artificial acrylic nails and painting them with colorful and elaborate designs in long nails is especially popular among African American women. Even when these nails hamper manual dexterity, their personal and social impact may be so rewarding as to compensate for this. Given the history of race and labor, African American hands that look as though they do not do manual labor or service work contradict and challenge much of the past. The individual reasons for this preference, however, are highly diverse, reflecting a myriad of emotional desires and aesthetic sensibilities. Everything from Black Power fists to floral designs are popular requests, depending on person and place. In this sense, nail beautification can be read as a means of resistance as well as inscribing identity, along with cosmetic and decorative art, in body aesthetics. Practices in nail beautification can be read as culturally coded styles of beauty that motivate and valorize particular expressions of differences.

See also: Manicurists and Nail Technicians; Nail Salons

Further Reading: Black, Paula. *The Beauty Industry: Gender, Culture, Pleasure.* New York: Routledge, 2004; Han, Jeong woo. "Eye To Eye, Nail To Nail: Body and Identity in Korean Nail Salon Workers in New York City." PhD diss., New School for Social Research, 2004; Morris, Desmond. *The Naked Woman: A Study of the Female Body.* New York: Macmillan, 2007; Schultes, Sue Ellen, and Deborah Beatty. *Milady's Standard: Nail Technology.* 4th ed. London: Cengage Learning, 2002; Willett, Julie. "'Hands across the Table': A Short History of Manicurists in the Twentieth Century." *Journal of Women's History,* 17 no. 3 (2005): 59–80.

Jeong woo Han

NAIL SALONS

Nail salons are beauty service establishments that offer nail care services such as manicures and pedicures, services once relegated to beauty salons and some barbershops. Today, nail salons also offer hand, foot, and back massages. Some nail salons provide skin care and/or **waxing** services, and some nail techs specialize in elaborate variations of **nail art**. According to *Nail Trade Magazine,* there are approximately 58,350 nail salons (2008) in the United States, doing some $6.4 billion in business each year; most of these are Korean or Vietnamese owner operated. Thanks to immigrant women's entrepreneurship, in particular, manicures, once done by women themselves in the privacy of their own home or a luxury item carried out at full-service hair salons, have become something that is paid for in nail salons.

Formation of a Niche

On the East Coast, New York City is the place where nail salons first appeared as a separate nail care establishment. In the late 1970s and early '80s Korean women who were employed as either **hairdressers** or manicurists in Manhattan hair salons took considerable initiative to start their own businesses and paved the way for other Korean women to enter the workforce. At the time, there were no specialty nail salons, and manicures were available only in upscale, full-service beauty salons, affordable only to an elite group of people, namely upper- and upper-middle-class white women. Innovative Korean manicurists caught on to this point and took this luxury service out of the beauty salons; they started creating the nail salon niche within the expanding sector of beauty industry there. The number of Korean-owned nail salons increased dramatically during the 1980s, and the price for a manicure in New York City fell to such extent that low-income women could afford to have the service.

Korean nail salons now form up to 90 percent of nail salons in New York City. The Korean-American Nail Salon Association estimated that 5,000 nail salons were run by Koreans in New York City and surrounding suburbs in 2006. Since the Korean nail salons began to appear in Manhattan in late 1970s, they have proliferated in such remarkable numbers that they have evolved into one of the signature icons of the city, an easily recognizable symbol on nearly every city block. The term *nail salon* in NYC and its neighboring suburbs evokes images of a specifically Korean establishment.

On the West Coast and in Texas, Vietnamese transformed the nail salon industry in similar ways. Since the mid 1970s and the fall of Saigon, Vietnamese immigrants began looking for an entrepreneurial niche and, in cities like Los Angeles, moved from offering cut-rate prices in salons to establishing their own businesses. In the 1970s an L.A. manicure may have cost as much as $60, and now one can get the same service for sometimes less than $20. In places like California, Vietnamese immigrants brought manicures to the masses and established the nail salon as a distinct beauty institution. Today, in California, approximately 80 percent of nail techs are Vietnamese and, nationally, 43 percent of nail salons are Vietnamese owned and operated. Their clientele, however, remains quite diverse. Due to mass production manicures, women from a broad range of social classes and occupations and across various ethnic and racial lines can easily afford to get their nails done. Although *manicurist* is not a word that translates directly into Vietnamese, Vietnamese manicurists found an ethnic niche similar to that of Indian-owned hotels and Cambodian doughnut shops.

As structural conditions necessary for the emergence and growth of nail salons in NYC and L.A. developed, the socioeconomic order of the global city, characterized by its development of service industries in the wake of the erosion of the urban **manufacturing** base, should be noted. This unique enterprise could not be successful without a steady supply of both nail workers who dedicated themselves to this type of body-related work and to their clients with the disposable income necessary to purchase the services offered by nail salons within the expanding sector of the beauty industry.

Another crucial factor of a successful ethnic business is the domination of one particular industry through vertical integration, which is defined as an interdependence among co-ethnic producers, suppliers, and retailers. Immigrant clustering in the nail salon niche has resulted in strong vertical integration in lines of nail-related businesses, namely the interdependence among co-ethnic nail salons, nail material suppliers, and nail training schools. As the number of nail salons rapidly increased, some immigrants with money thrust themselves into the nail supply business and nail schools. Ethnic clustering like this leads to advantages such as the ability to form business associations and negotiate with manufacturers to receive cheaper wholesale prices.

Business Incentives

Just as immigrant couples first found their economic niche in running vegetable stands or fish markets, women and increasingly entrepreneurs now find their niche in nail salons. This requires a relatively small initial investment, a simple command of English, a readily available supply of **labor**, and few professional skills. Koreans and Vietnamese can rent small spaces and need only make a few purchases to open a nail salon. Personal incentives include opportunities to socialize with coworkers and customers, to increase English skills, and to work in a beauty-related artistic field.

Shop Culture

The economic character of nail salons rests on higher profit margins coming from providing elaborate service for each customer. This is not the case with most immigrant-owned shops, which are characterized by low profit margins, high customer turnover, fleeting encounters, and general anonymity. Because a nail shop is a service enterprise, the ability to forge relationships with customers is an important component of success. Thus, service performances involving physical contact and face-to-face encounters with other racial groups are the conditions that shape nail shop culture.

This nail shop culture is highlighted by attitudes and feelings of social distance between manicurists and customers in struggles over language, tips, and competing as well as supporting relations among employees. It reveals conflict-laden relationships and a gulf between customers and nail women, as well as between American and Korean or Vietnamese cultures. Korean manicurists constantly straddle these deep conflicting divisions. In performing nail services, immigrant manicurists not only attend to the physical comfort and aesthetics of the customers' appearance, but also engage in complex relations with customers through which they are constantly challenging, accommodating, and/or reinforcing the status quo and hierarchical structure of the dominant society.

The nail salon is often more than just a place of business. For customers, it is a social space where they can spend time, relax, and socialize with the business owners, employees, and fellow customers. Because customers tend to assume that Korean and Vietnamese manicurists have a poor grasp of the English language, they do not expect to engage in conversations with their manicurists. Nail salons are social spaces where customers talk to one another, shoulder-to-shoulder at the manicure and drying table.

Safety Concerns

People generally believe that having one's nails done is harmful to healthy nails because of the use of harsh chemicals and cuticle removers. Manicurists often wear masks to protect themselves from the dust of nail buffing powder and other chemicals. This is especially the case among the manicurists who work in predominantly low-income African American neighborhood salons, where strong chemicals are frequently needed to achieve the intricate nail designs their customers request.

Recent scientific studies show that nontuberculous mycobacterial infections have been found to cause severe skin and soft-tissue infections in association with nail salon whirlpool footbaths. The Department of Health Services expects that rapidly growing mycobacterial infections related to pedicures may continue to occur in a sporadic fashion, and asks clinicians to inquire about recent pedicures in a patient with recurrent infections of furunculosis and the need for long-term polymicrobial therapy.

Interactions with Customers

Perhaps better known than the health concerns are the interactions between American customers and immigrant nail techs. The degree to which relationships are constructed through conversation between the manicurist and her customer varies with the location of the nail salon, which determines the race, ethnicity, and age of its main clientele. In upscale salons in Manhattan's commercial districts, where the clientele is predominantly white and middle or upper-middle class, conversation with customers is discouraged by the salon owner for the sake of speed and efficiency of service. Salons located in suburban spaces generally allow for more opportunity for conversation between manicurist and customer. The fact that many of the clients in these salons tend to be older and homemakers rather than career women is also a factor that is more conducive to conversations between client and worker. Such variations in levels of active conversation are the result of service expectations by both the customer and the worker according to race, class, and the neighborhood in which the salon is situated.

Customers' race and class are intertwined and become important factors in determining interactions with and perceptions of American women and American life for Asian manicurists. The manicurists' interactions with customers are at times characterized by tension over matters of the use of the native Korean or Vietnamese language. Some nail salons hang television monitors to distract the customer and further mitigate social interactions with nail workers. Yet, in some local shops, there is enough leeway in the emotional and physical demands of their work to allow for workers to get to know their American clientele, at least in terms of holidays and food recipes. The relative older age and free time of some contribute to a more relaxed atmosphere in the salon.

Ultimately, the nail salon is a common space where two different bodies, the manicuring and the manicured, come in physical contact and through which both are challenged, accommodated, negotiated, and acculturated. With their American salon names, immigrant manicurists are drawn into a commodified body industry, performing previously unimaginable work that involves encounters with unfamiliar racial and ethnic groups. Through daily service interactions, immigrant service providers construct and/or transform not only their own identity, learning where their place is in this society and culture, but also the meaning of black and white within the racial hierarchy of the United States. They create a space where it is not unusual to find, for example, a Vietnamese nail tech meticulously painting a black power fist salute on her clientele's fingernails. Both social interactions and touch reaffirm and redefine the nature of service work along with contemporary trends in the beauty industry.

See also: Health and Safety; Labor; Manicurists and Nail Technicians

Further Reading: Airriess, Christopher. *Contemporary Ethnic Geographies in America,* 5th ed. Lanham, MD: Rowman & Littlefield, 2007; Han, Jeong woo. "Eye To Eye, Nail To Nail: Body and Identity in Korean Nail Salon Workers in New York City." PhD diss., New School for Social Research, 2004; Kang, Miliann. *The Managed Hand: Race, Gender and the Body in Beauty Service Work.* Berkeley: University of California Press, 2010;

Lee, Jennifer. "Retail Niche Domination among African American, Jewish, and Korean Entrepreneurs." *American Behavioral Scientist,* 42 (1999): 1398–1416; Oh, Joong-Hwan. "Economic Incentive, Embeddedness, and Social Support: A Study of Korean-Owned Nail Salon Workers' Rotating Credit Associations." *International Migration Review,* 41 no. 3 (2007): 623–55; Tran, My-Thuan. "Vietnamese Nail Down the U.S. Manicure Business." *Los Angeles Times,* May 5, 2008; Willett, Julie. "'Hands across the Table': A Short History of Manicurists in the Twentieth Century." *Journal of Women's History,* 17 no. 3 (2005): 59–80; Winthrop, Kevin L., Kim Albridge, David South, Peggy Albrecht, Marcy Abrams, Michael C. Samuel, Wendy Leonard, Joanna Wagner, and Duc J. Vugia. "The Clinical Management and Outcome of Nail Salon-Acquired Mycobacterium fortuitum Skin Infection." *Clinical Infectious Diseases,* 38 (January 2004): 38–44.

Jeong woo Han

NATURAL LOOK

The natural look is a style of **cosmetics** use made to create the illusion of not wearing any beauty products at all. This style was first popular in the 1970s, when there was a desire articulated across the fashion world to return to a more simple and innocent time, with many **designers** looking to traditional and folk dress for inspiration. In turn, a wide variety of more subtle tones of lipstick, nail polish, eye shadow, and blusher appeared on the market. Untinted or subtly shaded lip gloss appeared on the market in 1971. Hairstyling was also a factor in this overall look. Many women began to wear their hair straight and long, a dramatic change from the **bouffant** and beehive styles popular in the 1960s. Although there was not a single defining trend in makeup during the 1970s, the natural look became very popular with women across a variety of population segments. The irony is that to correctly achieve this un–made up look, a lot of makeup must be used. Similarly, the natural style of hair worn long, loose, and straight was not possible for many women, and they used clothing irons to press the curls and waves out of their hair to achieve the desired natural look. African American women were encouraged to grow their hair into an **Afro**, a style that also appeared casual and careless but took a great deal of time and effort to achieve.

The natural look fell out of favor in the 1980s, when the trend focused on fluorescent colors, bright pastels, and anything that sparkled. By the mid 1990s, a more casual look was in favor. With the advent of casual Fridays, grunge, and shabby chic, and a revival of the Bohemian look, heavy makeup for women once more gave way to neutral shades of eye shadow and paler lipstick colors. Mascara ceased to be available in electric blue, purple, and hot pink; instead a wide variety of brown to black hues were sold.

In today's market, the natural look is once again popular. Tinted moisturizers and barely there shades create a minimalist look. Maybelline recently created a line of eye shadow sets intended to compliment and enhance the eye color instead of drawing attention to the makeup itself. Actress Drew Barrymore scolded the **advertising** audience that their "makeup was showing" in a 2008 television advertisement for **CoverGirl**, further telling them that they should "see the difference, not the makeup."

The natural look is also more than just an un–made up style; it also incorporates the use of natural products. Companies like Burt's Bees, Physician's Formula, and Bare Escentuals have made a name for themselves by providing natural-looking cosmetic styling created from minerals and organic ingredients. Because of their origins, these products have less variety of available colors and often do not provide the finish or lasting wear that many women desire in makeup. To bridge this gap, many mainstream cosmetics companies such as CoverGirl, **Avon**, L'Oréal, and **Mary Kay Cosmetics** have all launched mineral makeup lines or have added minerals to many of their existing products.

Today, the use of makeup is still required to achieve that natural look, but cosmetics companies have made great strides in creating makeup that is the next best thing to nothing at all. From natural minerals to mousse foundations, the idea is to use makeup to create a flawless complexion that looks like a woman is wearing nothing at all.

See also: Hairstyles

Further Reading: Gavenas, Mary Lisa. *Color Stories: Behind the Scenes of America's Billion-Dollar Beauty Industry*. New York: Simon & Schuster, 2002; Tortora, Phyllis, and Keith Eubank. *Survey of Historic Costume: A History of Western Dress,* 3rd ed. New York: Fairchild Publications, 2005.

Sara M. Harvey

ORGANIC TRENDS AND PRODUCTS

Organic trends and products within the beauty industry are produced according to organic standards: using ingredients derived from organically grown, natural botanicals. This is a growing trend in the beauty industry, with many beauty companies promoting a link between natural beauty and environmental health.

Principles

Organic products are those that use production methods and include materials that enhance and support the health of ecological systems. Organic agricultural practices aim to minimize pollution from air, soil, and water by avoiding pesticides. The primary goal of organic companies is to create products that support the health of plants, animals, and people by sustaining a healthy environment.

Chemicals in Cosmetics

Most synthetic makeup products are petroleum based and are processed using synthetic and potentially harmful chemicals. Fifty of the many chemicals included in American personal care products have been banned in Europe. Researchers argue that many of these chemicals are carcinogenic and have other negative health effects. Most of the products applied to the skin are absorbed and can enter the bloodstream. Synthetic or toxic ingredients in lotions, cleansers, and makeup may cause allergic reactions or have other effects on health. As the primary consumers of **cosmetics**, women are at particular risk for ingesting the harmful ingredients of cosmetics such as preservatives, fragrances, and other components like formaldehyde. A recent study found that 61 percent of 33 name-brand lipsticks contained unsafe amounts of lead.

Trends

Organic personal care products offer an alternative to the chemical-based conventional beauty lines. Such cosmetics and personal care products include organic ingredients and are produced without pesticides or other potentially hazardous chemicals. Advocates of organic personal care products cite the health benefits of using beauty products without harmful chemicals.

Organic products have risen in popularity and thus the number of products offered has increased dramatically. The organic beauty industry has grown at

15 percent for the past 15 years. In 2007, personal care products counted for 15 percent of the U.S. personal care market, with sales of $9 billion. Over 100 natural, organic, and environmentally friendly beauty lines have been developed since 2002. With the growth of the organic personal care industry, the importance of accurate labeling becomes more pressing to avoid greenwashing (misrepresenting a product as environmentally friendly).

With the rise in popularity of organic products, there is an increased risk for misleading **advertising** and labeling to cash in on the popularity of such products. Among consumers of the beauty industry, a common misconception is that *natural* is synonymous with *organic*. *Natural* is a term used to describe nonsynthetic ingredients, and this wording is not regulated, while organic products abide by strict regulations.

Some manufacturers use terms like *natural* instead of *organic* or *authentic* instead of *certified*. These terms are not regulated, and thus consumers may mistakenly believe they are buying organic products. While natural products do not themselves contain synthetic additives or chemical preservatives, they may contain ingredients that were genetically modified or treated with pesticides earlier in the production process.

Organic Standards

The United States Department of Agriculture's (USDA) organic standards regulate specific practices in the production and processing of organic agricultural ingredients used for both food and nonfood products. These standards include regulation of methods used in crop growing and harvesting, along with the processing of agricultural products. Organic standards include a list of approved synthetic substances that are sanctioned for use in the production of organic products, as well as a list of prohibited natural ingredients. Organic products are minimally processed without artificial ingredients or preservatives. Organic farming maintains and cultivates crops without the use of toxic pesticides or fertilizers. Finally, organic ingredients must be produced without the use of antibiotics or synthetic hormones, and cannot be genetically modified or irradiated.

There is no national certification body in the United States: certification of organic products must occur by state and local agencies approved by the federal government. The USDA regulates three levels of organic products. Products may be labeled *100 percent organic* if they are made entirely with certified organic ingredients. Those made with at least 95 percent organic ingredients may be labeled *organic*. Both 100 percent and 95 percent organic products may **display** the USDA organic seal on the label. Products containing at least 70 percent organic ingredients may use the label *made with organic ingredients*.

While the USDA has been regulating organic personal care products since 2004, the first organic standard specifically for the beauty and personal care industry emerged in 2008. The Organic and Sustainable Industry Standards (OASIS) certify personal care products that have at least 85 percent organic ingredients as organic. OASIS also certifies those products that are made with organic ingredients, which have a minimum of 70 percent organic content, with the remaining 30 percent of ingredients meeting additional criteria. The Organic Consumers Association (OCA) criticizes OASIS for allowing ingredients made from conventional agricultural materials, which may use pesticides.

Controversy and Certification

The organic food and product industry emerged in the 1960s, when it was composed of small, independent farmers selling to local consumers. These farmers had direct, personal relationships with their customers, who trusted them in their claims to be organic. In 1990, U.S. Congress passed the Organic Foods Production Act (OFPA) in a first attempt at a national program to regulate production of organic ingredients. In 2002, the National Organic Program (NOP) was implemented after 10 years of public input and debate. The NOP regulates the use of the term *organic,* restricting it to those products certified by state agencies and approved by the USDA.

Organic farmers and consumer groups alike protested that the new guidelines were unfair to those farmers who were already practicing organic farming and production, but would now be excluded based on the national standards. For example, farmers who had been raising crops organically would not be certified if they could not prove no pesticides have been used on their soil for 10 years. Some farmers and producers also view the labeling program as restrictive and potentially economically disadvantageous to their own livelihood. Certified organic ingredients are much more expensive, and the certification process is potentially burdensome for small farmers who do not have the resources to process through the bureaucracy. Consumer advocacy groups also argue that the certification debate is occurring in lieu of measures to educate consumers about the ingredients in their products. By focusing on labeling, consumers may ignore the complex principles and practices behind organic production and fall prey to manipulation.

Health and Environmental Benefits

Proponents of organic products note many benefits for the consumer's health and the environment. The most basic benefit of organic products is the reduction in toxicity. Contemporary research shows that American infants are exposed to hundreds of harmful chemicals such as pesticides and additives. The National Academy of Science cites potential neurological and behavioral effects from even low-level exposure to pesticides, while other research demonstrates that pesticides commonly used in nonorganic food are carcinogenic and may decrease fertility.

Organic agriculture, which produces ingredients for beauty products, reduces pollution by eliminating pesticides that cause air and water contamination. Organic production methods also build healthy soil. Organic farmers promote biodiversity by using pesticide alternatives such as crop rotation, avoiding monoculture (planting one crop over a vast space of land), and planting pest-repelling plants (for instance, geraniums repel insects that feast on tomatoes). Organic matter used to fertilize has been shown to increase nutrients in organic produce, whereas synthetic fertilizers deplete the soil's mineral content and cause leaching of excess nitrogen. Organic farming protects wildlife by respecting wetlands and fragile ecosystems. Finally, organic farming methods have proved to use an average of 30 percent less energy than conventional farming methods. Proponents argue that organic farming promotes healthy ecosystems and is safer for farmers and consumers alike.

Challenges

While the consumer demand for organic products is growing, these products are generally more expensive than conventional products because of the time and **labor** required to cultivate organic crops. Organic farmers do not receive federal subsidies as conventional farmers do, and many are small farmers who cannot offer lower prices achieved through efficiency, as can industrial agricultural producers. Organic ingredients are thus more expensive. This is seen particularly in organic beauty products because of specialty ingredients grown for cleansing, moisturizing, and other properties. Advocates of organic products argue that these are actually the true costs of these products, whereas conventional products do not reflect the environmental costs of the use of pesticides and other chemicals in the production of their ingredients.

See also: Cosmetics; Health and Safety; Natural Look; U.S. Food and Drug Administration

Further Readings: Associated Press. Organic Growth. *Seattle Times,* September 11, 2008. http://seattletimes.nwsource.com/html/businesstechnology/2008172156_stoxcenter11.html. (Accessed September 24, 2008); The Campaign for Safe Cosmetics. *A Poison Kiss: The Problem of Lead in Lipstick.* October 2007. http://www.safecosmetics.org. (Accessed September 24, 2008); Farlow, Christine H. *Dying to Look Good: The Disturbing Truth about What's Really in Your Cosmetics, Toiletries and Personal Care Products.* Escondido, CA: Kiss for Health Publishing, 2000; Gabriel, Julie. *The Green Beauty Guide: Your Essential Resource to Organic and Natural Skin Care, Hair Care, Makeup, and Fragrances.* Deerfield Beach, FL: HCI Books, 2008; "The Healthy Person's Guide to Personal Care Ingredients." http://www.terressentials.com/ingredientguide.html. (Accessed September 24, 2008); Natural Newswire. "Launch of OASIS: The First U.S. Organic Standard for the Beauty and Personal Care Industry." March 5, 2008. http://www.naturalnewswire.com/2008/03/launch-of-oasis.html#more. (Accessed September 24, 2008).

Anne Marie Todd

P

PACKAGING

Packaging is an essential component of product design and marketing, and integral to the **advertising** and distribution of consumer goods. In the beauty industry, packaging is highly important as a function of cosmetic products and the use of products on a regular basis by consumers. Many cosmetic products integrate packaging as a tool for storage and a method for product application. Typically, packaging design is tested through various stages of development to ensure ease of use, attraction to consumers, transportation and distribution reliability, and overall production protection.

In the early 20th century, **cosmetics** were sold in general use jars or boxes, but competition from firms and manufacturers in Paris led American manufacturers, like Weeks, to reconsider how the products were packaged. Looking to the art world, manufacturers and magazines such as ***Vogue*** redesigned and marketed the products according to the new packaging. The new containers eased application and acted as fashion components of the consumers' appearance and attire.

Since World War II, packaging has emerged as a major component of advertising and **branding**. Packaging allows manufacturers and advertisers to integrate the product and its brand into the lives of consumers. Advertisers incorporate images of models using the product and images of product use into packaging. These images are designed to demonstrate and educate consumers on product use, as well as to promote the continued use of the product. In cosmetics packaging, the name of the product may be incorporated into the package, but the package primarily operates as a tool for application and storage. Lipstick provides an obvious example as the package functions as both an easy container preserving the product and an application tool for consumers. Many cosmetics products also incorporate mirrors into packaging to further aid application and use.

Cosmetics use packaging in their functional design, and manufacturers use further packaging to sell a product or group of products. Packaging in direct contact with the product in question is considered primary, while packaging designed for easy sale of products is considered secondary. For example, powder compacts incorporate packaging for product use, but consumers purchase the item backed by cardboard and plastic. Secondary packaging denotes the state of the item, typically new or used, mint or not. Further packaging in this form, or bulk packaging of products, is used to ship mass quantities of products to sale from the manufacturer to the retailer. Tertiary packaging is often cardboard boxes or crates that also feature the name of the manufacturer or brand. Crates, boxes, and palettes are used to store products in warehouses, too.

Packaging can take advantage of color schemes to denote different product use or application and manage which product in a brand should be used for what type of feature, and so forth. Makeup foundation may be packaged in various colors to address different skin tones or conditions, indicating the product best suited to consumers with specific needs. The same is true of other products where color packaging denotes the color of the product or its specialized application. Critics have attacked packaging practices for developing these types of techniques and models because they appeal to younger consumers and increase the number of users of products. These critiques of packaging are akin to those leveled against advertising and branding.

Packaging is also used to promote a brand of products that together signify a particular ideology or meaning. Similar packaging between branded products may appeal to consumers because they associate functionality or product maintenance with packaging and associate different product lines by the same manufacturer or under the same brand. Modern practices of product **manufacturing** and consumption rely on packaging to maintain the product, make it appeal to more consumers, and create useful and easy functionality.

See also: Manufacturing

Further Reading: Beauty Packaging Magazine. http://www.beautypackaging.com/. (Accessed October 29, 2008); *Cosmetic and Personal Care Packaging Magazine.* http://www.cpcpkg.com/home/. (Accessed October 29, 2008); Peiss, Kathy. *Hope in a Jar: The Making of America's Beauty Culture.* New York: Metropolitan Books, 1998.

Richard D. Driver

PERFUMES AND FRAGRANCES

Perfumes and fragrances are products made from either natural or (usually) synthetic materials that are meant to appeal to the sense of smell. While consumers can choose from a range of fragrance options such as bath oils, splashes, toilet waters, aftershave lotions, body sprays, and colognes, perfumes are usually the most highly priced fragrances.

American companies began **manufacturing** essential oils for soaps and other products during the 19th century, especially after the discovery of oil in Pennsylvania boosted synthetic production. Most of the earliest American essential oil houses were based in New York City, given its access to crude spices, processed oils, and French fragrances. Despite the emergence of some domestic perfumeries, the French, with their reputation for high-class (and highly priced) scents, dominated the business. For decades, advertisements for the French perfume Joy employed the tagline "the costliest perfume in the world" as a selling point. During the mid 20th century, several American cosmetic companies successfully branched into perfumes, and they have marketed scents at prices affordable to a larger number of Americans, selling them in department stores and even drug stores rather than just exclusive boutiques. The California Perfume Company, which changed its name to **Avon** in the 1930s, was very successful at marketing inexpensive perfumes, fragrances, and **cosmetics** to the working classes through door-to-door sales. The American perfume

> "A woman who doesn't wear perfume has no future."
>
> *Coco Chanel*
>
> Source: Brainy Quote. http://www.brainyquote.com/quotes/authors/c/coco_chanel.html.

business, like cosmetics generally, led to economic opportunities for many non-traditional entrepreneurs. Some of the most successful American companies, such as **Elizabeth Arden**, **Helena Rubinstein**, and **Estée Lauder**, were started by women, and Arden and Rubinstein were both first-generation immigrants.

In recent decades, perfume companies have continued to expand their market into the middle classes by suggesting that perfume need not be reserved for special occasions. One of the most successful perfume ad campaigns was for Charlie, beginning in 1973. For this product, **Revlon** capitalized on the women's liberation movement by featuring a strong, liberated woman wearing pants in the ads. Sales of the fragrance exceeded 10 million dollars during the year of its launch. Throughout the 1970s, this type of lifestyle **advertising**, often featuring career women, was very popular.

During the 1980s, pricier fragrances marketed by **designers** and celebrities (such as Elizabeth Taylor and Joan Collins) became increasingly profitable. Taylor's Passion enjoyed long-term success; however, most celebrity scents, including Collins's Spectacular, Cher's Uninhibited, and Julio Iglesias's Only had a short shelf life. In the United States, designer **Calvin Klein** marketed Obsession with explicitly sexual black and white advertisements, and many other perfume advertisers followed his example. However, as Americans came to grips with the AIDS crisis in the late 1980s, advertisers began to tone down the nudity and sexuality in their advertisements. Through the 1990s, popular scents such as Estée Lauder's Beautiful and Calvin Klein's Eternity emphasized marital commitment in their advertising campaigns. In the 21st century, just as in the mid 20th century, perfume advertisements using appeals to sexuality, romance, and prestige dominate the pages of women's magazines during the months of November and December, in hopes of winning holiday customers' eyes.

Further Reading: Morris, Edwin. *Fragrance: The Story of Perfume from Cleopatra to Chanel.* New York: Charles Scribner's Sons, 1984; Turin, Luca. *The Secret of Scent: Adventures in Perfume and the Science of Smell.* New York: Ecco, 2006.

Beth Kreydatus

PERMANENTS

Although typically associated with blue-haired ladies and mullet-wearing hair bands of the 1970s and 1980s, perms have been a fashion trend that has helped to define the 20th-century beauty industry. Perming hair is a process that has made use of thermal and/or chemical combinations to alter the hair texture and to make it either curly or straight until regrowth. In African American beauty culture, straightening or relaxing curls is commonly referred to as a perm, but the vernacular is most notably associated with the beauty practices of Euro-American women and men with naturally straight hair looking for curly tresses. Everything from chicken bones to orange juice cans have been used to make curls, but a perm meant it didn't wash out. Over the past century, technology has helped to simplify processes, making perms more palatable to **hairdressers** and their clientele, but the popularity of curls also speaks to complex racial stereotypes. For centuries, racial identities have been based not only on skin color but also on hair texture. Distinctions based on hair type have provided the basis for lingering caricatures that defined black hair as kinky and coarse. In contrast, straight hair has long been a demarcation of Eurocentric notions of beauty, refinement, and conservativeness. Consciously or not, whites who curled their hair have engaged in a kind of racial cross-dressing in popular imagination that has intimately linked curls and kinks with sensuality and uncontrollability.

Technology and its Problems

In 1906 German inventor Charles Nessler patented the original electric permanent wave machine, which hung like a chandelier attached to heavy rods and weights designed to protect the scalp as the right current and chemical combinations were used to transform straight hair into ringlets. Although it initially took nearly half a day to achieve the new look and at times burned the skin and singed the hair, the odd-looking contraption became a mainstay of beauty shop services thanks to celebrity endorsements, free demonstrations, and the persuasive skills of countless numbers of beauty operators who eventually won over a loyal female clientele. More so than bobbing hair, permanents encouraged the growth of beauty shops in the 1920s and '30s as a distinct female social space that aided hairdressers looking to distinguish themselves and their professional identity from barbers. Still, there were problems with the contraption. Not every perm came out the same. Some looked like haystacks; others were simply too fuzzy. Since it was unbearably hot, many beauty shops found perms to be profitable only in the cooler months. Folklore has it that the occasional customer would faint from the heat and weight of the contraption and at least one tragic death was recalled when a not-so-quick-witted beauty operator electrocuted her customer when she tried to revive her by dousing the customer with water. More mundane problems could simply be solved by using the right amount of towels to support a woman's neck and supplying her with magazines and conversations to keep her occupied until the process was complete.

Changing Styles

The first wave of popularity for the perm came at the height of Jim Crow segregation. Flappers in the 1920s, who smoked cigarettes and shortened their skirts, famously challenged gender and racial boundaries by bobbing and frizzing their hair as they transgressed prescribed limits of proper femininity. At the same time, perms helped to define a new traditional female space—the beauty shop, a place distinct from the world of barbershops and a rough masculine milieu. Even during the Great Depression and World War II, beauty shop profits owed much to the permanent waves they offered—Shirley Temple curls were sometimes given in exchange for bartered goods and services. In an effort to maximize profits and minimize absentees, some war industries offered their employees free perms for their exemplary service. The 1950s, however, ushered in something new: a cold wave-perm process with chemical solutions that could be sold in drug and grocery stores. Toni and Lilt home perms were popular with do-it-yourselfers; however, salons suffered a little in the following decades because too many of the housewives with children underfoot could not attempt the process without interruption and were unable to keep up with the latest trends, sending many women back to their hairdressers. The 1960s and '70s witnessed the rise of a range of styles, from precision **Vidal Sassoon** cuts to the **natural look**, epitomized by straight, seemingly unprocessed hair and the iconic **Afro**. Men and women would achieve a similar look with perms that drove profits well into the 1980s, long after the Afro's political implications had faded. The 1980s boasted designer jeans, shoulder pads, and big hair that was often permed to achieve the desired volume. Perms once again may make a comeback for a younger generation looking for another walk on the wild side.

See also: African American Beauty Industry; The Bob; Hairstyles; Hairdressers

Further Reading: Blackwelder, Julia Kirk. *Styling Jim Crow: African American Beauty Training during Segregation*. College Station: Texas A&M Press, 2003; Buckley, Cara. "Turning the Male Perm into a Very Good Hair Day." *New York Times,* February 15, 2009; Walker, Susannah. *Selling Beauty to African American Women, 1920–1975*. Lexington: The University Press of Kentucky, 2007; Weitz, Rose. *Rapunzel's Daughters: What Women's Hair Tells Us about Women's Lives*. New York: Farrar, Straus and Giroux, 2004; Willett, Julie. *Permanent Waves: The Making of American Beauty Shop*. New York: New York University Press, 2000.

Julie Willett

PIERCING

Piercing is a type of semi-permanent body modification. In the technique most commonly used by piercing professionals today, a hollow-point needle is inserted in the skin to cut a small opening for the **display** of jewelry, usually a ring or a stud. Although vulnerable to infection, the flesh surrounding the puncture wound tends to heal within weeks. In the United States and Europe, the most widespread practice involves the ear lobe or the cartilage of the outer ear. The piercing of facial tissue is also an increasingly popular technique, especially nasal cartilage, the septum, the soft tissue around the eyebrow, the tissue around the lips, and the tongue. Other common forms include the nipple, the soft skin tissue around the navel, and the genitals, although any fleshy part of the body may theoretically be pierced.

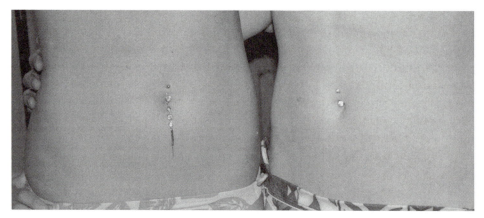

Kansas City teens show off belly rings. (Courtesy of Terri Merrigan)

Piercing in Human Culture

Piercing varies widely according to historical and cultural context. Archaeological evidence from sites in the Alps and the Indian subcontinent suggest that piercing, especially of the ears and nose, has been a part of human culture for as far back as 5,000 years, and it enjoyed widespread popularity in the ancient Mediterranean cultures. Although piercing fell out of practice in Medieval Europe, colonial contacts led to the spread of piercing during the European Renaissance, particularly in countries that had extensive maritime empires. Piercing remained popular among both men and women throughout the 16th and 17th centuries in Western Europe. The austerity of Victorian beauty standards led to the abandonment of the practice, particularly among middle-class Europeans who increasingly associated piercing with what they considered the primitive nonwhites who fell under colonial rule. However, piercings remained commonplace among sailors and merchant marines throughout the 19th and 20th centuries. As a result, piercing was often associated with the urban subcultures of prostitution, sailors, and burgeoning enclaves of homosexuals in industrialized cities.

The 20th Century

With the sexually uninhibited fashion of the 1920s and the early rise of the beauty industry among young and oftentimes single new women, earrings became a standard aspect of women's fashion, with offerings from high-end jewelers like Cartier. The advent of clip-on earrings in the 1930s led to a decrease in the number of actual piercings. When ear piercing again became popular in the 1950s, doctor's offices began to offer sterile techniques—including the piercing gun—as alternatives to home methods. After the late 1960s, when biker, gay, and sadomasochism subcultures began to influence high-fashion **designers** like Vivienne Westwood, more elaborate piercings began to break into the mainstream of American and European fashion. The punk scene of the 1970s also saw an explosion of piercings among young working-class men in England and North America. As male athletes, rock and roll musicians, and other celebrities began to display piercings in the 1970s and 1980s, increasing numbers of men found it socially acceptable to pierce. Body piercing has also become highly popular. Starting with Jim Ward's Gauntlet Studio, opened in 1978 in West Hollywood, body piercing studios, publications, and conferences have increased in size and number throughout the United States. Since the 1970s, it is increasingly common to see piercing among both women and men, and ear and body piercing have become a standard service offered by both accessories retailers and tattoo parlors.

Further Reading: Pitts-Taylor, Victoria. *In the Flesh: The Cultural Politics of Body Modification.* New York: Palgrave MacMillan, 2003; Rosenblatt, Daniel. "The Antisocial Skin: Structure, Resistance, and 'Modern Primitive' Adornment in the United States." *Cultural Anthropology,* 12 no. 3 (1997): 287–334; Steinbach, Ronald. *The Fashionable Ear: A History of Ear-Piercing Trends for Men and Women.* New York: Vantage, 1995.

Christopher A. Mitchell

PROCTER AND GAMBLE

Procter and Gamble (P&G) is an American manufacturer of soaps and beauty products that was first established in the 19th century and is now a billion-dollar business. P&G has introduced a myriad of common household beauty products that range from Ivory Soap to Oil of Olay.

In 1837, cousins William Procter and James Gamble founded P&G in Cincinnati, Ohio. Originally it produced candles and laundry soap. In 1879, P&G introduced Ivory Soap, a soap intended for both personal hygiene and laundry. It was not meant to be a beauty product and was sold on its purity and ability to float. In 1926, P&G introduced its first personal beauty soap, Camay, a perfumed soap. In 1933, P&G created a new beauty product, Drene, a liquid shampoo that cleaned oil off of hair. At around the same time, it developed a liquid dentifrice called Teel that it stopped selling during World War II.

In 1947, P&G started a division to concentrate on toiletries and opened a new factory in Cincinnati to develop and produce them. The company developed Personal Size Ivory, which was sold as a beauty product along with a number of soaps and shampoos. The company continued to sell Drene and created Shasta Cream Shampoo and Prell, which is still on the market. In 1948, P&G began **manufacturing** permanent kits. Lilt was the first one the company produced, followed by Pert and Party Curl. Finally, P&G developed Pin-it, a permanent that used bobby pins. They also tried manufacturing Lana for bleached or frizzled hair, but it proved unsuccessful, and they followed up that failure with another one, Wondra, a face-cleansing cream. In 1952, P&G began manufacturing Gleem toothpaste and the much more popular Crest, with fluoride added. Over the next few decades, the company would develop similar products and expand into new territory: the 1960s and 1970s, for example, saw experiments in men's **hair care products**, along with Head and Shoulders antidandruff shampoo, Secret and Sure deodorants, Scope mouthwash, and Coast, a deodorant soap bar.

By the end of the 1980s, the company began to look for ways to expand sales of **cosmetics** and beauty products and began to acquire other corporations: They purchased Noxell Corporation, manufacturers of Noxzema products and **Cover-Girl** cosmetics. They also acquired Bain de Soleil, a sun care product line, and in 1991 they bought **Max Factor** and Betrix from **Revlon**. By the end of the 1990s, they had control of the fragrance business belonging to Giorgio Beverly Hills and had introduced the world to Pantene Pro-V, which became the fastest-growing brand of shampoo across the globe. From 2001 to 2008, the company purchased the Clairol hair care line from Bristol-Myers Squibb, found an entrée into the professional hair care market by purchasing a controlling interest in Wella AG, a German company, and began to produce the Old Spice line of products and to sell Hugo Boss Baldessarini, a luxury fragrance brand for men. By the end of 2008, P&G's unaudited annual sales worldwide were $83.5 billion, and the company was one of the biggest manufacturers of soaps and beauty care products in the world.

P&G's corporate reach, however, has not gone unchallenged. Indeed, they have had to alter everything from their original logo to their global business practices. In the United States, rumors erupted that their longstanding moon and stars logo that dated back to middle of the 19th century was satanic. The company gradually transformed its logo to just its initials—a logo that remains one of the most recognizable in the global marketplace. Far more problematic was the company's venture into feminine hygiene products. In 1980, after P&G's Rely Tampons were linked to toxic shock syndrome, the product was taken off the market. More recently, the company has been accused of what is described as *greenwashing*—**branding** suspect detergents as environmentally sound. Above all else, the use of animals to test beauty products has outraged **animal rights** groups and other consumers, who have organized global boycotts and public protests. In 1999, the company announced that it would reduce animal testing to 20 percent of its consumer goods, but this number did not include new products and thus did little to resurrect the company's reputation. Indeed, during the Campaign for Safe Cosmetics in California in 2005, the company lobbied against efforts to implement a regulatory framework for the use of chemicals in beauty products that would require companies to report all toxic ingredients used in their products.

To be sure, P&G has put millions of dollars into researching alternatives to animal testing in response to consumer pressure and to a March 2009 European ban on animal testing. Thus, P&G may be a global powerhouse in the beauty industry, but the corporation is not immune to everyday concerns about product safety and other ethical business practices.

See also: Advertising; Hair Care Products; Health and Safety; Permanents

Further Reading: Canedy, Dana. "P. & G. to End Animal Tests for Most Consumer Goods." *New York Times,* July 1, 1999; Carval, Doreen. "A New Science, at First Blush." *New York Times,* November 20, 2007; Dyer, Davis, Frederick Dalzell, and Rowena Olegario. *Lessons from 165 Years of Brand Building at Procter and Gamble.* Boston: Harvard Business School Press, 2004; Left, Sarah. "Animal Rights: A Guide to the Movement." *Guardian,* July 12, 2004. http://www.guardian.co.uk/uk/2004/jul/21/animalwelfare.

world; Lief, Alfred. *"It Floats": The Story of Procter & Gamble.* New York: Reinhart & Co., 1958; Pearce, Fred. "Greenwash: The Responsible Business Awards Defy Parody." *Guardian,* July 9, 2009. http://www.guardian.co.uk/environment/cif-green/2009/jul/09greenwash-responsible-bus; Schisgall, Oscar. *Eyes on Tomorrow: The Evolution of Procter & Gamble.* Chicago: J. G. Ferguson, 1981.

Scott Sheidlower

QUEER EYE FOR THE STRAIGHT GUY

Queer Eye for the Straight Guy was an American reality television program developed for the Bravo television network that ran from 2003 to 2007. After its debut in 2003, the show became a surprise hit, and its rights were purchased by NBC. The program's executive producers, Dave Collins, who has been in a gay relationship for 14 years, and David Metzler, who is straight, sought to create a reality program in which five fashionably sensible gay men (dubbed the fab five) would advise straight men on fashion and style. In 2004, *Queer Eye for the Straight Guy* won an Emmy Award for outstanding reality program.

The show, moreover, played on the popular stereotypes of the effeminate and flamboyant gay male who advises straight men on how to dress, prepare food, style their hair, decorate their room, and on other fashion- and style-related topics. At its core level, however, Collins and Metzler envisioned *Queer Eye for the Straight Guy* as an opportunity for platonic bonding between gay and straight men. Perhaps the show's best example of platonic bonding between the fab five and straight men and the show's ability to portray the straight men's acceptance

Cast members from *Queer Eye for the Straight Guy,* 2003. (AP Photo/Mary Altaffer)

of gay advice on fashion and style can be seen in the special edition DVD, *Queer Eye: Queer Eye for the Red Sox*. For the episode, the fab five turned the Red Sox press box into a spa and gave five of the Red Sox ballplayers, striking examples of modern-day masculinity, facials, pedicures, back **waxing**, massages, and new clothes.

Despite the show's popularity and goal of creating a fashion-driven bond between gay and straight men, *Queer Eye for the Straight Guy* came under fierce attacks from politicians and journalists for promoting gay stereotypes. For men's fashion, *Queer Eye for the Straight Guy* symbolized a growing trend of straight men using traditionally feminine hair and beauty products and frequenting traditionally feminine spaces, such as fancy wine bars. Public figures, such as soccer's David Beckham, further promoted the image of the metrosexual with his perfectly filed nails and braided hair. In the early 21st Century, *Queer Eye for the Straight Guy* best represented Americans' shift from traditional notions of masculinity to an acceptance of fashion and beauty products previously reserved for women.

See also: Makeover Television; Metrosexuals

Further Reading: Cornetta, Louise K. "Red Sox Get Queer Eye Makeover." *ESPN,* June 7, 2005. http://espn.com. (Accessed September 15, 2008); Glitz, Michael. "Queer Eye Confidential." *Advocate,* September 2, 2003. http://www.advocate.com. (Accessed September 15, 2008); McGeveran, Tom. "Shmomo Erectus." *New York Observer,* July 22, 2003. http://www.observer.com. (Accessed September 15, 2008); "Outstanding Reality Program." *The Emmys,* 2004. http://www.emmys.org. (Accessed September 15, 2008); St. John, Warren. "Metrosexuals Come Out." *New York Times,* June 22, 2003. http://www.nytimes.com. (Accessed September 15, 2008).

Brian Robertson

QVC

QVC, Inc. is a television and **Internet** retailer with 1,150 products on offer each week. Merchandise categories include fashion, beauty, home furnishings, electronics, and toys and gifts. It is one of the largest multimedia retailers in the world, with net sales of $7.4 billion in 2007.

QVC (Quality, Value, Convenience) was founded in 1986 by Joseph Segel. A graduate of the Wharton Business School, Segel is also noted for founding the Franklin Mint and for serving on the United Nations General Assembly under Henry Kissinger. Inspired by the Home Shopping Network, he raised $20 million in capital and entered a two-year contract to sell products for Sears. On November 24, 1986, he launched QVC television, broadcast in over 7 million homes. Segel's concept for QVC was based on the idea of informing the viewer about a product, rather than pressing a customer to buy. To this day, QVC programming is characterized by lengthy descriptions of the products presented, usually accompanied by demonstrations of function, rather than the lightning-fast timeframe of a traditional commercial. While traditional commercials rely on the impulsiveness of the customer, QVC strives to sell the product based on merit and informed choice. Celebrity endorsements and personal testimonials are also common sales methods, and they too provide an opportunity for in-depth coverage of the product.

In 1996, QVC launched an Internet retailer, iQVC, which in 2001 became www.qvc.com. Internet sales in 2007 totaled over $1 billion, and sales continue to increase as www.qvc.com receives over 5 million visitors each month in the United States alone. QVC's international footprint is also large, with international broadcasting centers in Germany, Japan, and the United Kingdom. Its television programming reaches 160 million homes worldwide, and to date it boasts over 50 million customers. To further enhance its television programming, in April 2008 QVC launched QVCHD, tapping into the ever-growing market of high-definition television viewers.

Of the 1,150 products on offer each week, over 250 are brand new and exclusive to the QVC customer. Hundreds of brands sell through QVC, and many count a large portion of their sales through QVC. Brand leaders include philosophy, Dell, and Bare Escentuals. It has launched numerous **cosmetics** lines throughout its history, including the record-breaking debut of celebrity makeup artist **Bobbi Brown** in 2007, in which her products completely sold out in 45 minutes. To accommodate a diversified market, QVC's television programming is divided into various different shows catering to different products. Some, such as the QVC Fashion Channel, are devoted to specific products, like fashion, accessories, and beauty products. Others, like the QVC Morning Show, combine shopping with news and weather in collaboration with *USA Today*.

Throughout its history, QVC has placed a high value on philanthropy and made a commitment to giving back. Its employees and customers have raised millions of dollars for various charities, including the American Red Cross and the National Women's Cancer Research Alliance.

See also: Advertising; Endorsements of Products, Celebrity; Makeovers

Further Reading: Gumpert, Gary, and Susan J. Drucker. "From the Agora to the Electronic Shopping Mall." *Critical Studies in Mass Communication,* 9 (1992): 186–200; Shaw, Dan. "Journeys; For Sleep-Deprived Shoppers, a Pilgrimage to QVC." *New York Times,* September 6, 2002; QVC. http://www.qvc.com.

Abigail Mitchell

RELIGION AND BEAUTY

From the annual sales of Easter dresses to the popularity of rhinestone crosses, religion has been marketed for the masses. Nevertheless, religion and the beauty industry have had a contradictory relationship, in part because religion has been both a source of inspiration as well as condemnation. As men and women have fashioned their own identities, they have embraced, rejected, and reinterpreted their spirituality along with official religious dictums that are also bound to a larger political economy. Whether it is gender conformity or moral implications, beauty and style seem to threaten and reaffirm that which is often assumed to be divine.

In the 20th century, women and girls remained trapped in a virgin/whore dichotomy that in many ways set a double standard that profoundly shaped the direction of the beauty industry. Everything from the use of nail polish to skirt lengths has been the basis for special prayers, sermons, and a sense of righteousness. More often than their male counterparts, women have been cast as the keepers of family and religious traditions. To be sure, religious edicts of style have not been limited to female behavior. Nevertheless, whether it is the food consumed or the clothes adorned, women who embrace or deviate from tradition have shaped much of the public's discourse.

Hairstyles

Hairstyles have often reflected religious conviction and dedication. Because of women's submissive role to both men and God in traditional Christian religion, the hair is worn long and is occasionally covered to symbolize that submissiveness. These beliefs are based on 1 Corinthians 11:15 and 1 Timothy 2:9–15, which prescribe long hair for women and prohibit elaborate hairstyles. For Orthodox Jews, it is considered necessary for women to cover their hair at all times. For non-Orthodox Jewish women, it is sometimes necessary to cover the hair while in the synagogue or in other sacred/religious locations. Hairstyles for Muslims are determined based on the example of the Prophet. For example, the Prophet specifically forbade the shaving of only part of one's scalp. In addition, it is forbidden to imitate the style of nonbelievers, especially those who shave only part of the hair.

The degree to which a larger political economy reinterprets the religious take on fashion is also evident in the debates over changing hairstyles. In the 1920s, hair products that promised to aid in the growth of long hair were praised by evangelical women in churches because of the biblical teaching that a woman's hair is her glory. In African American congregations, however, ministers often opposed the emerging beauty industry that stressed standards of white beauty because they saw **hair straightening** or pressing as both unnatural and ungodly. The popularity of blondeness had for centuries been associated with purity and the fair sex. In the 20th century, being blonde and blue-eyed continued to suggest a hierarchy based on race and religion.

Perhaps no hairstyle captures the complexity of mixing religion and politics better than the popularity of Jesus hair against the backdrop of the Vietnam War. In the 1960s and '70s, a young generation of men came to reject what they perceived as the more militaristic crew cuts so popular in the decades after World War II. Most closely identified with hippies and challenges to the status quo, the Jesus look touted androgynous hair, lengthy beards, and a peace-loving aesthetic that seemed to represent at the very least a resurrection in style. Nevertheless, longhaired men and boys were kicked out of schools, businesses, and homes, ultimately condemned as unpatriotic and, ironically, as a threat to Christian values.

Cosmetics and Complexions

Religious concerns have also been a reflection of the development of the **cosmetics** industry. In the 1920s, the cosmetics industry received a boost when it gradually became acceptable for respectable women to wear makeup. By the 1930s, makeup came to be seen as an indicator of mood or a way in which a woman defined herself, regardless of morality. In the 19th century, the division between the lady and the painted woman was clear. Cosmetics were a symbol of female vice and generally indicated some sort of moral deficiency. In fact, self-titled old-fashioned women of the '20s and '30s refused to adopt the use of paint and emphasized their moral objections to anything that changed one's appearance. However, religious beliefs also urged women to embrace cosmetics. In the early 20th century, popular belief held that **acne** was a sign of some internal spiritual struggle or sexual immorality. This only fed the desire to cover up the blemishes with makeup and/or combat acne medically in the name of respectability.

Altering the hue of one's complexion or adding color to one's lips was not only an acceptance of artificiality and sensuality, but also an insult to one's lineage. Cosmetics were also cast as an attack on one's own family. For both Jewish and other immigrant girls in the 19th and early 20th centuries, participation in girl culture, including the emerging cosmetics industry, was a way in which they created an American identity and differentiated themselves from their parent's generation. This participation was often kept concealed from parents due to the perception that cosmetics were sinful. Immigrant parents especially found the use of cosmetics disturbing, and saw it as just another breakdown in family life and culture.

Weight Loss, Dieting, and Fasting

Dieting has been impacted greatly by spiritual concerns. In Western philosophy, humans are thought to be ruled by two competing powers: the soul and the body.

While the soul is concerned with spiritual matters, the body is weak and must be controlled in an effort to protect the soul. Hunger and overindulgence, in addition to sexuality, are sins that the body commits. In the 1830s, Sylvester Graham began to preach that health problems, including spiritual concerns, could be solved by eating a basic vegetarian diet. In addition to the diet, he encouraged other behaviors that would safeguard morality, such as regular cold showers, sleeping on hard mattresses, drinking pure water, and sexual abstinence. Graham created and lent his name to the graham cracker; he emphasized the consumption of bland foods like the crackers to combat passionate emotions that may lead to immorality.

By linking sin with obesity, many diet programs have been able to find support and participants among mainstream Christian groups. Today, religious diet culture is marked by both a dependence on prayer and the Bible. Gwen Shamblin, the author of *The Weigh Down Diet* (1997), advises that spirituality can be used to avoid overeating. Sales have totaled more than 1.2 million copies. Shamblin identifies a physical need and an emotional need that make people want to eat. She recommends eating only when physical hunger strikes and to stop eating when full. Overeating betrays greediness. Shamblin contends that praying and reading the Bible fill emotional needs. Thus, the beauty industry has benefited from the association of physical beauty or thinness with self-control and sexual purity. Early 20th-century **advertising** for beauty products often had a religious tone and spoke of the *religion of beauty* or the *sin of ugliness*. This same religious language is used today in discussions of weight loss and dieting. Fasting, for example, is the process by which one intentionally refrains from consuming all food or some particular foods for spiritual purposes. In medieval Europe, prolonged fasting was considered a female miracle. Fasting girls have since been linked to spirituality. The symbolic diet of a fasting maiden supported her image of purity and innocence. The history of fasting has forever linked together the ideas of spirituality, purity, and consumption. Women, however, have typically replaced the spiritual aspect of fasting with the desire to be beautiful. Among some religious groups, it is thought that to be overweight indicates a failure of personal morality and shows a lack of self-control that fits with the message of an industrial work ethic, reflects the ebb and flow of economic woes, and helps make billions for the dieting industry.

Building a better body has never been simply a female concern. During the Victorian era, Christian activism in combination with the idea of vigorous masculinity was stressed in the Christian church. This movement promoted both physical strength and a masculine lifestyle for Christian men. Muscular Christianity influenced the development of organizations such as the Promise Keepers and extracurricular groups for teens like the Fellowship of Christian Athletes. A renewed emphasis on muscular Christianity occurred during the evangelical resurgence of the 1970s, 1980s, and early 1990s and in response to the perceived feminization of the Christian church. The masculine Christian ideal in combination with the renewed idea that Christians had a moral obligation to participate in politics led to the emergence of the Christian Right and helped to propel conservative leaders like Ronald Reagan into the national spotlight. In this way, the ideal male body type captured the political ethos of unyielding strength, fueling the popularity of

Arnold Schwarzenegger, bodybuilding facilities like Gold's Gym, and a rich array of health supplements as well as the mainstream use of steroids, all of which has suggested that, once again, religion and the beauty industry would be fraught with contradiction.

See also: Hairstyles

Further Reading: Bordo, Susan. *Unbearable Weight: Feminism, Western Culture, and the Body.* Berkeley: University of California, 1993; Brumberg, Joan Jacobs. *The Body Project: An Intimate History of American Girls.* New York: Vintage, 1997; Brumberg, Joan Jacobs. *Fasting Girls: The History of Anorexia Nervosa.* New York: Vintage, 2000; Enstad, Nan. *Ladies of Labor, Girls of Adventure: Working Women, Popular Culture, and Labor Politics at the Turn of the Twentieth Century.* New York: Columbia University Press, 1999; Glenn, Susan A. *Daughters of the Shtetl: Life and Labor in the Immigrant Generation.* Ithaca, NY: Cornell University Press, 1990; Griffith, R. Marie. *Born Again Bodies: Flesh and Spirit in American Christianity.* Berkeley: University of California Press, 2004; Peiss, Kathy. *Cheap Amusements: Working Women and Leisure in Turn-of-the-Century New York.* Philadelphia, PA: Temple University Press, 1986; Peiss, Kathy. *Hope in a Jar: The Making of America's Beauty Culture.* New York: Metropolitan Books,1998; Putney, Clifford. *Muscular Christianity: Manhood and Sports in Protestant America, 1880–1920.* Cambridge, MA: Harvard University Press, 2001; Shamblin, Gwen. "What is the Weigh Down Workshop?" The Weigh Down Workshop. http://www.weighdown.com.

Krystal A. Humphreys

RETAIL

The modern retail fashion and beauty industry dates back to the 19th century. Begun from secondhand clothing stalls, the ready-made retail market grew from the slums into the highest echelons of society. Currently, both beauty products and clothing are sold in a wide variety of establishments, from grocery and convenience stores to high-end department stores and boutiques.

Segmented Market

The retail store is the last stop in a system that produces goods and sells them to consumers. At the **manufacturing** level, the raw materials are gathered and the goods produced. Whether it is clothing or **cosmetics**, the items must be properly manufactured at the lowest cost possible for the intended level of final sale. Goods that will be sold at lower-end stores such as Kmart, Walmart, dollar stores, drugstores, grocery stores, and the like must be produced with the least expensive raw materials possible and a minimal amount of **labor** to ensure that the price point will fall within the accepted range for those budget stores. Items can also be produced at a moderate level for stores that are slightly more upscale, such as Target, Sears, and many mall stores. Moderately priced items can either use slightly more expensive raw materials or take more time and effort to produce. The highest level of mass market production is better and includes most anchor or department stores such as Macy's, Nordstrom, Dillard's, and Saks. These manufacturers can produce goods that are made from moderate- to higher-priced materials and take more time and effort. Better items are considered to be of the highest quality available to the average consumer. Ready-to-wear, boutique, and designer items are the most expensive goods available, but the market for items of this quality and price is small.

Production

After the item is manufactured, the cost of goods is assessed. The manufacturer will take the cost of all raw materials and labor, add on any extra costs such as shipping and import duty, and then add 40–60 percent to cover overhead costs such as building maintenance, housekeeping, electricity, phone and **Internet** service, and so on. This is the price that the wholesaler will pay for the item.

At the wholesale level, the products are purchased, warehoused, and shipped to the appropriate location in the quantity that a retail outlet requires. The wholesaler is the middleman, often offering a variety of goods in general such as clothing, cosmetics, accessories, and furniture, or in a particular area, such as t-shirts, **perfumes**, and costume jewelry, to name a few examples. The retailer is able to purchase required merchandise directly from the wholesaler to be sold to the general public. The wholesaler will add 40–60 percent to cover overhead expenses, and this will be the price the retailer pays.

When the retailer purchases items at a wholesale price, the retailer must mark up the price further before it is sold to the consumer. The retail markup is generally higher than the markups at the **manufacturing** and wholesale level. The retailer usually has a higher rent to pay and more hourly employees. Additional costs are incurred by **advertising** and marketing, which are not necessary for manufacturers and wholesalers, in addition to standard costs such as electricity, phone and Internet service, and maintenance and housekeeping. In many higher-end shopping centers, the mall itself requires a percentage of sales over and above what the retailer pays to the mall in rent each month. These extra expenses at the retail level mean markups of 100 percent and more. An item that costs $5 in materials can end up with a retail price of $22.50 to $45, depending on the price point (budget, moderate, better, or designer).

Youth Markets

In general, items aimed at younger markets, especially tweens and juniors, fall into the budget or moderate category. These items are priced to meet the needs of customers with a limited income. These items can also be made of lesser quality materials, since they are fad oriented and less likely to be worn for longer than a few months. Adult customers have a larger disposable income and generally have a taste for more classic looks meant to last several months or even years. Adult customers are most likely to shop in the moderate to better categories. Stores such as Forever 21 and Charlotte Russe cater to a young, image-conscious female customer who is looking to purchase items at a low price to wear for a short amount of time. The garments purchased from these types of stores have an expectation of trendiness but not of lasting quality. Contrast this with stores like Talbot's and Brooks Brothers, which focus on the adult woman shopping for career wear meant to be investment pieces, worn for years in some cases, which must be able to withstand multiple uses and cleanings. The styling, construction, and price point of these two types of stores are markedly different from one another, but each is a necessity to its chosen target market.

Men's Market

Private-label apparel or direct-to-market manufacturing was used primarily in men's wear. This allowed a retail store to own and control the means of production and not only create items unique to its own brand, but increase the profit margin considerably by removing the steps between manufacturing and retail sale. The men's market is a niche market, with individual labels and stores catering to a specific target lifestyle group. This type of private-label marketing was a necessity, as men have been known for their brand loyalty and specific expectations from the brands they choose. Building on the success in the men's wear market, private-label retailers have become the single largest segment of the retail experience, with stores like Old Navy, The Gap, Anne Taylor, Lane Bryant, and most mall storefront retailers that sell nothing but their own label. While this may not be surprising to 21st-century shoppers, this marks a change in the retail atmosphere. Most department stores will still carry multiple brands and lines, including several in-house labels. This allows stores to spread their profit margin across several brands.

Sales

Private labeling also creates an opportunity for attention-generating sales. With no middleman to pay out to, a store can offer deep discounts when merchandise goes on sale and still make back the initial investment in the item. Sales like this have a multitude of positive effects for the retailer. First, they foster goodwill among consumers, who are always pleased to feel like they have gotten a good deal. Second, well-publicized sales of large percentage discounts are a major draw, bringing more customers in the door. These sales can help a retailer divest themselves of extra or unwanted merchandise as well as bring in a larger than normal crowd into the store. The sale merchandise is almost always placed at the rear of the store, creating an opportunity for the customer to pass by the new and regularly priced merchandise. Sale merchandise can also be placed directly beside the cash registers for impulse buys. Customers who find an item they were ready to purchase for regular price on sale are often willing to take the amount of money they saved and purchase another item. With markups on private-label goods as high as 500–800 percent over the cost of manufacture, this allows the retailer to continue to secure the required profit margin while still offering low prices to its customers.

Various Industries

The purpose of the fashion industry is to create and sell the clothes that a particular market group desires in a style they want to wear and at a price they are willing to pay. The adult woman customer, or missy customer, accounts for the vast majority of all clothing, shoes, and accessories sales worldwide, which totals in the hundreds of billions of dollars each year.

The cosmetics segment of the retail world is not much different. Beauty products like makeup and perfumes are a multibillion dollar business, even before including profits for hygiene-based items such as lotions, cleansers, and other necessities. The segment of the makeup industry devoted strictly to boutique and department store sales alone makes up a substantial percentage of that amount. Beauty's rise to prestige began after World War I. It did not become socially acceptable for women to wear makeup until the 1920s, but between Hollywood and relaxing social mores, cosmetics became a mainstay for American women.

With such a variety of available cosmetics choices, makeup companies have resorted to two marketing techniques. The first of these is the establishment of seasonal colors. These colors were not only seasonal, with different shades for spring, summer, fall, or winter, but they changed annually. Each cosmetics company also had to set their own shades apart from their competitors and did so with creative and clever names such as Indian Love Call, Cherries in the Snow, Jezebel, Fearless, Where's the Fire? and the like. Some nail polish companies like OPI take this to an even more unique level with such titles as Aphrodite's Pink Nightie, I'm Not Really a Waitress, You're Such a Kabuki Queen, My Chihuahua Bites! and Hoodoo Voodoo?! This marketing technique gives OPI a retail edge by giving them a singular presence among more mundane names like Curtain Call Red and Shy Violet.

Gaining Customer Attention

Another great marketing technique is exclusivity. Even Walmart carries exclusive colors, scents, and gift sets not available in other stores. Holiday time is especially important for this technique, with stores vying for customer dollars. Christmas and New Year's celebrations also put an emphasis on makeup with sparkle, giving an extra incentive for women to shop for something special.

Once in the retail environment, regardless of the type of store, the customer is subjected to the art of cosmetic advertising. The images and sales personnel are geared toward not just selling an item but selling a story or an image that will in some way improve the life of the customer. Many department store cosmetics counters use video monitors, music, and hands-on displays to entice women to their specific brand. But regardless of gimmick, once a woman settles on a brand, more often than not she is loath to abandon it. The idea then becomes to tempt an established customer to buy something new, something that before that moment, she did not know she could not live without.

In both market segments, the retail world exists to present a perfected version of the world, a story into which the customers can insert themselves. Successful brands connect to their customers on an emotional level, creating more than a great item but an entire experience that surrounds that item. Truly exceptional retail brands are those that positively impact the consumer's life beyond the moment of the sale, whether through exceptional price, quality, or customer service.

See also: Teen Market; Tween Market

Further Reading: Gavenas, Mary Lisa. *Color Stories: Behind the Scenes of America's Billion-Dollar Beauty Industry.* New York: Simon & Schuster, 2002; Hunter, Victoria. *The Ultimate Fashion Study Guide.* Pasadena, CA: Hunter Publishing, 2007; Lincoln, Keith, and Lars Thomassen. *How to Succeed at Retail: Winning Case Studies and Strategies for Retailers and Brands.* London: Kogan Page, 2007.

Sara M. Harvey

REVLON

Beginning as a producer of unique nail enamels, Charles Revson (1906–75) founded a mass production **cosmetics** firm that he built into an international corporation. Revson was known for his creativity and perfectionism. The Revlon Company modernized cosmetics **advertising** techniques, and was an early practitioner of the color story.

Early Career

Born in Boston, Revson was the middle son of working-class parents living in tenement housing. Brought up in Manchester, New Hampshire, Revson moved to New York City as a young man and worked for a dress company before joining a **cosmetics** company that sold nail polish. Along with his brother Joseph and chemist Charles Lachman, Revson founded the Revlon Cosmetics Company in 1932. Using pigments instead of dyes, their unique nail enamel was first sold to beauty salons and later department stores.

Marketing Philosophy

Revson and the Revlon Company are well known as the proponents of the modern beauty ad, letting the picture tell the story, and like other beauty mavens **Elizabeth Arden** and **Helena Rubinstein**, following the philosophy of beauty products as a necessary luxury. Their first consumer advertisement came out in 1935 and, by 1939, Revlon had introduced a matching nail polish and lipstick line. The Revlon Company had grown to multimillion dollar status by the beginning of World War II. Revlon was one of the early leaders in the color story **advertising** technique by 1944, and after 1945 the company began its growth as a general cosmetics firm. This expansion has included developing different product lines for varying age, race, and gender groups. By 1970, the Revlon Company was the second largest cosmetics corporation in the world (behind **Avon**). In 1973, Revson helped launch the supermodel phenomenon when he hired Lauren Hutton as the face of Revlon. Further mass media successes were the Charlie Perfume ads of the early 1970s.

Legacies

Revson's personal life often gained attention, as he married three times and was known to be a harsh employer. Revson remained the president of Revlon until 1962, and served as chairman until his death in 1975. After his death, the company continued to flourish. The Revlon Company surpassed one billion dollars in sales in 1977. MacAndrews and Forbes Holdings bought the company in 1985.

In 1956, Revson established the Charles H. Revson Foundation, which concentrates philanthropic efforts in New York City among the Jewish community, health, and educational institutions. The Charles H. Revson Fellowship program selects 10 fellows each year for a year of enrichment study at Columbia University. Foundation grant disbursements as of 2008 total more than $127 million with an endowment of over $200 million.

See also: Perfumes and Fragrances

Further Reading: Charles H. Revson Foundation. http://www.revsonfoundation.org; Gavenas, Mary Lisa. *Color Stories: Behind the Scenes of America's Billion-Dollar Beauty Industry.* New York: Simon & Schuster, 2002; Peiss, Kathy. *Hope in a Jar: The Making of America's Beauty Culture.* New York: Metropolitan, 1998; Perutz, Kathrin. *Beyond the Looking Glass: America's Beauty Culture.* New York: William Morrow, 1970.

Christina Ashby-Martin

RUBINSTEIN, HELENA (C. 1870–1965)

Helena Rubinstein, a female pioneer in the **cosmetics** industry, made her reputation based on face creams. Rubinstein's glamorous public persona and her own natural complexion were her best **advertising** for women's beauty routines. Like her rival, **Elizabeth Arden**, she became known as a groundbreaking cosmetics entrepreneur, philanthropist, and prominent international businesswoman.

Early Years and Immigration

Born the eldest of eight children to a Jewish family in Cracow, Poland, Rubinstein studied medicine for a short time before immigrating to Australia sometime in the 1890s. Working as a governess and possibly a waitress, Rubinstein sold face creams made by her family's friend, Jacob Lykusky. Rubinstein opened her own beauty salon in Melbourne around 1900, and she was shortly thereafter joined by her sisters Ceska and Manka. With a $100,000 stake, Rubinstein traveled to London where she met and married her first husband, American journalist Edward Titus. She opened a shop in Paris in 1912, but at the beginning of World War I she and her family immigrated to New York City, where Rubinstein opened a Fifth

Avenue beauty salon. Shortly thereafter, her skin care products were selling in department stores across the country.

Beauty and Professional Philosophy

The Rubinstein reputation was built on skin care products, specifically face cream. Rubinstein's promotion of the beauty routine took the Puritan work ethic and adapted it to the beauty industry, but especially toward the regularity of individuals' beauty routines, centered on the use of the triad: cold cream, astringents, and moisturizers. Like her rival grande dame, Arden, Rubinstein pushed the beauty culture into high-volume sales and high-end advertising. Much of Rubinstein's success was to be found in her salon personnel's personal touch. This effort was directed at luring middle-class customers into the use of specialty cosmetics. She also helped develop the 1920s view of the New Woman, specifically, the beauty specialist as a professional. Rubinstein herself became a model for the new sophisticated and independent woman.

Later Years and Legacy

In 1928, Rubinstein sold her American interests to Lehman Brothers and then bought the company back after the stock market crash in 1929. Rubinstein divorced Titus in 1938 and married Prince Artchil Gourielli-Tchkonia, lending an additional European, aristocratic element to her image. Her personal migrations from Poland to Australia, London, Paris, and New York City, gave Rubinstein a truly international background. Other immigrant or working-class women could aspire to these heights of success. Rubinstein maintained control of her extensive business interests through direct involvement and family members until her death in 1965.

However, the later period in Rubinstein's life involved a shift in focus to include a growing reputation as an art collector and patron and supporter of Israel. As an art patron, her collection illustrated her eclectic tastes; African sculpture, Oceanic and Oriental art, Egyptian, as well as modern paintings are a prominent legacy of her artistic eye. Because she believed that education was an important avenue for career development, especially for women, she focused many of her philanthropic efforts in areas that encouraged young women to pursue higher education and nontraditional careers. The Helena Rubinstein Foundation was created in 1953 and supports education, the arts, and special programs for women. The foundation also continues Rubinstein's commitment to the welfare of Israel through cultural programs and scholarships. L'Oréal bought Helena Rubinstein's rights in 1988 and relaunched the company in the United States in 1996.

Further Reading: Gavenas, Mary Lisa. *Color Stories: Behind the Scenes of America's Billion-Dollar Beauty Industry.* New York: Simon & Schuster, 2002; Helena Rubinstein Foundation. http://www.helenarubinsteinfdn.org; Peiss, Kathy. *Hope in a Jar: The Making of America's Beauty Culture.* New York: Metropolitan Books, 1998; Perutz, Kathrin. *Beyond the Looking Glass: America's Beauty Culture.* New York: William Morrow, 1970.

Christina Ashby-Martin

S

SALLY'S BEAUTY SUPPLY

Founded in 1964 with one store in New Orleans, Sally's Beauty Supply has grown to be the world's largest retailer of professional beauty supplies. Specializing in well-known as well as hard to find products, Sally's carries over 6,000 products for hair, skin, and nails and are available to **retail** customers and salon professionals in over 2,700 store locations throughout the United States and internationally. Sally's Beauty Supply came of age in the era of small neighborhood beauty salons, and although it has never been associated with haute couture, it has been the mainstay for small businesses, students, and especially do-it-yourselfers who are happy to pay less money for knock-off brands that, in the eyes of many consumers, achieve the same result. Although the name alone suggests that Sally's is far from trendy, it has recently incorporated new features in its sales strategies to access younger and computer-/**Internet**-savvy customers. Sally's has added both a Facebook page and Twitter sites that keep customers apprised of sales, and sites where they can download additional savings coupons. Its sales strategy appears to be working as more customers join the Beauty Club and are thereby encouraged to visit the stores more frequently.

History and Holdings

Headquartered in Denton, Texas, Sally's has grown dramatically and steadily since the late 1960s through acquisitions of other national and international beauty supply enterprises. Sally's Beauty Holdings comprises Sally's Beauty Supply, the retail portion, and Beauty Systems Group, which sells 9,500 professionally branded products targeted exclusively for professional and salon use. The combined holdings sell and distribute to over 3,300 stores, including 170 franchise units. Beauty Systems Group began aggressive acquisitions of other businesses in 1985, and its portion of the holdings comprises approximately 825 stores throughout most of the United States and Canada. Sally's Beauty Holdings is a freestanding company traded on the New York Stock Exchange (SBH).

Sally's Beauty Supply has gained a large share of the distribution market. Besides its 2,200 stores in the 48 contiguous states, it owns 9 stores in Canada, 180 stores in the United Kingdom and Ireland, 25 in Germany, 30 in Japan, and 40 in Mexico. In addition, in 2008 they acquired 40 stores in Belgium, France, and Spain, giving the company a foothold in Western Europe.

The recent U.S. and worldwide recession has affected Sally's Beauty Holdings, yet the company has remained strong enough to continue paying its acquisitions debt and plans to continue opening more stores. While direct-to-salon sales have dropped modestly, 4.1 percent in the third quarter of 2009, the holdings company has posted a 7 percent profit. A significant portion of this profit is due to a 3.2 percent increase in Sally's Beauty Supply store sales. This increase is attributed to the accessibility of its generic beauty brands and the use of do-it-yourself products by many of its customers in preference to visiting salons for more expensive beauty treatments. Gross profits continue to rise but are being offset by the cost of acquisitions, hovering in the $1.2 billion range, while total revenue for the holdings remains close to double that amount.

Commerce and E-Commerce

Through its acquisitions and opening of new locations, Sally's Beauty Supply stores are readily located in many medium-sized and larger cities. Easily accessed through both online locator sites and Sally's own Web site, store locations are by company policy open seven days a week and for extended hours, to enable shopping by all sectors of customers and especially those who work full-time. The company offers loyalty incentive plans through Beauty Club Cards for its nonprofessional clients and a Sally ProCard for its professional customers with discounts on items throughout the stores.

Publicized through *SallyBeauty* magazine, launched in 2000, and its Web site (www.sallybeauty.com), launched in 2001, Sally's targets three customer areas: the working beauty professional, the beauty school student, and the general consumer.

SallyCares

Created in 1996, SallyCares endeavors to provide personal care assistance and guidance to women in need. SallyCares is divided into four areas of focus; the SallyCares Shelter program focuses on aiding over 50 women's domestic abuse shelters nationwide through donations of grooming and beauty products, and through monetary contributions through the SallyCares Anniversary Fund. Breast cancer research is the focus of the second endeavor; launched in 1991, the City of Hope canister fundraising campaign and the annual gala have to date contributed over $3 million to breast cancer research. The two other foci—SallyCares Seminars and the funding of 10 National Cosmetology Association scholarships, demonstrate the company's policy of career building and education for future professionals. In recent years, the holding company has contributed scholarship donations to the University of North Texas and grants to Texas Women's University, furthering the company's goals of encouraging women's careers. The benefits for Sally's employees are four major areas of insurance coverage, time off earned in the first year of employment (three weeks), paid holidays, tuition reimbursement, and 401(k) with company matching contributions.

Further Reading: Halkias, Maria. "Sally Beauty Holdings' 3Q sales, Earnings Rise." *Dallas Morning News,* August 1, 2009. http://finance.yahoo.com. (Accessed August 7,

2009); Sally Beauty Holdings Inc. (SBH). Income Statement. August 7, 2009; Sally Beauty. http://www.sallybeauty.com; http://www.sallybeautyholdings.com.

Christina Ashby-Martin

SASSOON, VIDAL (1928–)

As a hairdresser, Vidal Sassoon promoted a belief that the structure of the cut should provide the style; this led to the development of his signature wash-and-go geometric cuts of the 1960s. Though all his cuts are visually distinct, he is most often associated with the 5-point cut, a short geometric cut with one point over each ear and three visible points at the nape of the neck. A crucial player in the vibrant Swinging London scene of the 1960s, Sassoon promoted simplicity of line that was visually analogous to the minimalist, geometric lines of mid '60s fashions. Sassoon's most famous cut is that worn by Mia Farrow in the 1967 **film** *Rosemary's Baby*.

Sassoon was born in the East End of London on January 17, 1928 to parents of Sephardic Jewish ancestry. His father abandoned the family when Sassoon was very young, and his mother placed Sassoon and his brother in an orphanage until 1939, when the family was reunited. At age 14, Sassoon was apprenticed

Vidal Sassoon is surrounded by models, showing his new cuts for 1976, in London. The styles are called, clockwise from lower left: The Hummingbird, Question Mark, Feathers, Tomboy, and Silver Lady. (AP Photo)

"Had I gone to a university . . . I probably would have been an architect because that was my first love. But, hair was fascinating to me! It was this organic material that you could flow with and could cut shapes into."

Vidal Sassoon

Source: Gordon, Michael. *Hair Heroes.* New York: Bubble and Bubble Press, 2002, 239.

to a hairdresser named Professor Cohen. He spent the next several years honing his skills at a series of gradually more prestigious London salons. During the same period, Sassoon was also involved with the 43 Group, an antifascist Jewish group in London. In April 1948, Sassoon joined the Israeli Army and spent several months fighting in the Arab-Israeli War before returning to London. Upon his return to London, Sassoon returned to work as a hairdresser, eventually opening his own London salon in 1954.

Though Sassoon quickly built a name for himself, it was not until 1963 that he experienced the creative breakthrough that led to his signature geometric cuts. Asked by London fashion designer Mary Quant to develop a new look for her models in an upcoming fashion show, Sassoon gave all the models haircuts reminiscent of **the bob** of the 1920s. Quant also volunteered her own hair and the Sassoon cut was born.

Like an artist, Sassoon named his creations, giving them names such as Eye-Eye, a cut that covered one eye, or the Curly Geometric, a permed version of his geometric cut. Fashion-forward women such as model Peggy Moffit, designer Emmanuelle Khanh, and actor Nancy Kwan quickly adopted the avant-garde Sassoon look. As his reputation spread, Sassoon began collaborating with fashion **designers** such as Rudi Gernreich, Mila Schon, Paco Rabanne, and Emanuel Ungaro to create **hairstyles** to complement their designs.

Sassoon eventually opened salons and hair academies in New York and London, while also developing a line of **hair care products**. In 1982, Sassoon founded the Vidal Sassoon International Center for the Study of Anti-Semitism at Hebrew University in Israel, an organization dedicated to studying and documenting anti-Semitism throughout the world. By 2004, Sassoon was no longer associated with any of the salons, hair academies, or products that bear his name. He lives in Los Angeles and devotes his time and financial resources to various philanthropic efforts.

See also: Beauty Shops and Salons; Endorsements of Products, Celebrity; Hair Care Products; Hairdressers; Hairstylists, Celebrity

Further Reading: Cox, Caroline, and Lee Widdows. *Hair and Fashion.* London: V&A Publications, 2005; Sassoon, Vidal. *Cutting Hair the Vidal Sassoon Way.* Burlington, MA: Butterworth-Heinemann, 1984; Sassoon, Vidal. *Sorry to have Kept you Waiting, Madam.* New York: G. P. Putnam's Sons, 1968; Sassoon, Vidal, Gerald Battle Welch, Luca P. Marighetti, Werner Moller. *Vidal Sassoon and the Bauhaus.* New York: Distributed Art Publications, 1994.

Rachel Harris

SEVENTEEN

Seventeen magazine, for teen girls, was first published in 1944. Publisher Walter Annenberg and *Seventeen's* first editor Helen Valentine created a magazine that has now become the queen of the teenage magazine market stand. This service magazine for young women was the first of its kind in the United States. Since the inception of *Seventeen*, the magazine has been sold to the Rupert Murdoch family of businesses, to Primedia Company, and to its present owner, the Hearst Corporation.

Content

Researchers of *Seventeen* have found the main emphasis of the magazine to be the importance of beauty. The magazine provides a variety of content but still focuses the majority of its effort on beauty problems. It gives information and advice about fashion and trends, celebrities, beauty, and lifestyle. There are sections on skincare, hair and makeup, health, nutrition and exercise, sex and the body, quizzes, and horoscopes. Also strewn within the covers are sections on colleges and education and an exclusive cover-to-cover issue on prom.

Demographics

In the beginning stages of *Seventeen*, market research showed that its young female readers were between the ages of 16 and 17 and were influential in the family purchases. They had enough money to see movies and purchase sodas, makeup, and clothing, and what they could not cover they knew their middle-class parents would. As the magazine progressed, the content stayed the same, but the target market branched out to include girls between the ages of 14 and 21. Today, with an emerging **tween market** there have been some complaints that the once exclusively teen magazine is now attracting a prepubescent readership.

Goals

The main goal of *Seventeen* was to help young female consumers find the right products to purchase to be successful, popular, and most importantly beautiful. *Seventeen* was designed as a shopping guide; a source where young girls could reference current trends and learn where to find these products. The teenage girl was also spotlighted as having a viable economic market value and the ability to become a consumer extraordinaire, making it much easier to sell the magazine to both advertisers and young women.

Critique

Seventeen magazine faces competition from a range of publications and Web sites that often seem less dated and more suited for a generation of teens raised on *Sex and the City*, reality shows, and designer brand labels. *Cosmo Girl* and *Elle Girl* (now exclusively Web sites), as well as *Teen **Vogue*** and *YM Magazine*, offer edgy articles on topics that range from music divas to male hotties, as well as high-end fashion.

In the face of competition, *Seventeen* has opted out of any kind of real makeover. Instead, the magazine touts what can best be defined as a heartland aesthetic with familiar suburban mall styles and mainstream content. While *Seventeen* may offer articles on teen icons and advice on boys, it avoids the more titillating tabloid trends, thus making the magazine quaintly retro—hawking simple beauty and style.

See also: Advertising; Fashion Magazines; Teen Market

Further Reading: Carr, David. "Reinviting Seventeen with a View to Middle America." *New York Times*, November 24, 2003; Labre, Magdala Peixoto, and Kim Walsh-Childers. "Friendly Advice? Beauty Messages in Web Sites of Teen Magazines." *Mass Communication & Society* 6 (2003): 379–96; Mazzarella, Sharon K., and Norma Odom Pecors, eds. *Growing Up Girls: Popular Culture and the Construction of Identity*. New York: P. Lang, 1999; McRobbie, Angela. *Feminism and Youth Culture: From 'Jackie' to 'Just Seventeen.'* Boston: Unwin Hyman, 1976.

Nicolette Cosburn

SKIN CARE LINES, MEN'S

Men's skincare, like all aspects of **male grooming**, has a long and complicated history. In the ancient Egyptian world, men practiced a beauty and health regimen that included the application of skin conditioners and moisturizers. **Cosmetics**, especially those intended to protect, shadow, and enhance the appearance of the eyes, were also routinely used in life and death among the Egyptians. Additionally, they applied ingenious concoctions made from ingredients like olive oil, Cyprus bark, and oil of fenugreek to their faces in an effort to eliminate freckles and wrinkles. In the Classical Greek and Roman worlds, men paid special attention to the appearance of the skin and the face. In Roman baths, they received facial treatments with ointments that were intended to beautify and replenish. The importance of this particular ritual of personal hygiene was reflected in the fact that these ointments were applied by a special masseuse, known as an *aliptes,* in a purpose-specific room referred to as an *unctuarium.* Roman men also used a chalk-based powder to render their complexions more youthful and frequently dyed their hair to achieve a fairer look.

In other regions, men and women alike used a broad range of facial treatments that were intended to improve the appearance of the skin. In the Islamic world, from the 9th through the 12th centuries, physicians and alchemists used their specialized forms of knowledge to devise skin care treatments. These included skin cleansers made of almond oil and facial masks composed of rice, grains, seashells, lime, egg, and other ingredients that removed layers of dead skin from the face. Despite a tendency on the part of the medieval Christian church in Europe to condemn the practices of excessive adornment and the use of cosmetics, evidence suggests that men persisted in their efforts to beautify their faces. During the Renaissance, the physician and alchemist Theophrastus Paracelsus (1493–1541) drew on his knowledge of botany and plants from the New World to prescribe the use of artichokes and aloe to treat **baldness** and the application of wine vinegar to eliminate wrinkles. It was within this period, as well, that Europeans began to be exposed to other forms of skin care and adornment, such as facial **tattoos**, found in places like the Yucatan peninsula of Mexico.

United States

Men in the American colonies and the early United States continued to care for the skin and treat problems such as **acne** with a broad array of concoctions and home remedies, though the impact of Puritanism in the New England colonies and the exigencies of colonial life often precluded excessive vanity or indulgence. Still, some American men in the 18th century affected the powdered and primped appearance of the European macaroni, who was known for his excess, indulgence, and the extravagant adornment of his person. By the mid 19th century, men were seeking remedies for skin ailments, as well as a host of internal or neurological problems, in the form of unregulated patent or quack medicines. Hundreds of remedies, frequently alcohol- or opium-based, were advertised in the pages of American magazines and newspapers throughout the 19th century. Concoctions like Acker's Blood Elixir, advertised in a Bloomington, Illinois, newspaper in 1888, for example, promised to cure ulcers, eruptions, and syphilitic poisoning, the aesthetic effects of which could be quite devastating. A similar potion, advertised in a Montrose, Pennsylvania, publication in 1880, extolled the pimple-eliminating virtues of vegetable balm. Whatever the intended use, the marketability of cure-all elixirs appealed, in part, to the male and female desire to beautify the skin and create as pleasing an appearance as possible to secure success in business, courtship, and marriage. Some men, in seeking a competitive edge in life during this period, also sought out the services of beauticians like Madame Velaro in New York City to have their wrinkles treated and their mustaches tinted.

Men's skin care was most affected by one late-19th-century development: the introduction of the safety razor and the emergence of self-shaving in the 1880s. Accompanying this important technological change was the emergence of a host of new products meant to ease shaving and cleanse, nourish, and beautify the skin. By the 1920s, producers were offering a range of new products, in often highly masculinized advertisements in magazines like *Fortune* (f. 1930) and *Esquire* (f. 1933), which promised to improve facial appearance. New lines of lotions, powders, and moisturizers like

"The men who uphold the standards of American sport today are clean men—clean of action and clean of face. Your baseball star takes thought of his personal appearance—it's part of his team ethics. He starts the day with a clean shave—and, like all self-reliant men, he shaves himself."

Gillette Advertisement, 1910

Source: Peiss, Kathy. *Hope in a Jar: The Making of America's Beauty Culture.* New York: Metropolitan Books, 1998, 161.

Florian were directed specifically at the male beauty consumer. In the 1930s, market research firms were beginning to study white-collar workers to determine how frequently they used products like aftershave lotions and moisturizers. In one survey from 1936, they discovered that one in two middle-class New York men was using at least some sort of beauty product. Some of these men relied on skin care services offered by their barbers, and some used female-oriented products like Ponds to treat acne or Covermark to hide embarrassing blemishes. A few even took to visiting the beauty culture studios of industry entrepreneurs **Elizabeth Arden** and **Helena Rubinstein**, both of whom entered the lucrative beauty business in the 1910s. This embrace of new skin care regimens was not entirely unproblematic for those who were concerned about the gendered implications of this form of consumption. Some heterosexual men worried that behaviors of this sort might lump them in with what were viewed as the painted fairies of New York (and other cities), who used makeup as a way to visually express their sexual identity.

During World War II, American men in the armed forces were expected, as a component of military discipline, to keep their hair neat and short, their faces clean shaven, and their clothes and shoes pressed and polished. With this new emphasis on fastidious male grooming came a dramatic expansion of the men's shaving and skin care industry. In the 1950s and 1960s, companies concerned primarily with female consumers began to develop lines of aftershave products and skins lotions that were marketed to men as ways to achieve the desired aesthetic effect of cleanliness. This development really took off as companies like Clinique and Lancôme began to market products, previously confined exclusively to a female audience, to male consumers in magazines like *Gentlemen's Quarterly (GQ)* (f. 1957) and *Esquire*. By the mid 1980s, Clinique was selling products like Scruffing Lotion to a new, large market of men who were increasingly comfortable requesting male beauty aids in department stores and specialty shops.

Since the 1990s, features on men's skin care have been fairly standard fare in a broad range of magazines directed at different segments of the male market, including youthful heterosexuals (*Maxim*, f. 1995) and gay men (*Out*, f. 1992). Discussions of dry skin, acne, shaving techniques, **tanning**, and aging not only punctuate the pages of these popular magazines but, since the late 1990s, have also appeared on countless Web sites and online publications. One such Web site, www.menessentials.com, bills itself as "the Internet's first male grooming site and the premiere online destination for men of style and substance" and offers products for sale and a broad range of advice on skin and hair care, as well as shaving. In some instances, discussions of men's skincare have taken on a critical edge or brought up potentially controversial topics like the use of cosmetics. In a 2007 article that appeared in the online publication *Salon.com*, for example, the virtues, as well as potential pitfalls, of guyliner and mancake were discussed in relation to Zac Efron, the teen-idol star of *High School Musical*. While controversies about the excesses of male vanity (especially as they relate to the frequently discussed and much-maligned metrosexual) continue, it would appear that the current obsession with male skin care is here to stay.

See also: Advertising; Anti-Aging Products and Techniques; Barbers and Barbershops; Magazines, Men's; *Men's Health;* Metrosexuals; *Queer Eye for the Straight Guy*

Further Reading: Blanco-Dávila, Feliciano. "Beauty and the Body: The Origins of Cosmetics." *Plastic and Reconstructive Surgery,* 105 no. 3 (2000): 1196–2004; Chauncey, George. *Gay New York: Gender, Urban Culture, and the Making of the Gay Male World, 1890–1940.* New York: Basic Books, 1994; Kim, Kibum. "Bronzer Gods: Does Teen Heartthrob Zac Efron's Love of 'Mancake' Foundation and 'Guyliner' Put Him on the Edge of a New Men's Makeup Breakthrough?" *Salon.com,* October 30, 2007. http://www.salon.com/mwt/feature/2007/10/30/mens_makeup; Luciano, Lynne. *Looking Good: Male Body Image in Modern America.* New York: Hill and Wang, 2001; Peiss, Kathy. *Hope in a Jar: The Making of America's Beauty Culture.* New York: Metropolitan Books, 1998; Vail, G. A. *A History of Cosmetics in America.* New York: Toilet Goods Association, 1947.

Paul R. Deslandes

SPAS

The term *spa* is commonly thought to be derived from the name of the town of Spa in Belgium, where a natural hot springs has been a site of healing since before Roman times. Evidence of human visitation to hot and cold springs can be traced to prehistoric times, and many people worldwide have believed in the healing power of certain springs and of bathing and purification in general. Most spas were established at sites that had been used for centuries for health and well-being, often built around natural hot springs or near lakes. The ancient Greeks and Romans were well known for their medicinal bathing and the vast complexes they built to accommodate this pastime.

Spas and sanitariums in the United States blossomed in the 1800s along with a resurgence in values associated with the Greco-Roman period: a focus on physical exercise, hygiene, disease prevention, and overall well-being. European and British colonialists brought to the New World an interest in the medicinal use of bathing and hot and cold springs. In addition, many learned about local hot and cold springs from Native Americans. Colonial doctors began recommending water cures in the 18th century, establishing famous spas such as Saratoga Springs in New York, as well as in Pennsylvania and Virginia. Entrepreneurs built hotels where visitors could lodge, eat, and visit the hot springs, thus giving rise to the U.S. health resort industry. Industrialization gave rise to a prosperous middle class in the United States that could also afford to use upper-class spas and sanitariums, mostly to treat ailments under a physician's recommendation.

Use Statistics

In the United States, the spa industry grew and prospered in the late 20th century, with a 24 percent growth rate between June 2007 and June 2008 and $10.9 billion of revenue according to the International Spa Association (ISPA) (Figure 1).

Oceans Spa and School in Lubbock, Texas, blurs divisions between health and beauty by offering services that range from pedicures and facials to specialized massages for cancer patients, 2009. (Courtesy of Julie Willett)

One in four Americans has been to a spa, with 138 million spa visits estimated in 2007 (Figure 2). In a 2002 American Massage Therapy Association survey, 28 percent of Americans who said they had received a massage in the previous five years said the reasons were relaxation or stress reduction (23%), other health reasons (53%), and pampering themselves (15%). Twenty-seven percent preferred to receive a massage at a spa compared with 19 percent in the therapist's office.

Corporate Wellness Culture

Founded in 1991, ISPA is the first professional organization to represent the industry. It represents 3,200 health and wellness facilities and providers in 83 countries. Members include resorts, hotels, medical spas, mineral springs, and cruise ships, as well as service providers such as physicians, massage therapists, and product suppliers. Its mission is to forward the industry's mission to promote the spa experience, demonstrating that the spa is not a luxury but a lifestyle. The organization offers directories, a job bank, promotions, and outreach programs to promote wellness to communities through education, research, and scholarship. ISPA has also conducted ethnographic consumer trends research into spa use, exploring why the spa experience is becoming a sought-after lifestyle focused on wellness and connection to self.

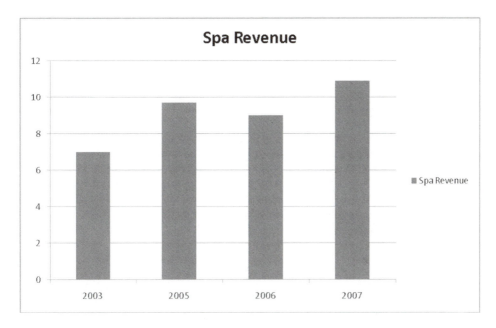

Figure 1   U.S. Spa Industry Revenue from 2003 to 2007 (in billions)
Source: Compiled from data from International Spa Association Web site (www.experience
ispa.como/education-resources/facts-and-figures/industry-stats/)

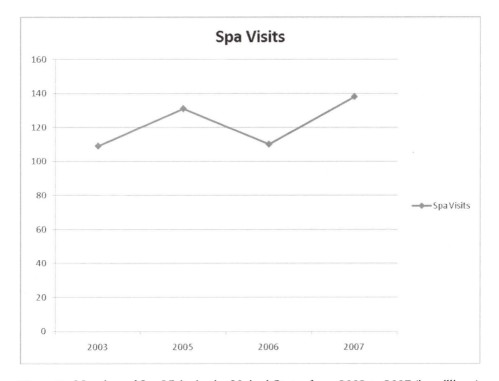

Figure 2   Number of Spa Visits in the United States from 2003 to 2007 (in millions)
Source: Compiled from data from International Spa Association Web site (www.experience
ispa.como/education-resources/facts-and-figures/industry-stats/)

Worksite wellness programs advanced in the 1990s focused on employee wellness. In particular, corporations often funded retreats for their top-level employees at spas with the intent to enhance company performance. This helped to fuel the burgeoning spa industry, which caters increasingly to corporate culture and high-income clients. Recent news reports suggest that executives from firms receiving bailout money from U.S. taxpayers spent hundreds of thousands of dollars on expensive spa retreat weekends, angering the public.

Labor

The spa industry employs a range of workers, including massage therapists, nutritionists, physicians, wellness educators, cosmetologists, and cleaning staff. Most employees in the spa industry are part-time or contract employees, numbering 160,500 in comparison to 143,200 full-time employees.

Massage therapists have always been part of the spa industry, but were employed in greater numbers in day spas and beauty salons as the industry boomed during the early 20th century and again in the 1990s. Although most massage therapists, according to the American Massage Therapy Association (AMTA) practice privately, 22 percent of AMTA members say they are employed in a spa or salon, compared to 43 percent who travel to client locations, 33 percent who have a home office, 16 percent who have an office with other massage therapists, 30 percent who are in private practice with their own office, and 19 percent who work in a medical setting.

Most massage students tend to train in regions where there is a large potential market for massage services. Increasing numbers of students, however, are likely to become employees in the burgeoning spa industry rather than practicing for themselves. Changing licensing laws and increasing educational standards are more likely to affect the provision of massage in the enormous day spa industry. Hotel spas and large corporate day spas typically pay between 20–30 percent commissions to massage therapists.

Another reason for the burgeoning spa industry has been a ready supply of cheap **labor**, allowing spa business to make a hefty profit. For many workers in day spas and salons, $10–$12/hour is the industry maximum, although some contract massage workers make more. Being non–English speaking means lower wages, sometimes $50 a day, well below minimum wage, and up to 20 percent of spa-worker income can be based on commissions. At times, spa owners may change the percentage of the treatment price they pay employees or change or stop paying the hourly rate altogether. In some spas, there is no hourly rate and employees are not paid at all for no-shows. Plaintiffs in a lawsuit against two **nail salons** on the Upper West Side of New York City were awarded $250,000 for overtime violations and wrongful terminations; these salon workers were routinely putting in 10-hour days, often without a break, six days a week.

Day Spas

A spa environment offering services to customers on a day-use basis is usually built in a stand-alone facility, without lodging or restaurants. Most day spas offer massage services, and cosmetology services such as facials, **waxing**, body treatments, manicures, pedicures, and sometimes hairstyling.

Medical Spas

A medical spa operates under the supervision of a licensed health care professional and integrates complementary and alternative therapies with typical spa services. In addition, many medical spas offer the latest dermatological skin treatments that can be practiced by technicians under the supervision of a licensed medical professional, such as microdermabrasion, a tool that exfoliates the top layer of skin from the face, medical chemical peels, and Restylane and **Botox** injections.

Mineral Springs Spas

A mineral springs spa is a spa that is built around a natural mineral hot or cold spring that offers hydrotherapy treatments. They can be day spas or may also include a hotel or resort spa environment with lodging, restaurants, and a full range of spa services. Some of the most famous include the Spring Resort and Spa in Desert Hot Springs, CA; Colorado's Hot Sulphur Springs Resort and Spa; the Ojo Caliente Mineral Springs Resort and Day Spa in Northern New Mexico; and the Hot Springs Resort in North Carolina.

Hotel/Resort Spa

Hotel/resort spas are hotels or resorts that offer spa services or a spa environment within the facility; this may include fitness and wellness services, as well as special meals. Examples of the best known spas in the country include Canyon Ranch (Tucson, Arizona), The Spa at the Mandarin Oriental (New York), Mii Amo (Sedona, Arizona) and Lake Austin Spa Resort (Austin, Texas).

Further Reading: Calvert, Robert Noah. *The History of Massage.* Rochester, VT: Healing Arts Press, 2002; Dobson, Marnie. *Professionalizing Touch: Gender, Sexuality, the Law and Massage Work.* Ann Arbor, MI: UMI Dissertation Services, ProQuest Information and Learning Company, 2006; International Spa Association. http://www.experienceispa. com/education-resources/facts-and-figures/industry-stats/. (Accessed May, 7, 2009); Kang, Miliann. *The Managed Hand*: *The Commercialization of Bodies and Emotions in Korean Immigrant-Owned Nail Salons. Gender and Society,* 17 (2003): 820–39; Nussbaum, Emily. "A Revealing Look at the Spa Industry." *New York Magazine,* November 25, 2007.

Marnie Dobson

TANNING

Tanning refers to the natural or artificial process of darkening one's skin color. Typically, tanned skin is achieved via sun exposure but, in recent years, tanning beds delivering ultraviolet rays or booths that cover users with a topical spray that mimics a natural tan have become increasingly popular.

History

The debate about altering one's skin color has been going on for centuries; in some cultures, darkened skin color and cosmetic use were seen as markers of wealth and attractiveness, while in others, darkened skin was seen as primitive and uncivilized. In 18th-century Europe and America, cosmetic skin whiteners and home remedies to cure accidental tans were popular. As the Industrial Revolution took hold, however, Western notions about skin color began to change. In Europe, as the working class headed indoors to do factory work, the wealthy started associating darkened skin with leisure time and wealth. This new association did not take hold in America until the early 20th century because Victorian propriety forbade skimpy bathing costumes and daywear and looked down upon any alteration of one's skin color.

America in the 20th Century

By the turn of the 20th century, however, new ideas surfaced about leisure time, skin color, and appropriate dress and behavior for women. In particular, women of the 1910s and 1920s began challenging female stereotypes and limitations by putting off marriage and childbearing, donning skimpier clothing (including bathing costumes and dresses that showed off arms, legs, and chests), and wearing **cosmetics**, which had previously been associated with oversexualized women. These changes, coupled with the accidental tan of European fashion icon **Coco Chanel** in the early 1920s, paved the way for the rising popularity of tanning in America. Advertisers and other social conduits began associating tanning with health, personal and national strength, female beauty, and female liberation. Advertisements for skin products began focusing on how the products enhanced a tan; this was a departure from ads prior to the 1920s that promoted products that preserved white skin. As tanning's popularity grew, advertisers from the 1930s to the 1960s promoted obvious products, like tinted face powder and nylons, as well as unobvious products like silverware, by drawing connections between a tan and patriotism, anticommunism, and an acceptance of civil rights activity and the feminist movement. During the 20th century, most products and advertisements related to tanning targeted women, though advertisements for alcohol and car makers, vacation spots, and even a few cosmetic preparations like Man Tan, a 1950s tinted cosmetic, encouraged tanning for men. Despite a discussion of the health risks of tanning, which began in the 1960s, Americans continued associating tans with leisure time, wealth, beauty, and health through the end of the 20th century; accordingly, advertisers and producers continued promoting tans.

"Several times a week, Jaclyn, 22, drives to a tanning bed lined with 100-watt UV bulbs for 15 minutes. It's a routine she's been loyal to since her senior year in high school. 'I hate being pale,' she says. 'It makes me feel ghostly and sick. I look healthier with a tan.' But what about the potential effects on her skin-the age spots, the wrinkles, the *cancer*? 'By the time I have to worry about that, they'll have something to fix it.'"

Source: "Tanning Junkie." *Oprah Magazine,* August 2009, 146.

Tanning Booths

Because of tanning's reputation for giving good health, Americans started looking for easier and faster ways to get sun exposure. Tanning beds (machines using artificially produced ultraviolet rays to tan users' skin) were introduced in the 1930s. These beds were originally advertised to tubercular Americans, for whom sun exposure was considered healing, and even as a home appliance for adventurous sorts, but by the 1970s, tanning beds were available to the general public in commercial tanning salons. Through the 1980s and 1990s, tanning salons sprung up across the nation, offering Americans quick and intense tans. When scientists made connections between skin cancer and outdoor sun exposure, tanning bed manufacturers promoted beds as safe alternatives. But through the 1990s, studies consistently demonstrated higher risks of skin cancer among tanning bed users because of the intensity of ultraviolet exposure in tanning beds. Despite the risk, there is currently still a large culture of Americans, particularly young women, who use tanning beds.

Skin Cancer Risks

In the 1960s, many Americans became aware of the strong links between sun tanning and skin cancer, among other less serious maladies like wrinkles. Though literature connecting tanning with skin cancer began showing up in popular magazines as early as 1941, it was not until the early 1960s that a serious challenge to tanning's popularity emerged. And though advertisers continued to encourage tanning to sell products, the late 1960s and early 1970s saw the emergence of increasing studies and reports about the dangers of tanning, as well as the introduction of alternative products, such as leg creams and other cosmetic substitutes that gave the appearance of a tan. Similarly, sunscreen became widely popular, particularly after the sun protection factor (SPF) rating system was implemented in the 1970s. And yet, Americans continued to ignore the warnings of physicians and prescriptive literature and tan, often with low SPF sunscreen or no sunscreen at all; the association of a tan with good health and beauty was too strong to reverse overnight. It took a concerted effort by scientists, doctors, and others from the 1980s to the present day, armed with frightening statistics about skin cancer mortality rates, to get the word out and convince more Americans to either use stronger sunscreen or avoid sun exposure altogether.

America in the 21st Century

In the 21st century, Americans seem more informed about the risks associated with sun tanning. There is copious literature about the risks of sun exposure and the problems associated with darkening one's skin. The positive associations tied to tanning, however, continue to hold strong in the national psyche. As a result, new products have emerged to alter one's skin color safely; most notably, self-tanning lotions and booths that spray a topical tanning product have become popular and safe alternatives. Additionally, there is much greater attention to sunscreen and sun safety in popular literature and culture, signaling a slowly developing awareness of the dangers of sun tanning and attention to preventative measures.

See also: Dermatology; Feminism

Further Reading: Hansen, Devon. "Shades of Change: Suntanning and the Twentieth Century American Dream." PhD diss., Boston University, 2007; Peiss, Kathy. *Hope in a Jar: The Making of America's Beauty Culture.* New York: Metropolitan Books, 1998; Segrave, Kerry. *Suntanning in 20th Century America.* Jefferson, NC: McFarland & Company, 2005.

Devon Atchison

TATTOOS

A tattoo is a type of body modification in which dye is injected into the skin to alter the pigment. Tattooing is prominent throughout the world, and there is anthropological evidence of some sort of tattooing for the past 10,000 years. Techniques vary, but the most common form of tattooing involves pricking the skin and inserting ink beneath the dermis. The word tattoo derives from a word in the Samoan language meaning "open wound." The word, like the practice, was introduced to Europe during the 17th and 18th centuries by mariners. The historical meanings of tattoos vary from culture to culture and, increasingly, from individual to individual. Tattoos may be taboo in some cultures and signs of esteem in others. In various cultural groups and historical periods, tattoos have held varying religious, political, and social significance.

Custom tattoo. (Courtesy of James Barber)

Origins in Western Cultures

In human cultures and human history, tattooing practices varied from rubbing ash, plant dyes, and ink into open wounds to create distinctive markings. Archeological evidence suggests that tattooing has been a distinctive part of human culture for at least the past 5,000 years. In Europe, ancient Germanic, Scandinavian, Celtic, and other tribes often used tattooing for religious significance as well as markers of class. The introduction of Christianity in the first century C.E. incorporated the Jewish prohibition against tattoos from Leviticus. The gradual Christianization of Europe in the first millennium C.E. led to the widespread ban of the practice, as well as numerous other cultural elements identified with pre-Christian paganism. During European colonization, from roughly the 16th to the 19th centuries, sailors witnessed tattooing among the cultures they encountered around the world, particularly in Japan, Inuit areas of the Arctic, Australia, and Oceania. As a consequence, European and North American sailors reintroduced the practice to European culture, sometimes even by exhibiting the bodies of the colonized as an exotic or primitive aspect of European fashion. By the 18th century, tattooing had become an established aspect of the commercial economies that appeared in port cities across Europe.

Commercial Tattooing

Because of the introduction of tattoos by sailors and dockworkers, tattoos held strong associations with working-class masculinity in European port cities of the 18th century. As a consequence, tattoos remained socially unacceptable among the burgeoning middle classes as well as the gentry, particularly for women. Nonetheless, tattoos became a common practice in many branches of the military, often as a rite of passage, and many middle- and upper-class European and North American veterans were tattooed during terms of military service. Furthermore, the turn-of-the-century rise of primitivism—an artistic movement marked by the adaptation of cultural elements, including tattoos, from colonized peoples—meant that tattoos held a certain cultural cachet in European and North American fashion. Despite widespread antipathy toward tattoos from the respectable classes, gossip magazines in Europe speculated that large numbers of the gentry, including women, wore tattoos concealed beneath oftentimes elaborate Victorian clothing. Indeed, by the early 20th century, society magazines began to estimate that large numbers of the English gentry had tattoos.

The rise of a commercial culture in the late 19th and early 20th century also led to the proliferation of tattoo parlors based on small business models, helping to fuel demand. Because of the associations with maritime workers, most early tattooing designs followed styles adopted from abroad, such as Maori or Japanese patterns, or signs associated with sailing. Increasingly, practitioners in the 19th and early 20th centuries also began to tattoo religious symbols, references to family and romantic relationships, and insignia from the military. Until the period following World War II, the most common tattoos outside the maritime commercial economy marked service in a specific branch or company of the military. As a result, mass militarization in the first half of the 20th century saw unprecedented numbers of tattoos among young men in the United States. As commercial tattoos gained in popularity in the 20th century, tattoo parlors spread from port cities to most major metropolitan areas in Europe and North America. Unlike tattooing in other cultures, where markings tended to designate specifically shared cultural meanings, commercial tattoo parlors allowed for much greater leeway for individual choice.

New Yorker Samuel O'Reilly patented the first electronic tattoo machine in 1891 as a modification of Thomas Edison's electronic engraving machine. The introduction of electronic tattoo machines in the early 20th century decreased the amount of time, **labor**, and physical discomfort involved in tattooing. Practitioners became skilled technicians and introduced major technological innovations throughout the 20th century, which facilitated the growth of tattooing as a major cosmetic industry. After World War II, tattoos also became strongly associated with urban subcultures. For example, members of organized crime, motorcycle gangs, and gay men who participated in the bondage and sadomasochism subculture each developed their own rituals and distinctive styles that incorporated tattooing as a form of cultural identification and bonding. As the rebel image became an ideal model of masculinity in the 1950s and 1960s—largely influenced by filmic portrayals of bikers and rock and roll musicians—tattoos began to become more and more commonplace. In the 1970s, tattoo artists such as Don Hardy of San Francisco became famous for their designs. In many ways, the artisanal nature of tattooing has established the practice in mainstream fashion and popular culture. Indeed, tattooing has become commonplace across lines of class, race, and gender, even if certain religious taboos remain for some observant Jews, Christians, and Muslims. By the 21st century, tattooing has become the subject of reality television even as the practice has grown into a multibillion dollar a year industry.

Most importantly, the industry has become highly regulated by public health authorities, particularly as epidemiology connected unsanitary tattooing practices and viral infections such as hepatitis and HIV. In the United States, many cities and states have banned the practice altogether during epidemic crises. In New York City, for example, health authorities suspended tattooing in the 1960s due to associations with a hepatitis outbreak and in the late 1980s due to associations with the spread of HIV.

Further Reading: Caplan, Jane, ed. *Written on the Body: The Tattoo in European and American History.* Princeton, NJ: Princeton University Press, 2000; Lautman, Victoria. *The New Tattoo.* New York: Abbeville, 1994; Long, Gayle E., and Leland S. Rickman. "Infectious Complications of Tattoos." *Clinical Infectious Diseases* 18 no. 4 (1994): 610–19.

Christopher A. Mitchell

TEEN MARKET

The teen market refers to a representative group of the population made up of girls and boys aged 14 to 18 years. Tradition has it that the teenager was born of the 1950s rockers and beatniks. However, increasingly America began referring to adolescent youth aged 14 to 18 as teenagers. From its inception, the term *teenager* has been a marketing buzzword embraced by advertisers and manufacturers to reflect a group of newly economically viable adolescents.

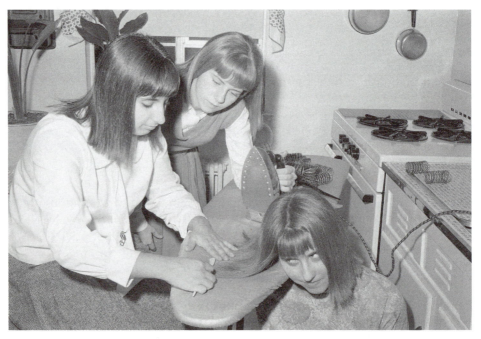

Girl, 14, has her hair ironed straight on an ironing board by her friends in her Glen Oaks, New York, home, 1964. (AP Photo)

History

The concept of teenagers can be traced back to the late 19th century. The difference between adulthood and childhood was made notable during the 1890s with the rise in legislation surrounding youth, such as the Illinois Juvenile Court Act and other government policies designed to contain delinquent youth. The idea was that those now defined as teenagers were more mature than children, but not as mature as adults.

The 1910s saw a growth in cross-media promotion of movie stars and musicians. Those same celebrities were found to influence the styles of the time. Commercial media has represented and influenced the lives of American women since the late 1870s, when the housewife was found to be the model consumer. Young women, or teenagers, were found to be brand loyal and influenced by advertisements and peers. Advertisers and manufacturers were finding new ways to influence the purchase of goods, not just in the short term, but in creating a lifelong symbiotic relationship between the teen and the brand.

Hollywood movies and popular music profoundly shaped the American beauty industry. Hollywood producers offered young women exactly what they wanted. The visuals exposed were premarital sexual encounters, drinking, and a handful of other nontraditional female activities such as nude swimming.

Movie and musical stars influenced purchasing decisions. For example, studies showed that high school and college students attended the movies at least once per week. Therefore, media consumption was highest among teenagers who were free from the full-time workforce and of social and economic responsibilities.

Post-World War I

World War I saw the shipment of young men overseas to the front lines. Young girls were no longer enthralled by the idea of finding a husband and making a life for themselves within the home. Young women entered the workforce to help with the war effort. After World War I, life changed considerably—women had entered the workforce and a new democratic American family was being built. Teenagers started to venture out into the world chaperon-free. As a result of this freedom, teens developed social networks, peer groups, and their own flavor of popular culture different from younger siblings and adults. It was during the post–World War I years that music, movies, and **advertising** campaigns were directed at youth groups.

1920s

By the 1920s, a separate youth culture had emerged with its own fashion, language, and behavior. Youth was extended through government policies and the acceptance into college. Attending high school became the rule rather than the exception. With more time spent outside the home with like-minded peers, female youth were positioned as a special group in society and, as such, were entitled to their own forms of media and activities. The Roaring Twenties produced the first teenage fashion styles pronounced through music and movies: the flapper, a gal about town known for her bobbed hair, short skirts, makeup, and svelte look. The 1920s flapper trend became associated with the selling of soft drinks (mainly Coca-Cola), perfumes, movies, music, and dancing. It was also associated with a particular nonchalant behavior and an uninhibited sexuality. By 1923, female teen styles were being observed, recreated, and displayed in media forms—movies, magazines, radio, advertising, and the music industry. Teens received money from part-time jobs and indulgent parents to support their new teen consumerism (and materialism), and were different from the rest of the adult or child population. They were able to drape themselves in trendy clothing and enjoy extravagant social activities.

1930s

The Great Depression brought the idea of a teenage lifestyle to a halt. With the focus on financial crisis, teenagers found themselves without income from part-time jobs or parents. Government policies requiring children to stay in school until the age of 16 helped further a teen culture outside the home. While major changes in the teen lifestyle occurred, the term *teenager* was itself coined.

World War II and the 1940s

World War II saw a mass exodus of teenage boys to the front lines. Female teens and their mothers were left to pick up the financial burden and enter the workforce yet again. The government policies in place requiring youth to remain in school became relaxed to accommodate their entrance into positions previously held by their older male counterparts. By the 1940s, the teenager had arrived as a new stage in life; teens were still dependent on parents, but were yet a part of a teen market that situated them as special and different.

In September 1944, **Seventeen** magazine was launched as a publication marketed to the teenage girl. This service magazine was designed to offer the teenage girl a place to find her own style and identity and most importantly to spend her share of the $750 million in teen spending capacity. Teenage girls were virtually an untapped market. *Seventeen* launched the ad campaign about Teena, a girl with an allowance, a self-conscious personality, a trendsetter and a trend follower. Teena was savvy. Teena was the average girl who needed to be catered to through magazine advertisements and informed of where to find the latest teenage girl trends within her budget.

The 1940s also represented a period of character-building novels that advised teenage girls on how to act, how to set and achieve their long-term goals, and how to keep a healthy, open family atmosphere to earn more leisure and dating time. The high school girl was more independent and interested in finding her own way to adulthood. She relied on the teen market as a place of inspiration and of friendship, taking all she could from magazines such as *Seventeen*.

The teen market of the 1920s and 1930s focused on upper-class young women, while the 1940s expanded the definition of the teen marketplace to be more inclusive. Items designed for the upper class were becoming basic essentials for the 1940s teenage girl. *Seventeen,* for example, capitalized on white middle-class youth, but by the late 1940s the teen market started shifting to represent working-class teenagers with little intention to follow the character stories and complacent middle-class young women of the early 1940s.

1950s

The 1950s continue to represent the quintessential teenage era. The symbols that identify the teen market are the 1950s generation: *American Bandstand,* poodle skirts, letter sweaters. Rock 'n' roll dominated record players, radio stations, and concert stages. Elvis Presley's hip thrusts sent female teens into a frenzied state of buying Elvis paraphernalia, including concert tickets and posters. Their teen magazines were focused on pop idols like Elvis and Frank Sinatra, offering pinup posters for their bedrooms. The magazines wrote on how to get a boyfriend like Elvis, the characteristics that Elvis sought from his girlfriends and alongside these pages on Elvis's life were the products that could assist girls in meeting Elvis's expectations.

In addition, television became dominant in the family home. With teen programs such as *American Bandstand* and *The Mickey Mouse Club* dominating the set, advertisers consistently aimed products to the teenage girl. Bobby-soxers, as they were often called, often associated the new teen market with white, middle-class ideals, but the new rock 'n' roll music also broadened the definition of the teen market to include advertising to both black and white working-class teens.

1960s to Today

Not much has changed in the teen market since the 1960s—white, middle-class youth still dominate the teen market. The magazines have become more focused on beauty and advertising and on the possibility of finding a heterosexual partner through the purchase of the right products. Teenagers today are younger than ever. Their entrance into a teen society has been dropped to the age of 9. This new generation of youth aged 8 to 12 makes up a new marketing segment called tweens. Research has found that the money afforded to teenage and tween girls is spent on the beauty industry—**cosmetics**, hair dye, fashion, **perfumes and fragrances**, skin care, and hygiene products. The majority of the pages of teen magazines focus on beauty; television shows for teenage girls create dialogue about shopping and the commercials within television programs distinctly focus on beauty efforts for girls.

"Fashion isn't about impressing the rest of the world, it's about impressing ourselves. We dress the way we do because this is how we want to look like, because this is our idea of beautiful, and when someone tries to take that away from us it's taking away our identity and then we're lost forever."

Liza Willett, high school sophomore

Source: Willett, Liza. "What are We Going to Do: Tank Tops and Flip Flops." *The Individual,* August 10, 2009. http://individualink.org/main/index.php/editorials/

Critiques of Emphasis on Beautification

Throughout history, the teen market has been met with criticism and a host of media effects research has focused on its negative aspects. While some researchers believe the teen market is a place where girls build their individuality and create an identity for themselves, others have studied the effects of media consumption on body satisfaction and self-esteem. Media effects research assumes that exposure to the American beauty industry through popular culture has the ability to mentally and physically morph one's ideals, beliefs, behavior, and language, ultimately leading to a homogeneous group of female teens. The teen market is dominated by high-gloss images of fashion trends and thin young models. Researchers believe these images reinforce the traditional tropes of a patriarchal society.

See also: Fashion Magazines; Film; Manufacturing; Tween Market

Further Reading: Driscoll, Catherine. *Girls: Feminine Adolescence in Popular Culture and Cultural Theory.* New York: Columbia University Press, 2002; Fiske, John. *Understanding Popular Culture.* Boston: Unwin Hyman, 1989; Fornas, Johan, and Goran Bolin, eds. *Youth Culture in Late Modernity.* London: SAGE Publications, 1995; Savage, Jon. *Teenage: The Creation of Youth Culture.* New York: Penguin Group, 2007.

Nicolette Cosburn

TONI&GUY

Toni&Guy is an international hairstyling company that consists of salons, hair products, hairdressing academies, an Italian-style café chain, and specialized companies related to the salon business. The Toni&Guy hair design brand reflects current trends in fashion and style, emphasizing training, education, and innovative products. Known for their fashion-forward approach to styling hair, their salons are popular for the latest trends. They reflect marketing trends in the music industry, especially **hip hop**, and place their **hairstyles** within an urban, edgy overall look. Their hairstyles are put into collections and shown at fashion shows. They are also known for creating some popular looks like the *mink,* the *mouvant,* the *la vera,* and the *undercut.* Toni&Guy's commitment to excellence and expertise in the hairdressing industry has made it one of the most recognized hairstyling brands in the world.

History

Toni&Guy was founded in London in 1963 by Italian brothers Toni and Guy Mascolo, with brothers Bruno and Anthony joining later. Their string of salons focused on hair demonstrations, hair fashion shows, and a vision for **branding** the Toni&Guy name. The first hair academy for training stylists opened in 1983. The first salon in the United States opened in Dallas in 1985. Toni&Guy are located in 41 countries and operate 402 salons and 28 educational academies, which train close to 100,000 **hairdressers** annually. They have their own books, magazine, TV station, and professional **hair care products**. Numerous awards and achievements have been won by the company for hairdressing and product excellence.

Products

Toni&Guy sell hair products and have their own makeup line. The TIGI line includes **Bed Head**, Essensuals, and Classic. Catwalk, S-Factor, and Hardcore are popular brands. The signature hair products are divided into three areas: curly, straight, and textured hair. They include shampoos, styling gels, and sculpting tools; makeup products include eye shadows and liners, lipsticks, foundations, and powders. Their brand philosophy is seen in their products: cutting-edge modernity that positions the brand within fashion and style. Unilever purchased TIGI hair products for $411.5 million dollars in 2009.

Charity

The Toni&Guy Charitable Foundation was started by Toni Mascolo in 2003. It is seeking donations to renovate the Toni&Guy ward of the Variety Club Children's Hospital in London. The Terrence Higgins Trust, the United Kingdom's largest HIV charity, is also supported by the foundation. The Fondazione Oasi Regina Degli Angeli in Italy, which houses victims of abuse, is another beneficiary of the Toni&Guy Charitable Foundation.

Further Reading: Davidson, Andrew. "Toni Mascolo: King of the Hairdressers." *Sunday Times* (London), October 26, 2008. http://business.timesonline.co.uk/tol/business/industry_sectors/leisure/article5014558.ece. (Accessed May 4, 2009); King, Ian. "Unilever Gels with Brothers over $411m TIGI Deal." *Times* (London), January 27, 2009. http://www.mediapost.com/publications/?fa=Articles.showArticle&art_aid=99180. (Accessed May 4, 2009).

Corye Perez Beene

TRADE JOURNALS AND PUBLICATIONS

Specialized magazines, newsletters, and trade journals devoted to beauty include product information, reports on the status of the profession, and various beauty association interests and activities—including government lobbying actions, articles on trends, and professional advice for both new practitioners and seasoned entrepreneurs.

Catering to a wide range of beauty industry interests, trade journals may be geared toward specialties within the profession or the broader professional market. Published in both printed and online formats, these trade journals have a long history as being guides for professional development and expansion of the industry. Published by both trade associations, such as the Professional Beauty Association, and private companies such as Creative Age Publishing, trade journals are not geared toward the mass market, or even the **retail** market, but rather toward manufacturers, distributors, spa owners/operators, and entrepreneurs who have broader influence than the corner drug store beauty aisles.

Mass market magazines for the beauty consumer often overlap in appearance and sometimes in content. In the United States, the oldest fashion or ladies' magazines were *Godey's Lady's Book* (1830) and *Peterson's Magazine* (1842). Many current magazines cater to specific audiences, such as **Vogue, Seventeen**, and *Essence,* and with the proliferation of online versions, the content lines between professionally targeted trade journals and mass market beauty magazines is becoming blurred.

Large Publishing Companies

Creative Age Publishing (www.creativeage.com), established in 1971 by Deborah Carver, targets special segments of the beauty industry. The beauty publishing section launched in 1989 is now one of the largest beauty publishers in the nation. Its journals include *Launchpad, DAYSpa,* and *NailPro.*

Launchpad provides up-to-date information on hair, makeup, and fashion trends, and features the launch of new products geared toward salon professionals. It has a circulation of around 60,000.

DAYSpa has been in publication since 1996 and is targeted to day spa owners and managers, providing information on products, service trends, treatments, staffing, client retention, marketing, money management, industry news, and legal issues.

NailPro is the original beauty industry magazine, and was launched by Carver in 1989. With a circulation of 61,000, it is geared towards salon owners and professionals interested in building or maintaining a successful nail care business.

Modern Salon Media is a subsidiary of Vance Publishing (www.vancepublishing.com), founded in 1937, which serves business-to-business markets, including 20 magazines. Modern Salon Media publishes *First Chair Success Guide, Modern Salon,* and *Salon Today.*

First Chair Success Guide is a biannual publication and Web site (www.firstchair.com) geared to new salon and spa professionals. It is designed to help new professionals build a career and connect with effective salon and industry partners.

Modern Salon was first published in February 1924 as *Modern Beauty Shop*. It circulates to 117,000 stylists, salon and spa owners, managers, professional hair colorists, and estheticians in the United States and Canada. It includes articles and features that provide step-by-step education for hairstylists. In 2008, *Modern Salon* became the official publication of America's Beauty Show.

Salon Today Magazine is a monthly for salon and spa owners. It includes business-to-business ideas and strategies for growing businesses and has several special annual issues, including the Salon Today 200 award issue.

The Professional Beauty Association (www.probeauty.com) (PBA) is a nonprofit trade association representing the beauty industry, including manufacturers, distributors, salons, and **spas**. It serves as the source for information on business tools, education, government advocacy, networking, and **trade shows** to improve individual businesses and promote the professionalization of the industry. It publishes approximately 15 guides and reports, both online and in print.

One of its publications is *PBA Progress,* the association's quarterly newsletter, which keeps salon professionals up to date on industry news and the association's activities, including its government advocacy efforts. The journal is subdivided into sections targeting the general membership, distributors/stores, manufacturers/representatives, and salons/**spas**.

Another PBA publication is *National Profile of the Salon Industry,* which annually provides a national profile of the U.S. salon industry based on data from the U.S. Census Bureau and the Department of Labor's Bureau of **Labor** Statistics. First commissioned in 2005, the report includes the number of salon-industry establishments, sales volume, number of employees, weekly hours and wages, workforce diversity, and other relevant industry information.

PBA Beauty Industry Guide is an online resource published jointly by the PBA and Multiview. It provides access to an extensive directory of industry-specific products and services.

Portrait of the U.S. Salon/Spa Industry by Congressional District is a PBA report including salon establishment and employment estimates and the names of the congressional representatives for all 435 congressional districts in the 50 states plus the District of Columbia.

Salon and Day Spa Consumer Trend Report, first published in 2007, reports the findings of studies commissioned by the PBA. It provides information about the target audiences of salons and day spas in the United States and Canada, to help industry professionals target their marketing strategies to identify, recruit, and retain customers.

Questex Media Group (www.questex.com) is a print and digital media publication group catering to business and professionals in 11 different markets, with linkages to marketing clients in the field. In the beauty and wellness market, Questex publishes *American Salon, American Spa Magazine,* and *The Green Book*.

American Salon (www.americansalonmag.com) is the official trade magazine of the National Cosmetology Association. Approximately 130 years old, with a monthly circulation of 123,000, it targets salon owners, managers, and beauty professionals. It addresses trends in hair, nails, skincare, and other treatments.

American Spa Magazine, first published in 1997, has a monthly circulation of 28,000 spa owners, managers, and skincare professionals. It provides information on spa products and services.

The Green Book is an annual comprehensive listing of all hair product and tool manufacturers and distributors, **beauty schools**, professional and trade organizations, and trade shows. Compiled from industry statistics and reports from 21 trade associations, the journal has a circulation of 35,000.

Other popular trade journals are listed below.

The Beauty Industry Report (www.bironline.com) is a monthly newsletter started in 1997 that provides information to management about the professional beauty business, leading companies, and professionals.

Estetica is an international trade publication for the hairdressing industry that comes out four times a year in the United Sates and five in the United Kingdom. It was first published in Italy in 1946 and is now has 24 different editions around the world; it is one of the largest trade magazines. The magazine features the latest hairstyling trends, news and events, technical advice, interviews with international and local professionals and stylists, and product and accessory information.

Hairdressers Journal International (www.hji.co.uk) is one of the oldest trade journals, with a 125-year history. It is a weekly publication containing a range of information including techniques, trends, product news, business news, advice, and job listings. It is published in the United Kingdom by Reed Business Information.

Les Nouvelles Esthetiques, first published in Paris in 1952, is a monthly publication (www.nouvelles-esthetiques.com/) with a worldwide circulation. It is published in 30 countries, including the United States, Brazil, France, Italy, Russia, China, Japan, South Africa, and Australia. It provides the latest information on the spa industry, including skin care, body care, nails, makeup, hair care, therapies, and business management.

Nails Magazine (www.nailsmag.com) is a monthly trade journal for nail professionals and salon owners. It has been published for over 25 years by Bobit Business Media in Torrance, California.

OTC Beauty Magazine is a monthly bilingual (Korean and English) trade publication. It was established in 2002, and is geared toward beauty supply retail store owners, manufacturers, distributors, and industry professionals.

Salon is published monthly in Canada in English and French by Salon Communications, Inc., for hair professionals. *Salon 52* is a weekly online version (www.salon52.ca).

Salon Business magazine (www.salonbusiness.co.uk/index.htm) is published monthly by Salon Gold Publishing in the United Kingdom. It provides industry news, previews the latest products, and offers reviews, editorials, and business advice for U.K. salon owners and professional hairdressers.

Salon Life is the quarterly trade journal published by the National Cosmetology Association (NCA, founded in 1921) for its new members. Its articles address the heath, wealth, and well-being of salon professionals. Accessed through the NCA Web site, http://www.cares.org/, it is supplemented by a blog and video library.

Skin Inc. (www.skininc.com) is intended for day spa, medical spa, and wellness professionals. Published monthly by Allured Business Media, it includes information about spa business solutions, skin science, and spa treatment trends.

Increasingly, trade publications are being made available in online formats. Interactive Web portals are emerging for use by the hairdressing industry as well.

Some of the largest include www.salonchannel.com, www.behindthechair.com, www.beautytech.com, and www.spatrade.com.

See also: Hairdressers; Health and Safety; Internet; Manicurists and Nail Technicians; Manufacturing; Nail Salons; Trade Shows

Further Reading: American Salon. http://www.americansalonmag.com/americansalon/; Gavenas, Mary Lisa. *Color Stories: Behind the Scenes of America's Billion Dollar Beauty Industry*. New York: Simon & Schuster, 2002; Canadian Hairdresser International. http://www.canhair.com; http://www.estetica.co.za/default.asp; Fashion Products. http://www.fashionproducts.com/beauty-tools-publication.html; Salon Today. http://www.salontoday.com/aboutus/tabid/82/Default.aspx; Sherrow, Victoria. *Hair: A Cultural History*. Westport, CT: Greenwood Press, 2006.

Lauren P. Steiner

TRADE SHOWS

Trade shows are designed for beauty industry professionals to energize the workforce, communicate new trends and demonstrate new products, market **packaging** and product lines, and organize industry interests related to consumers and government policies. Trade shows may be huge international and national conferences open only to professional trade associations, regional and local shows catering to a wide range of specialties within the industry, or company conventions specifically targeting their own workforce and product lines.

Professional and Company Shows

Among the largest of trade shows are those that cater to industry professionals only. Premiere Vision, held biannually outside of Paris, is a textile show that has tremendous influence on U.S. beauty companies seeking to determine the upcoming trends and colors. The attendance at this show helps explain the somewhat uniform and similar direction of the product lines developed by the largest beauty manufacturers; they all get their inspiration at the same place. Cosmoprof, which has been held in Italy each April for over 40 years, has an attendance of approximately 100,000 and showcases mostly European suppliers with a side emphasis on packaging. This show attracts those companies with a more international clientele or that have a significant European market share. Cosmoprof has expanded beyond its strictly European locales to Hong Kong, Shanghai, and Las Vegas.

The Health and Beauty America (HBA) Global Expo, launched in 1993, is the largest industry gathering in the United States, held annually in June in New York, and concentrates on U.S.-made products and suppliers. It holds seminars on current industry lobbying efforts, has large packaging displays, and illustrates the intense organization that is a hallmark of the trade associations' efforts to further the interests and profit of the industry. This show is not known for the glitz and glamour frequently associated with other events open to the general public, but concentrates on the no-nonsense side of the industry. The HBA also offers mid-year conferences focusing on specific areas: the marketing, technical, and other aspects of the business.

Specific companies also run their own conferences and seminars in the trade show format that highlight their individual product lines, host training seminars, and usually include inspirational sessions to boost and build enthusiasm in their sales representatives. The top pyramid-structure companies such as **Avon** and **Mary Kay Cosmetics** are especially effective in their use of company gatherings. Avon has had great success through three specific small shows: Grand openings are promotional events for Avon representatives to build their individual business by publicizing new market locations and starting business demonstrations, and also act as localized **focus groups** for representatives to monitor their customers' interests. Boot camps target new representatives with training sessions to help them develop their businesses and to establish sales goals. Beauty bashes focus on demonstrations of how to use Avon **cosmetics**. Mary Kay runs huge seminars for their annual conventions. Their sales force has become so big that the company has split the conventions into five separate gatherings, titled Sapphire, Ruby, Emerald, Pearl, and Diamond. These jewels in Mary Kay's crown heavily emphasize company promotion, inculcation of company philosophy, and building the sisterhood that characterizes their sales force. Their support system for sales representatives has created a strong network of women in control of their own businesses and that illustrate strong diversity across the nation.

Specialty Shows

Specialty shows cater to salon professionals, students, and consumers in specific areas of the beauty industry, such as hair, nails, and product lines. Specialty shows often also target localized markets, such as those held in particular states. They may be combination shows such as Natural Products Expo West, which highlights both beauty and food products made from natural ingredients. The natural cosmetics market is believed to be growing by as much as 20 percent per year. The World Natural Hair Show demonstrates chemical-free hair treatments and special-interest grooming for ethnic customers. The Proud Lady Beauty Show, held in Chicago, was founded by American Health and Beauty Aids Institute in 1981; it represents one of the few American industries mainly founded and fueled by African Americans. The show is the largest in the Midwest dedicated to the needs of the black beauty community of cosmetologists, barbers, and nail technicians.

Beauty industry trade shows, like other professional conferences, demonstrate a clear purpose: building the industry. They are quite effective tools for professional networking, recruitment, the spread of innovation, and marketing. They also illustrate the broad diversity of the industry's interests, customers, and sales force, and the pervasiveness of grooming interests in all walks of life. Trade shows are big business. Because of the organizational skill necessary to run large conventions, beauty trade shows are organized and run by small and large companies that specialize in them; these companies market the shows and publicize their locations, registration, and accommodation information on the World Wide Web.

See also: Internet; Manicurists and Nail Technicians

Further Reading: American Health and Beauty Aids Institute. http://www.ahbai.org; Biz Trade Shows. http://www.biztradeshows.com; Bonika.com. http://www.bonika.com; COSMOPROF. http://www.cosmoprof.com; Gavenas, Mary Lisa. *Color Stories: Behind the Scenes of America's Billion-Dollar Beauty Industry.* New York: Simon & Schuster, 2002; Global Expo. http://www.hbaexpo.com; Klepacki, Laura. *Avon: Building the World's Premier Company for Women.* Hoboken, NJ: John Wiley & Sons, 2005; Malkan, Stacy. *Not Just a Pretty Face: The Ugly Side of the Beauty Industry.* Gabriola Island, BC: New Society Publishers, 2007; HBA Naturalhairshow.com. http://www.naturalhairshow.com.

Christina Ashby-Martin

TWEEN MARKET

Although young girls have long played dress up, paraded around at home in their mother's high heels, and nagged for sweets in grocery store check-out lines, only in the last couple of decades have they constituted a new marketing niche known as tweens. No longer defined in the **advertising** world as a child, yet not quite a teenager, girls in the 8–12 age range have captured the attention of fashion and beauty businesses, seeking brand loyalty from the Y generation. Key to corporate success is the ability to sell teenage sensuality and attitude to preadolescent youth culture. Perhaps most symbolic of this shift is the rise of Bratz dolls, a sassy, street-smart makeover of Barbie that embraces not the cosmopolitan lifestyle of a single girl, but rather teenage moxie. While Barbie has increasingly become the play toy of three and four year olds, a whole host of manufactured teenage icons, ranging from Brittney Spears to Hannah Montana, has been selling everything from toys to fashion. However, tween culture is not simply about marketing bliss. As this newest stage of the lifecycle has become part of the everyday vernacular, tweens have troubled parental and consumer groups who worry that the youngest generation may simply be growing up too fast.

Recent History

In some ways, selling beauty products and stylish clothes to tweens is not so new. Although unimaginable before World War II, baby boomers quickly came into their own as head-to-toe beauty consumers, easily finding everything from clothing stores for teenagers to magazine advice columns. By the late 1980s, a similar pattern began to take shape with a somewhat younger crowd. Shopping had already become an all-American past time, and suburban malls were seen as safe and exciting spaces for young girls to pal around with their peers and to try on the latest fashions. In the 1980s, with conspicuous consumption no longer a taboo, a younger generation of Madonna wannabes saw their embracing of the material girl as a means of empowerment, at least in the realm of consumption. At the same time, there were several factors that seemed to intensify the commercialization of childhood. **Advertising** to children was becoming ubiquitous; even public schools were no longer off-limits to advertisers. New FCC regulations, for example, allowed children's cartoons to be transformed into advertisements designed to sell far more than just breakfast cereal. PBS children's programming, for example, increasingly seemed to be teasers for the fast food and toy industries. The mass marketing of Teletubbies, Strawberry Shortcake, and the Care Bears paved the way for Bratz, Britney Spears, and the Backstreet Boys. In the 1990s, not only was tween consumption undeniable in shopping malls across the country, but market surveys found that tweens had surprising influence over the family expenditures, often outspending their teenage counterparts. Tweens were now a marketing factor to be reckoned with and experts in the fashion industry also relished their sophistication and brand loyalty. For the children of the well-to-do, it is no longer simply Hillary Duff but Louis Vuitton and Juicy Couture that capture their attention.

Parental Concerns

The commercialization of tweens, however, has renewed fears of exploitation. Stores often titillate tweens with pop aesthetics that mix the latest music with girlhood accessories that range from flavored lip gloss to bras. Claire's, Justice for Girls, and Limited Too have had huge success, along with Abercrombie, a once teenage clothing store that has taken flak for marketing thong underwear to 10 year olds. The mixing of Webkinz (stuffed animals with virtual lives) and lingerie has struck many parents as disturbing. Preadolescent girls seem to have adopted more sensual styles of beauty and glamour associated with their teenage counterparts. They casually flip through the pages of *Seventeen*, once marketed to the age implied, and they follow the romances of 20-something actors who play high-schoolers in their favorite Disney movies. Some question whether kids are growing up too quickly thanks to Madison Avenue, or whether this is a recurring cliché that has troubled every generation since Vladimir Nabokov's 1955 novel *Lolita*.

Since tween culture and consumption tend to be gendered female, a familiar and often uncomfortable double standard is easily resurrected. Although boys are also part of the tween market and are susceptible to the influence of the latest trends or complaints about baggy pants, hair length, and violent video games, protecting a girl's virtue remains front and center of both public and private debates. Adding to that discourse are the latest

---

"For many people, the very word 'Lolita' no long denotes Nabokov's fictional twelve-year-old but exists as an all-purpose signifier for the underage sexual temptress. 'Precociously seductive girl' is Webster's definition—and images from the fashion world have given the archetype a visual form."

Susan Bordo, philosopher

Source: Bordo, Susan. *The Male Body: A New Look at Men in Public and in Private*. New York: Farrar, Straus and Giroux, 1999, 300.

scientific findings attempting to understand why American girls begin menstruating at increasingly younger ages. White American girls, on average, begin to menstruate at the age of 10, while for African American, girls the average age is now 9. Whether it is higher fat content in the American diet or the liberal use of hormones in dairy cattle, girlhood seems at risk and marketing to tweens demands balancing childhood dreams with parental anxiety.

Acquiescence

Despite a litany of concerns, marketing to tweens has been a tremendous success, bringing billions of dollars to the beauty industry. To understand what appears to be a parental contradiction, scholars define consumption as a complicated response to an ever-changing social economic landscape. Some have insisted that parental guilt has driven the pace of consumption. Thanks to family speed-ups that typically require mothers and fathers to work outside the home for longer hours, parents turn to shopping and presents as a quick fix when they cannot spend enough time with their children. At the same time, consumption is a process; mothers and daughters still shop, get their hair done, and frequent **nail salons** together. Planning a birthday party at a tween spa facilitates familiar kinds of conversation that in previous years helped organize a backyard get-together or sleepover. It is a shift in **labor** that is most profound. Mothers and fathers may hold the video camera, but in the commercial setting they do not have to provide the entertainment or the food or clean up. Again, the growth of tween culture is bound to larger changes in the political economy that also shape the adult world of work and responsibility. Amid a global recession, tween consumption may face some limits, but a shrinking pocketbook does not mean the end of tween culture. Tweens who have the kind of savvy to distinguish between knock-off and designer brands will more than likely piece together good bargains as they continue to hone their skills in the world of consumption and style.

See also: Teen Market

Further Reading: Hulbert, Ann. "The Way We Live Now: Tween 'R' Us." *New York Times Magazine,* November 28, 2004; Linn, Susan. *Consuming Kids: Protecting Our Children from the Onslaught of Marketing and Advertising.* New York: Anchor Books, 2005; Mitchell, Claudia, and Jacqueline Reid-Walsh, eds. *Seven Going on Seventeen: Tween Studies in the Culture of Girlhood.* New York: Peter Lang Publishing, 2005; Seymour, Lesley Jane. "Tweens 'R' Shoppers." *New York Times,* April 22, 2007; Schor, Juliet. *Born to Buy: The Commercialized Child and the New Consumer Society.* New York: Scribner, 2004.

Julie Willett

UNDERGARMENTS

Undergarments or underwear have been coded as delicates, underthings, intimates unmentionables, and underclothes, suggesting the cultural mystique underpinning these most provocative and private garments. While men's undergarments have remained relatively unchanged throughout most of the 20th century, women's undergarments have shaped and reshaped women's bodies since the dawn of fashion in the Middle Ages.

The influence of fashion on the shaping of women bodies is perhaps no better illustrated than by the case of the merry widow, a foundation garment that was invented for and worn by Lana Turner in the 1952 **film** bearing the same name. The merry widow foundation garment brought a renewed focus to the breasts while cinching the waistline, producing the ideal hour-glass figure popularized during the 1950s. The merry widow exemplifies the intertwined relationship of the American beauty industry, the fashion industry, and the American film industry, sometimes referred to as the beauty/fashion industrial complex.

Model Tyra Banks wears lingerie at the Victoria's Secret fashion show, 2003, in New York. (AP Photo/Louis Lanzano)

Foundation Garments

Foundation garments like the merry widow structured external silhouettes by shaping women's bodies from underneath. The New Look, designed by Christian Dior in 1947, was produced by foundation garments that sharply defined the breasts and narrowed the torso. In an effort to revamp the ideal feminine silhouette after World War II,

Dior is said to have declared that without foundations, there could be no fashion. Hence, according to Dior, women's fashion was dependent on foundation garments to fashion female bodies into desirable silhouettes. Other famous foundation garments include the corset, which until the 1920s reigned as the single most shape-enhancing garment in Western beauty and fashion culture from the 1350s onward.

Corset

The corset produced a myriad of figures throughout the centuries and tended to focus on the waist, although in some cases the hips and even the breasts were dramatically altered by the application of the corset. Fashioned on the Greek *zoné* or girdle, which shaped the lower torso, the corset similarly cinched the waist. Corsets were made of many materials, including steel and iron in the 16th century and heavy linen and whale bone in the 17th century. Whale bone continued to be the main material used in corsets until the 1929 invention of Lastex, a rubber elastic thread developed by the Dunlop Rubber Company. Corsets also came in many shapes, such as the swan-bill corsets of 1895 and the Edwardian s-bend corsets popularized by the Gibson Girl, which shaped women into the letter S. Straighter, longer corsets followed the s-bend corsets and hinted at the end of the Victorian era and the move toward more modern undergarments in the 20th century.

Corselette

The all-in-one undergarment known as the corselette solved the figure dilemmas of 1920s woman who wanted to look like girlish imps in flapper apparel. By flattening the breasts, slimming the hips, and deemphasizing the waist, the corselette created a tubular effect. The ideal feminine flapper form was lithe, with graceful arms, legs, and collarbones all exposed, but this body ideal gave way to the more curvaceous and womanly figure of the 1930s.

In the United States, the silver screen goddesses Marlene Dietrich, Jean Harlow, Mae West, Joan Crawford, and Greta Garbo exemplified fashion's ideal body, and Lastex made undergarments sleeker, more streamlined, and sexier without bumps or bulges. The motion picture industry glamorized and sexualized women's bodies, figures, and silhouettes, and the bust again became a saleable commodity. Warner introduced cup sizing in 1935 and revolutionized the brassiere industry. Separating the breasts became a key focus of brassieres in the 1930s. DuPont's invention of Nylon just before World War II foretold the role technology and **manufacturing** would play in developing stronger but lighter undergarments. The undergarment industry was poised for growth, but wartime production of parachutes, tents, and tarpaulins took precedence, and fashion waited until the war was over.

Foundations after World War II

With the end of World War II, inventions such as Nylon, Lastex, and power net could be brought to bear on women's fashions and figures. Christian Dior's New

Look dominated postwar fashion. Women in the late '40s and '50s embraced the conical shaping of the breast. While technology in the form of foam rubber continued to contribute to bra padding, the use of wire and underwire to achieve conical breast shape intensified. Girdles and bras began to be worn in tandem in the 1950s, creating voluptuous figures.

> "Vital to your figure's future. .the bra and girdle you wear now . . . in the formative teen years. So choose wisely! Get Bobbies by Formfit—a name you can trust. Designed specially for teenagers. Bobby Bras and Britches give you trim, smooth, natural lines you want today. Plus the healthful support, the freedom and comfort your figure needs to develop best for the future!"
>
> *Bobbie by Formfit, Post-World War II advertisement*
>
> Source: Jacobs Brumberg, Joan. *The Body Project: An Intimate History of American Girls.* New York: Random House, 1997. Photo Insert 39.

Girdle

The girdle, a cousin of the corset, is an elasticized or rubberized lightweight corset extending from waist to upper thigh. The girdle arrived along with an increase in women's physical activity; however, the history of girdles has been somewhat tempestuous. They were simultaneously embraced and required in the '40s and '50s because they controlled jiggling and bulging while keeping stockings up. Fabrics such as Lastex, Nylon, and finally DuPont's Lycra in 1959, increased the comfort, construction, and design of girdles during this time. Such new technologies spurred on by the progress of postwar industrialization showed up in an array of styles to fit the varying sizes of waists, thighs, and bottoms.

The end of the '60s and early '70s meant a decline in girdles and a virtual end to their prescribed rituals and practices. Although this garment underwent many changes—from open-bottom, to boy-leg, to panty-girdle; from rubber, to Lastex, to Lycra; from paneled, to single-seamed, to seamless—girdles continued to hold up stockings, flatten tummies, and shape American women for three decades. What happened in the late '60s was a social upheaval, a feminist movement, and a fashion coup. Girls in particular wore dresses and girdles less often, preferring pants, pantyhose, and miniskirts, and many women flirted with the idea of wearing little or no underwear. The '60s also signified a moment of social change in which the rules for everything from fashion to politics were broken. The decline of the girdle was part of this social change.

Breasts and Bras

Like the waist, breasts were constantly subjected to fashion's ideal silhouette. While flapper's breasts were flattened, Hollywood's leading ladies of the 1930s and 1940s allowed breasts to take center stage. Jane Russell's appearance in the first ever cantilever-engineered wire bra in Howard Hughes's then infamous 1943 film, *The Outlaw,* caused quite a stir. Hughes built a bra based on the theory that a bra is nothing more than a suspension bridge for the breasts. Russell has been said to have made a career of her breasts and appeared through the '70s as the spokesmodel for Playtex's 18 Hour Bra. Conical bras were replaced with cantilevered bras and other 1950s female movie stars followed Russell's lead. Marilyn Monroe, Elizabeth Taylor, and Brigitte Bardot all rose to fame as their voluptuous figures projected fashion for the masses.

Like the fate of the girdle, the bra was threatened by dress reform in the late 1960s. Earlier dress reform movements, such as Amelia Bloomer's 1851 promotion of bloomers, Turkish trouser–like pantaloons that gained popularity in the early 1900s when many women took up cycling as a leisure activity, would serve as a reminder of the relationship between women's rights and gender-restricted dress. During the American women's rights movement of the late 1960s and '70s, many women sought to free themselves physically and metaphorically from the trappings of femininity. While bra burning was part of feminist protests and rallies, contrary to popular misconception, there were no bras burned at the 1968 or 1969 Miss America Pageant protests.

However, unlike the girdle, the bra survived the political, social, and cultural upheaval galvanized by the antiwar movement, the gay rights movement, the feminist movement, and the civil rights movement. The fitness craze of the 1970s kept women locked in the cult of the slender body launched by the 1960s model Twiggy. As breasts again came to be the focus of gendered fashion in the late 1980s and 1990s, push-up bras and breast implants rose to ascendancy while tall, narrow-hipped, broad-shouldered supermodels were in vogue.

Thongs

Thong underwear, along with its closely related G-string, was once associated only with the risqué; yet, by the end of the 20th century it quickly became mainstream, but still controversial, fashion. Since the late 1990s, the underwear that literally hides in the crevasses of the body may not show panty lines, but the straps that follow the lines of the hips can be evocatively visible. Indeed, the first controversy to bring the thong to the attention of the masses came in 1998, when President Bill Clinton's affair with Monica Lewinsky received full media exposure, as did her admission of the thong's flirtatious role in her tryst with the president. In 1999, what had been a relatively small share of the undergarment market witnessed a 100 percent increase. In 2000, for example, 40 percent of underpants sold at Victoria's Secret were either thongs or G-strings. But the undergarment was also turning profits at stores that ranged from Macy's to Kmart, suggesting a range of consumers that now considered thongs to be everyday apparel. So popular had undergarments become, that rhythm and blues artist Sisqo realized growing success with his pop chart simply titled "Thong Song." While the 2000 hit song, just like the fashion statement, seemed to be everywhere in American culture, there were some limits with the consuming public. Indeed, in 2002, clothing chain Abercrombie & Fitch faced a backlash after briefly attempting to market thongs to tweens, something that struck a nerve, especially with parents' associations and Christian organizations. Finally, in 2005, the thong was again involved in a political scandal involving another tainted presidency. This time, the sensual garment became not a means to tease but to torture, designed to break Muslim detainees held at Abugraib. Mixing religion and sex, the underwear became a device of female interrogation that left much of the American public questioning military procedure and the ethics of the entire Bush administration. The thong is just one of many undergarments throughout history that has engendered controversy while exposing the contradictions that have given shape to society.

See also: Designers; Feminism; Film

Further Reading: Bressler, Karen W., Karoline Newman, and Gillian Proctor. *A Century of Lingerie*. Edison, NJ: Chartwell Books, 1997; Burns-Ardolino, Wendy. *Jiggle: (Re) Shaping American Women*. Lanham, MD: Lexington, 2007; Dowd, Maureen. "Torture Chicks Gone Wild." *New York Times,* January 30, 2005; Ewing, Elizabeth. *Dress and Undress: A History of Women's Underwear*. New York: Drama Book Specialists, 1978; Farrell-Beck, Jane, and Colleen Gau. *Uplift: The Bra in America*. Philadelphia: University of Pennsylvania Press, 2001; Fields, Jill. *Intimate Affair: Women, Lingerie and Sexuality*. Berkeley: University of California Press, 2007; Hass, Nancy. "Noticed; For Women Great and Small, Briefs Can't Get Much Briefer." *New York Times,* August 30, 2000; Kaufman, Leslie. "National Briefing-Consumers: Dispute over Thongs for Youths." *New York Times,* May 24, 2002. Presley, Ann Beth. "Fifty Years of Change; Societal Attitudes and Women's Fashions, 1900–1950." *The Historian,* Winter 1998, 307–24; Squiers, Carol. "Lingerie: A Brief History." *American Photo,* 6 (1995): 46–57; Steele, Valerie. *The Corset: A Cultural History*. New Haven, CT: Yale University Press, 2001.

Wendy A. Burns-Ardolino

U.S. FOOD AND DRUG ADMINISTRATION

The U.S. Food and Drug Administration (FDA) is a scientific and regulatory agency of the federal government charged with protecting public health through overseeing the safety of consumer products. The FDA has various departments that serve to regulate the beauty industry: Office of **Cosmetics** and Colors, Plastic and Reconstructive Surgery Devices Branch, and Center for Drug Evaluation and Research. The primary laws pertaining to cosmetics marketed in the United States are the Federal Food, Drug, and Cosmetic Act (FD&C Act) and the Fair **Packaging** and Labeling Act (FPLA).

Federal Food, Drug, and Cosmetic Act

The FD&C Act defines products by their intended uses, including cosmetics, drugs, and medical devices. The FDA defines cosmetics as products applied to the human body for cleansing, beautifying, or altering appearance, without affecting the body's structure or function. These include **hair care products**, skin care products, makeup, and perfume. The FDA defines drugs as products intended for the diagnosis, cure, treatment, or prevention of disease by affecting the structure or function of the body. According to the FDA, medical devices such as surgical implants are products that are intended to affect bodily structure or function but do not achieve this through the chemical action of a drug.

A product's intended use as a drug, cosmetic, or medical device is established by claims made in its product labeling, and advertisements. Some products marketed

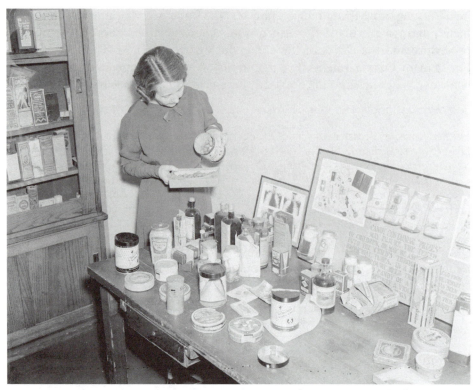

In the 1930s, when members of Congress introduced bills on a new drug and food legislation, they often requested the aid of Ruth Lamb, chief of public relations of the Department of Agriculture Food and Drug Administration. Her display, which she called the "Chamber of Horrors," was composed of before and after pictures, showing how women had been disfigured by the unknowing use of dangerous cosmetics. Death certificates and testimonials are side by side, 1937. (Courtesy of Library of Congress)

as cosmetics may be considered drugs if claims establish their intended use to affect the structure or functions of the human body. For example, hair products that claim to restore hair or prevent hair loss, which may seem to be cosmetic goals, are considered drugs because of the mechanism they use to invigorate hair growth. Other products marketed as cosmetics that are considered drugs include those that eliminate **cellulite** or reduce varicose veins, **acne** medicine, sunscreen, and products designed to treat hair and skin ailments.

When a product has two intended uses, it must comply with the requirements for both cosmetics and drugs. For example, an antidandruff shampoo is considered both a cosmetic and a drug: it is used to treat **dandruff** (and alter the structure of the hair follicle) and clean hair. Other examples of products with both cosmetic and drug applications are fluoride toothpastes, antiperspirant deodorants, and moisturizers or makeup that include sunscreen.

Each type of product is subject to different laws and regulations. Drug companies must register with the FDA and list their various drug products, while cosmetics companies may choose to register under the FDA's Voluntary Cosmetic Registration Program (VCRP). While the FDA reviews and approves drugs and medical devices before they enter the consumer market, cosmetic products and their ingredients are not reviewed before they are publicly available.

Soap is a special category under the FD&C Act. Soap products are considered neither cosmetics nor drugs and are exempt from the FD&C Act. The FDA assigns the term *soap* to a product only when it is labeled and sold exclusively as soap and consists primarily of alkali salt of fatty acids. Cleansing products that include detergents and are intended for cosmetic or health uses are regulated as cosmetics or drugs, respectively.

Fair Packaging and Labeling Act

The Fair Packaging and Labeling Act (FPLA) is designed to protect consumers from potential health hazards that may result from cosmetics and also to guard against deceptive practices by ensuring accurate labeling that can help consumers make informed decisions about their cosmetics and drug purchases. Every label must include an identity statement indicating the nature and use of the product, an accurate statement of the contents, and any applicable safety warnings. Misbranding occurs when a label is false or misleading or fails to properly give required information. Products with two intended uses, such as drugs that have cosmetic purposes, must comply with label regulations for both drug and cosmetic ingredient labels.

Cosmetic Alterations

The FDA reviews products implanted into the body that could have health consequences. These include surgical and nonsurgical cosmetic alterations. Surgical alterations are categorized as medical devices. The FDA regulates the use of silicon implants for breast augmentation; surgical procedures such as stomach flattening, or tummy tucks; and facial **cosmetic surgery**. The FDA also regulates products that affect the structure of the face and could have such health consequences. For example, soft tissue fillers such as Restylane (hyaluronic acid) are approved by the FDA to treat facial wrinkles. The regulation of such treatments typically falls under the FDA's regulation of a drug. For example, Tretinoin (retinoic acid) is not banned from use in cosmetics, but when applied to the skin to treat acne, sun damage, and other skin conditions, it alters the skin's cellular makeup by increasing collagen, and thus the FDA regulates it as a drug. When evaluating such cosmetic treatments, the FDA uses a benefit-to-risk ratio. The FDA may allow greater risk from products intended to treat medical conditions than from those that are approved for cosmetic purposes. While cosmetic products regulated by the FDA are supposed to be extraordinarily safe, some consumer groups criticize the regulation of products as too lenient: for example, since fragrance formulas are considered trade secrets, companies are not required to reveal fragrance ingredients on the label. The FDA bans 10 chemicals from use in cosmetics, but many of the thousand ingredients used in cosmetics are considered toxic. A recent study by the Campaign for Safe Cosmetics found that 15 of 33 popular lipsticks had detectable traces of lead. The FDA claims that it does not tolerate high risk for a drug with a primary use as a cosmetic; nevertheless, what is safe and the degree to which beauty products are taken as seriously as other commodities is continually debated.

FDA Globalization Act

The FDA Globalization Act of 2008 is intended to provide the FDA with the authority to regulate food, cosmetics, drugs, and medical devices in a global marketplace. Under the act, companies must register all cosmetic facilities serving American consumers, and these facilities must report adverse events resulting from the use of their products. Such companies must comply with American **manufacturing** practices, and the FDA may monitor foreign facilities producing food, drugs, devices, and cosmetics for American consumers.

See also: Advertising; Animal Rights; Health and Safety; Organic Trends and Products; Vitamins and Beauty Supplements

Further Reading: The Campaign for Safe Cosmetics. "A Poison Kiss: The Problem of Lead in Lipstick." October 2007. http://www.safecosmetics.org; Miller, Kristen. "Proposed Cosmetic Regulations Act Concerns Small Beauty Industry." *Herald Journal,* September 15, 2008. http://www.herald-journal.com/archives/2008/stories/niemela.good. thymes.html. (Accessed October 20, 2008); Rados, Carlos. "Science Meets Beauty: Using Medicine to Improve Appearances." *FDA Consumer Magazine,* March–April 2004. http://www.fda.gov/FDAC/features/2004/204_beauty.html. (Accessed October 20, 2008); Schmidt, Julie. FDA "Fees Eyed to Boost Food, Drug Safety." *USA Today.* http://www.usatoday.com/money/industries/food/2008-04-17-fda-dingell_N.htm. (Accessed October 20, 2008); U.S. Food and Drug Administration (Center for Safety and Nutrition/Office of Cosmetics and Colors). *Cosmetic Labeling: An Overview.* April 25, 2006. http://www.cfsan.fda.gov/~dms/cos-lab4.html. (Accessed October 20, 2008); U.S. Food and Drug Administration (Center for Safety and Nutrition/Office of Cosmetics and Colors). *Authority over Cosmetics.* March 3, 2005. http://www.cfsan.fda. gov/~dms/cos-206.html. (Accessed October 20, 2008).

Anne Marie Todd

V

VIDAL SASSOON. *SEE* **SASSOON, VIDAL**

VITAMINS AND BEAUTY SUPPLEMENTS

Vitamins are organic compounds essential for growth and activity in small amounts. Dietary supplements are minerals, herbs, and vitamins taken to help increase nutritional intake and daily food consumption. Today, American consumers spend millions of dollars each year on vitamins and supplements that promise everything from sexual vigor and increased body mass to clear complexions and more youthful skin. Indeed, today's hope in a jar is often a magic pill or supplement that touts scientific authority.

Historical Uses

The use of minerals, health supplements, and vitamins stretches back to the herbal remedies of the Sumerian, Chinese, and Greek societies. European apothecaries and Native American medicine men were the predecessors to the modern herbalist. In the late 1880s, experiments were conducted to determine the purpose of vitamins and how they affected the body. Scurvy became one of the first diseases viewed as a vitamin deficiency disease. The lack of a micronutrient was determined to be the cause of scurvy, as physicians realized that the intake of citrus fruits would eliminate the deadly disease's effects. Continued research led medical doctors to conclude that vitamin B deficiency caused the disease known as beriberi. Other vitamins and minerals would soon be discovered and would lead to a compiled list of the essential micronutrients known today, including their effects on the body. By the early 1900s, American businesses began to mass market vitamins and beauty supplements.

During the early 20th century, scientists began to associate vitamins with an array of remarkable cures. The focus was primarily on health concerns compounded by war, poverty, and the effects of modern food processing, which threatened healthy diets. Advertisers and manufacturers, however, quickly played to middle-class consumers, who were unlikely to be suffering from any real deficiencies. Nevertheless, the tenets of scientific motherhood ensured that middle-class female authority was based on running the household and that included understanding nutritional needs such as what vitamins and foods her family needed. From Cream of Wheat breakfast cereal to a daily dose of Squibb's Cod Liver Oil, advertisements in the early 20th century successfully mixed fear with scientific discourse to ensure their products became part of a family's day-to-day consumption.

Manufacturers soon made the leap from concerns over the family's health to personal beauty. In 1937 Vitamins Plus, a mixture that included vitamins, liver extract, and iron, was sold to middle-class female consumers, but this time through the department store cosmetic counter. A month's supply cost a little less than three dollars and, according to the advertisements, it helped a woman's makeup stay in place, her hair to hold a curl, and her nail polish to resist chipping. At the same time, vitamin D soap was advertised to reduce wrinkles, blackheads, and pimples. From cures for **acne** to anti-aging, beauty and health would make profits for vitamins and supplements manufacturers, who continued to insist what they were hawking was scientifically proven. With all the false claims, when in the 1960s and '70s a derivative of vitamin A, retinoic acid, was discovered to be a successful treatment for acne, it was celebrated as an iconic moment. Marketed as Retin-A by Johnson and Johnson, the skin care product was not only effective in diminishing acne, but also helped smooth skin texture and reduce some signs of aging.

Contemporary Significance

Since the 1990s, there has been increasing interest in vitamins and herbal supplements for health and beauty. Hormones and steroids were included in the definition of dietary supplements when potential uses for weight loss (synephrine), regulating sleep function (melatonin), anti-aging (estrogen), and muscle maintenance (creatine) were discovered. Whether the prolonged use of hormones or their derivatives is safe is controversial and debated by scientists; many health studies continue to study them for their beneficial effects. The herbal market extends into natural supplements produced or isolated from plant extracts or herbs. Phytotherapy is highly popular in European markets, and is still practiced among modern apothecaries. In underdeveloped regions, plant derivatives are often the only form of pharmaceutical applications still in use. General Nutrition Center (GNC) is an example of the many nutrition companies that sell health supplements. This company began selling in health food stores and is now commonly found in malls.

Vitamins have found their niche in the diet as cofactors for enzymes and micronutrients that the body cannot make on its own. These include vitamin A, E, K, D, and the B complexes. Most vitamins are provided by bacteria or normal daily food intake. Minerals and metals like zinc and iron are usually only taken in prescribed amounts for deficiencies, but are commonly found in multivitamins. Herbal supplements are commonly used in place or as the source of essential micronutrients. The organic compounds are digested by the body more easily than chemically synthesized drugs. Hormones and proteins are continually used in bodybuilding and for chemical imbalances, such as in stress relief and sleeping aids; they are also used to ease the effects of menopause and stunted growth. Vitamins and supplements can be found for weight loss (green tea, chromium picolinate), skin treatments (vitamin E), antioxidants (CoQ), acne treatment (Echinacea), sexual enhancement (ginseng), and gender-specific treatments (pomegranate extract for prostate care). Honey, cinnamon, eucalyptus, garlic, and ginger are a few of the many food supplements used for skin treatments or herbal medicines. The market has been so diverse and expanded that a health or beauty supplement can be found for practically any condition.

Scientists, however, especially those not promoting their own products, often question the effects of many of the supplements and other products, such as crèmes, sold on the market today and even warn that many of them are unproven or unsafe. For example, excessive amounts of vitamin D and E can be dangerous. One of the more recent trends (although something that was practiced in the ancient world) is the use of healthy foods transformed into miracle creams. Brands such as Origins, for example, boast the creations of Dr. Andrew Weil, who uses mushrooms, ginger, and turmeric, as well as other food stuffs. Similarly tomatoes, spinach, pumpkin, cucumbers, and chili peppers have all found their way into cosmetic lines. How much of a nutrient can be absorbed through the skin is debated. Even more problematic, some medical professionals note that skin allergies are quite common, and foodstuffs applied to the body can often be the culprit. Nevertheless, cosmetic counters, grocery stores, and specialized businesses like GNC provide outlets for many nutrition companies who supply and sell beauty supplements that attempt to blur beauty and health benefits.

See also: Cosmetics; Health and Safety; U.S. Food and Drug Administration

Further Reading: Apple, Rima D. *Vitamania: Vitamins in American Culture*: New Brunswick, NJ: Rutgers University Press, 1996; "More Than One-Third of U.S. Adults Use Complementary and Alternative Medicine, According to New Government Survey." Press release, May 27, 2004. http://www.cdc.gov/nchs/pressroom/04news/adultsmedicine.htm. (Accessed July 17, 2009). Schillinger, Liesl. "Skin Deep: Smart Enough to Understand Your Moisturizer?" *New York Times,* December 22, 2005; Torgovnick, Kate. "Beauty Tools Plucked from Produce Aisles." *New York Times,* December 24, 2008; Valhouli, Christina. "Take 2 and Call Your Cosmetician in the Morning." *New York Times,* May 6, 2005.

McKellan Binkley and Julie Willett

VOGUE

Vogue is the world's preeminent fashion periodical, functioning as an authoritative voice on all things fashion related. Throughout its history, *Vogue* has set the standard for fashion coverage, innovating and changing with the times in a way that has managed to ensure its continued relevance. Over the years, this has meant the inclusion of varying amounts of social and cultural commentary, though the consistent focus of the magazine has always been informed coverage of the fashion world.

Begun in 1892 as a weekly journal intended to appeal to the elite of New York City, it was purchased by Condé Nast in 1909. The original formula for the magazine was a primary focus on coverage of New York's wealthy elite, including some fashion coverage. Nast gradually introduced various changes, including more extensive coverage of Paris and London fashions. Visually, Nast introduced more color to the magazine, including color covers, which quickly placed *Vogue* at the forefront of women's magazines. These innovations altered *Vogue*'s reputation from a magazine targeted specifically at the aristocratic classes to a magazine purveying the possibility of an aristocratic lifestyle for all.

Though Nast's innovations helped push *Vogue* into a prominent position; this prominence has been sustained by a series of charismatic women who served as both editors-in-chief and tastemakers. Edna Woolman Chase (1914–51) guided Vogue through the early years of the 20th century. Jessica Daves (1952–62) is remembered for her interest in incorporating more serious journalism and coverage of the arts. This melding of fashion with more traditionally accepted artistic practices was the first step towards the melding of the fashion and art worlds that is so prevalent in the 21st century.

Vogue's most flamboyant editor, Diana Vreeland (1963–71), was notorious for her vision of fashion as pure escapist fantasy. This view of fashion as excess resulted in her ousting in favor of Grace Mirabella (1971–88), who was considered more responsive to the fashion needs of the 1970s working woman. Anna Wintour (1988–present) not only documents styles, but sets them through her promotion of relatively unknown fashion talent. Wintour has also aligned the magazine with various philanthropic causes, including AIDS activism and the Metropolitan Museum of Art's Costume Institute.

Throughout its history, *Vogue* has been associated with top illustrators and photographers such as Edward Steichen, Cecil Beaton, Lee Miller, Irving Penn, William Klein, David Bailey, Richard Avedon, Steven Meisel, and Georges Lepape. Capturing images of models garbed in the fashions of the moment, these artists have provided the high-quality images that ensure the continued success of the magazine.

In 2008, the *Vogue* empire included 12 international editions, along with the magazine *Teen Vogue*. *Men's Vogue* ceased publication in 2008 due to financial pressures on the parent company. *Vogue* also has a Web page that provides readers with inter-issue updates on the fashion world.

See also: Designers; Fashion Magazines

Further Reading: Angeletti, Norberto, and Alberto Oliva. *In Vogue: The Illustrated History of the World's Most Famous Fashion Magazine*. New York: Rizzoli, 2006; Dwight, Eleanor. *Diana Vreeland*. New York: William Morrow, 2002; Vogue. http://www.style.com/vogue/.

Rachel Harris

W

WALKER, MADAM C. J. (1867–1919)

African American beauty entrepreneur Madam C. J. Walker, originally named Sarah Breedlove, was born in 1867 in Delta, Louisiana, to sharecropper parents who had recently been freed from slavery. Walker experienced considerable hardship in the early years of her life. Orphaned at the age of seven and obliged to live with her older sister and an unkind brother-in-law, Walker married Moses McWilliams when she was 14 and lived with him and their daughter Lelia in Vicksburg, Mississippi, until Moses died in 1888. In 1889, Walker moved to St. Louis and, like many African American women at the time who needed to earn a living while caring for small children, worked as a laundress in her home.

Creating Opportunity

In 1894, Walker married John Davis, and theirs was an unhappy union that had ended in separation by 1903. After more than 10 years of backbreaking **labor** as a washerwoman, Walker was frustrated with the lack of economic opportunity and distressed at how stress and lack of proper care had given her short, brittle hair, bald spots, and a dry scalp. When relating the story of her entry into the hair care industry, Walker claimed that the formula for her Wonderful Hair Grower came to her in a dream; however, it is more likely that she got the idea for creating her own preparation after she began working as an agent for the Poro company of **Annie Turnbo Malone** sometime in 1903. Walker became a successful hairdresser and sales agent in St. Louis, focusing mostly on using shampoos and scalp salves to promote hair health, rather than selling the hair straighteners that were becoming more popular at the time. By 1904, Walker had begun to produce her own products and sell them in person and by mail order. Around this time, Sarah Breedlove McWilliams Davis became Madam C. J. Walker when she married newsman Charles Joseph Walker. (They divorced in 1912.) In 1905, the Walkers moved to Denver, where Madam Walker expanded her business. By 1907, they had moved to Pittsburgh, before finally settling in Indianapolis, the city that would become the Madam C. J. Walker **Manufacturing** Company's permanent headquarters, in 1919.

Selling Her Own Success

Madam Walker's business grew steadily through the 1910s. By 1911 she had built a factory, laboratory, and salon in Indianapolis. The mail order business was

Madam C. J. Walker advertising, 1920. (Courtesy of Library of Congress)

thriving, due in part to a widespread **advertising** campaign in African American newspapers that appealed to racial pride as well as touting the effectiveness of the products. Just as important to the Walker company's success was Madam Walker's effectiveness at recruiting and training African American women across the United States to do hair and sell her products. In promotional literature and in the lectures that she gave to audiences of black women across the country, Walker emphasized her own humble beginnings and told African American women that they, too, could free themselves from ill-paying, unsatisfying, grueling work, and gain financial independence as beauticians and saleswomen. The message was particularly appealing to working-class black women who had few employment options beyond working as laundresses or domestic servants. As the rolls of Walker agents expanded, reaching 10,000 by 1916, the company built Walker **beauty schools** in major cities, provided modest insurance through the

Walker Clubs it sponsored, and even published a company newsletter. Around this time, Walker expanded her product line to include hair oils designed to straighten hair using a heated iron comb. Publicly, Walker deflected African American critics who accused her of promoting a white beauty ideal by downplaying this growing part of her business, emphasizing instead the effectiveness of her products in improving hair health and her own contributions to the African American community as a businesswoman and a philanthropist.

"A HAVEN OF HOPE FOR MILLIONS In these times, when we are so greatly concerned about jobs, it is refreshing to know that here is one company where the color of one's skin in not a bar to employment. Countless women have availed themselves of the ever widening opportunity as Walker agents, and have learned what it means to be economically free and financially independent. MADAM C. J. WALKER'S PREPARATIONS *Made* by Colored People . . . *for* Colored People. . . . By their secret formula, especially conceived for the peculiar texture of Race hair and skin, Mme. C. J. Walker's preparations have renewed the hopes, brightened the future and increased the self respect of our entire Race."

1920s Madam C. J. Walker advertisement

Source: Walker, Susannah. *Style and Status: Selling Beauty to African American Women, 1920–1975.* Lexington: The University Press of Kentucky, 2007, 53.

Quest for Respectability

In spite of her impressive yearly sales (up to six figures by 1916), her army of agents, and her substantial contributions to the YMCA and several African American educational institutions, Walker had a hard time initially gaining respect from black political and business leaders. Educator Booker T. Washington, for example, repeatedly rebuffed her proposals to establish a beauty culture course of study at the Tuskegee Institute and in other contexts expressed disapproval of the beauty industry, going so far as trying to eliminate cosmetic and hair product advertising from newspapers he supported and opposing, for a time, beauty enterprises joining the National Negro Business League (NNBL). In 1912, Madam Walker attended the annual conference of the NNBL, and Washington, who had delivered the keynote address and was presiding over proceedings that included speeches from various successful black business owners, refused to allow her to speak. On the last day of the conference, Walker stood up in the middle of the audience and told her story to enthusiastic applause, but it would be several more years before Washington would publicly recognize Walker's contribution to black enterprise and the financial betterment of African American women.

In 1916, Walker moved to Harlem and devoted herself to building the national reputation and cohesiveness of her business, including hosting a national Walker agent conference in 1917, as well as throwing herself into the social, cultural, and political life of black New York. In these years, Walker became involved in a number of social activist causes, joining the National Association for the Advancement of Colored People, NAACP, participating in anti-lynching campaigns, and speaking out for civil rights during and after World War I. Walker moved into her Irvington-on-Hudson mansion, Villa Lewaro, in 1918. She died on May 25, 1919, from a long-term kidney illness. At her death, she was the wealthiest black woman in the world. Walker's daughter, Lelia, became president of the Madam C. J. Walker Manufacturing Company, which continued to be among the most recognized names in the **African American beauty industry** for many decades.

See also: Beauty Shops; Hair Care Products; Hairdressers; Hair Straightening; Hairstyles

Further Reading: Bundles, A'Lelia. *On Her Own Ground: The Life and Times of Madam C. J. Walker.* New York: Scribner, 2001; Peiss, Kathy. *Hope in a Jar: The Making of America's Beauty Culture.* New York: Metropolitan Books, 1998; Rooks, Noliwe. *Hair Raising: Beauty, Culture, and African American Women.* New Brunswick, NJ: Rutgers University Press, 1996.

Susannah Walker

WAXING

Waxing is a semipermanent hair removal process that pulls hair out by the root. A solution of wax is applied to the skin over the hair and removed in the direction of the hair growth. Hair does not grow back for 2–8 weeks, depending on the area of the body being waxed and the individual's rate of hair growth. Any body hair can be waxed, but the hair should be at least 1/4 inch in length for ease of removal. Women most commonly wax eyebrows, the upper lip, legs, and the bikini area, while men typically wax their back and chest, although the pubic area is becoming increasingly popular for men. Other common areas include arms, toes, armpits, and knuckles.

People have used waxing to remove body hair for thousands of years. Ancient Egyptians, Greeks, Romans, and Turks used waxing or sugaring (a similar process involving a honey emulsion) to remove body hair, especially pubic hair. Modern waxing is performed using the strip wax technique or hard wax. Strip waxing involves spreading a wax solution thinly over the area chosen for hair removal. This wax is typically warm, although cold wax solutions are available. A strip of cloth or paper is pressed over the wax and ripped off quickly, removing both wax and hair from the skin. Hard waxing is similar but instead of using a strip, the wax is allowed to cool and the hardened wax is removed directly from the skin. Hard wax is recommended for sensitive skin and is typically used to remove hair in the bikini area and almost always used for Brazilian waxing.

Brazilian waxing refers to the process of removing most to all of the hair from the genital area, including the inside of the buttocks. A strip of hair above the genitals, sometimes referred to as a *landing strip* is optional. The J. Sisters Salon in New York City, a salon owned by seven Brazilian sisters, first offered the Brazilian wax in the United States in 1994. They named the technique after their home country, where more extreme forms of bikini waxing are common in order to accommodate the smaller bikini bottoms favored by Brazilian women. The practice was quickly popularized by Hollywood celebrities like Gwyneth Paltrow, known to frequent the J. Sisters Salon.

The benefits of waxing include that it removes large amounts of hair at one time and lasts longer than shaving or depilatory creams because it removes hair from the root. Additionally, hair typically grows back softer than with shaving, which can result in rough, coarse stubble. Waxing does have other disadvantages. It can be painful, particularly in sensitive areas like the upper lip or bikini area. The pain generally recedes quickly, however, and most women find that avoiding waxing during menstruation helps decrease the pain. Waxing can be done at home with over-the-counter supplies, but many prefer to have professional aestheticians perform waxing services, particularly for the bikini and facial areas, making the process expensive. Waxing is not recommended for people suffering from diabetes, varicose veins, or poor circulation because of the risk of infection, excessive irritation of the skin, and broken blood vessels. Users of prescription and over-the-counter **acne** medications are also advised to avoid waxing.

See also: Metrosexuals

Further Reading: Bickmore, Helen. *Milady's Hair Removal Techniques: A Comprehensive Manual.* Albany, NY: Milady/Thompson Learning, 2003; *Get Waxing: Your Guide to the World of Waxing.* 2005. http://www.getwaxing.com/index.htm; Valhouli, Christina. "Faster Pussycat, Wax! Wax!: A Brazilian Bikini Wax Changed Gwyneth Paltrow's life; It can Change Yours Too!" September 2, 1999. http://www.salon.com/health/feature/1999/09/03/bikini/index.html.

Kym Neck

WHAT NOT TO WEAR

What Not to Wear (*WNTW*) on The Learning Channel (TLC) is a personal **makeover television** show that teaches unstylish individuals how to dress and style themselves according to middle-class norms. The original *WNTW* is British and began airing on the BBC Two in 2001. The American version of *WNTW* began airing on TLC in 2003 and is now in its sixth season. At this time, *WNTW* is the longest running of any U.S. makeover show.

Participants are nominated for the show by their friends and family, who contend that the participant's lack of style interferes with her career and/or love life. Nearly all of the participants are women; most are white and middle class. In exchange for appearing on *WNTW*, participants receive the expertise and advice of the hosts of the show, Stacy London and Clinton Kelly; a free trip to New York City; a paid hotel stay; and $5,000 with which to buy a new wardrobe.

As in all makeover shows, the participant must be humiliated and broken down. First, the participant watches her secret footage—clips of her going about her ordinary life, unaware that she is being filmed—with Stacy and Clinton. She is humiliated by Stacy and Clinton's critical commentary on her outfits. Stacy and Clinton examine the participant's wardrobe and throw away the clothes deemed bad. The participant then enters the 360-degree mirror, a tiny mirrored room. Here, humiliation and teaching occur at the same time. After the participant views herself in a favorite outfit from all angles in the mirror, the hosts enter and explain why those particular clothes make her look bad.

In *WNTW,* the participant must also learn how to appropriately dress herself. After establishing that the participant does not know how to dress herself, Stacy and Clinton explain the rules the participant should follow in order to make her body look good—long, lean, and curvy—and show her three example outfits. The participant exercises her new knowledge by spending a day alone shopping for a new wardrobe in Manhattan. After watching her struggles, Stacy and Clinton join her on the second day to help her shop.

In the third part of the show, the participant is remade. Nick Arrojo styles and cuts the participant's hair, while Carmindy applies the participant's makeup. The participant then must put her final look together for Stacy and Clinton. The hosts invariably compliment her on both her physical transformation and mastery of the rules. Having passed their test, she returns home to present her new look to her admiring friends and family. In the final scene, the participant reflects on how the makeover has changed her life.

WNTW teaches women to value themselves through their appearance and that they must appropriately care for their appearance in order to move ahead at work and to attract a good (middle-class) man. The show promotes the ideology that you are what you wear; one can improve one's life through dressing well. Ambition requires consumption, much to the profit of the beauty industry.

See also: Makeovers

Further Reading: Heller, Dana, ed. *The Great American Makeover: Television, History, Nation.* New York: Palgrave Macmillan, 2006; Heller, Dana, ed. *Makeover Television: Realities Remodelled.* London: I. B. Tauris, 2007; McRobbie, Angela. "Notes on *What Not to Wear* and Post-Feminist Symbolic Violence." *Sociological Review,* 52 no. 2 (2004): 99–104; Palmer, Gareth. "'The New You': Class and Transformation in Lifestyle Television." In *Understanding Reality Television,* ed. Su Holmes and Deborah Jermyn. New York: Routledge, 2004; Redden, Guy. "Makeover Morality and Consumer Culture." In *Makeover Television: Realities Remodelled,* ed. Dana Heller, pp. 150–64. London: I. B. Tauris, 2007; Roberts, Martin. "The Fashion Police: Governing the Self in What Not to Wear." In *Interrogating Postfeminism: Gender and the Politics of Popular Culture,* ed. Yvonne Tasker, 227–48. Durham, NC: Duke University Press, 2007; Roof, Judith. "Working Gender/ Fading Taxonomies." *Genders,* 44 (2006): 1–33; Sherman, Yael D. "Fashioning Femininity: Clothing the Body and the Self in *What Not to Wear.*" In *Exposing Lifestyle Television: The Big Reveal,* ed. Gareth Palmer, pp. 49–63. Burlington, VT: Ashgate Press, 2008.

Yael D. Sherman

WHITENING, BRIGHTENING, AND BLEACHING

The obsession with all things bright and shiny, from hair to teeth, from face to body, inspired the beauty industry to take on the vintage, sepia tones associated with age and ripeness and offer beauty products and treatments that could offer a clear, blank, and often brightened slate to celebrities and regular consumers alike. Although certainly the plethora of products and treatments available now are more varied and the options more copious, the desire to erase the signs of sun damage, age, wrinkles, spots, lines, and uneven skin tone is not a contemporary phenomenon.

Precedents

In ancient Egypt, Cleopatra was known to use aloe to heal and nurture her face from the African sun and to enjoy milk baths because the lactic acid exfoliated and softened her skin. In ancient China, fair, porcelain skin was a sign of beauty and elegance and perhaps more importantly, of social status—only the wealthy and the aristocratic could stay indoors protecting their complexions while peasants labored under the sun. Chinese women would swallow remedies of ground pearl from seashells to maintain their pale skin tones. In Japan, nightingale droppings were originally used to remove stains from kimonos and other silk garments. Its use was so effective that soon geishas began using the droppings to remove their heavy makeup and to brighten their complexions. (Nightingale droppings have experienced a revival. Cutting-edge **spas** such as Ten Thousand Waves Japanese Spa and Resort in Santa Fe, New Mexico, Shikuza New York Day Spa and London's Hari's Salonare now offering nightingale facials that incorporate dried, pulverized, and ultraviolet-light-sanitized droppings.) Queen Elizabeth I protected her pale skin at all costs, wearing hats in the sun and using bright red dyes on her cheeks and lips to emphasize the lightness of her complexion. Elizabethan women attempted to emulate the queen by using her favorite mixture of white lead and vinegar, known as ceruse, to lighten their skin; this was a highly poisonous but aesthetically effective concoction. In the 19th century, the Brothers Grimm told of queens who longed for baby princesses, sighing, "Oh, how I wish that I had a daughter that had skin white as snow, lips red as blood, and hair black as ebony." Even in the golden age of cinema, movie stars and ingénues had the smoothest of complexions, the palest of skins—from Marlene Dietrich to Judy Garland, from Marilyn Monroe to Audrey Hepburn. Marlene Dietrich even sold her secret of achieving beautiful skin, becoming one of the first modern-day celebrities to endorse beauty products—Lux Soap and Woodbury Cold Cream.

Race in the 20th Century

The obsession with light or lighter skin and the social advantages that came from having a paler complexion played a dramatic role in the development of African American aesthetic sensibilities. The legend of the turn of the 20th century's *paper bag parties,* in which only African Americans with skin color at least as light as a paper bag were admitted, still permeates and perpetuates the hierarchy of complexion. The idea of *passing,* when light-skinned African Americans could pass as white and hide their ethnic/racial identities and hence move more freely within the American social and class structures, seemed to support the caste system within American society. What were seen as stereotypically African American physical traits, from skin tone to hair type, from body shapes to voice timbres, were characterized as undesirable, unattractive, and unpleasant. Advertisements played on racial fears and prejudices. Products promised "Lighter skin makes you more popular," and "Quickly, the dark, ugly tones of the skin give way, shade by shade, to light-toned beauty." It has been argued that although some African American women may have used the creams and concoctions that promised to mask or mute or mutate the objectionable dark tone to a more agreeable, paler shade, the color of their complexion was not enough to guarantee these African American women entry into a more equitable, less prejudiced world. Most recently, L'Oréal Feria was accused of having lightened the complexion of African American singer/actress Beyoncé in a hair color ad to make her more accessible and more palatable to a wider public. L'Oréal Feria has denied this claim vehemently.

> "Will turn the skin of a black or brown person four of five shades lighter, and a mulatto person perfectly white. In forty-eight hours a shade or two will be noticeable."
>
> *"Black Skin Remover" 1903 Advertisement, Crane and Co. of Richmond, Virginia.*
>
> Source: Peiss, Kathy. *Hope in a Jar: The Making of America's Beauty Culture.* New York: Metropolitan Books, 1998, 42

Global Trends

Although the post–World War II world soon became enamored with the sun-kissed skin associated with the jet set, beach vacations, and the healthy glow of a tan, and although the beauty industry concentrated its efforts on bronzing powders, **tanning** liquids, and the tanning bed, the whitening/brightening/bleaching world was still in full swing in the Asian markets. And with the concern over skin cancer and melanoma, and sun damage and aging, more emphasis has been placed on the marketing and researching of whitening and brightening products in the 1990s and the 2000s. Most major **cosmetics** firms, especially if they have an interest in the East Asian markets, have recently invested their capital in researching and creating products for the whitening and brightening of the face. Although most of these products are marketed as offering whitening capabilities to Asian clients, in the Caucasian markets, these same products are relabeled as brightening. The racial overtones of these words have forced industry executives to sensitize their marketing campaigns in more multicultural areas, where the term whitening is perceived as being more offensive and demeaning.

Skin-lightening creams are among the most popular cosmetic and skin care product purchases in East Asia. Asian beauty companies have been producing products that are geared toward the Asian market and their desire for paler, fairer complexions since the 1970s. Shiseido, SK-II, and Kanebo have all been on the cutting edge of research in anti-aging, skin-brightening, complexion-lightening products and procedures. These products boast such names as Blanc Expert, White-Plus, WhiteLight, Future White Day, Blanc Purete, Fine Fairness, Active White, White Perfect, and Snow UV.

Health Concerns

In their desire to look like the pale Asian models in magazines and billboards, women in Hong Kong stormed the department store beauty counters to purchase two new whitening creams in 2002. Soon afterward, a news report warned that these two creams had between 9,000 and 65,000 times the level of mercury content recommended for safe usage. More than a thousand women were on the phones to health department hotlines. Despite these health alerts, the market is enormous and is growing as the rest of the world becomes increasingly interested in whitening and brightening as anti-aging treatments.

Whitening and brightening products are offered by both department store and drugstore brands—from Shiseido, Christian Dior, **Elizabeth Arden**, and Lancôme to Maybelline, L'Oréal, and Boots. The most popular ingredient in whitening products is hydroquinone, a topical medication that has been used to reduce the discoloration of the skin. It is banned in the European Union. Serious medical debates about the safeness and side effects of the chemical are still raging today. Other products that have been touted as having brightening effects are soy, vitamin A, alpha and beta hydroxyl acid products, vitamin C, and peptides. Treatments that were once reserved for dermatologists and special skin clinics, such as glycolic acid peels, are now widely available.

Cosmetic Dentistry

Whitening, brightening, and bleaching products have also found a niche in cosmetic dental work. Tooth whitening is one of the most popular dental treatments available today. The bleaching of teeth, which can involve using oxidizing agents such as hydrogen peroxide or carbamide peroxide, penetrates the enamel of the tooth and helps to oxidize the stains. While originally only available in dentists' offices, tooth whitening has become an at-home endeavor as well. Toothpaste companies offer whitening toothpastes and mouthwashes. Other companies offer do-it-yourself kits of strips, mouth guards, and paint-on liquids, such as those available from Crest White Strips and Go Smile. The rise of cosmetic dentistry has even produced a few celebrities. The featured dentist on ABC's *Extreme Makeover,* Bill Dorfman, has appeared on *The Jay Leno Show, The Today Show, Entertainment Tonight,* and *EXTRA.* Actress Terri Hatcher even noted that she had a crush on him. VH1's Best Week Ever called Dr. Dorfman the Dentist to the Stars after pop star Britney Spears reportedly rushed to his office to have an emergency tooth whitening procedure in 2008.

See also: Anti-Aging Products and Techniques; Cosmetics; Endorsements of Products, Celebrity; Film; Health and Safety; Makeover Television

Further Reading: Adrian, Bonnine. *Framing the Bride: Globalizing Beauty and Romance in Taiwan's Bridal Industry.* Berkeley: University of California, 2003; Eco, Umberto, ed. *History of Beauty.* New York: Rizzoli, 2004; Hunter, Margaret L. *Race, Gender, and the Politics of Skin Tone.* New York: Routledge, 2005; Miller, Laura. *Beauty Up: Exploring Contemporary Japanese Body Aesthetics.* Berkeley: University of California, 2006; Mire, Amina. "Pigmentation and Empire: The Emerging Skin-Whitening Industry." http://www.counterpunch.org/mire07282005.html; Mire, Amina. "Skin-Bleaching: Poison, Beauty, Power, and the Politics of the Colour Line." *Resources for Feminist Research,* 28 no. 3/4 (2001: 13–38); O'Farrell, Mary Ann. *Telling Complexions: The Nineteenth Century*

Novel and the Blush. Durham, NC: Duke University Press, 1997; Peiss, Kathy. *Hope in a Jar: The Making of America's Beauty Culture.* New York: Metropolitan Books1998; Phillips, Alberta. "Let the Truth Out of the Bag." http://www.statesman.com/opinion/content/editorial/stories/02/08/0208phillips_edit.html; Walker, Susannah. *Style and Status: Selling Beauty to African American Women, 1920–1975.* Lexington: University Press of Kentucky, 2007.

Aliza S. Wong

WIGS AND HAIRPIECES

Wigs have been worn by both men and women since ancient times. Wigs are worn for a variety of different reasons, including protection, adornment, disguise, ritual, social or professional status, health or hygiene, and religious strictures. Wigs can be used to change hair color as well as make dramatic shifts in hairstyle from short to long and vice versa. The word *wig* is a shortening of the 17th century word *periwig*, which in the Anglicized version of the older French word *perruque*. The function of a wig is to cover the head with natural or synthetic hair fibers in an approximation of hair that grows out of the scalp. The intention might be to approximate or augment a natural head of hair or to create a completely new and fantastical look.

Precedents

Wigs in ancient Egypt were worn at first for hygienic reasons. Heads of men, women, and children were shaved to protect against lice and other insect infestations. Wigs made from human or animal hair were also worn as adornment and as protection from the sun. The ancient peoples of Greece, Japan, China, and the Americas wore wigs for ritual or theatrical purposes. In Rome, a fondness for blonde and red hair created a fashion for wigs of these colors that continued through the Renaissance. Throughout the 17th and 18th centuries, wigs were a mark of status for both men and women, often created as towering confections powdered white and heavily decorated. Although wig size and interest declined in the 19th century, some members of British society still wore wigs into the 21st century, most notably attorneys and judges.

Contemporary Trends

In today's fashion, wigs are not necessarily seen as a mark of rank or profession, but as an ordinary part of fashion. Women and men of all ages and backgrounds wear wigs for fun, to liven up their looks. Others require wigs to cover **baldness** or thinning hair caused by disease or genetics. Patients undergoing chemotherapy usually lose their hair and wigs can bring a sense of normalcy back into their lives. This is especially important for children who have lost their hair, and many charities specialize in making wigs to fit their small heads.

Styles and Materials

Wigs for all sizes can be made in a variety of ways. The most natural-looking method is to use real human hair attached individually or in small groups onto a mesh base. These wigs are also the most costly. Human hair can also be sewn to strips called wefts and arranged in horizontal rows around a mesh cap. This gives the appearance of a balanced head of hair, but the style cannot be altered easily as the gaps between each row would show through. Human hair wigs require a great deal of attention and special cleaning and care to retain their **natural look**. Wigs meant to be worn daily must be cleaned at least once every two weeks. Hair that is removed from the head will start to dry out and break down, and although human hair wigs have a long life, they must be replaced after long-term wearing.

Hair of European origin is the most expensive and most prized for wig making because of the wide range of colors and textures available. Hair from India is one of the leading types available today because it is plentiful and relatively inexpensive, but there are limits to the color and texture and it can be difficult to work with.

Synthetic hair dominates the wig market today. Nylon and acetate are used to create realistic-looking hair fibers, as is Dynel, a synthetic fiber developed specifically for wig making. Occasionally, animal hair such as horse, sheep, or yak is blended with synthetic fibers to create a more realistic look. Synthetic wigs are much less expensive and easier to care for than natural hair wigs, but they have their drawbacks. Synthetic hair is much more difficult to style, as certain **hair care products** might cause a chemical reaction that can damage the color or texture of the wig. Synthetic hair is also flammable and much less tolerant of heat than natural hair; it can easily be melted with a curling iron or blow-dryer.

The wig market also includes a wide variety of smaller hairpieces such as wiglets, falls, pastiches, and novelty add-ons connected to combs or clips. Wigs for men are also quite common and known toupees. Regardless of their availability, wigs and toupees remain largely taboo, and individuals attempting to cover up hair loss are often ridiculed.

Further Reading: Love, Toni. *The World of Wigs, Weaves, and Extensions.* Albany, NY: Milady/Thompson Learning, 2002; Sherrow, Victoria. *The Encyclopedia of Hair: A Cultural History.* Westport, CT: Greenwood Press, 2006.

Sara M. Harvey

WOLF, NAOMI (1962–)

Naomi Wolf is an influential feminist and is considered a founder of third-wave **feminism**. Wolf was born in San Francisco and attended Yale University, earning a bachelor of arts degree in English literature (1984); she then spent a term as a Rhodes scholar at Oxford (1985 to 1987). She garnered international acclaim in 1991 with the publication of *The Beauty Myth,* now considered a classic work of American feminism.

Writer Naomi Wolf, 2003. (AP Photo/Jennifer Graylock)

In *The Beauty Myth,* Wolf argued that the goals of the women's movement were co-opted by the beauty and fashion industry. Wolf contended that when women made advances in science, economics, and politics, they threatened the Western social order that positioned women as lesser beings. The result was the creation of the beauty myth that maintained women's oppression by imprisoning them in an unrealistic and unattainable body of flawless beauty. According to Wolf, the beauty myth was a socially constructed system that physically and psychologically punished women for their inability to maintain this beauty standard. Through the beauty myth, the patriarchal system replicated its own hegemony by creating beauty-based norms in several aspects of women's lives: work, sex, violence, hunger, and religion. Wolf's work also provided numerous statistics demonstrating the danger of the beauty myth, as well as a historical overview of the beauty myth and its origins. *The Beauty Myth* was a call to dismantle the beauty myth by refusing to follow its impossible standards. "What I support in this book, " Wolf wrote in the 10th anniversary edition, "is a woman's right to choose what she wants to look like and what she wants to be, rather than observing what market forces and a multibillion dollar advertising industry dictate" (2).

Wolf followed *The Beauty Myth* with *Fire with Fire,* a book considered the first publication of third-wave feminism. *Fire with Fire* presented Wolf's argument that feminism in the 1960s and 1970s hinged on a victim mentality, and it advised women of the 1990s to embrace their will to power by taking control over media representations of women. Wolf continued to build her reputation as a leading feminist scholar and activist with *Promiscuities* (1998), which argued that stories of female adolescent sexuality were suppressed by patriarchy. In *Promiscuities*, Wolf encouraged women to regain authority over their own sexuality. Wolf also became heavily involved in American mainstream politics in the late 1990s. She served as an advisor to President Bill Clinton during his 1996 reelection campaign and worked on Al Gore's bid for the presidency in 2000. Wolf continued to write as well: *Misconceptions* (2001) advocated a return to midwifery, and her most recent books, *The End of America* (2007) and *Give Me Liberty* (2008) are handbooks for political change. Wolf continues to be an influential and controversial voice of American feminism, with regularly published essays and a blog on www.huffingtonpost.com. Her greatest contribution to date, however, is *The Beauty Myth*, which remains one of the most influential treatises on the beauty industry ever written.

Further Reading: Wolf, Naomi. *The Beauty Myth: How Images of Beauty are Used against Women*. New York: Harper, 1991; Wolf, Naomi. *The End of America: A Letter of Warning to a Young Patriot*. New York: Chelsea Green Publishing, 2007; Wolf, Naomi. *Fire with Fire*. New York: Ballantine, 1994; Wolf, Naomi. *Give Me Liberty: A Handbook for American Revolutionaries*. New York: Simon & Schuster, 2008; Wolf, Naomi. *Misconceptions: Truth, Lies, and the Unexpected on the Journey to Motherhood*. New York: Anchor, 2001; Wolf, Naomi. *Promiscuities: The Secret Struggle for Womanhood*. New York: Ballantine Books, 1998; Wolf, Naomi. *The Tree House: Eccentric Wisdom from My Father on How to Live, Love, and See*. New York: Simon & Schuster, 2006; Wolf, Naomi. Blog on *The Huffington Post*. http://www.huffingtonpost.com/naomi-wolf.

Amber R. Clifford

Appendix 1: Percentage of U.S. Beauty Industry Employees by Occupation, Sex, Race, and Ethnicity, 2007

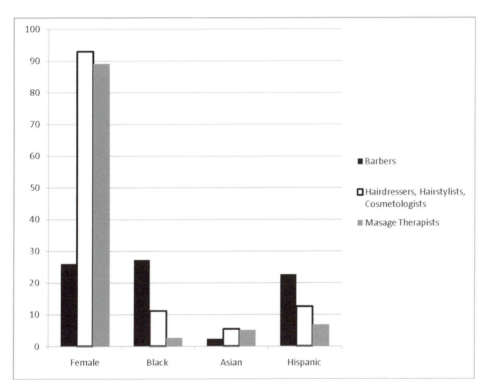

Source: Data from U.S. Bureau of Labor Statistics, "Employment and Earnings Online," January 2008.

Appendix 2: Number of Salon-Type Establishments in the United States with Payroll Employees

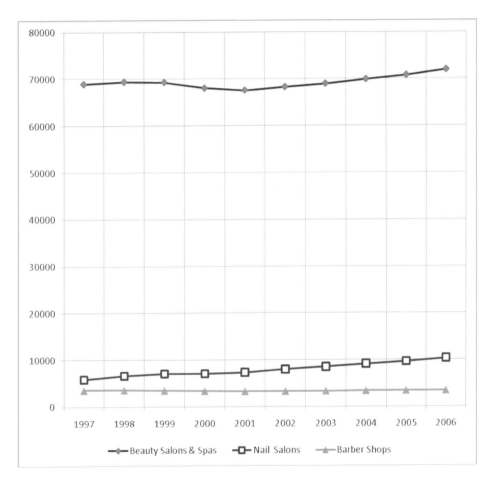

Source: Compiled from data from Professional Beauty Association, "2008 National Profile of the Salon Industry."

Selected Bibliography

Books

Adrian, Bonnine. *Framing the Bride: Globalizing Beauty and Romance in Taiwan's Bridal Industry.* Berkeley: University of California Press, 2003.

Allen, Margaret. *Selling Dreams: Inside the Beauty Business.* New York: Simon & Schuster, 1981.

Allman, Jean. *Fashioning Africa: Power and the Politics of Dress.* Bloomington: Indiana University Press, 2004.

Alvarez, Julia. *Once Upon a Quinceanera: Coming of Age in the USA.* New York: Viking Adult Press, 2007.

Angeletti, Norberto, and Alberto Oliva. *In Vogue: The Illustrated History of the World's Most Famous Fashion Magazine.* New York: Rizzoli, 2006.

Asante, M. K. *It's Bigger than Hip Hop: The Rise of the Post-Hip-Hop Generation.* New York: St. Martin's, 2008.

Ash, Mary Kay. *Mary Kay.* 1st ed. New York: Harper and Row, 1981.

Aucoin, Kevyn. *Face Forward.* Boston: Little, Brown and Company, 2001.

Aucoin, Kevyn. *Making Faces.* Boston: Little, Brown and Company, 1999.

Banet-Weiser, Sarah. *The Most Beautiful Girl in the World: Beauty Pageants and National Identity.* Berkeley: University of California Press, 1999.

Banks, Ingrid. *Hair Matters, Beauty, Power, and Black Women's Consciousness.* New York: New York University Press, 2000.

Banner, Lois. *American Beauty.* New York: Knopf, 1983.

Basten, Fred E. *Max Factor: The Man Who Changed the Faces of the World.* Baltimore, MD: Arcade Press. 2009.

Basten, Fred E., Robert Salvatore, and Paul Kaufman. *Max Factor's Hollywood: Glamour, Movies, Make-Up.* Toronto: Stoddart, 1995.

Baumgardner, Jennifer, and Amy Richards. *Manifesta: Young Women, Feminism, and the Future.* New York: Farrar, Straus and Giroux, 2000.

Benson, Susan Porter. *Counter Cultures: Saleswomen, Managers, Customers in American Department Stores, 1890–1940.* Urbana: University of Illinois Press, 1986.

Benwell, Bethan. *Masculinity and Men's Lifestyle Magazines.* Malden, MA: Blackwell, 2003.

Berry, Bonnie. *Beauty Bias: Discrimination and Social Power.* Santa Barbara, CA: Praeger, 2007.

Berry, Sarah. *Screen Style: Fashion and Femininity in 1930s Hollywood.* Minneapolis: University of Minnesota Press, 2000.

Biggart, Nicole Woolsey. *Charismatic Capitalism: Direct Selling Organizations in America.* Chicago: University of Chicago Press, 1989.

Black, Paula. *The Beauty Industry: Gender, Culture, Pleasure.* New York: Routledge, 2004.

Blackwelder, Julia Kirk. *Styling Jim Crow: African American Beauty Training during Segregation.* College Station: Texas A&M Press, 2003.

Bordo, Susan. *The Male Body: A New Look at Men in Public and in Private.* New York: Farrar, Straus and Giroux, 1999.

Bordo, Susan. *Unbearable Weight: Feminism, Western Culture, and the Body.* Berkeley: University of California Press, 1993.

Bressler, Karen W., Karoline Newman, and Gillian Proctor. *A Century of Lingerie.* Edison, NJ: Chartwell Books, 1997.

Bristol, Doug. *Knights of the Razor: Black Barbers in Slavery and Freedom.* Baltimore, MD: Johns Hopkins University Press, 2009.

Brown, Bobbi. *Bobbi Brown Living Beauty.* New York: Springboard, 2007.

Brown, Patty, and Janett Rice. *Ready-to-Wear Apparel Analysis.* Upper Saddle River, NJ: Pearson/Prentice Hall, 2001.

Brumberg, Joan Jacobs. *The Body Project: An Intimate History of American Girls.* New York: Vintage, 1997.

Brumberg, Joan Jacobs. *Fasting Girls: The History of Anorexia Nervosa.* New York: Vintage, 2000.

Bryer, Robin. *The History of Hair: Fashion and Fantasy down the Age.* London: Philip Wilson Publishers, 2003.

Bundles, A'Lelia. *On Her Own Ground: The Life and Times of Madam C. J. Walker.* New York: Scribner, 2001.

Burke, Timothy. *Lifebuoy Men, Lux Women: Commodification, Consumption, and Cleanliness in Modern Zimbabwe.* Durham: University of North Carolina Press, 1996.

Burns-Ardolino, Wendy. *Jiggle: (Re)Shaping American Women.* Lanham, MD: Lexington, 2007.

Byrd, Ayana D., and Lori L. Tharps. *Hair Story: Untangling the Roots of Black Hair in America.* New York: St. Martin's Griffin, 2001.

Calvert, Robert Noah. *The History of Massage.* Rochester, Vermont: Healing Arts Press, 2002.

Caplan, Jane, ed. *Written on the Body: The Tattoo in European and American History.* Princeton, NJ: Princeton University Press, 2000.

Chang, Jeff, and D. J. Kool Herc. *Can't Stop Won't Stop: A History of the Hip-Hop Generation.* New York: Picador, 2005.

Chauncey, George. *Gay New York: Gender, Urban Culture, and the Making of the Gay Male World, 1890–1940.* New York: Basic Books, 1994.

Chenoune, Farid. *Hidden Underneath: A History of Lingerie.* New York: Assouline Publishing, 2005.

Coad, David. *Metrosexual: Gender, Sexuality, and Sport.* Albany: State University of New York Press, 2008.

Cole, Louise, and Giles Vichers-Jones. *Professional Modeling.* London: New Holland Press, 2009.

Condry, Ian. *HIP-HOP Japan.* Durham, NC: Duke University Press, 2006.

Cook, Alan, ed. *Skin Disorders Sourcebook.* Detroit, MI: Omnigraphics, 1997.

Corner, John, and Dick Pels. *Media and the Restyling of Politics: Consumerism, Celebrity and Cynicism.* Thousand Oaks, CA: Sage Publications, 2003.

Corson, Richard. *Fashions in Hair: The First Five Thousand Years.* 3rd ed. London: Peter Owen Ltd., 2000.

Cox, Caroline, and Lee Widdows. *Hair and Fashion.* London: Victoria and Albert Museum, 2005.

Craig, Maxine B. *Ain't I a Beauty Queen? Black Women, Beauty, and the Politics of Race.* New York: Oxford University Press, 2002.

Crewe, Ben. *Representing Men: Cultural Production and Producers in the Men's Magazine Market.* Oxford: Berg, 2003.

Davis, Fred. *Fashion, Culture, and Identity.* Chicago: University of Chicago Press, 1992.

De La Haye, Amy, and Shelley Tobin. *Chanel: The Couturiere at Work.* New York: Overlook Press, 1994.

De Marly, Diana. *Worth: Father of Haute Couture*. 2nd ed. New York: Holmes & Meier, 1990.

Deslandres, Yvonne. *Poiret: Paul Poiret, 1879–1944*. New York: Rizzoli, 1987.

Driscoll, Catherine. *Girls: Feminine Adolescence in Popular Culture and Cultural Theory*. New York: Columbia University Press, 2002.

Eakin, Julie Sinclair. *Salons and Spas: The Architecture of Beauty*. Beverly, MA: Rockport Publishers, 2007.

Eco, Umberto, ed. *History of Beauty*. New York: Rizzoli, 2004.

Ehrenreich, Barbara. *Nickel and Dimed: On (Not) Getting By in America*. New York: Holt, 2002.

Elsner, Peter, and Howard I. Maibach, eds. *Cosmeceuticals and Active Cosmetics: Drugs versus Cosmetics*. 2nd ed. Boca Raton, FL: Taylor & Francis, 2005.

Engasser, Pat, John Gray, and Steve Sheil. *Dandruff and the Sensitive Scalp*. London: Royal Society of Medicine, 2004.

Enstad, Nan. *Ladies of Labor, Girls of Adventure: Working Women, Popular Culture, and Labor Politics at the Turn of the Twentieth Century*. New York: Columbia University Press 1999.

Entwistle, Joanne. *The Fashioned Body: Fashion, Dress and Modern Social Theory*. Malden, MA: Blackwell Publishers, 2000.

Escoffery, David S. *How Real Is Reality TV? The Role of Representation in Reality Television*. Jefferson, NC: McFarland, 2006.

Espiritu, Yen Le. *Asian American Women and Men: Labor, Laws, and Love*. New York: Rowman and Littlefield, 2007.

Ewing, Elizabeth. *Dress and Undress: A History of Women's Underwear*. New York: Drama Book Specialists, 1978.

Farlow, Christine H. *Dying to Look Good: The Disturbing Truth about What's Really in Your Cosmetics, Toiletries and Personal Care Products*. Escondido, CA: Kiss for Health Publishing, 2000.

Farrell-Beck, Jane, and Colleen Gau. *Uplift: The Bra in America*. Philadelphia: University of Pennsylvania Press, 2001.

Fields, Jill. *Intimate Affair: Women, Lingerie and Sexuality*. Berkeley: University of California Press, 2007.

Fishman, Diane, and Marsha Powell. *Vidal Sassoon: Fifty Years Ahead*. New York: Rizzoli, 1993.

Flyin, Natalia. *Blonde Like Me: The Roots of the Blonde Myth in Our Culture*. New York: Simon & Schuster, 2000.

Freedman, Rita. *Beauty Bound*. Lexington, MA: Lexington, 1986.

Frieda, John. *Hair Care*. Seattle, WA: Bay Books, 1983.

Frieda, John. *John Frieda Precision Styling System*. Darien, CT: Zotos International, 1989.

Friedan, Betty. *The Feminine Mystique*. New York: Dell, 1963.

Furman, Frieda Ke. *Facing the Mirror: Older Women and Beauty Shop Culture*. New York: Routledge, 1997.

Gabriel, Julie. *The Green Beauty Guide: Your Essential Resource to Organic and Natural Skin Care, Hair Care, Makeup, and Fragrances*. Deerfield Beach, FL: HCI Books, 2008.

Gaines, Steven, and Sharon Churcher. *Obsession: The Lives and Times of Calvin Klein*. New York: Avon Books, 1995.

Gamber, Wendy. *The Millinery and Dressmaking Trades, 1860–1930*. Urbana: University of Illinois Press, 1997.

Gavenas, Mary Lisa. *Color Stories: Behind the Scenes of America's Billion-Dollar Beauty Industry*. New York: Simon & Schuster, 2002.

George, Nelson. *Hip Hop America*. New York: Penguin, 2005.

Gill, Tiffany M. *Beauty Shop Politics: African American Women's Activism in the Beauty Industry.* Urbana: University of Illinois Press, 2009.

Gilman, Sander, L. *Making the Body Beautiful: A Cultural History of Aesthetic Surgery.* Princeton, NJ: Princeton University Press, 1990.

Glenn, Susan A. *Daughters of the Shtetl: Life and Labor in the Immigrant Generation.* Ithaca, NY: Cornell University Press, 1990.

Glock, Ruth E., and Grace I. Kunz. *Apparel Manufacturing: Sewn Product Analysis.* 4th ed. Upper Saddle River, NJ: Pearson/Prentice Hall, 2005.

Golbin, Pamela. *Fashion Designers.* New York: Watson-Guptill Publications, 2001.

Gordon, Michael. *Hair Heroes.* New York: Bumble and Bumble, 2002.

Griffith, R. Marie. *Born Again Bodies: Flesh and Spirit in American Christianity.* Berkeley: University of California Press, 2004.

Gundle, Stephen. *Glamour: A History.* New York: Oxford University Press, 2008.

Haiken, Elizabeth. *Venus Envy: A History of Cosmetic Surgery.* Baltimore, MD: Johns Hopkins University Press, 1997.

Harris-Lacewell, Melissa Victoria. *Barbershops, Bibles and BET: Everyday Talk and Black Political Thought.* Princeton, NJ: Princeton University Press, 2004.

Haugen, David M., ed. *Animal Experimentation.* San Diego, CA: Greenhaven Press, 2000.

Heil, Scott, and Terrance W. Peck, eds. *The Encyclopedia of American Industry.* 2nd ed. Detroit, MI: Gale Research, 1998.

Heller, Dana, ed. *The Great American Makeover: Television, History, Nation.* New York: Palgrave, 2006.

Heller, Dana, ed. *Makeover Television: Realities Remodeled.* London: I. B. Tauris, 2007.

Hill, Daniel Delis. *Advertising to the American Woman, 1900–1999.* Columbus: Ohio State University Press, 2002.

Hilts, Philip. *Protecting America's Health: The FDA, Business, and One Hundred Years of Regulation.* Charlotte: University of North Carolina Press, 2004.

Hix, Charles (with Michael Taylor). *Male Model: The World behind the Camera.* New York: St. Martin's, 1979.

Hodges, Graham, *Anna May Wong: From Laundryman's Daughter to Hollywood Legend.* New York: Palgrave, 2004.

hooks, bell. *Black Looks: Race and Representation.* Toronto: Between the Lines, 1992.

Hozic, Aida. *Hollyworld: Space, Power and Fantasy in the American Economy.* Ithaca, NY: Cornell University Press, 2002.

Huff, Toby. *The Rise of Early Modern Science: Islam, China, and the West,* Cambridge: Cambridge University Press. 2003.

Hunter, Margaret L. *Race, Gender, and the Politics of Skin Tone.* New York: Routledge, 2005.

Hunter, Victoria. *The Ultimate Fashion Study Guide.* Pasadena, CA: Hunter Publishing, 2007.

Jackson, Peter, Nick Stevenson, and Kate Brooks. *Making Sense of Men's Magazines.* Cambridge: Polity Press, 2001.

Jewell, Richard. *The Golden Age of Cinema: Hollywood, 1929–1945.* Malden, MA : Blackwell, 2007.

Johnson, Fern L. *Imaging in Advertising: Verbal and Visual Codes in Advertising.* New York: Routledge, 2008.

Jones, Geoffrey. *Multinationals and Global Capitalism: Multinationals and Global Capitalism from the Nineteenth to the Twenty-First Century.* Oxford: Oxford University Press, 2005.

Kang, Miliann. *The Managed Hand: Race, Gender, and the Body in Beauty Service Work.* Berkeley, CA: University of California Press, 2010.

Kay, Gwen. *Dying to Be Beautiful: The Fight for Safe Cosmetics.* Columbus: Ohio State University Press, 2005.

Kefgen, Mary, and Phyllis Touchie-Specht. *Individuality in Clothing Selection and Personal Appearance.* New York: Macmillan Publishing Company, 1986.

Kellogg, Ann, Amy T. Peterson, Stefani Bay, and Natalie Swindell. *In an Influential Fashion: An Encyclopedia of Nineteenth- and Twentieth-Century Fashion Designers and Retailers Who Transformed Dress.* Westport, CT: Greenwood Press, 2002.

Kidwell, Claudia Brush, and Valerie Steele. *Men and Women: Dressing the Part.* Washington, D.C.: Smithsonian Institution Press, 1989.

Kimura, Margaret. *Asian Beauty.* New York: Collins, 2001.

Kitwana, Bakari. *Why White Kids Love Hip Hop: Wankstas, Wiggers, Wannabes, and the New Reality of Race in America.* New York: Basic Civitas, 2006.

Klein, Naomi. *No LOGO: Taking Aim at the Brand Bullies.* New York: Picador, 2002;

Klepacki, Laura. *Avon: Building the World's Premier Company for Women.* Hoboken, NJ: John Wiley & Sons, 2005.

Koda, Harold, and Kohle Yohannan. *The Model as Muse: Embodying Fashion.* New York: Metropolitan Museum of Art, 2009.

Kolmar, Wendy K., and Frances Bartkowski. *Feminist Theory: A Reader.* 2nd ed. Boston: McGraw Hill, 2005.

Kuczynski, Alex. *Beauty Junkies: Inside our $15 Billion Obsession with Cosmetic Surgery.* New York: Doubleday, 2006.

Lautman, Victoria. *The New Tattoo.* New York: Abbeville, 1994.

Lee, Robert G. *Orientals: Asian Americans in Popular Culture.* Philadelphia, PA: Temple University Press, 1999.

Lewis, Tania, ed. *TV Transformations: Revealing the Makeover Show.* New York: Routledge, 2008.

Linn, Susan. *Consuming Kids: Protecting Our Children from the Onslaught of Marketing and Advertising.* New York: Anchor Books, 2005.

Lister, Maurice. *Men's Hairdressing: Traditional and Modern Barbering.* Albany, NY: Thomson Learning, 2004.

Love, Toni. *The World of Wigs, Weaves, and Extensions.* Albany, NY: Milady/Thompson Learning, 2002.

Luciano, Lynne. *Looking Good: Male Body Image in Modern America.* New York: Hill and Wang, 2001.

Madsen, Axel. *Chanel: A Woman of Her Own.* New York: Holt, 1990.

Malkan, Stacy. *Not Just a Pretty Face: The Ugly Side of the Beauty Industry.* British Columbia: New Society Publishers, 2007.

Marsh, Lisa. *The House of Klein: Fashion, Controversy, and a Business Obsession.* Hoboken, NJ: John Wiley and Sons, 2003.

Marshall, P. David, ed. *The Celebrity Culture Reader.* New York: Routledge, 2006.

Massey, John. *American Adonis: Tony Sansone, The First Male Physique Icon.* New York: Universe, 2004.

Maurer, Donna, and Jeffery Sobal, eds. *Weighty Issues: Fatness and Thinness as Social Problems.* Piscataway, NJ: Aldine Transaction, 1999.

Mazzarella, Sharon K., and Norma Odom Pecors, eds. *Growing Up Girls: Popular Culture and the Construction of Identity.* New York: P. Lang, 1999.

McGracken, Grant. *Culture and Consumption II: Markets, Meaning, and Brand Management.* Bloomington: Indiana University Press, 2005.

Mendible, Myra. *From Bananas to Buttocks: The Latina Body in Popular Film and Culture.* Austin: University of Texas Press, 2007.

Milbank, Caroline Rennolds. *Couture: The Great Fashion Designers.* London: Thames & Hudson, 1985.

Miller, Laura. *Beauty Up: Exploring Contemporary Japanese Body Aesthetics.* Berkeley: University of California Press, 2006.

Mitchell, Claudia, and Jacqueline Reid-Walsh, eds. *Seven Going on Seventeen: Tween Studies in the Culture of Girlhood.* New York: Peter Lang Publishing, 2005.

Molinary, Rosie. *Hijas Americanas: Beauty, Body Image & Growing Up Latina.* Berkeley, CA: Seal Press, 2007.

Moore, Pamela. *Building Bodies.* New Brunswick, NJ: Rutgers University Press, 1997.

Morris, Desmond. *The Naked Woman: A Study of the Female Body.* New York: Macmillan, 2007.

Morris, Edwin. *Fragrance: The Story of Perfume from Cleopatra to Chanel.* New York: Charles Scribner's Sons, 1984.

O'Farrell, Mary Ann. *Telling Complexions: The Nineteenth Century Novel and the Blush.* Durham, NC: Duke University Press, 1997.

Oliver, Richard, and Tim Leffel. *Hip-Hop, Inc.: Success Strategies of the Rap Moguls.* Cambridge, MA: Da Capo, 2006.

Osgerby, Bill. *Playboys in Paradise: Masculinity, Youth Culture, and Leisure-Style in Modern America.* Oxford: Berg, 2001.

Paglia, Camille. *Sexual Personae: Art and Decadence from Nefertiti to Emily Dickinson.* New York: Vintage, 1991.

Parfrey, Adam. *It's a Man's World: Men's Adventure Magazines, the Postwar Pulps.* Los Angeles, CA: Feral House, 2003.

Peiss, Kathy. *Cheap Amusements: Working Women and Leisure in Turn-of-the-Century New York.* Philadelphia, PA: Temple University Press, 1986.

Peiss, Kathy. *Hope in a Jar: The Making of America's Beauty Culture.* New York: Metropolitan Books, 1998.

Pendergast, Tom. *Creating the Modern Man: American Magazines and Consumer Culture, 1900–1950.* Columbia: University of Missouri Press, 2000.

Perutz, Kathrin. *Beyond the Looking Glass: America's Beauty Culture.* New York: William Morrow, 1970.

Pitman, Joanne. *On Blondes.* New York: Bloomsbury, 2003.

Pitts-Taylor, Victoria. *In the Flesh: The Cultural Politics of Body Modification.* New York: Palgrave, 2003.

Pitts-Taylor, Victoria. *Surgery Junkies: Wellness and Pathology in Cosmetic Culture.* New Brunswick, NJ: Rutgers, 2007.

Plitt, Jane R. *Martha Matilda Harper and the American Dream: How One Woman Changed the Face of American Business.* Syracuse, NY: Syracuse University Press, 2000.

Postle, Martin, and William Vaughan. *The Artist's Model: From Etty to Spencer.* London: Merrell Holberton, 1999.

Prashad, Vijay. *Keeping Up With Dow Joneses: Debt, Prison, Workfare.* Cambridge, MA: South End Press, 2003.

Putney, Clifford. *Muscular Christianity: Manhood and Sports in Protestant America, 1880–1920.* Cambridge, MA: Harvard University Press, 2001.

Quart, Alissa. *Branded: The Buying and Selling of Teenagers.* New York: Basic Books, 2004.

Rechelbacher, Horst. *Aveda Rituals: A Daily Guide to Natural Health and Beauty.* New York: Owl Books, 1999.

Regan, Thomas. *The Case for Animal Rights.* Berkeley: University of California Press, 2004.

Riordan, Teresa. *Inventing Beauty: A History of the Innovations that have Made Us Beautiful.* Broadway, 2004.

Rooks, Noliwe. *Hair Raising: Beauty, Culture, and African American Women.* New Brunswick, NJ: Rutgers University Press, 1996.

Rose, Tricia. *The Hip Hop Wars: What We Talk About When We Talk About Hip Hop—and Why It Matters*. New York: Basic Civitas, 2008.

Ruiz, Vicki, and Virgina Sanchez Korrol, eds. *Latina Legacies: Identity, Biography, Community*. New York: Oxford University Press, 2005.

Sassoon, Vidal. *Cutting Hair the Vidal Sassoon Way*. Oxford: Butterworth-Heinemann, 1984.

Sassoon, Vidal. *Sorry to have Kept You Waiting, Madam*. New York: G. P. Putnam's Sons, 1968.

Sassoon, Vidal, Gerald Battle Welch, Luca P. Marighetta, Werner Moller. *Vidal Sassoon and the Bauhaus*. New York: Distributed Art Publications, 1994.

Savage, Jon. *Teenage: The Creation of Youth Culture*. New York: Penguin Group, 2007.

Scanlon, Jennifer. *Bad Girls Go Everywhere: The Life of Helen Gurley Brown*. New York: Oxford University Press. 2009.

Schisgall, Oscar. *Eyes on Tomorrow: The Evolution of Procter & Gamble*. Chicago: J. G. Ferguson, 1981.

Schor, Juliet. *Born to Buy: The Commercialized Child and the New Consumer Society*. New York: Scribner, 2004.

Segrave, Kerry *Endorsements in Advertising: A Social History*. Jefferson, NC: McFarland, 2005.

Segrave, Kerry. *Suntanning in 20th Century America*. Jefferson, NC: McFarland, 2005.

Sennett, Robert. *Hollywood Hoopla: Creating Stars and Selling Movies in the Golden Age of Hollywood*. New York: Watson-Guptill, 1999.

Shah, Sonia, ed. *Dragon Ladies: Asian American Feminists Breathe Fire*. Cambridge, MA: South End Press, 1999.

Sherrow, Victoria. *The Encyclopedia of Hair: A Cultural History*. Westport, CT: Greenwood Press, 2006.

Simon, Diane. *Hair: Public, Political, Extremely Personal*. Thomas Dunne Books, 2000.

Simpson, Mark. *Male Impersonators: Men Performing Masculinity*. New York: Routledge, 1994.

Steele, Valerie. *The Corset: A Cultural History*. New Haven, CT: Yale University Press, 2001.

Steele, Valerie, ed. *Encyclopedia of Clothing and Fashion*. Vol. 1–3. New York: Charles Scribner's Sons, 2005.

Steele, Valerie. *Paris Fashion: A Cultural History*. New York: Oxford University Press, 1988.

Steinbach, Ronald. *The Fashionable Ear: A History of Ear-Piercing Trends for Men and Women*. New York: Vantage, 1995.

Stern, Remy. *But Wait . . . There's More! Tighten Your Abs, Make Millions, and Learn How the $100 Billion Infomercial Industry Sold Us Everything But the Kitchen Sink*. New York: Collins Business, 2009.

Stinson, Kandi. *Women and Dieting Culture: Inside a Commercial Weight Loss Group*. New Brunswick, NJ: Rutgers University Press, 2001.

Stokes, Melvin. *Hollywood Abroad: Audiences and Cultural Exchange*. London: British Film Institute, 2008.

St. Pierre, Mark, and Tilda Long Soldier. *Walking in the Sacred Manner: Healers, Dreamers, and Pipe Carriers—Medicine Women of the Plains*. New York: Simon & Schuster, 1995.

Sunstein, Cass R., and Martha C. Nussbaum. *Animal Rights: Current Debates and New Directions*. New York: Oxford University Press, 2005.

Torr, James D., ed. *The Internet: Opposing Viewpoints*. Farmington Hills, MI: Greenhaven Press, 2005.

Tortora, Phyllis, and Keith Eubank. *Survey of Historic Costume: A History of Western Dress*. 3rd ed. New York: Fairchild Publications, 2005.

Tremper, Ellen. *I'm No Angel: The Blonde in Fiction and Film*. Charlottesville: University of Virginia Press, 2006.

Troy, Nancy J. *Couture Culture: A Study in Modern Art and Fashion*. Cambridge, MA: MIT Press, 2003.

Turin, Luca. *The Secret of Scent: Adventures in Perfume and the Science of Smell*. New York: Ecco, 2006.

Turudich, Daniela. *1960s Hair: Hairstyles for Bouffant Babes and Swingin' Chicks*. Long Beach, CA: Streamline, 2003.

Underwood, Jim. *More than a Pink Cadillac: Mary Kay Inc.'s Nine Leadership Keys to Success*. New York: McGraw-Hill, 2003.

Verma, Himanshu. *The Metrosexuals: Exploring the Unexplored*. New Delhi: Red Earth, 2004.

Walker, Juliet. *The History of Black Business in America: Capitalism, Race, Entrepreneurship*. New York: Macmillan Library Reference USA, 1998.

Walker, Susannah. *Style and Status: Selling Beauty to African American Women, 1920–1975*. Lexington: University Press of Kentucky, 2007.

Wann, Marilyn. *Fat? So!: Because You Don't Have to Apologize for Your Size*. Berkeley, CA: Ten Speed Press, 1999.

Watkins, S. Craig. *Hip Hop Matters: Politics, Pop Culture, and the Struggle for the Soul of a Movement*. Boston: Beacon Press, 2006.

Watson, Elwood, and Darcy Martin, eds. *"There She Is, Miss America": The Politics of Sex, Beauty, and Race in America's Most Famous Pageant*. New York: Palgrave, 2004.

Weber, Brenda R. *Makeover TV: Selfhood, Citizenship, and Celebrity*. Durham, NC: Duke University Press, 2009.

Weber, Brenda R. *Subject to Change: Becoming a Self on Makeover TV*. Durham, NC: Duke University Press, 2009.

Weber, Bruce. *Calvin Klein Jeans*. New York: Condé Nast, 1991.

Weems, Robert. *Desegregating the Dollar*. New York: New York University Press, 1998.

Weingarten, Rachel C. *Hello Gorgeous!: Beauty Products in America '40s–'50s*. Portland, OR: Collectors Press, 2006.

Weitz, Rose. *Rapunzel's Daughters: What Women's Hair Tells Us about Women's Lives*. New York: Farrar, Straus and Giroux, 2004.

White, Carolyn L. *American Artifacts of Personal Adornment, 1680–1820: A Guide to Identification and Interpretation*. Lanham, MD: AltaMira Press, 2005.

Willett, Julie A. *Permanent Waves: The Making of the American Beauty Shop*. New York: New York University Press, 2000.

Wolf, Naomi. *The Beauty Myth: How Images of Beauty are Used against Women*. New York: Harper, 1991.

Woodhead, Lindy. *War Paint: Madame Helena Rubinstein and Miss Elizabeth Arden, Their Lives, Their Times, Their Rivalry*. Hoboken, NJ: Wiley, 2004.

Zukin, Sharon. *Point of Purchase: How Shopping Changed American Culture*. New York: Routledge, 2005.

Web Sites

Alliance of Professional Tattooists
http://www.safe-tattoos.com
Forums and information for trade professionals.

American Academy of Dermatology
http://www.aad.org

American Academy of Facial Plastic and Reconstructive Surgery
http://www.aafprs.org
Provides information on procedures, newsletters, and training.

American Hair Loss Association
http://www.americanhairloss.org
Provides information on types of hair loss, reasons for hair loss, and treatment plans.

American Men's Studies Association
http://mensstudies.org
Links to archives, blogs, and association news.

Association of Professional Piercers
http://www.safepiercing.org
Provides links, legislation, conferences, and educational information for industry professionals.

The Beauty Industry Report
http:// www.bironline.com.
Monthly subscription newsletter providing information about the professional beauty business, including its leading companies and professionals.

Bureau of Labor Statistics, U.S. Department of Labor. "Barbers, Cosmetologists, and Other Personal Appearance Workers." *Occupational Outlook Handbook, 2008–2009.*
http://www.bls.gov/oco/ocs 169.htm
Job descriptions, working conditions, and opportunities, as well as information about training for beauty workers.

Campaign for a Commercial-Free Childhood
http://comercialfreechildhood.org
Advocacy, education, and research related to the harmful effects of marketing on children.

The Campaign for Safe Cosmetics
http://safecomestics.com
Information on products, companies, laws, and campaigns for nontoxic cosmetics, bath, and body products.

CorpWatch
http://www.corpwatch.org
A nonprofit organization with news, articles, and resources about corporations. It advocates multinational corporate accountability for industries such as retail, manufacturing, and pharmaceuticals.

Dove's Campaign for Real Beauty
http://www.campaignforrealbeauty.com/
Dialogue and fund designed to challenge beauty stereotypes.

Environmental Working Group's Skin Deep: Cosmetic Safety Database
www.cosmeticsdatabase.com
Information and data on the safety of various cosmetics.

Euromonitor International
www.euromonitor.com.
Offers reports on global trends from industries, ranging from cosmetics to clothing.

The Humane Society of the United States
http://www.hsus.org
Information on animal testing that includes the beauty industry.

International Spa Association
http://www.experienceispa.com/education-resources/facts-and-figures/industry-stats/
Provides statistics on industry growth.

Johnson Products Heritage
http://www.johnsonproducts.com/heritage.html
Provides an engaging look in pictures and text of the company's history.

Madam C. J. Walker Official Web Site
http://madamcjwalker.com
Provides an engaging look at the entrepreneur and her legacy.

The Mayo Clinic
http://www.mayoclinic.com
Definitions and information on a range of diseases, products, and procedures related to beauty, body, and health.

The Metropolitan Museum of Art: The Costume Institute
http://www.metmuseum.org/works_of_art/department.asp?dep=8
Provides a wealth of information on the history of fashion.

Nails Magazine
http://www.nailsmag.com
An informative monthly trade journal designed for nail professionals and salon owners offering information on the latest trends.

The Naked Truth Project
http://www.thenakedtruthproject.org
A consumer guide to nontoxic products that includes clothing and body products.

National Alopecia Areata Foundation
http://www.naaf.org
Free information on the coping with and treatments of the disease.

National Black Cosmetology Association
http://www.nationalblackcosmetologycaassociation.com
Provides information on resources, legislation, and upcoming events.

National Cosmetology Association
http://www.ncacares.org
Provides information such as blogs, videos, links, newsletters, and information on licensing.

National Latino Cosmetology Association
http://www.nlcamerican.org
Offers industry information on careers and events, as well as a brief history.

The National Organization for Women
http://www.now.org
Information on legislation and campaigns, blogs, links, and articles on issues that include women's health and self-image.

National Tattoo Association
http://nationaltattooassociation.com
Designed for professionals in the tattoo industry and includes history, conventions, and examples of art.

The National Women's Studies Association
http://www.nwsa.org
Paid membership provides information on conferences, blogs, and a range of resources on women's body issues.

Organic Consumers Association
http://www.organicconsumers.org
A wealth of resources on production and labor processes, companies, legislation; includes everything from clothing to body products.

People for the Ethical Treatment of Animals (PETA)
http://www.peta.org
A resource for activism that provides information on the exploitation of animals in various industries, including beauty and fashion.

U.S. Department of Health and Human Services. "The National Girl's Health Information Center"
http://www.girlshealth.gov
Provides information on topics that range from nutrition and fitness to acne and other body and health concerns. Designed for girls 10 years and older.

U.S. Department of Health and Human Services. "The National Women's Health Information Center"
http://www.womenshealth.gov
Provides up-to-date articles and information on a range of topics connected to the beauty industry such as cosmetics, plastic surgery, sun exposure, and body image.

U.S. Food and Drug Administration
http://www.fda.gov
Under "Cosmetics" information can be found, for example, on product recalls, product content, and labeling.

Women's Wear Daily
http://www.wwd.com
Provides up-to-date headlines and article summaries and (with a subscription) in-depth information on markets, people, companies, and fashion trends.

Index

Note: Page numbers for main entries are in **bold** type.

About the Editor and Contributors

Christina Ashby-Martin teaches at Texas Tech University. She specializes in the cultural and social history of the late 19th and early 20th centuries.

Devon Atchison is an assistant professor at Grossmont College in San Diego, California. She teaches early and modern American history and American women's history. She is also the archivist for the Women's History Museum & Educational Center.

Corye Perez Beene is a PhD student in history at Texas Tech University. Her dissertation explores 20th century legal history, focusing on civil rights, women, and sports.

McKellan Binkley researches the intersection of medical discourse and social history through the Honors College Undergraduate Research Mentorship Program at Texas Tech University.

Kate Brinton is a journalist in the United Kingdom. She has studied fashion forecasting and the history of textiles and dress. Her research includes trends in eco textiles, the cultural importance of the flapper dress, the consumption and social life of textiles, and the effects of gay men's style on trends in heterosexual men's fashions.

Doug Bristol is an associate professor of the Department of History at the University of Southern Mississippi and the author or *Knights of the Razor: Black Barbers in Slavery and Freedom* (2009).

Wendy A. Burns-Ardolino is assistant professor and director of the Master of Arts in Liberal Studies program at Clayton State University in Atlanta, where she teaches interdisciplinary courses in women's studies, media studies, and liberal studies. She is the author of *Jiggle: (Re)Shaping American Women* (2007).

Amber R. Clifford teaches cultural anthropology and museum studies, and curates museum collections, at the University of Central Missouri. Her research interests are gender and sexuality in popular music scenes, and textile interpretation and conservation.

Nicolette Cosburn has a background in popular culture and media and culture communications. Her research focuses on female youth cultures and the adoption of popular feminism. She is interested in how young women use music, television, and film to construct personal realities and understand a personal feminism.

Paul R. Deslandes is associate professor of history at the University of Vermont, Burlington. He is the author of *Oxbridge Men: British Masculinity and the Undergraduate Experience, 1850–1920* (2005), and is researching the cultural history of male beauty in Britain from the 1840s to the present.

James I. Deutsch is a program curator at the Smithsonian Institution's Center for Folklife and Cultural Heritage. In addition, he serves as an adjunct professor, teaching courses on American film history in the American Studies Department at George Washington University.

Perlita Dicochea is an assistant professor in the Ethnic Studies Program at Santa Clara University, where she teaches environmental racism, gender, and justice. Dicochea's research explores race and class relations along the transnational Salton Sink, which is situated both in Imperial Valley, California, and Mexicali Valley, Baja California.

Marnie Dobson is a research associate at the Center for Occupational and Environmental Health at UC Irvine and associate director of the Center for Social Epidemiology in Los Angeles, California. Her research interests focus on gender, work, and health; emotional labor; and work organization. She is the co-editor of *Unhealthy Work: Causes, Consequences and Cures* (2009).

Richard D. Driver is a PhD student in history at Texas Tech University. His research examines the place and role of rock and roll music and the media in the cultural and social history of the 1950s to the 1980s, with a focus on the images of masculinity.

Priya Dua is a PhD student in sociology at the University of Missouri–Columbia. Her research focuses on the identity construction and maintenance of women experiencing hair loss.

Tiffany M. Gill is an assistant professor in the Department of History and the Centers for African and African American Studies and Women's and Gender Studies at the University of Texas at Austin. She is the author of *Beauty Shop Politics: African American Women's Activism in the Beauty Industry* (2009).

Jeong woo Han is lecturer of history and political science at Chestnut Hill College, Philadelphia. She is an anthropologist who specializes in gender studies, feminist discourses on the body, culture and political economy, globalization, and race/ethnicity.

Mary Thomasine Harkins is an associate professor and head of the theatre design/technology program at Emerson College, Boston. Harkins is a costume designer and fashion historian and primarily teaches and researches the visual elements of American clothes as a direct expression of social, economic, and historical events.

Rachel Harris is a fashion historian and educator based in Seattle. Her research is primarily focused on the intersections of fashion and culture in the 20th century.

Laura Harrison is a doctoral student and associate instructor in the gender studies program at Indiana University. Her research analyzes the implications of new reproductive technologies on family formation, women's reproductive freedom, and the changing meaning of race in the United States, with attention to representations of fetal personhood and maternal-fetal conflict.

Sara M. Harvey teaches fashion design and fashion history at the International Academy of Design and Technology in Nashville.

Shana Heinricy is an instructor in communication studies at Xavier University in New Orleans. Her research focuses on television and the body.

Krystal A. Humphreys is a PhD student in history at Texas Tech University. Her research looks at the culture of the 1970s and '80s in relation to the rise of modern conservatism and the political awakening of the Christian Right, specifically evangelical Christian definitions of gender.

Gwen Kay is an associate professor of history at the State University of New York at Oswego. She is the author of *Dying to be Beautiful: The Fight for Safe Cosmetics* (2005).

Beth Kreydatus is an assistant professor of history at the University College at Virginia Commonwealth University. Her research interests include 20th-century feminism, business history, and beauty culture.

Malia McAndrew is an assistant professor of history at John Carroll University. Her research centers on the history of gender, race, business, and beauty culture in the 20th-century United States.

Abigail Mitchell is a graduate student at Indiana University, Bloomington.

Christopher A. Mitchell is a PhD candidate at Rutgers University. His dissertation looks at the effects of gay and lesbian-feminist liberation on the illicit queer subcultures of New York City's consumer culture from 1966 to 1977.

Kym Neck is a doctoral candidate in cultural anthropology at the CUNY Graduate Center. Her work focuses on the anti–border wall movement in Brownsville, Texas, and examines the production of space on an international border and the impact of moral panics on local populations.

Caryn E. Neumann is a visiting professor of history at Miami of Ohio and the author of the *Term Paper Guide to African American History* (Greenwood, 2009).

De Anna J. Reese is an assistant professor in the Department of History and the Africana and American Indian Studies Program at California State University, Fresno. Her areas of specialization include 20th century U.S., African American, women's, social, and urban history. She is researching black female entrepreneurship, beauty culture, and social welfare activism in St. Louis, Missouri.

Brian Robertson is a doctoral candidate at Texas Tech University studying the rise and fall of Richard Nixon through the lens of masculinity, diplomacy, and the political crisis of the 1960s and '70s.

Scott Sheidlower is an assistant professor and a librarian in the library at York College/CUNY, Jamaica, New York.

Yael D. Sherman recently earned a PhD. Her dissertation was titled "Fashioning Our Selves: Gender, Power and Normalization in Personal Makeover Television Shows."

Lauren P. Steiner teaches film studies at Cleveland State University. In 2006 she wrote, directed, and produced *The Corner Shop,* a short documentary film about women and their relationships with their hairdressers.

Danica C. Tisdale is a PhD candidate in the Department of Women's Studies at Emory University. Her research interests include beauty, the body, and popular culture; her dissertation is titled "The Pageant Politic: Race and Representation in American Beauty Contests and Culture."

Anne Marie Todd is an associate professor in the Communication Studies Department at San Jose State University. She teaches and researches in the areas of environmental communication, media criticism, and social movements discourse.

Susannah Walker is an associate professor at Virginia Wesleyan College in Norfolk. Her teaching focuses on African American history, women's history, and the history of consumer culture. She is the author of *Style and Status: Selling Beauty to African American Women, 1920–1975* (2007).

Brenda R. Weber is an assistant professor in the Department of Gender Studies, with adjunct appointments in English, cultural studies, and American studies at Indiana University in Bloomington. She is the author of *Makeover TV: Selfhood, Citizenship, and Celebrity* (2009).

Bernadette Wegenstein, an Austrian linguist and filmmaker, is associate research professor in the Department of German and Romance Languages and Literatures at the Johns Hopkins University, where she teaches media and film theory. She is the author of *Getting under the Skin: Body and Media Theory* (2006) and articles on body criticism, performance art, and film theory. She also produced a feature-length documentary film on the topic of the technologies and culture of bodily makeover, *Made Over in America* (2007).

Julie Willett is an associate professor of history at Texas Tech University, where she teaches courses on the history of gender, labor, and sexuality. She is the author of *Permanent Waves: The Making of the American Beauty Shop* (2000). She has also researched and published on race, gender, and the history of the manicurist.

Aliza S. Wong is associate professor of history at Texas Tech University. She works in modern Italian history, with a specialization in race, nation, and identity. She teaches popular culture and history, 19th- and 20th-century European history, and diaspora and immigration.